REBELLIOUS PRUSSIANS

Rebellious Prussians

*Urban Political Culture under Frederick
the Great and his Successors*

FLORIAN SCHUI

OXFORD
UNIVERSITY PRESS

OXFORD
UNIVERSITY PRESS

Great Clarendon Street, Oxford, OX2 6DP,
United Kingdom

Oxford University Press is a department of the University of Oxford.
It furthers the University's objective of excellence in research, scholarship,
and education by publishing worldwide. Oxford is a registered trade mark of
Oxford University Press in the UK and in certain other countries

First Edition published in 2013
Impression: 1

British Library Cataloguing in Publication Data
Data available

ISBN 978–0–19–959396–5

Printed in Great Britain by
MPG Books Group, Bodmin and King's Lynn

For Rita

Acknowledgements

This book brings together different aspects of my research on the Prussian and European history of ideas. I began exploring the history of fiscal debates in the eighteenth century as a postdoctoral research student in Cambridge and Galway. I should like to thank St Edmund's College, the Centre for Research in the Arts, Social Sciences and Humanities (CRASSH) in Cambridge, and the Hans Böckler-Stiftung as well as the Moore Institute at the National University of Ireland, Galway, and the Irish Research Council for the Humanities and Social Sciences (IRCHSS) for their support. I owe an enormous intellectual debt to colleagues and participants in research seminars in Cambridge, Galway, and elsewhere who commented on my work in this period and subsequently. In particular I should thank Nicholas Canny, Chris Clark, and Martin Daunton for their comments and suggestions.

Later, after having taken up a lectureship at Royal Holloway, University of London, a fellowship at the Herzog August Bibliothek, Wolfenbüttel allowed me to take additional research leave and conduct further research into the history of religious debates of the period. I am grateful for the financial support of the library, for the kind and competent support of the librarians, and for the inspiring conversations I had with colleagues working there. I would especially like to thank Ulrike Gleixner and the other participants in the library's research seminar for their thoughtful comments and suggestions.

During the preparation of the manuscript I incurred further intellectual debts that I am happy to acknowledge. In particular, I should thank William O'Reilly for a close reading and invaluable comments and suggestions on the text. A number of other colleagues have also commented on the whole manuscript or parts of it. I wish to thank Greg Claeys, Avi Lifschitz, Michael Kwass, Emma Rothschild, Mark Spoerer, and the anonymous readers for their comments, which helped me greatly to improve the manuscript and sharpen the argument. I also benefited from the generosity of colleagues in other ways: Michael Kwass shared a forthcoming article with me, Mark Spoerer gave me access to the statistical data on which the graph about Prussia's state revenue is based, and Daniel Beer critically reviewed the translations of source material that are included in the text. I would also like to thank Stephanie Ireland at Oxford University Press for her suggestions and for guiding me through the practical process of completing the manuscript. Any remaining errors in the book are of course solely the author's responsibility.

I should also express my gratitude for access to the collections of libraries, archives, and museums without which it would have been impossible to complete this project. In particular I wish to thank the following institutions and their staff: Geheimes Staatsarchiv, Preussischer Kulturbesitz (Berlin), the British Library (London), Biblioteca Braidense (Milan), Biblioteca delle Science della Storia e della documentazione Storica (Milan), Staatsbibliothek, Preussischer Kulturbesitz (Berlin), and the University Library (Cambridge).

The following institutions generously made illustrations available for this book: Bildarchiv Preussischer Kulturbesitz, Klassik Stiftung Weimar, Kupferstich-Kabinett, Staatliche Kunstsammlungen Dresden, and LWL-Landesmuseum für Kunst und Kulturgeschichte Münster (Westfälisches Landesmuseum). Detailed acknowledgements can be found in the captions. Cambridge University Press allowed me to reproduce parts of an article published in the *Historical Journal*. Details are given in the notes to Chapter 4.

Finally, I should also express my gratitude to friends and family. Writing can be a lonely business and I doubt that I would have been able to complete the manuscript without the many chats, coffee breaks, and other distractions that pleasantly interrupted the writing routine. However, inevitably, writing a book also puts a burden on those who are closest to the author and who do not necessarily share his fascination with the historical world of eighteenth-century Prussia. Reading dusty volumes got in the way of playing with my daughter Cecilia far too often (but those extra stickers and bedtime stories partly made up for that, right?) and my absences left my wife with many jobs to do that should have been shared more evenly. It is to her that this book is dedicated in loving gratitude.

Table of Contents

List of Illustrations   xi

Introduction   1
   Historiography   7
   Sources   14

1. The Paradoxes of State Building   16
   The father of the Prussian state   17
   The growing financial appetite of the state   19
   Town vs. country   21
   The making of Prussian burghers   24
   The military–fiscal state as seen from the towns   25
   The economics of the excise   29
   Soldiers in the town   32
   Religion and state building   34
   Sex and the Prussian town   40
   The 'state-free' schools of Prussia's towns   45
   'Where individual life carries its own centre of gravity within itself'   47

2. Urban Navel-Gazing   48
   Urban growth   50
   The causes of urban growth   54
   The wealth of towns   57
   Epicurean Prussians   58
   'Wealth is a mother of poverty'   60
   The perils of wealth   61
   The perils of poverty   64
   The dangers of religious individualism   66
   Recalibrating relations with the state   68

3. Official Perspectives on the Towns   75
   Knowing the towns   76
   For whose benefit?   81
   Tranquillity   82
   Prosperity   83
   The visible hand of the Prussian state   85
   Guided consumers   90
   The utility of specie   91
   An English bank for Prussia   93
   The long shadow of Colbert   95
   Start-up industry protection   95

4. Taxation and its Discontents   101
    Membranes made of stone   102
    Making an administration one official at a time   104
    The creation of the Régie   107
    Taxpayer opposition   111
    The power of the written word   118
    The fall of the Régie   126
    After the end   133
    Reaping the benefits   134
    Long-term outcomes   138
    A soft landing for the Prussian state   139

5. Religion and the State   144
    A new hymnal for Prussia   145
    Forms of resistance   147
    Frederick the Great flees from a flock of burghers   148
    The causes of rebellion   151
    Religious *Realpolitik*   153
    Woellner's machinations   155
    The intellectual origins of the edicts   157
    The dangers of 'self-thinking'   160
    Opposition to the edicts   165
    A people of 'self-thinkers'   172
    Woellner, Voltaire, and subversiveness   174

6. A Prussian on Liberty   176
    On religion   178
    On education   182
    On scarcity and abundance   184
    On change   189
    On the limits of state action   191

Conclusion: 'Le *Sonderweg* est mort, vive le *Sonderweg*?'   195

Bibliography   199
Index   217

List of Illustrations

Map

Prussia in 1786. The principal Hohenzollern territories in 1786 with the main towns mentioned in the text.

Illustrations

2.1. Daniel Nikolaus Chodowiecki, 'Leben eines Lüderlichen' (Life of a good-for-nothing), one of six motifs in this series (Blatt 6), etching, 1773. Published in 'Berlinischer genealogischer Calender', 1774. Reproduced with permission from Klassik Stiftung Weimar, Museen, Inv. DK 416/84.   63

2.2. Daniel Nikolaus Chodowiecki, 'Der Mond Doctor' (The moon doctor), one of twelve motifs in the series 'Modethorheiten' (The follies of fashion), etching, 1788. Reproduced with permission from Kupferstich-Kabinett, Staatliche Kunstsammlungen Dresden, Foto: Herbert Boswank.   67

3.1. The structure of state revenue in Brandenburg Prussia, 1653 to 1913. The graph is based on data kindly made available by Mark Spoerer. See Mark Spoerer, 'The revenue structures of Brandenburg-Prussia, Saxony and Bavaria (fifteenth to nineteenth centuries): are they compatible with the Bonney-Ormrod Model?', in Simonetta Cavaciocchi, ed., *La fiscalità nell'economia europea secc. XII-XVIII* (Florence, 2008), pp. 781–91.   87

4.1. Daniel Nikolaus Chodowiecki, 'Das Brandenburger Thor in Berlin' (The Brandenburg Gate in Berlin), etching, 1764. Reproduced with permission from Klassik Stiftung Weimar, Museen, Inv. DK 208/84.   103

4.2. Daniel Nikolaus Chodowiecki, 'Die Einwanderung der Franzosen zur Errichtung der Regie' (The arrival of the French for the creation of the Régie), etching, 1771. Reproduced with permission from Klassik Stiftung Weimar, Museen, Inv. DK 293/84.   108

5.1. Anonymous, 'Samuel Lobegott Apitzsch, Kaufmann zu Berlin' (Samuel Lobegott Apitzsch, merchant in Berlin), etching, 1781. Reproduced with permission from LWL-Landesmuseum für Kunst und Kulturgeschichte Münster (Westfälisches Landesmuseum) / Porträtarchiv Diepenbroick.   149

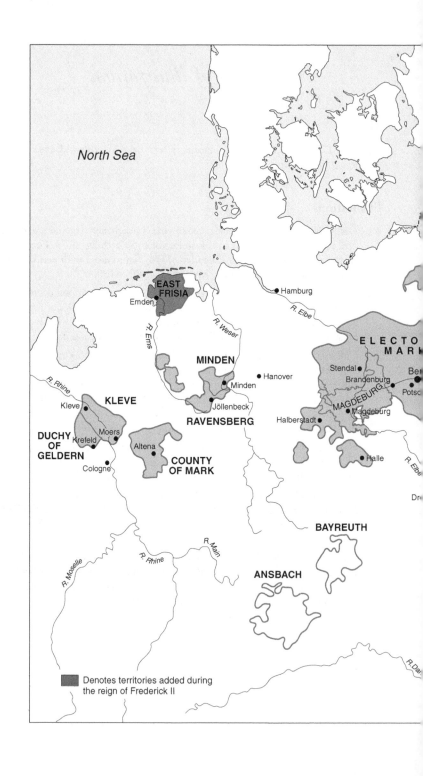

North Sea

EAST FRISIA
Emden

Hamburg
R. Elbe

R. Ems
R. Weser

MINDEN

Hanover

Minden

R. Rhine

KLEVE

Kleve

Jöllenbeck

RAVENSBERG

Moers

DUCHY
OF
GELDERN

Krefeld

Altena

Cologne

COUNTY
OF MARK

Halberstadt

ELECTO
MARK

Stendal
Brandenburg

MAGDEBURG

Magdeburg

Ber

Potsc

R. Elbe

Halle

Dr

BAYREUTH

R. Main

R. Moselle

R. Rhine

ANSBACH

R. Da

Denotes territories added during
the reign of Frederick II

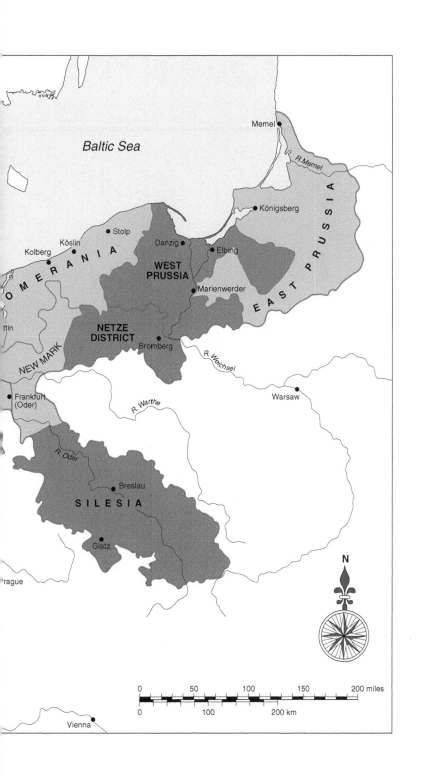

Introduction

Prussian discipline is legendary. However, the notion of deeply engrained authoritarian structures in Prussian society is not only a topos of popular culture but has also played an important role in shaping political developments and historiographical debates. When the remnants of the Prussian state were dissolved in 1947, the Allied Control Council described Prussia as an entity that 'from early days has been [a] bearer of militarism and reaction in Germany'.[1] Similar views were also influential in historiographical debates of the post-war period and linger, to some extent, even today. One of the prime 'exhibits' of historians arguing the case of an authoritarian tradition in Prussia has always been the absence of a bourgeois revolution or other clear sign of civic emancipation in the late eighteenth century.[2] While the self-reliant bourgeoisies of England and France developed a culture of critical debate and eventually crushed—or at least chipped away at substantial portions of—the power of their monarchies and aristocratic elites, the argument went, Prussians were standing to attention awaiting orders from their monarchs. Various explanations have been put forward for the lack of a more forceful challenge to the political status quo. The earliest and most influential pointed to the alleged weakness of the Prussian bourgeoisie. In this view, most notably associated with the *Sonderweg* (special path) thesis, a retarded economic development meant that the middle class remained smaller and weaker in Prussia than in Western Europe. As a result, the development of critical public discourses and of an effective political challenge to the status quo was crippled and the unbroken rule of traditional elites set Prussia and Germany on a path of development that led directly to the failure of liberal democracy in the twentieth century and to the subsequent rise of national socialism.[3] As this view began to be increasingly questioned,

---

[1] Allied Control Council, 'Law no. 46. Abolition of the state of Prussia, 25 Feb. 1947', in Office of Military Government for Germany (US) Legal Division, ed., *Enactments and approved papers of the Control Council and Coordinating Committee* (1947), vol. 6, p. 28.

[2] David Blackbourn and Geoff Eley, 'Introduction', in David Blackbourn and Geoff Eley, eds., *The peculiarities of German history: bourgeois society and politics in nineteenth-century Germany* (Oxford, 1984), p. 13.

[3] There are several excellent surveys of this debate. Dieter Groh, 'Le "Sonderweg" de l'histoire Allemande: mythe ou réalité?', *Annales. Histoire, Sciences sociales*, 38 (1983), pp. 1166–87. Blackbourn and Eley, *German history*. Jürgen Kocka, 'German history before Hitler: the debate about the German Sonderweg', *Journal of Contemporary History*, 23 (1988), pp. 3–16. William Hagen, 'Descent of the Sonderweg: Hans Rosenberg's history of Old-Regime Prussia', *Central European History*, 24 (1991), pp. 24–50. Jürgen Kocka, 'Asymmetrical historical comparison: the case of the German Sonderweg', *History and Theory*, 38 (1999), pp. 40–50.

alternative explanations were put forward. In 1985, for example, Catherine Behrens argued that the absence of social conflict was not due to the weakness of the potential revolutionaries but, rather, to the lack of a cause for revolution. In this view, the superior performance of the Prussian *ancien régime* compared with its European counterparts spared the country a revolutionary escalation. In contrast to the string of failed reforms that characterized for example the French polity in the eighteenth century, the Hohenzollern mounted well-organized and effective responses to the political, economic, and military challenges of this period, thereby reducing the potential for social conflict and the need for revolutionary change.[4] More recently, another explanatory paradigm that has gained currency among historians interprets the absence of political conflict in this period as the result of the proximity of many leading members of civil society with the state. According to this view, many of the well-educated members of the middle class, as well as public commentators, did not see themselves in a conflictual relationship with the state. On the contrary, often they were employed by the state, linking for it the prospects of political stability and individual prosperity. Moreover, this proximity also meant that leading members of civil society did not see the state as an obstacle to achieving reform but rather as a tool that could be used to this end. The cosiness between the state and many exponents of civil society prevented public debates from taking a subversive turn in the way that they did in France in the same period, and the Prussian public therefore did not pose a threat to the state, but instead accepted the leadership of the state.[5]

The present study presents a fresh perspective on this period of Prussian history. It differs from old and new orthodoxies about the relation between state and urban civil society in Prussia. As I argue, this relationship was characterized by the strength of civil society and its ability to impose its will politically in several instances of conflict with the state during the eighteenth century. Urban dwellers were neither too weak to challenge the state nor were they overinvested in it. Instead, they prevailed in conflicts between themselves and the state, and the absence of a full-blown revolution must be understood in light of these gradual political successes of civil society and the corresponding defeats of state power.[6] These instances of the successful rebellion of members of civil society lie at the centre of this study. The causes of these conflicts and the means that Prussians used to confront the state, as well as the causes that led to the weakness of the state on these particular occasions and the long-term impact on political culture in Prussia and beyond, form the focus of this study.

In particular, focus is placed on fiscal and economic conflicts associated with the introduction of a new urban tax regime by Frederick II in 1766 and on religious conflicts that were associated with the introduction of a new hymnal under

---

[4] C. B. A. Behrens, *Society, government and the enlightenment* (London, 1985).
[5] Most prominently Tim Blanning, *The culture of power and the power of culture: old regime Europe, 1660–1789* (Oxford, 2006). Michael Sauter, *Visions of the Enlightenment: the Edict on Religion of 1788 and the politics of the public sphere in eighteenth-century Prussia* (Leiden, 2009).
[6] For a discussion of the relation of revolutionary and incremental change to the rise of bourgeois society see Blackbourn and Eley, 'Introduction', pp. 13–17.

Frederick in 1781. Additionally, we consider the attempt of Frederick William II's minister Johann Christoph von Woellner to impose religious dogma on the Protestant clergy and the wider public from 1787. The monarchs and their officials attached great importance to these reforms, which were eventually repealed as a result of the various forms of resistance raised by the public.

These conflicts shared two related characteristics that determine the perspective adopted in this study. Each of these conflicts gave rise to extensive public debates, and while they were associated with other forms of opposition including passive resistance and violence, the rise of critical public debates was central to the defeats of the state. The other shared feature of these conflicts was their predominantly urban nature. This is most strikingly evident in the fiscal conflicts, since the tax that was the core bone of contention was mainly levied in towns. However, in the religious conflicts too, urban dwellers were often leading the opposition. This was partly because the state's reforms were felt more intensely in the towns, where the government's administrative reach went further than in the countryside. Perhaps more important was the higher level of literacy and the culture of printing in the towns, facilitating the development of political debates in general, but also in particular leaving traces of evidence for historians. This study mainly examines public commentary in the urban context. (We discuss the meaning of the term 'urban' in this period in more detail later in this Introduction, together with the selection of sources.) The urban focus should not be taken to imply that conflicts between authority and ordinary Prussians were not also unfolding in the country-side. On the contrary, William Hagen's forensic study has shed light on the complexity of power relations in the Prussian countryside.[7]

In order to understand fully both the causes of the state's reform attempts that provoked urban resistance, and the reaction of civil society, it is necessary to examine the synchronous and interrelated development of both spheres. The roots of these conflicts lie in the duplicitous nature of the process of state building that accelerated in Prussia after the Thirty Years War (1618–48). As a result of the existential threats that Prussia and other nascent states experienced during this conflict the state concentrated its efforts on expanding military power. This process was associated with an increase in fiscal and administrative capabilities and, in some areas, with an extension of the state's power. However, perhaps less well understood is another aspect of this process, the increasing withdrawal of the state from economic and religious matters. The decrease in the state's involvement in urban economies was directly linked to an attempt to develop urban commerce and manufacturing on the Dutch model and use taxation as a means to fund military expansion. At the same time, the retreat from involvement in religious affairs in the guise of far-reaching religious toleration aimed to defuse the destructive power of religious discord that had been amply demonstrated by the religious wars of Europe. This attempt to insulate the state from the principal source of political destabilization of the period was of particular urgency in Prussia where a Reformed

---

[7] William Hagen, *Ordinary Prussians* (Cambridge, 2002).

dynasty ruled over a majority of Lutheran subjects and where the effects of war and occupation had been devastating. Paradoxically, the flip side of the process of state building was thus an increase in individual autonomy in important areas. This dual process is explored in Chapter 1 for the period between the Thirty Years War and the beginning of the reign of Frederick the Great in 1740.

As a result of this retreat of the state a sphere of individuality developed in the towns which contemporaries referred to as 'civil society' ('bürgerliche Gesellschaft'). Urban dwellers used their increasing liberty to pursue their private interests and desires, and they also began to think of urban society in terms of an individualistic culture. When using the word 'individualism' and its variations here, this should not be understood as a reference to the development of a more heterogeneous society. Instead, the term refers to a society in which individual actions were mostly, or at least more so than previously, guided by individual interests and preferences. However, the fact that individual motivations and desires played a greater role does not necessarily imply a greater variety of outcomes. The rise of the concept of 'fashion' in the eighteenth century illustrates this well. Being fashionable was crucially about individual desires and choices, but the result was not diversity, rather homogeneity. Indeed, where individual freedom did not lead to a self-regulating order but to a fragmentation and heterogeneity, as in the case of religious dissenters, this caused deep concerns among contemporaries. The outlook of urban commentators on the rise of individualism was thus not always optimistic, but those who warned of its dangers and those who embraced it still shared a vision of the realities of urban society as fundamentally gravitating around individuals and their needs and desires. In particular, religious freedoms, and also autonomy in choices about participation in an increasingly varied material culture and a vibrant commercial sphere, were seen as central to urban individuality. Chapter 2 examines these self-perceptions of urban dwellers and the fears and hopes that were associated with discourses about rising individualism mainly in the areas of the production and consumption of goods and in religious matters during the reign of Frederick the Great from 1740 to 1786.

While urban self-perceptions saw the individual at the centre of society, official perspectives remained substantially different. These views are examined in Chapter 3. From the state's point of view individual autonomy could be tolerated, it was even encouraged as a means to achieve greater prosperity or avoid religious bickering, but it was not an end in itself. The principal aim remained the creation of prosperity and the preservation of quiet order in religious matters. Where greater individual freedom, rather than direct regulation of individual behaviour, was more efficient in achieving these goals, it was promoted and protected. But where individual freedom produced undesired economic outcomes or religious fragmentation and instability state officials saw no reason why individual freedom should not be curtailed. Overarching, long-term interests of the greater whole, mostly equated with the military–fiscal interests of the state, dominated the discourses of Frederick the Great and his officials concerning the towns. It may be tempting to see this as a contrast between an enlightened public and a state apparatus clinging to retrograde views. But officials cherished the values of rationality, efficiency, and the systematic use of empirical information as much as members of civil society did. The two spheres were not differentiated by their preferred means and epistemological values but by the interests pursued. Whereas urban dwellers thought of certain areas as their prerogatives, state officials saw themselves legitimized, if necessary, to interfere with individual freedoms for the protection of the state's interest. While they were committed to discourses about balancing private and state interests, they also saw it as their task to preserve and determine the nature of this balance. This was particularly true in economic matters but also regarding religious toleration, which was rarely embraced out of principled commitment but rather because of political expediency. Officials increasingly armed themselves with the tools of rationality and empiricism in this period, reinforcing their faith in the legitimacy of their actions but doing little to lessen the differences in outlook between state and civil society.

The conflicts between urban civil society and the state that unfolded during the second half of the eighteenth century emerged as a result of the different outlooks of officials and urban dwellers analysed in Chapters 2 and 3. Frictions developed because of attempts by the state to increase its reach in certain areas. Partly as a result of the fiscal crisis after the Seven Years War (1756–63) and partly because individual autonomy in religious matters came to be seen as a political threat rather than as a guarantee of stability, the Prussian state tried to reduce individual autonomy in matters related to the consumption, circulation, and production of goods and in religious and educational questions. The conflicts often happened at the same time and were interrelated on many levels. However, for the sake of clarity they are explored here in two separate chapters, one on economic and fiscal conflict (Chapter 4) and one on religious conflict (Chapter 5). In these conflicts, urban dwellers deployed a variety of methods of resistance, including petitions, passive resistance, violence, and, most importantly, public commentary, that forced the state to retreat and confirm the individual liberties that it had sought to limit. The wide variety of forms of opposition makes these conflicts particularly interesting, but also more difficult to write their history. In his critique of Jürgen Habermas, Geoff Eley has drawn our attention to the existence of multiple publics in the nineteenth century and his arguments raise important questions for our period.[8] Should the different types of responses—often adopted by urban dwellers in different cities of a polity with an extremely fragmented geography—be treated as a unified movement or public? Should acts of resistance be distinguished from verbally expressed opposition? And should the latter be treated as a whole when publicly voiced critique differs in important ways from that expressed in petitions and complaints to officials? Such questions have been discussed by modern historians but they were also asked by contemporaries.[9] Perhaps not choosing his examples entirely at random, Immanuel Kant (1724–1804) argued in 1784, in his *What is enlightenment?*, that it was acceptable to complain about taxes so long as

---

[8] Geoff Eley, 'Nations, publics, and political cultures: placing Habermas in the nineteenth century', in Craig Calhoun, ed., *Habermas and the public sphere* (Cambridge, MA, 1992), pp. 289–339.

[9] For a theoretical framework see Albert Hirschmann, *Exit, voice and loyalty: responses to decline in firms, organizations and states* (Cambridge, MA, 1970).

one kept paying them. Printed commentary on taxation was even part of the commendable 'public use of reason' that was bound to promote the progress of enlightenment. In this way, Kant distinguished between the social utility of different responses to conflict, but also acknowledged their inherent connection. Disobedience and reasoning were both possible reactions to conflict and both could be observed in Königsberg at the time Kant was writing. Kant's arguments sought to convince fellow Prussians that reasoning was the 'enlightening' reaction to grievances and to alleviate official fears that freedom of thought was inherently associated with subversion or rebellion. Despite the varied forms that resistance took, the underlying conflicts thus emerge as the unifying element of disparate forms of response that originate in civil society.

The serial defeats of the state in the face of resistance from urban civil society should not only lead us to reconsider our understanding of the balance of political power in the Hohenzollern polity in this period. The outcomes of these conflicts were also part of a structural shift in the long-term rise of bourgeois society in Prussia. As Eley and Blackbourn have argued, the concern with revolutionary change has often led historians to overlook the incremental structural change that allowed the bourgeoisie to become the dominant social class.[10] In late eighteenth-century Prussia we can observe shifts of this kind that were not revolutionary in nature, but the development was still driven by direct confrontation with the state. It is often argued that far-reaching reform was bequeathed on Prussians by a combination of military defeat at the hands of Napoleon and a set of liberal officials fortuitously in the right place at the right time. However, this overlooks the way in which urban dwellers forced Prussian absolutism to make gradual but significant steps towards concessions in the preceding decades. The outcome of these conflicts not only led to structural political shifts, but also gave rise to discourses about individualism, feeding directly into the development of liberal political thought in Prussia and the rest of Europe. Crucial for this connection between rebellious Prussian burghers of the eighteenth century and liberal thinkers of the nineteenth were the early political writings of Wilhelm von Humboldt (1767–1835). The conflicts and debates explored here formed the original historical context in which Humboldt developed his views in *On the limits of state action* which he wrote in the early 1790s and which subsequently influenced John Stuart Mill (1806–73) and other liberals across Europe. These European connections are explored in Chapter 6, but it is a central concern of this study to discuss the Prussian developments in a European and Atlantic context in the preceding chapters. In all chapters reference is made to the many instances in which ideas, publications, and individuals that moved between Prussia and other European countries and North America played a crucial part. This interconnectedness points to structural similarities in European history. The advice of French tax officials would have been meaningless in Prussia, as a Prussian tract on the limits of state action would have been in Britain, without the existence of structural similarities in the challenges

---

[10] Blackbourn and Eley, 'Introduction', pp. 13–18.

and developments that contemporaries faced. By employing a connective approach instead of looking at comparisons, I suggest that the European history of this period might best be approached as an integrated whole rather than as a bundle of special paths. This is one of the central arguments of this book and hopefully it will emerge clearly from the following chapters along with the details and complexities that have been omitted here for the sake of clarity and brevity.

HISTORIOGRAPHY

The arguments put forward in this book build on the work of generations of historians. Rather than acknowledging specific debts—this is done in the notes in the usual way—I point out here where I see the place of this contribution among the existing historiography. This book relates, principally, to three overlapping historiographical debates that centre on the issues of state building, the rise of a critical public, and the development of Prussian towns.

The process of state building is the point of departure of the analysis presented here and in doing so I am responding to some extent to the recurring plea to bring the state back into historiography and the social sciences, as formulated by Theda Skocpol and others in 1985.[11] However, while this was an important call in the light of the preponderance of social history and a lingering Marxist influence, at times reducing the state to a puppet of the ruling class, it certainly did not resonate in the Prussian case in the same way as it did in other national contexts. Perhaps no other historiography has a richer tradition of engagement with the process of state building. Otto Hintze, Gustav von Schmoller, and Hans Rosenberg are among the giants on the shoulders of whom Prussian historians of the state can stand.[12] Rather than bringing the state back in, it may therefore be a matter of bringing society, specifically urban society, into the historiography of Prussia. Often the focus on institutional development and its inner logic has obscured the social context in

---

[11] Theda Skocpol, 'Bringing the state back in: strategies of analysis in current research', in Peter Evans, Dietrich Rueschemeyer, and Theda Skocpol, eds., *Bringing the state back in* (Cambridge, 1985), pp. 3–43.

[12] See among others Gustav von Schmoller, *Der preußische Beamtenstand unter Friedrich Wilhelm I.* (Berlin, 1870). Gustav von Schmoller, *Das brandenburgisch-preußische Innungswesen von 1640–1806 hauptsächlich die Reform unter Friedrich Wilhelm I.* (Berlin, 1887). Gustav von Schmoller, *Über Behördenorganisation, Amtswesen und Beamtenthum im Allgemeinen und speciell in Deutschland und Preußen bis zum Jahre 1713* (Berlin, 1894). Gustav von Schmoller, *Der deutsche Beamtenstaat vom 16.–18. Jahrhundert. Rede gehalten auf dem deutschen Historikertag zu Leipzig am 29. März 1894* (Leipzig, 1894). Gustav von Schmoller, *Preußische Verfassungs-, Verwaltungs- und Finanzgeschichte* (Berlin, 1921). Gustav von Schmoller, *Das Merkantilsystem in seiner historischen Bedeutung staedtische, territoriale und staatliche Wirtschaftspolitik* (Frankfurt, 1940). Otto Hintze, *Die Hohenzollern und ihr Werk: fünfhundert Jahre vaterländischer Geschichte* (Berlin, 1915). Otto Hintze, 'Staatenbildung und Verfassungsentwicklung', in Gerhard Oestreich, ed., *Staat und Verfassung* (Göttingen, 1970), pp. 34–51. Otto Hintze, 'Der österreichische und der preußische Beamtenstaat im 17. und 18. Jahrhundert', in Gerhard Oestreich, ed., *Staat und Verfassung* (Göttingen, 1970), pp. 321–58. Otto Hintze, 'Der Commissarius und seine Bedeutung in der allgemeinen Verwaltungsgeschichte', in Gerhard Oestreich, ed., *Staat und Verfassung* (Göttingen, 1970), pp. 242–74. Hans Rosenberg, *Bureaucracy, aristocracy and autocracy: the Prussian experience, 1660–1815* (Cambridge, MA, 1958).

which the process of state building took place. This is perhaps most apparent in the studies of fiscal institutions that often achieve the remarkable feat of discussing taxation almost entirely in the absence of any consideration of reaction and agency of taxpayers in relation to the institutional change, while, at the same time, devoting extraordinary attention to the organization of the administrative structure.[13] Here the historiography of state building in Prussia needs to broaden its perspective and take inspiration from the tradition of fiscal sociology pioneered by Rudolf Goldscheid and others.[14] The present study thus seeks to emphasize the way in which the objectives of the state—the preservation of security and more broadly speaking the creation and maintenance of order—led it to act, in part, independently of the interests of the social groups on which its power rested. Actions of the state took place in a context that consisted of motives related to its self-preservation and the interests of the main actors who were directly invested in it, in this period mainly the ruler and administrators. However, the agency of the state must also be seen as conditioned by imperatives and tensions at the level of the administrative and communicative practices through which it interacted with its citizens.[15] It is therefore crucial to understand the development of the state and its actions in the context of the simultaneous and corresponding evolution of civil society. The complex interrelation between the two processes in the area of the regulation of sexuality has recently been discussed by Isabel Hull in an innovative study and it has been the ambition of this present volume to bring some of her dialectical perspective to the analysis of the changes in the interaction between state and individuals in economic and religious matters.[16]

If Prussian civil society has often received short shrift at the hands of historians of the state, it initially did not fare much better among those studying conflicts between civil society and the state. In his seminal work on the rise of the bourgeois public sphere in Europe, Habermas explicitly excluded Prussia from his analysis on the grounds that the weak local bourgeoisie never mustered the strength to challenge the state in this way.[17] Habermas' thesis—closely linked to the *Sonderweg* argument—led to a protracted debate that unfolded essentially in two waves

[13] Gustav von Schmoller, 'Die Epochen der preußischen Finanzpolitik', *Jahrbuch für Gesetzgebung, Verwaltung und Volkswirtschaft im Deutschen Reich*, 1 (1877), pp. 32–114. Walther Schultze, *Geschichte der preussischen Regieverwaltung von 1766 bis 1786, ein historisch-kritischer Versuch* (Leipzig, 1888).

[14] See among others Rudolf Goldscheid, *Staatssozialismus oder Staatskapitalismus* (Wien, 1917). Joseph Schumpeter, 'The crisis of the tax state', in Richard Swedberg, ed., *Economics and sociology of capitalism* (Princeton, 1991), pp. 99–140. Edwin Seligman, *Essays on taxation* (New York, 1913). Isaac Martin et al., eds., *The new fiscal sociology* (Cambridge, 2009).

[15] Peter Becker, 'Sprachvollzug: Kommunikation und Verwaltung', in Peter Becker, ed., *Sprachvollzug im Amt* (Bielefeld, 2011), pp. 9–44.

[16] Isabel Hull, *Sexuality, state and civil society in Germany, 1700–1815* (Ithaca, NY, 1996). A lucid discussion of the interrelation of state and civil society building can be found in Schumpeter, 'The crisis of the tax state'. However, Schumpeter's article remained a largely theoretical treatment which lacked the detail expected of professional historians.

[17] Jürgen Habermas, *The structural transformation of the public sphere: an inquiry into a category of bourgeois society* (Cambridge, 1989). Jürgen Habermas, *Strukturwandel der Öffentlichkeit. Untersuchungen zu einer Kategorie der bürgerlichen Gesellschaft; mit einem Vorwort zur Neuauflage 1990* (Frankfurt am Main, 2009).

following the publication of the original work in 1962 and its English translation in 1989.[18] Apart from being a testimony to the lack of globalization in the world of professional historians, the trajectory of the debates also meant that it became even more sprawling than was perhaps necessary: one reviewer counted over 12,000 contributions.[19] We concentrate on those aspects of the debate that are directly relevant to our project.

Most relevant is Habermas' claim that a critical public never developed in Prussia. This view has been proved wrong many times and in arguing that public criticism was the primary form of opposition helping urban dwellers to prevail over the state's power, this work agrees with the critics.[20] However, we hope to do more than this and shed light on a blind spot in the revisionist historiography about Prussia's public. Oddly, the many studies that have discussed the vibrant political debates that existed in Prussia have studiously ignored fiscal debates and the important role that economic issues played in contemporary exchanges.[21] This is surprising, because fiscal debates are one of the focal points of the historiography of contemporary public debates in France, the North American colonies, and elsewhere. In particular, governmental efforts to fiscalize growing consumption and social resistance against them have recently been the subject of innovative studies.[22] The omission of this subject in Prussian historiography may well reflect a lingering notion that the Prussian public was only politicized up to a certain degree, but ultimately preferred loftier discourses to the mundane and potentially confrontational questions of public finance. This work will contribute to a more rounded view of the Prussian public.

[18] For a survey and critique see Andreas Gestrich, 'The public sphere and the Habermas-Debate', *German History*, 24 (2006), pp. 413–31.

[19] Stéphane Van Damme, '"Farewell Habermas"? Deux décennies d'études sur l'ancien régime de l'espace public', in Patrick Boucheron and Nicolas Offenstadt, eds., *L'espace public au moyen âge: débats autour de Jürgen Habermas* (Paris, 2011), pp. 42–55.

[20] Summarizing the revisionist research about the politicization of the German public: Eckhart Hellmuth, 'Towards a comparative study of political culture', in Eckhart Hellmuth, ed., *The transformation of political culture: England and Germany in the late eighteenth century* (Oxford, 1990), pp. 1–38.

[21] Contemporary commentary on fiscal matters is occasionally mentioned but never systematically explored. See, for example, Günter Birtsch, 'Die Berliner Mittwochsgesellschaft', in Hans Bödeker and Ulrich Herrmann, eds., *Über den Prozess der Aufklärung in Deutschland im 18. Jahrhundert* (Göttingen, 1987), pp. 94–112, at p. 101. Eckhart Hellmuth, 'Aufklärung und Pressefreiheit: zur Debatte der Berliner Mittwochsgesellschaft während der Jahre 1783 und 1784', *Zeitschrift für Historische Forschung*, 9 (1982), pp. 315–45. Horst Möller, 'Wie aufgeklärt war Preußen?', *Geschichte und Gesellschaft*, Sonderheft 6 (1980), pp. 176–201. Rudolf Vierhaus, 'The Prussian bureaucracy reconsidered', in Eckhart Hellmuth, ed., *Rethinking Leviathan* (Oxford, 1999), pp. 150–64, at p. 163. Even Ingrid Mittenzwei who examines fiscal conflicts in the western provinces in some detail argues that economic discourses did not play an important role in the Prussian context and takes this as an indication of the retarded development of Prussia compared with England. Ingrid Mittenzwei, *Preußen nach dem Siebenjährigen Krieg: Auseinandersetzungen zwischen Bürgertum und Staat um die Wirtschaftspolitik* (Berlin, 1979), p. 71.

[22] Michael Kwass, *Privilege and the politics of taxation in eighteenth-century France: liberté, égalité, fiscalité* (Cambridge, 2000). William Ashworth, *Customs and excise: trade, production and consumption in England, 1640–1845* (Oxford, 2003). T. H. Breen, *The marketplace of revolution: how consumer politics shaped American independence* (Oxford, 2004). Nicolas Delalande, *Les batailles de l'impôt: consentement et résistances de 1789 a nos jours* (Paris, 2011).

Another criticism that had been levelled against Habermas was associated with his narrow focus on conflicts over economic questions as a driving force behind the rise of a critical public and the ensuing neglect of the important religious debates of the time.[23] The question of the development of religious publics is largely absent from the *structural transformation*, although Habermas has recently discussed similarities in the state's disengagement from economic and religious matters in the process of state building.[24] Nonetheless, despite the critique of Habermas' neglect of religion and the publication of important work on the development of religious publics, historians of Prussia have not been successful in integrating and relating the development of the religious public with other contemporary publics. The rich literature on the interaction between state building, the two Prussian reformations, and the emergence of public debates about religious matters has remained disconnected from other strands of research.[25] Where a connection has been made, the emphasis is mainly on how certain forms of religiosity, mainly Pietism, contributed to increasing the power of the state and forming an obedient and malleable civil society.[26] The emancipatory impulses that originated in religious life and in particular in forms of communication championed by Pietism have been explored in recent studies. In this book we examine the development of the religious public in the context of the emergence of public debates about other issues, most notably about fiscal and economic questions.[27] In this way an artificial

---

[23] Among others, see David Zaret, 'Religion, science, and printing in the public spheres in seventeenth-century England', in Craig Calhoun, ed., *Habermas and the public sphere* (Cambridge, MA, 1992), pp. 212–35. James van Horn Melton, 'Pietism, politics and the public sphere in Germany', in James E. Bradley and Dale K. Van Kley, eds., *Religion and politics in enlightenment Europe* (Notre Dame, IN, 2001), pp. 294–333.

[24] Jürgen Habermas, '"The political": the rational meaning of a questionable inheritance of political theology', in Judith Butler, Eduardo Mendieta, and Jonathan Van Antwerpen, eds., *The power of religion in the public sphere* (New York, 2011), pp. 15–33.

[25] An impressive body of research on the Prussian case has been produced by historians of religion and Pietism in particular. Klaus Deppermann, 'Pietismus und die moderne Welt', in Kurt Aland, ed., *Pietismus und die moderne Welt* (Witten, 1974), pp. 75–98. Bodo Nischan, *Prince, people, and confession: the Second Reformation in Brandenburg* (Philadelphia, 1994). Mary Fulbrook, *Piety and politics: religion and the rise of absolutism in England, Württemberg, and Prussia* (Cambridge, 1983).

[26] Carl Hinrichs, *Preußentum und Pietismus* (Göttingen, 1971). Richard Gawthrop, *Pietism and the making of eighteenth-century Prussia* (Cambridge, 1993). Benjamin Marschke, *Absolutely Pietist: patronage, fictionalism, and state-building in the early eighteenth-century Prussian army chaplaincy* (Tübingen, 2005). Much of the literature on the Woellner controversy has equally emphasized the successes of the authoritarian policies and paid less attention to the successful resistance against it. Dirk Kemper, 'Obskurantismus als Mittel der Politik. Johann Christoph Wöllners Politik der Gegenaufklärung am Vorabend der Französischen Revolution', in Christoph Weiß, ed., *Von 'Obscuranten' und 'Eudämonisten'. Gegenaufklärerische, konservative und antirevolutionäre Publizisten im späten 18. Jahrhundert* (St Ingbert, 1997), pp. 193–220. Christina Stange-Fayos, *Lumières et obscurantisme en Prusse* (Bern, 2003). Sauter, *Visions*. Uta Wiggermann, *Woellner und das Religionsedikt Kirchenpolitik und kirchliche Wirklichkeit im Preußen des späten 18. Jahrhunderts* (Tübingen, 2010).

[27] Martin Schmidt, 'Der Pietismus und das moderne Denken', in Kurt Aland, ed., *Der Pietismus und die moderne Welt* (Witten, 1974), pp. 9–74. Christina Rathgeber, 'The reception of Brandenburg-Prussia's new Lutheran hymnal of 1781', *Historical Journal*, 36 (1993), pp. 115–36. Martin Gierl, *Pietismus und Aufklärung: theologische Polemik und die Kommunikationsreform der Wissenschaft am Ende des 17. Jahrhunderts* (Göttingen, 1997). Melton, 'Pietism, politics and the public sphere in Germany', pp. 294–333. Marschke, *Absolutely Pietist*. Ulrike Gleixner, *Pietismus und Bürgertum: eine historische Anthropologie der Frömmigkeit, Württemberg 17.–19. Jahrhundert* (Göttingen, 2005).

divide is bridged through a discussion of the emergence of economic and religious publics as interrelated and mutually reinforcing phenomena. This is done by treating economic and religious matters as integral parts of the sphere that individuals came to see as an area of their autonomy in this period. State interference with both was equally resented and provoked similar forms of reaction, most notably public criticism but also passive resistance and violence or threats of violence. In adopting this perspective some important claims of Habermas about the weakness of the Prussian public are rejected, while also using and further developing some of the hermeneutical tools that he provides. In particular, Habermas offers a useful framework in which to think about the historical development of ideas in the context of changing socio-economic realities. Approaches that seek to explain the development of ideas by placing them in the context of other ideas have done much to further our understanding of intellectual change but they also have obvious limitations. In the area of economic thought, in particular, where the relation of ideas to the material realities of their time is obvious, a limited contextualization must remain frustrating.[28]

Treating economic and religious debates together further complicates the answer to another central question regarding the Habermas debate, relating to the bourgeois nature of the public sphere. Habermas' characterization of the public as 'bourgeois' ('bürgerlich') has provoked widespread criticism based on a careful counting and categorization of active members of the Prussian public in different settings such as debating or reading societies. Painstaking enquiries of this kind revealed that many members of the public were on the state's payroll and were not just independent, upstanding businessmen.[29] However, the implications of such findings for Habermas' theory have perhaps sometimes been overestimated. This is partly because one may question them on methodological grounds. We do not know anything about how the social compositions of the examined samples relate to the composition of the Prussian public as a whole. It therefore remains doubtful whether we can extrapolate the composition of the whole public from the composition of the samples. But even more importantly, Habermas himself argues that while the public sphere was in principle open to all (educated) individuals, 'officials of the rulers' administrations were its core'.[30] However, if everyone, including Habermas, seems to agree that there were few proper bourgeois—at least in the narrow economic definition of the term—should we not then think about correcting the English translation of 'bürgerliche Öffentlichkeit' from 'bourgeois' to 'civic' or 'urban public sphere'? This question should also be examined from another angle. The bourgeois nature of many public debates of this period did not derive

---

[28] On this question see Paul Cheney's remarks in the introduction to his *Revolutionary commerce: globalization and the French monarchy* (Cambridge, MA, 2010).

[29] Möller, 'Wie aufgeklärt war Preußen?', pp. 178–82. Richard Van Dülmen, *Die Gesellschaft der Aufklärer* (Frankfurt, 1986). Birtsch, 'Mittwochsgesellschaft'. Hans Bödeker, 'Prozesse und Strukturen politischer Bewußtseinsbildung der deutschen Aufklärung', in Hans Bödeker and Ulrich Herrmann, eds., *Aufklärung als Politisierung* (Hamburg, 1987), pp. 10–31, at p. 10. Blanning, *Culture of power*, p. 12. For a variation of the quantitative approach see Sauter, *Visions*, pp. 141–66.

[30] Habermas, *Public sphere*, p. 22.

from the social origin of the contributors but from the fact that the issues that were debated would not have arisen had it not been for the rise of commercial capitalism and consequently of a bourgeois class. This is a convincing argument in the context of fiscal and wider economic debates, developed further in Chapter 4, which made up a central part of public debates in Prussia and elsewhere. The same, however, cannot be said of religious debates. What remains is a compounded picture in which only the emergence of a part, albeit a central one, of public debates may be linked to the socio-economic transformations associated with the long-term rise of the bourgeoisie. One might go so far as to argue that the public as a whole would not have evolved with the same dynamism and political power had it not been for this partial link with socio-economic change. It could also be argued that even the sections of the public who did not have 'bourgeois' origins contributed to the development of cultural traits that subsequently became crucial aspects of bourgeois society. There can be no doubt that any analysis of the origin of the public that focuses exclusively on a socio-economic link must remain incomplete. Rather than trying to privilege one or the other, this study engages in a connective way with the multiple sources that supplied the public with forms of communication, dynamism, and political power. In the Prussian case, it is possible to get away with this eclecticism, even in the eyes of the most hardened historical materialist. After all, Friedrich Engels once declared that it was impossible to understand Prussian history purely in the light of economic factors.[31]

Closely linked to the question of its bourgeois nature is that of the alleged subversiveness of the public. In contrast to Habermas, it has been argued that because many members of the public were in the pay of the state their public commentary did not constitute a challenge to the state. Rather, public debates were, to some extent, a continuation of considerations that occurred within the corridors of power, and leading members of the public had a vested interest in the stability of the state because it was linked with their own career prospects and because they saw the state as a means, not an obstacle, to carrying out their reformatory agenda.[32] This nexus was, allegedly, particular strong in Prussia and as a result its public—unlike the French—did not pose a serious challenge to the state.[33] The notion of a close relationship between state and public in Prussia does not sit easily with the evidence discussed in this book. In several instances Prussians publicly attacked the state and the state eventually acceded to these attacks and fulfilled the demands of the critics. Moreover, some of the most vicious attacks were written by employees of the state, which calls into question the notion that critical capability ceased with state employment. Even the additional argument that critical voices only made up a part of the public and that, seen as a whole, it was therefore politically neutral vis-à-vis the state is ultimately not convincing as it

---

[31] Friedrich Engels, 'Letter to J. Bloch, 1 Oct. 1895', in T. Borodulina, ed., *On historical materialism* (Moscow, 1972), pp. 294–6, at p. 294.

[32] Blanning, *Culture of power*, pp. 11–14. Sauter, *Visions*, pp. 1–14.

[33] Blanning, *Culture of power*, p. 13. Sauter, *Visions*, p. 82.

misunderstands the nature of the threat that public debates posed to the state.[34] Even supporters of the state's position challenged its authority when they expressed their views publicly because, either explicitly or implicitly, they claimed to have a say in the matter under consideration and thus challenged the state's monopoly on political power. Moreover, an even more basic nexus applied in Prussia and elsewhere. The power of early modern states was extremely precarious. Their administrative and military apparatus was still fragile and they feared nothing more than disorder. For this reason, uncontrolled and uncontrollable public debates that might spill over into other forms of disorder were perceived as menacing quite independently from the contents of the arguments that made up the debates.

The notion of a lack of subversiveness in the Prussian public is also difficult to reconcile with another characteristic of the conflicts explored here. Although the argument about the cosy relationship between public and state in Prussia is usually couched in terms of a revision of Habermas' thesis, it supports his central point about the fundamental difference of the Prussian case from the French and other western experiences. Perhaps the main difference between the two arguments lies in their perspective. While many historians in the generation of Habermas asked whether Prussia had been on a special path of development, some of today's historians seem inclined to declare France to be an exceptional case.[35] Many eighteenth-century writers might have dismissed this kind of dispute as sophistry, but there are also some substantial issues associated with it. Prussian development was closely linked with development in other parts of Europe and the Atlantic world through movements of individuals, ideas, and goods. Similarly, close connections have been shown to have existed between other regions in this period. The ease with which such exchanges were possible calls into question how useful the resurgence of an insistence on 'national distinctiveness' can be to our understanding of this period. This argument builds on a large body of recent research on European transnationality, transfers, and exchanges, research that has also spurred a considerable theoretical debate.[36] However, this argument, that successful exchanges were indicators of structural similarity, goes further than many existing contributions to this field.

Works on Prussia's towns form the last body of literature directly relevant to this study. Although this is a very small field of historiography it is a deeply divided one. Some authors seek to show the weakness and oppressed existence of Prussian towns and their inhabitants under the Hohenzollern yolk, while others have sought to paint a more optimistic, and therefore perhaps more realistic, picture.[37] However,

---

[34] Blanning, *Culture of power*, pp. 12–13.

[35] Blanning, *Culture of power*, p. 13. Sauter, *Visions*, p. 82.

[36] For a summary and commentary on parts of the debate see Holger Nehring and Florian Schui, 'Introduction: global debates about taxation: transfers of ideas, the challenge of political legitimacy and the paradoxes of state-building', in Holger Nehring and Florian Schui, eds., *Global debates about taxation* (London, 2007), pp. 1–18.

[37] Firmly in the former category are Johannes Ziekursch, *Das Ergebnis der friderizianischen Städteverwaltung und die Städteordnung Steins am Beispiel der schlesischen Städte dargestellt* (Jena,

many of the important contributions to the field, such as Schmoller's upbeat *Deutsches Städtewesen in älterer Zeit* or the rather depressing panorama of Friedrich Ziekursch's *Die friderizianische Städteordnung*, are now almost a hundred years old.[38] More recently the most important impulses for urban history in the Prussian context have come from the efforts of economic historians to revise the view of Prussia's economy of this period as backward and static. In his revisionist studies Rolf Straubel has revealed the economic vibrancy of several Prussian towns and the importance of larger merchants and manufacturers, which points to a dynamic development that was rapidly outgrowing traditional patterns of the urban economy.[39] In a similar way, recent scholarship about the self-perceptions of urban dwellers and contemporary notions of urbanity, such as the innovative studies of Matt Erlin and Yair Mintzker, emphasizes the dynamism and vibrancy of the urban environment in Prussia.[40] Beyond these studies the most important recent contribution is perhaps Christopher Clark's chapter on urban life in *Iron kingdom*. Using an innovative iconographic approach, Clark captures some of the cultural and political strength that characterized Prussian towns and their burghers. However, even more telling than the findings that he presents is perhaps his remark that the towns are a 'world that is often overlooked in general accounts of the Prussian lands'.[41] This present study makes a contribution to changing this situation.

SOURCES

In accordance with the focus of this study on the political power of the urban public, sources used here consist mainly of published commentaries on Prussian towns written by inhabitants of those towns. In addition, works from other parts of

1908). Andreas Nachama, *Ersatzbürger und Staatsbildung: zur Zerstörung des Bürgertums in Brandenburg-Preussen* (Frankfurt, 1984). More balanced accounts can be found in Gerd Heinrich, 'Staatsaufsicht und Stadtfreiheit in Brandenburg-Preussen unter dem Absolutismus (1660–1806)', in Wilhelm Rausch, ed., *Die Städte Mitteleuropas im 17. und 18. Jahrhundert* (Linz, 1981), pp. 155–72. Beate Engelen, 'Fremde in der Stadt. Die Garnisonsgesellschaft Prenzlaus im 18. Jahrhundert', in Klaus Neitmann and Jürgen Theil, eds., *Die Herkunft der Brandenburger* (Potsdam, 2001).

[38] Gustav von Schmoller, *Deutsches Städtewesen in älterer Zeit* (Aalen, 1964). Ziekursch, *Städteverwaltung.* Ernst Fidicin, *Die Territorien der Mark Brandenburg oder Geschichte der einzelnen Kreise, Städte, Rittergüter, Stiftungen und Dörfer in derselben, als Fortsetzung des Landbuchs Kaiser Karls IV* (Berlin, 1858). Ernst Fidicin, *Berlin, historisch und topographisch dargestellt* (Berlin, 1852).

[39] Rolf Straubel, *Kaufleute und Manufakturunternehmer: eine empirische Untersuchung über die sozialen Trager von Handel und Großgewerbe in den mittleren preußischen Provinzen (1763 bis 1815)* (Stuttgart, 1995). Rolf Straubel, *Frankfurt (Oder) und Potsdam am Ende des Alten Reiches Studien zur städtischen Wirtschafts- und Sozialstruktur* (Potsdam, 1995). Rolf Straubel, *Die Handelsstädte Königsberg und Memel in friderizianischer Zeit ein Beitrag zur Geschichte des ost- und gesamtpreußischen 'Commerciums' sowie seiner sozialen Träger (1763–1806/15)* (Berlin, 2003).

[40] Matt Erlin, *Berlin's forgotten future: city, history, and enlightenment in eighteenth-century Germany* (Chapel Hill, NC, 2004). Yair Mintzker, 'What is defortification? Military functions, police roles, and symbolism in the demolition of German city walls in the eighteenth and nineteenth centuries', *Bulletin of the German Historical Institute*, 48 (2011), pp. 33–58.

[41] Christopher Clark, *Iron kingdom: the rise and downfall of Prussia, 1600–1947* (London, 2007), p. 148.

Germany and Europe that were read and discussed by Prussian burghers are drawn into the discussion. However, the geographic limitation of the scope of this enquiry is less clear than it may seem. 'Prussian towns' are not easy to define for our period and were subject to change. We take the term Prussia to denote all territories under the control of the Hohenzollern ruler at any given time. In the eighteenth century this is largely consonant with contemporary usage, although the collection of provinces that were comprised in the Hohenzollern polity came to be known under this collective name only gradually. Equally, we follow the contemporary usage of the word 'town', although in many cases settlements that were considered to be towns by contemporaries would hardly be considered as such today. One of the leading geographers of the time, Anton Friedrich Büsching (1724–93), drew up a tentative list of characteristics that we may refer to. For him the most important attribute of a town was to do with the way that its inhabitants sustained themselves economically. The right to 'make a living in a burgher-like fashion' ('bürgerliche Nahrung treiben') was seen as a crucial element of urbanity. The definition was somewhat circular but it still points to an environment that was economically and fundamentally different from the agrarian context of the countryside. The two other distinguishing features that Büsching names were the existence of a magistrate, implying some degree of political self-rule, and the presence of a wall or similar barrier that visibly delimited the territory of the town from the surrounding countryside.[42] Crucially, the size of the settlement did not matter, which means that a wide range of towns of different sizes formed the objects of contemporary commentary, although much attention was devoted to the largest and fastest growing towns such as Berlin. A Berlin-centric bias has been avoided as much as possible, but this was not always feasible because of the prominent role that the capital played in contemporary debates. We have also drawn on non-published sources in some instances, in particular to reconstruct official discourses. The material used comes mostly from the Geheimes Staatsarchiv Preußischer Kulturbesitz in Berlin. References are to edited versions of the documents in the *Acta Borussica* and other editions, even if the originals have been consulted. The volumes of *Acta Borussica*, in particular those edited by Hugo Rachel, bring together many of the important documents for Prussia's fiscal history in this period. However, while they are valuable tools it should be remembered that, in keeping with the spirit of contemporary German historiography, the selection and comments on documents often show a 'pro-state' bias. This must be borne in mind and anyone intending to work on the role of non-state actors is well advised to carefully contextualize Rachel's selection. Finally, in order to make this book more accessible all citations and titles that appear in the main text have been translated by the author (unless stated otherwise). The original titles and text—mostly in German and French—are given in the notes.

---

[42] Anton Friedrich Büsching, *Topographie der Mark Brandenburg* (Berlin, 1775), p. 57. For an excellent discussion of contemporary perceptions and functions of walls see Mintzker, 'What is defortification?', pp. 33–58.

1

The Paradoxes of State Building

Only where individual life carries its own centre of gravity within itself, where its meaning lies in the individual and his personal sphere, where the fulfilment of the personality is its own end, only there can the state exist as a real phenomenon.

Joseph Schumpeter, *The crisis of the tax state* (1918).[1]

Much has been written about the process of state building in Prussia but little attention has been paid to the corresponding process of 'civil society building'. Every step on the road to state building meant that ordinary Prussians were confronted with larger and more powerful state organs, particularly in areas associated with the exercise of military power. But as the state consolidated its grip on certain areas it also withdrew from others, or at least confined its activities to better-defined limits. In economic and religious matters in particular, it left more space for choices to be made by individuals and for private interests to be pursued. It is important to understand that greater diversity was not the objective of this increased individual freedom. Individuals were not given greater freedom in order to become more different. Rather it was hoped that reliance on individual choices and motivations would yield well-ordered prosperity and stable religious peace more efficiently than direct intervention. The double-faced process of state and civil society building was accelerated in the aftermath of the Thirty Years War and defined in many respects the front lines of conflict between state and urban dwellers that emerged in the late eighteenth century. This chapter sketches how the relations between individuals and state changed in Prussian towns as a result of the Thirty Years War until the beginning of the reign of Frederick II in 1740. First, the origins of the process of state building and its different trajectories in country and towns are explored. Second, focus is placed on the impact of institutional change on urban civil society in fiscal, economic, and military matters, then in matters of religion, and the related spheres of sexuality and education.

---

[1] Joseph Schumpeter, 'The crisis of the tax state', in Richard Swedberg, ed., *Economics and sociology of capitalism* (Princeton, 1991), pp. 99–140, at p. 119.

THE FATHER OF THE PRUSSIAN STATE

Although we will try to look at the process of state building from the perspective of a Prussian burgher, it is necessary to start in a rather traditional way. The everyday life of urban Prussians was altered in many ways by the creation of a more powerful and centralized state, but the process of state building still had its origins in great power politics or, more precisely, with one form of it: warfare. The Thirty Years War should be regarded as the father of the Prussian state. Prior to and during this European conflict nothing seemed to suggest that the territories of the Hohenzollern rulers would be unified into a single state that would, eventually, be on a par with the great powers of Europe. Division and partial annexation by unfriendly neighbours seemed a more likely outcome on more than one occasion during the war. The lands of the Elector George William (1595–1640), who ruled throughout most of the conflict, were geographically disconnected, lacked easily defendable borders, and did not share a common historical or cultural heritage. Nonetheless, during the 150 years after the Thirty Years War the Hohenzollern rose from being Electors of Brandenburg and Dukes of Prussia (in addition to a host of other titles), to becoming first Kings in Prussia (that is in East Prussia which lay outside the empire) in 1701 and then Kings of Prussia in 1772. These changes were in part symbolic and driven by dynastic rivalry. The electors of Hannover and Saxony had acquired royal titles outside the empire around the same time. However, the new titles of the Hohenzollern dynasty also reflected a real increase in power and a greater unity of their realm. The collection of territories that they ruled began to turn into an entity that was increasingly known under the single collective name of Prussia.

The remarkable ascendancy of Prussia was in part due to its dynasty's relentless pursuit of glory and political power. Like all rulers of the time the Hohenzollern were keen to increase their prestige and power. There may be some truth in the argument that at least some members of the family had a particular gift for this quest. However, what motivated the rulers of Prussia more than the pursuit of greatness was fear. During the Thirty Years War they had to watch helplessly as Swedish and imperial troops took turns to occupy and loot their territories. George William ineptly tried to manoeuvre between the different sides in the war but in the course of events it became clear that he did not exercise any real power. Frederick II later remarked that his ancestor had been 'incapable of governing'.[2] This comment was meant as a personal insult but it probably captures the historical reality better if we read it differently from how it was intended: George William's main problem was not that he lacked political insight but that he did not have the means to make his decisions count. Lucky circumstance meant that the Hohenzollern came out of the war with their territories not only intact but even enlarged. However, the experience of utter powerlessness impressed itself not only on George William's

---

[2] 'Incapable de gouverner'. Frederick II, 'Mémoires pour servir à l'histoire de la maison de Brandenbourg', in Johann D. E. Preuss, ed., *Oeuvres de Frédéric le Grand* (30 vols., Berlin, 1848), vol. 1, p. 36.

immediate successor, Frederick William, the Great Elector (1620–88), but also on subsequent monarchs who had to suffer similar if less threatening situations. The keen interest that the 'soldier king' Frederick William I (1688–1740) took in reforming the military derived to some extent from his experience as a military commander during the wars against Louis XIV. In these conflicts Prussia's military was once again too weak to prevent foreign invasion and the young crown prince was not only humiliated by military defeat but also by disparaging remarks about Prussia's military from his own allies.[3] The Thirty Years War and subsequent conflicts made it clear that unless Prussia acquired a significant military force its existence would remain precarious.

This was a strong motivation for the ruling house to build a more powerful army. Prior to this time any moves in this direction had collided with the interests of the nobles, prelates, and towns that were represented in the estates. The antagonism between estates and crown was not as marked in Prussia as in other European polities but the estates still resisted change that would to lead to an increase in the power of the ruler.[4] However, the Thirty Years War altered the traditional lines of domestic political conflict. Members of the estates suffered substantially during the war, mainly at the hands of Swedish invaders who did not show much respect for traditional rights and privileges. The occupiers imposed tax payments by force and ruled with an iron fist.[5] Clearly the vulnerability to foreign invasion was not only a threat to the dynasty but also to the estates. Any rights and prerogatives that they held were only as good as the power of the ruler who granted them. Compared with a ruthless foreign invader, the prospect of a strengthened central dynasty was a lesser evil. The Swedish troops that invaded Prussia during the Thirty Years War and in subsequent conflicts thus became the 'hammer' (Perry Anderson) that forged change on Prussia.[6]

One of the first steps was taken in 1653 when the estates agreed to the temporary introduction of new taxes for the funding of a standing army. The charter was the starting point of a protracted process that allowed the Prussian rulers to raise the financial means to keep a larger, better equipped, and more thoroughly trained army. The right to tax for a standing army was made permanent in 1662 and the first concrete results became visible in 1666 when for the first time soldiers were not sent home after a military campaign but instead became the nucleus of Prussia's standing army.[7] The further development of this army was an uphill struggle for the Hohenzollern despite the fact that the relationship between estates and rulers was in many respects one of cooperation rather than

[3] Wolfgang Neugebauer, 'Epochen der preußischen Geschichte', in Wolfgang Neugebauer, ed., *Handbuch der preußischen Geschichte. Das 17. und 18. Jahrhundert und große Themen der preußischen Geschichte* (Berlin, 2009), pp. 113–410, at p. 248.

[4] Edgar Melton, 'The Prussian Junkers, 1600–1786', in Hamish Scott, ed., *The European nobilities in the seventeenth and eighteenth centuries* (London, 1995), pp. 71–109.

[5] Gustav von Schmoller, *Deutsches Städtewesen in älterer Zeit* (Aalen, 1964), pp. 246–8.

[6] Perry Anderson, *Lineages of the absolutist state* (London, 1975), p. 198.

[7] Neugebauer, 'Epochen', p. 182. Beate Engelen, 'Fremde in der Stadt. Die Garnisonsgesellschaft Prenzlaus im 18. Jahrhundert', in Klaus Neitmann and Jürgen Theil, eds., *Die Herkunft der Brandenburger* (Potsdam, 2001), p. 114.

confrontation.[8] This was most notably the case in the countryside where their friendly relationship with the nobility formed one of the pillars of Hohenzollern rule. Nonetheless, opposition to the standing army and the associated financial demands was significant. In Königsberg, for example, resistance could be broken only by military force.[9] In a rather ironic way such instances of domestic use of the military confirmed fears of the opponents of a standing army that it was not only a tool to defend the country but also one that could be used to establish a more absolute monarchy at home.

Already when the first steps towards the creation of a standing army were taken it became clear that the crucial issue in warfare was money. Soldiers and weapons could be bought if only the necessary funds were available. The ability to tax, therefore, ultimately decided over triumph and defeat on the battlefield. The whole process of state building can only be understood in the light of this nexus.[10] It is a classic argument that bears repeating: the creation of the administrative capabilities that came to constitute a state were initially only by-products of the efforts to raise funds for warfare.[11] At this stage state building was anything but a conscious effort. It was what happened as dynastic rulers were scrambling to survive amid fierce international military competition.

THE GROWING FINANCIAL APPETITE OF THE STATE

Driven by international military competition financial needs grew rapidly: Prussia's total budget in 1640 was 35,000 thaler. By 1740 it had reached 7 million.[12] Not all of this money came from taxes and not all of it was spent on the army. A substantial part (about half in the middle of the eighteenth century) was raised from the income of the royal domains, and while military expenditure dominated the budget other forms of expenditure also increased.[13] Among them were the costs of the

---

[8] Wolfgang Neugebauer, 'Staatsverfassung und Heeresverfassung in Preußen während des 18. Jahrhunderts', in Peter Baumgart, Bernhard Kroener, and Heinz Stübig, eds., *Die preußische Armee* (Paderborn, 2008), pp. 27–44, at p. 39.

[9] Derek McKay, *The great elector* (Harlow, 2001), p. 62. Volker Press, 'Vom Ständestaat zum Absolutismus', in Peter Baumgart, ed., *Ständetum und Staatsbildung in Brandenburg-Preussen: Ergebnisse einer internationalen Fachtagung* (Berlin, 1983), pp. 280–336, at p. 324. Otto Nugel, 'Der Schöppenmeister Hieronymus Roth', *Forschungen zur brandenburgischen und preussischen Geschichte*, 14 (1901), pp. 19-105, at p. 32. Gustav Droysen, *Der Staat des Großen Kurfürsten* (3 vols., Leipzig, 1861–3), vol. 2, pp. 402–19, vol. 3, pp. 191–212.

[10] See the exploration of this nexus in the English context in John Brewer, *The sinews of power: war and the English state, 1688–1783* (London, 1989).

[11] Otto Hintze, 'Staatenbildung und Verfassungsentwicklung', in Gerhard Oestreich, ed., *Staat und Verfassung* (Göttingen, 1970), pp. 34–51, at p. 48. Theda Skocpol, 'Bringing the state back in: strategies of analysis in current research', in Peter Evans, Dietrich Rueschemeyer, and Theda Skocpol, eds., *Bringing the state back in* (Cambridge, 1985), pp. 3–43, at p. 8. Charles Tilly, 'War making and state making as organized crime', in Peter Evans, Dietrich Rueschemeyer, and Theda Skocpol, eds., *Bringing the state back in* (Cambridge, 1985), pp. 169–91, at pp. 170–2.

[12] Schmoller, 'Epochen', p. 61.

[13] Hans-Peter Ullmann, *Der deutsche Steuerstaat: Geschichte der öffentlichen Finanzen vom 18. Jahrhundert bis heute* (München, 2005), p. 19.

court, which fluctuated with the tastes of the ruler, and spending for the promotion of economic activity and infrastructure. However, growing military spending contributed most significantly to the increase in expenditure and a sizeable part of it had to be met through taxation. This rapid growth of expenditure forced equally rapid change on the political and administrative structures through which taxes were collected in the Hohenzollern polity.

The central principle of the system of estates government was that political power was exercised through a cascading distribution of duties and powers. The monarch ruled over his subjects through the estates. However, the need to raise large sums of money made it necessary for the Great Elector to establish a direct administrative connection with taxpayers. Demands and payments had to travel directly between ruler and individuals because—as many historians of the state have pointed out—a fiscal administration involving different competing entities was highly inefficient.[14] While this is true, one should not imagine that contemporaries were led by abstract considerations about administrative efficiency. More concretely, many members of the estates were opposed to the ruler's plans to raise more revenue and would have obstructed the workings of such an administration if these tasks had been left to them. This was not only a matter of resisting the expansion of the ruler's power, it was also a reaction against a competing claim to a share in the incomes of villagers and townspeople. Financial demands of the ruler almost inevitably limited the ability of the nobility to make good on its own claims or to expand them.[15] Since the middle of the seventeenth century new administrative structures loyal to the ruler slowly supplanted and bypassed older ones that relied on the estates. This was not a linear or homogeneous process. It happened in slow incremental steps in response to local conditions. The lack of major caesuras should not obscure the significance of the transformation.

The new administrative conduits between ruler and individuals became the tangible manifestations of the nascent state. As we shall see, they did not remain mere tools in the ruler's hands. They also developed a 'life of their own'. Along with the unfolding of the administration's capabilities came its growing power. The interests of the administration as an institution, and of the individuals within it, began to matter.[16] The developments we are concerned with here were primarily conflicts between ruler and administration on one side, and the administered individuals on the other. However, relations between ruler and administration were often less than harmonious. On more than one occasion conflict took the form of a three-way negotiation among ruler, administration, and administered.[17]

---

[14] Max Weber, *Economy and society* (2 vols., Berkeley, 1978), vol. 1, p. 223.

[15] Ullmann, *Steuerstaat*, p. 15.

[16] See the classic studies Hans Rosenberg, *Bureaucracy, aristocracy and autocracy: the Prussian experience, 1660–1815* (Cambridge, MA, 1958) and Hubert Johnson, *Frederick the Great and his officials* (New Haven, 1975).

[17] This triangle captures, in many ways, the reality of the Prussian polity better than Rosenberg's view of a Prussian polity dominated by an 'authoritarian power triad' composed of Junkers, the Prussian bureaucracy, and the aristocratic army officer corps. See William Hagen, 'Descent of the Sonderweg: Hans Rosenberg's history of Old-Regime Prussia', *Central European History*, 24 (1991), pp. 25–50, at p. 26. Florian Schui, 'French figures of authority and state building in Prussia', in Peter

In this context it is important to bear in mind that the state's administration was still a very minor body. For most of this period the central organs of the Prussian state, excluding the military, were made up of only a few hundred officials.[18]

TOWN VS. COUNTRY

For all their 'newness', the administrative organs of the nascent state still betrayed the political and economic order from which they were born. This is particularly visible in the different treatment that was reserved for towns and country. Although the estates included representatives of church, town, and landed nobility, the latter was by far the most influential group.[19] In practice political power was even more narrowly concentrated. In Brandenburg, for example, the formal distinction between upper and lower nobility as well as the great difference in wealth meant that a 'power elite' of fifteen families dominated the estates.[20] This internal balance of power within the estates was reflected in many of the political deals that were struck with the Hohenzollern dynasty and which shaped the process of state building. Nowhere is this more apparent than in the different ways in which the new administrative organs developed in town and country.

The difference is evident when one looks at the financial flows for which these administrations served as conduits. In 1653 the nobility had agreed to the general introduction of new taxes but it had not agreed to pay them. The fiscal privileges exempting nobles and prelates from most taxes were jealously guarded. Prussian villagers and burghers thus bore the brunt of the new taxes, with a substantially larger proportion falling on the latter. Until 1641 the towns had paid two-thirds of the principal tax—the *Contribution*—but after this date their share was reduced to 59 per cent.[21] Considering the population of the towns was significantly smaller than that of the countryside, this still resulted in a disproportionally high tax burden for urban dwellers. In Electoral Mark (Kurmark), for example, two-fifths of the population thus paid three-fifths of the *Contribution*.[22]

The differences were exacerbated as different modes of tax collection emerged in town and country. Traditionally, only the total sum of taxes was negotiated between ruler and estates. Nobles, magistrates, and prelates were then responsible for the collection of the respective shares from 'their' taxpayers.[23] This system was now slowly replaced by a centrally directed fiscal administration. These fiscal

Becker and Rüdiger von Krosigk, eds., *Figures of authority: contributions towards a cultural history of governance from 17th to 19th century* (Oxford, 2008), pp. 153–76.

[18] Christopher Clark, *Iron kingdom: the rise and downfall of Prussia, 1600–1947* (London, 2007), p. 111.

[19] Melton, 'Prussian Junkers', pp. 71–5.

[20] Peter Michael Hahn, *Struktur und Funktion des brandenburgischen Adels im 16. Jahrhundert* (Berlin, 1979), pp. 239–44.

[21] Benno Gliemann, 'Die Einführung der Accise in Preussen', *Zeitschrift für die gesamte Staatswissenschaft*, 29 (1873), pp. 180–217, at p. 183.

[22] Population statistics from Schmoller, *Städtewesen*, p. 288.

[23] Schmoller, 'Epochen', p. 55.

structures were part of a system of administrative offices known as *Kommissariats-behörden* (war offices) which formed the administrative backbone of the Prussian state.[24] During the Thirty Years War, the *Kriegskommissar* (war official) had been an officer in charge of controlling the numbers, quality, and equipment of troops, who were often supplied by private military 'entrepreneurs'. By the reign of Fredrick William I the office had developed into a centralized administration that was not only responsible for all matters related to the maintenance and enlargement of the army but also for the procurement of the means to achieving this: it was put in charge of taxation and the general economic welfare of the country. The office was structured in three layers: one central administration, the *Generalkriegskom-missariat* (general war office), an administration for every province, the *Oberkriegs-kommissariat* (main war office), and finally an official who represented the administration at the local level, the *Kriegskommissar*. The latter post existed mainly in two forms: the *Kreiskommissar* (district official), who later came to be known as the *Landrat*, was responsible for rural areas, while the *Commisarius loci* or *Steuerrat* (tax official) was responsible for a number of towns.[25] Formally they were repre-sentatives of the same administrations but in practice they were very different entities. Otto Hintze's incisive characterization of the two types of administrator deserves to be quoted at length:

> The *Landrat* in the rural districts is at the same time chosen by the estates of the district as well as being appointed a royal official: close in rank and spirit to the Junkers whose neighbour he is as a resident of the district, an official of questionable loyalty, but more of a nobleman and landlord than an official, comparably independent and deeply connected with the interests of the local nobility of the district. In contrast, the *Steuerrat* is the original image of a purely bureaucratic official, a travelling official foreign to town and region, wholly absorbed by his duties, dependent on his superiors and in the full awareness of his responsibilities uncompromising and meticulous towards those below him, the magistrates, mayors and treasurers who are under his control.[26]

Recent scholarship has revised Hintze's characterization of the *Steuerrat* and his rural colleague. Gerd Heinrich notes—and this is true of virtually all areas where early modern states were active—that there was often a significant difference

---

[24] It is hardly possible to translate the Prussian terms for administrative offices. The English terms in brackets are more explanations than translations of the original terminology.

[25] Hintze, 'Der Commissarius und seine Bedeutung in der allgemeinen Verwaltungsgeschichte', in Gerhard Oestreich, ed., *Staat und Verfassung* (Göttingen, 1970), pp. 242–74.

[26] 'Der Landrat in den ländlichen Kreisen ist zugleich ein Erwählter der Kreisstände und ein königlicher Beamter: ein Standes- und Gesinnungsgenosse der Junker, deren Nachbar er als Kreiseingesessener ist, ein Beamter von unzweifelhafter Loyalität, aber doch mehr Edelmann und Gutsbesitzer als Beamter, verhältnismäßig unabhängig und mit den ritterschaftlichen Interessen des Kreises verwachsen. Der Steuerrat dagegen ist das Urbild eines rein bürokratischen Beamten, ein stadt- und landfremder reisender Kontrollbeamter, ganz in seinem Dienst aufgehend, abhängig nach oben und im Gefühl seiner Verantwortlichkeit scharf und peinlich nach unten gegen über den Magistraten, den Bürgermeistern und Kämmerern, die er zu kontrollieren hat.' Hintze, 'Der österreichische und der preußische Beamtenstaat im 17. und 18. Jahrhundert', in Gerhard Oestreich, ed., *Staat und Verfassung* (Göttingen, 1970), pp. 321–58, at p. 353.

between theory and practice. To some extent also the *Steuerräte* worked within the existing power structures: deals were cut, controversial orders delayed or only partly executed. The *Steuerrat* did not act solely as an executer of monarchical will, but also as a representative of local interests to the central administration. It is probably true to say that *Steuerkommissare* did not always fulfil their orders to the letter, but on the whole they worked hard and often successfully to achieve the objectives of these orders. There are thus some caveats to remember, but at the same time new research also confirms the main thrust of Hintze's argument: Heinrich describes the *Landräte* as 'centaurs' who divided their loyalty between estates and state, and contrasts them with the zeal of the urban commissars to carry out government-led reforms.[27] The greater distance that the urban representatives of the Prussian state kept from the local elites is important for the future developments that we shall be concerned with. As Skocpol has pointed out, it was precisely this distance that enabled the apparatus of modern states to act autonomously.[28] In our period, the Prussian state developed this autonomy to a much greater extent in the towns than in the country. The result was not only a greater ability of the state to implement reforms in the towns but also a greater potential for conflict with the urban population.

The political causes of the different treatment of town and country are easy to see. The nobility were able to put up much greater resistance against any infringements of their prerogatives. Once they consented to increased taxes on the rural population the Hohenzollern refrained from undermining the power that they exercised locally. This was also in the interest of the ruling dynasty whose power ultimately relied on the support of the nobility. Hohenzollern and nobles may have been locked in political struggles for centuries but they also shared a strong political and social affinity.[29] As historical figures they were cut from the same wood, only in different forms. The towns, in contrast, were politically weak and were robbed of any remaining political autonomy in the process of state building. The imposing figure of the *Steuerrat* was only part of a development that weakened the institutions of local government. They were ultimately destroyed and substituted with a tight control by the central administration through the reforms promulgated in the *Rathäusliche Reglements* (town hall regulations) of Frederick William I and the subsequent reforms of Fredrick II.[30]

This is not to say that practices and individuals associated with the estates government did not also continue to play a role in urban administration. Such continuities contributed to the acceptance and legitimacy of the new branches of administration. However, the disciplines, routines, and hierarchies of the new administrations formed an increasingly rigid framework that did away with

[27] Gerd Heinrich, 'Staatsaufsicht und Stadtfreiheit in Brandenburg-Preussen unter dem Absolutismus (1660–1806)', in Wilhelm Rausch, ed., *Die Städte Mitteleuropas im 17. und 18. Jahrhundert* (Linz, 1981), pp. 155–72, at pp. 165–7.

[28] Skocpol, 'Bringing the state back in', p. 10.

[29] Neugebauer, 'Staatsverfassung'.

[30] Johannes Ziekursch, *Das Ergebnis der friderizianischen Städteverwaltung und die Städteordnung Steins am Beispiel der schlesischen Städte dargestellt* (Jena, 1908).

inherited forms of government, even where continuities existed at the individual level. Although a *Steuerrat* might come from the social environment of the estates, the disciplinary mechanisms of his office let him function efficiently as part of the machinery that slowly replaced the estates government.[31] This process happened much more quickly and efficiently in the towns than in the countryside. Consequently, the long-term effects of administrative change for the economy, society, and political culture differed substantially between town and country.

THE MAKING OF PRUSSIAN BURGHERS

In financial terms the firmer grip of the state's administration on the towns meant that the already skewed distribution of the tax burden was tilted further against the burghers. They had to shoulder a disproportionate and increasing share of the rapidly rising financial demands of the state. Politically, the destruction of local government left the townspeople without meaningful representation or intermediary forms of government. Increasingly they dealt directly with offices of administration that were part or wholly dependent on central government. The fate of Prussian towns under Frederick William I was thus not dissimilar to the experience that French towns underwent only slightly earlier at the hands of Jean-Baptiste Colbert (1619–83).[32] As in France, the consequences for political culture were far-reaching. Alexis de Tocqueville famously argued that administrative reforms of the *ancien régime* made Frenchmen more similar and individualistic at the same time, thus undermining the very basis of political and social order.[33] Tocqueville's thesis has been challenged on many levels and it can certainly not be applied to Prussia in its original form. Nevertheless, administrative change made the ways in which Prussian burghers interacted with the state more similar across different regions and at the same time furthered the development of greater individualism among urban dwellers. Again, as Tocqueville pointed out, greater individualism does not necessarily mean greater heterogeneity or variety, but rather that individual desires and decisions play a more important role. In the new, more individualistic societies, individuals were generally more selfish and allowed to act on their selfish impulses, but this did not mean a greater difference among them.

As a result of the reforms the *Steuerrat* and his subordinates became the face of the state for most Prussian burghers, irrespective of the province in which they lived. Local political traditions and differences became less marked the longer the shared daily experience with the centralized administration continued. The inhabitants of towns ceased, at least to some extent, to be primarily Magdeburgers, Berliners, or Königsbergers and became instead Prussian burghers with a shared political and legal position vis-à-vis the state. Administrative unification created a common identity and unity of the administered. It did so objectively by putting

---

[31] Neugebauer, 'Epochen', p. 182.
[32] Hintze, 'Commissarius', p. 250. Schmoller, *Städtewesen*, p. 427.
[33] Alexis de Tocqueville, *L'ancien régime et la revolution* (2 vols., Paris, 1954), vol. 2, pp. 143–58.

them in similar legal and fiscal conditions, but it also created a subjective perception of unity that made possible the collective political debates, demands, and actions examined here. Prussian state building thus created conditions in which the urban population developed into a more unified and stronger political subject.[34]

In France, according to Tocqueville, the tendency towards greater similarity was also associated with the emergence of greater individualism.[35] In Prussia a similar rise in individualism, above all in the towns, can be observed but circumstances were once again different. The first step towards a more individualistic culture was taken with the separation of town and country. Administrative reforms meant that towns became more similar to each other but it also meant that collectively they became more different from the countryside. Under the auspices of traditional, established government, different interests existed among nobility, clergy, and towns. However, these groups still encountered the ruler as part of a single political entity that purported to represent collective interests. Political arrangements were compromises between ruler and estates but also between the various groups within the estates. This changed with the decline of the estates government and the emergence of openly different fiscal and administrative treatment of town and country. Town and country now confronted the ruler separately and to some extent competitively. Every thaler that was not raised through rural taxation had to be raised through taxes on the towns. We cannot examine further the implications of this development in the present context, but the question must be asked as to whether the break-up of collective political structures contributed to the diffusion of a vision of society in which antagonistic interests took on a much more prominent role than the collective pursuit of a 'common good'.

THE MILITARY–FISCAL STATE AS SEEN FROM THE TOWNS

Administratively the towns were now treated differently from the surrounding countryside in many respects. The distinctive way in which the process of state building developed in the towns led to the emergence of greater individual freedom and a more individualistic society in the urban setting. In what follows we first examine the impact of fiscal, economic, and military reforms before turning to the effects that the changing relationship between state and religion brought about on individualism in the areas of faith, sexuality, and education.

The single most important process of administrative change that falls into the first category was the transformation of the fiscal system of the towns. From 1667 onwards, the Great Elector gradually introduced an excise tax that was levied only in the towns. The tax was the most up to date of its kind in Europe at the time. Much of the economic success of the United Provinces was credited to the use of the excise as the principal source of state revenue, and other countries—among

---

[34] Hintze, 'Staatenbildung', p. 50.
[35] Tocqueville, *L'ancien régime*, vol. 2, p. 158.

them Prussia—copied the model with greater or lesser success. In principle the excise was a sales tax: every time an excisable good was sold a certain fixed sum or share of the price had to be paid to the state. (The excise was, in a way, a primitive version of the modern value added tax, and not dissimilar to the sales taxes levied in some states of the USA.) The Prussian variant of this levy, the *Accise*, was peculiar in that it was only payable in the towns or, to be precise, in the 'excisable' towns which included all larger towns and most of the smaller ones. Because it was a purely urban tax it was often levied when the goods entered the towns rather than at the point of sale. In practice the Prussian excise often appeared much like a customs duty except that it was not levied at a foreign border, but between town and country. However, the excise was not only levied on goods imported and exported by the towns but also on goods produced there for local consumption. This part of the excise was levied at the point of production or sale in the towns. The excise also included customs duties proper to be paid upon entry to Prussian territory, and transit levies on goods that crossed Prussian lands. This part of the excise was collected either at a border town or port of entry. Finally, the excise officers administered a number of other levies and duties that, strictly speaking, were not part of the excise. The amount of excise due was usually not a share of the price but a fixed sum per item, volume, or weight. There was a specific excise tariff for almost every product so that tax officials were equipped with long tariff lists. In practice, however, the bulk of the revenue came from just a handful of products, mainly from payments for the consumption of beer, brandy, wine, grain, meat, and wood. From 1683, the excise became the principal tax for most Prussian towns. As with many 'innovations' in history the excise was not really new. Sales taxes had been levied on various products—often on alcoholic drinks—in many towns before that. Towns used the tax increasingly throughout the seventeenth century to raise their share of the *Contribution*. What changed around 1683 for most towns was that the excise replaced the *Contribution*. Towns were now submitted to an entirely different tax system from that in the countryside where a land tax remained the main form of taxation. As a result of the reforms not only the type of fiscal official encountered in the towns, but also the very nature of taxation, began to diverge from the rural situation.[36]

From the point of view of the ruler the excise had many advantages. It was comparatively easy to collect because it did not require land registers or detailed knowledge about private fortunes or revenues. Only a keen eye cast on sales and purchases at the moment of transaction was required. This mode of collection also meant that taxpayers were never behind in their payments and collection of arrears by force was mostly unnecessary. The tax was paid in small increments at moments when the taxpayer had sufficient liquidity to make a purchase. Perhaps most importantly the introduction of the excise meant that the tax burden on the towns could now be fixed independently of that on the country. This fiscal 'decoupling', together with the fact that the collection of the excise was at first supervised by the *Steuerräte* and later actually administered by them, meant that the

---

[36] Ullmann, *Steuerstaat*, p. 20. Gliemann, 'Accise', pp. 178–87. Gustav von Schmoller, *Preußische Verfassungs-, Verwaltungs- und Finanzgeschichte* (Berlin, 1921), pp. 92–105.

Hohenzollern were much less constrained by the old intermediary institutions of the estates in their fiscal policy. In practice this new flexibility of the ruler meant mainly that they had the ability to increase taxes in the towns.[37]

While it is easy to see why the Great Elector was keen to make the excise the principal form of urban taxation, it is less obvious why urban taxpayers should have welcomed it. And yet the tax enjoyed broad popular support when it was proposed. In more than one town, taxpayers sided with their ruler and forced acceptance of the new tax regime on reluctant magistrates.[38] Contemporary writers praised the advantages of the 'gentle excise' over the 'violent' *Contribution*.[39] What inspired the enthusiasm of this generation of taxpayers for a levy that a hundred years later became the target of public outrage? Most important was perhaps a perception that the introduction of the excise would lead to greater fiscal justice. Under the *Contribution* the overall tax burden was negotiated between estates and ruler. In the towns it then fell to the magistrates to decide how to raise the necessary sums. However, the political structures of most towns had become decadent as a result of the massive indebtedness. Venality of offices, corruption, and dependence on private creditors meant that magistrates often represented the interests of only a small group of wealthy and influential families.[40] The distribution of the tax burden was accordingly biased against a great number of taxpayers. The excise offered a more universal and equitable alternative. In principle it had to be paid by all consumers, and the individual tax burden did not depend on individual status or political protection but simply on consumption habits. In practice the excise included notable exemptions, too. Initially nobles, clergymen, university professors, and other groups frequently benefited from privileges.[41] However, despite these holes in the universality of the tax the excise was still seen as more equal than any previous form of taxation. At first it was a matter of creating greater equity within urban societies, but as excise rules became more homogeneous across Prussian territories and as the administrative procedures were further centralized, the excise also meant that taxpayers in different towns were treated more equally by the state.[42] Local and regional differences withered away and taxpayers everywhere were put on a more similar footing.[43]

The uniform and centralized character of the excise profoundly changed the playing field, and the players, of urban fiscal politics in Prussia. Increasingly, taxpayer grievances were no longer concerned with local arrangements pitting the

---

[37] Fritz Karl Mann, *Steuerpolitische Ideale* (Jena, 1937), pp. 50–61.

[38] Mann, *Steuerpolitische Ideale*, pp. 50–61. Schmoller, 'Epochen', p. 61. Schmoller, *Städtewesen*, p. 256. Gliemann, 'Accise', pp. 201–2.

[39] 'Sanftmüthige Accise'; 'gewaltsame Contribution'. Friedrich Wilhelm Tenzel, *Entdeckte Gold-Grube in der Accise* (Magdeburg, 1685), p. 4.

[40] Schmoller, *Städtewesen*, pp. 298–324.

[41] Schmoller, *Preußische Verfassungs-, Verwaltungs- und Finanzgeschichte*, p. 96.

[42] Walther Schultze, *Geschichte der preussischen Regieverwaltung von 1766 bis 1786, ein historisch-kritischer Versuch* (Leipzig, 1888), pp. 171–81. Mann, *Steuerpolitische Ideale*, pp. 72–3. Schmoller, *Preußische Verfassungs-, Verwaltungs- und Finanzgeschichte*, pp. 94–7.

[43] For similar processes in Britain see William Ashworth, *Customs and excise: trade, production, and consumption in England, 1640–1845* (Oxford, 2003), p. 10.

magistrate of a single town against all or a section of the urban population. Conflicts were now likely to occur in a similar fashion in all towns and 'the opposition' as seen from the taxpayer's perspective was no longer a particular local magistrate in one town, but a branch of the same central administration representing the state. In this way the introduction of the excise prepared the way for greater pan-Prussian conflicts in the long term, but in the short term it suited the interests of urban tax payers and Hohenzollern rulers.

Another motive for positive contemporary attitudes towards the excise were the limits that it posed to the intrusion of the state into private affairs. The new tax seemed to solve an old problem: the trade-off between protecting the privacy of taxpayers and efficient tax collection. As the *Kameralist* and ardent defender of the excise Wilhelm von der Lith highlighted, earlier attempts to solve this problem had not been successful. He cited the example of a wealth tax in Nürnberg where citizens made tax payments by depositing coins under a rug in the city hall. In this way the amount of tax paid and hence the size of the fortune owned by each individual remained secret. In order to ensure that the right amounts were paid, every citizen had to make a written calculation of the tax payment and keep these calculations at home. Upon departure from the city or after death the accounts could be inspected and taxpayers and heirs were subject to punishments if calculations were found to be faulty or incomplete. According to von der Lith the complicated procedure was a failure in every respect: the rug was too thin to conceal the amounts paid by each individual and the methods of control proved to be inefficient.[44]

Von der Lith, like other contemporaries, was aware of the problems caused by this kind of inefficient tax collection but he also knew that harsher and more intrusive fiscal controls were bound to raise other issues. 'What will happen', he asked, 'if vicious and inept people are given the power to inspect the papers of their fellow citizens and even of persons who are far above them in rank, and to rummage through the most hidden secrets of their revenues and expenses and pry on all other circumstances regarding their families?'[45] He warned of disastrous consequences for state and taxpayers. The tax inspectors were likely to be influenced by the rank of the taxpayer or by bribes, and tax collection would become arbitrary and ineffective. Even more importantly, taxpayers would find the obligation to reveal detailed information about their private economic affairs intrusive. For merchants and other businessmen in particular, such an obligation could be very damaging. Their creditworthiness could suffer and the harsh fiscal treatment was likely eventually to drive them to cease trading or to take their business elsewhere, thus harming the economic outlook for everyone in the local town.[46]

---

[44] Wilhelm von der Lith, *Politische Betrachtungen über die verschiedenen Arten der Steuern* (Breslau, 1751), p. 114.

[45] 'Was wird demnach erfolgen wofern lasterhaften und ungeschickten Leuten die Gewalt anvertrauet wird, in ihrer Mitbürger, ja in so vieler öfters dem Stande nach über sie weit erhabener Personen Schriften zu wühlen, und die innersten Geheimnisse ihrer Einnahme und Ausgabe, ja aller anderer ihre Familie betreffender Umstände einzudringen?' Von der Lith, *Politische Betrachtungen*, p. 145.

[46] Van der Lith, *Politische Betrachtungen*, p. 117.

The introduction of the excise thus offered a way out of many practical problems that the expanding tax state had encountered, but the excise did not completely solve the dilemma that resulted from the trade-off between efficient tax collection and the protection of privacy. Even with the excise in place tax officials still had to make sure that only 'excised' goods were consumed. This meant goods had to be prevented from being smuggled into towns or across the Prussian border. Controls of local producers were equally necessary to prevent them from selling a share of their production untaxed in order to undercut competitors. Ordinary consumers were subject to controls that became necessary, but merchants and manufacturers were the main focus of fiscal oversight.

Moreover, the mode of assessment of the excise gave rise to another potentially explosive question. As a result of the universality of the tax the tax burden to some extent shifted from the poorer to the wealthier urban dwellers. The latter had often paid little in taxation under the old fiscal regime and because of their higher expenditure on consumption they paid more excise than the poor. However, the extent of this effect depended largely on the tariff structure of the excise. Many writers sought to reinforce the shift of the tax burden towards wealthier burghers by advocating low or no taxes on 'necessary' goods and high duties on 'luxuries'.[47] Inevitably, the question of which products belonged in which category became one of the most controversial issues in the economic and moral debates that accompanied the introduction and evolution of the excise. However, these finer issues of fiscal privacy and justice caused little concern when the tax was first introduced. Despite its shortcomings the excise was more suitable to contemporary conceptions of privacy and justice than the 'violent *Contribution*' that was still fresh in the memories of urban dwellers.

THE ECONOMICS OF THE EXCISE

The introduction of the excise was not merely a technical change in fiscal policy. Along with the new tax the Hohenzollern also embraced a model for economic development for the towns that was based on initiative and effort from private individuals. It is hardly a coincidence that the Great Elector modelled his fiscal reform—like many of his other modernizing efforts—on the Dutch experience.[48] The United Provinces were Europe's commercially most advanced and most prosperous country. The decision to follow the fiscal example of the United Provinces was also a decision to import some of the economic dynamism of its commercial economy into Prussia's towns. In the Prussian context, the introduction

---

[47] Karl Theodor von Inama-Sternegg, 'Der Accisestreit deutscher Finanztheoretiker im 17. und 18. Jahrhundert', *Zeitschrift für die gesamte Staatswissenschaft*, 21 (1865), pp. 515–34. Mann, *Steuerpolitische Ideale*, pp. 50–79.

[48] Gliemann, 'Accise', pp. 187–93. Schmoller, 'Epochen', p. 62. Ingrid Mittenzwei, *Preußen nach dem Siebenjährigen Krieg: Auseinandersetzungen zwischen Bürgertum und Staat um die Wirtschaftspolitik* (Berlin, 1979), pp. 129–34. See the comprehensive discussion of the influence of the Netherlands on the German states in Heinz Schilling, *Höfe und Allianzen: Deutschland 1648–1763* (Berlin, 1989).

of the excise was thus the central institutional nexus linking the twin processes of state building and the development of mercantile capitalism.[49]

The excise was not only a good way to tap the wealth that was created in commerce and manufacturing but—perhaps more importantly for Prussia—it was also an ideal tool to steer and promote the development of these sectors. Königsberg, Memel, Magdeburg, and Kleve had strong mercantile traditions, but many Prussian towns compared poorly with these more advanced commercial hubs and with the wheeling and dealing of urban centres in Western Europe.[50] To most contemporaries it was a matter of course that customs and excise tariffs could be used to narrow this gap if tweaked in the right way and an excise-based fiscal system was a well-suited tool for this purpose.[51]

However, protective tariffs were only a part of the Hohenzollern's economic reform projects. In order to take full advantage of the powers of commerce, Prussia's urban economies had to become more similar to the great commercial centres of Western Europe and the United Provinces in particular.[52] Under Frederick William I, a whole set of economic reforms revised the institutional framework of urban economies. These reforms were in many respects a corollary of fiscal change and were often overseen by the same officials. The term 'corollary' can be understood quite literally in this context. In Frederick William's instruction to his *Steuerräte* in 1712 only the first half of the document was devoted to taxation. The second half dealt with economic and other matters.[53] No doubt the order of appearance implied a hierarchy of priorities (fiscal extraction over economic development) but at the same time the monarch was clearly aware that the abundance of his fiscal revenues depended on the economic prosperity of his towns.

Central to Frederick William's efforts was a revision of the rules that governed urban economies. The foundations for this transformation had been laid under the Great Elector, who had curtailed the power of corporations and guilds in the same edict that introduced the excise in the *Kurmark* in 1684. More reforms followed during his reign: children of shepherds, bailiffs, guardians, and urban servants were no longer excluded from guilds; fees payable in order to become a master guildsman were lowered; the requirement to produce excessively expensive masterpieces was abolished.[54] The changes were small and the state often lacked the power to enforce them. However, they give a clear idea of the monarch's intention to facilitate access to the guilds and hence to manufacturing.

The successor to the Great Elector continued with similar reforms. Frederick I tried to abolish the rules of certain guilds that imposed maximum numbers of masters in towns. When this proved impossible he decided that *Freimeister*—masters who were not members of a corporation—should be allowed to work in

[49] Tilly, 'War making and state making', p. 170.
[50] Schmoller, *Städtewesen*, p. 293.
[51] Mann, *Steuerpolitische Ideale*, p. 55.
[52] For a discussion of the Dutch economic model in the thinking of Prussian administrators see Mittenzwei, *Preußen nach dem Siebenjährigen Krieg*, pp. 129–34.
[53] Cited in Schmoller, *Städtewesen*, p. 401.
[54] Schmoller, *Städtewesen*, p. 262.

professions where closed numbers had been imposed. Similarly, in the Duchy of Prussia rules limiting the right to set up a business to homeowners were abolished. Frederick I summarized the principle behind this eclectic mix of measures: 'We believe that monopolies should be abolished in all forms and that freedom of commerce and trade should be promoted'.[55]

Frederick William I continued the work of his predecessors with new vigour. In 1730 he promulgated new statutes for all Prussian corporations. For the most part the new rules were identical for all trades.[56] The administrative and political effects of this centralizing reform led to greater homogeneity across Prussian towns and thus contributed to furthering a process that was associated with the reforms of urban fiscal structures. The economic effect was that it became more difficult for corporations to exclude anyone from becoming a master. Closed numbers were outlawed and rules that required new masters to be of irreproachable moral standing were abolished. The latter had often been used improperly to limit the number of competitors. Instead, only the insufficient quality of the masterpiece remained a legitimate reason to reject a new master. External supervision and an appeals procedure were introduced in order to ensure the rules intended to serve quality were not abused in order to limit competition.[57]

Many of these reforms reduced the monopolies and restrictions that prevented newcomers from setting up businesses. Prussian artisans and merchants gained more space to make their own decisions and there is perhaps no better example than the reform of guild regulations for the process of 'decorporatization', which according to Thomas Nipperdey led to the 'individualization' and 'emancipation' of society.[58] However, the Hohenzollern's objective was not simply less regulation. They successfully strove to abolish or change traditional rules that often dated from medieval times and that benefited specific groups or individuals. However, as the administrative capacities of the state grew, new forms of regulation began to appear. The main difference was that the new rules were less localized and more uniform, and that—at least in the opinion of those who made them—they served the common good rather than special interests.

The fiscal and economic reforms that we have discussed here did not mark the end of economic regulation and fiscal intrusion. Nevertheless, they do show how in Prussia's towns the process of state building was inseparable from the development of a growing private sphere of economic activity that was more clearly separated from the state and offered more opportunity to pursue private interests. How far-reaching this change was is perhaps best understood by comparing it to the

---

[55] 'Wir halten gnädigst dafür, daß die monopolia auf alle Weise abzschaffen und dahingegen die libertas commerciorum et negotiorum zu befördern sei.' Cited in Schmoller, *Städtewesen*, p. 262.

[56] Dietmar Peitsch, *Zunftgesetzgebung und Zunftverwaltung Brandenburg-Preußens in der frühen Neuzeit* (Frankfurt am Main, 1985), pp. 116–42.

[57] Schmoller, *Städtewesen*, p. 262. On the guilds' concerns with legitimacy: Isabel Hull, *Sexuality, state and civil society in Germany, 1700–1815* (Ithaca, NY, 1996), pp. 41–3.

[58] Thomas Nipperdey, 'Verein als soziale Struktur in Deutschland im späten 18. und 19. Jahrhundert. Eine Fallstudie zur Modernisierung', in Thomas Nipperdey, ed., *Gesellschaft, Kultur, Theorie gesammelte Aufsätze zur neueren Geschichte* (Göttingen, 1976), pp. 176–205, at p. 180.

development in the countryside. While the excise became the principal way of generating state revenue from towns, taxation represented only a part of the income extracted from the country. There the main revenue came from the royal domains: landed properties that were originally personally owned by the monarch and that had become state property. The state acted as a private landowner as well as a political entity and profits from the domains constituted a substantial part of government funding. In particular, under Friedrich Wilhelm I revenue from the domains increased as a result of a more efficient exploitation and of the systematic extension of the domains.[59] The different ways of generating state revenue from town and country marked an important divergence of economic structures. In the rural economy the state owned substantial and increasing amounts of what today might be called 'productive capital'. It was a large, in some areas dominant, actor in the rural economy. In the towns the state did not have a comparable role. Here economic matters were, to a greater extent, left to private initiative despite the fact that regulations and taxation interfered with many aspects of economic life. These instruments were in part designed to limit and channel private decision-making. However, the ownership of 'productive capital' was in the hands of private individuals and so, too, was the power to take economic decisions that came with it.

SOLDIERS IN THE TOWN

As well as a secure stream of revenue, the other fundamental need of the Hohenzollern's standing army was a steady supply of recruits. As with fiscal and economic reform the military reorganization that resulted from the creation of a standing army profoundly altered the relation between urban individuals and the state. During the Thirty Years War military entrepreneurs supplied monarchs with mercenaries and looting was in many cases the principal way to provide for the upkeep of the army in wartime. In peace time soldiers returned more or less successfully to civilian occupations and employment. From the point of view of local populations this form of military organization meant that it was not just foreign armies that were seen as a threat. In the experience of many, the armies of their own ruler often posed as much a danger for life and livelihood as those of other monarchs. With the introduction of the standing army, soldiers were recruited and maintained in a different way, but from the perspective of Prussia's burghers the new standing army was in many respects little better than its predecessor. The practices of recruitment were often brutal, sometimes resembling kidnapping, because of the need for new soldiers and the competition between regiments for the best recruits. Existing laws banning the forced recruitment of family fathers and artisan masters were regularly disregarded.[60]

[59] Peter Baumgart, 'Friedrich Wilhelm I.—ein Soldatenkönig?', in Peter Baumgart, Bernhard Kroener, and Heinz Stübig, eds., *Die preussische Armee* (Paderborn, 2008), pp. 3–26, at p. 15.
[60] Engelen, 'Garnisonsgesellschaft', p. 118.

Once soldiers had been 'made' they needed lodgings and supplies. Given the new permanent nature of the army this was also necessary in peacetime. Troops began to be quartered in the towns. As in fiscal and economic matters, the interaction with the military was fundamentally different for urban dwellers and rural populations. The procedures for securing lodgings and supplies for the army were often as haphazard and brutal as for the draft. Magistrates were forced to identify private homes where soldiers, officers, and their families could be housed. This happened without any system in place to ensure that the accommodation was suitable or that the burden of quartering was distributed in an equitable way. Often military officers simply knocked on the door of private homes and obliged the occupants to supply food and lodgings. Apart from the economic costs that were inflicted on the civilian population it is hard to imagine a more intrusive and disruptive way for the state to interfere with the lives of individuals. Enthusiasm for the army was, accordingly, low.[61]

It was under Frederick William I that the reforms occurred, which transformed the relation between army and urban society into a 'relaxed' and even symbiotic one.[62] Crucial for this change was the reorganization of draft and quartering procedures. In 1733 the introduction of the *Kantonalsystem* for the draft was completed. Regiments were now assigned cantons from which they could recruit soldiers. In principle, all young men in the districts had to serve and were entered into draft rolls. Notable exceptions included, among others, young nobles (although some were obliged to serve as officers), bourgeois sons of parents with a fortune of 10,000 thaler or more, and certain professionals, such as wool-manufacturers. Inhabitants of the city of Berlin (and some other towns) were largely exempted. The process of drafting also became more transparent and less arbitrary, and the burden of military service was distributed more evenly. In an attempt to further reduce this burden soldiers were allowed to take holidays during the harvest months.[63] These features of the new system went a long way to reduce resentment in the population. Just as the excise administration led to a more uniform treatment of taxpayers in Prussia's towns, the *Kantonalsystem* meant that treatment of young men in different territories became more uniform. Urban populations benefited, in particular, from the introduction of the more equitable system for quartering soldiers. Each company was now assigned a specific street where soldiers and their families were lodged, and regulations were put in place that stipulated what had to be provided by the hosts. Poorer families received financial aid in order to reduce the burden of quartering.[64]

These administrative reforms went a long way to making this burden more acceptable for urban dwellers. As time passed, burghers grew used to the alien presence in their homes and began to see the positive sides of this involuntary hospitality. Artisans and merchants appreciated the soldiers and their families as

---

[61] Engelen, 'Garnisonsgesellschaft', p. 117.

[62] Engelen, 'Garnisonsgesellschaft', p. 116.

[63] Max Lehmann, 'Werbung, Wehrpflicht und Beurlaubung im Heere Friedrich Wilhelm's I', *Historische Zeitschrift*, 67 (1891), pp. 254–89, at pp. 269–72.

[64] Engelen, 'Garnisonsgesellschaft', pp. 119–20.

consumers. Brewers and bakers seem to have benefited in particular. The new burghers were also welcomed as workers. Many of the soldiers and their wives worked in the towns, often for their hosts. This kind of employment also brought conflict with local corporations but in many cases it was a welcome addition to the local pool of skill and manpower.[65]

Not least, soldiers started to be seen as a source of protection rather than as a threat. As a result of the drill and training that the Prussian army copied from the Dutch military, soldiers became more disciplined and less menacing to the populations of the towns that hosted them.[66] At the same time they also became a more effective deterrent against attacks by foreign troops.[67] The presence of troops in every major town was increasingly seen as a welcome phenomenon, despite the fact that it gave the Hohenzollern rulers an effective tool for the further reduction of municipal autonomy. However, given the decadence of urban political structures, political autonomy was probably not missed by many. Even after these reforms quartering and military service remained among the most dramatic ways in which the state interfered with the lives of Prussian burghers. In particular, the permanent presence of the military in civilian life has often been cited as one of the factors that allegedly squashed the development of an autonomous bourgeois culture.[68] Many of the reforms that made the Prussian military stronger also made it a more bearable burden for urban populations, however. Compared with the situation before the reforms they were better protected from violence of their own and foreign troops, their homes were better protected from unregulated intrusions, and military service disrupted their lives less and in more foreseeable ways. However, the symbiotic relationship between civilian and urban military populations that developed in the first half of the eighteenth century remained precarious. The military was one of the principal 'incarnations' of the state that urban populations experienced on a regular basis and a substantial potential for conflict remained.

RELIGION AND STATE BUILDING

The process of state building in Prussia was in many respects a textbook example of the development of a military–fiscal state and yet the process was not only about money and soldiers. Prayers, priests, and churches played equally important roles. The Thirty Years War had clearly demonstrated the potential of religious strife to destabilize and destroy countries and dynasties. From the perspective of emerging early modern states it was therefore crucial not only to prepare for war, but also to

---

[65] Engelen, 'Garnisonsgesellschaft', p. 120.

[66] For the relation to the Dutch model see most recently Michael Rohrschneider, 'Leopold I. von Anhalt-Dessau, die oranische Heeresreform und die Reorganisation der preußischen Armee unter Friedrich Wilhelm I', in Peter Baumgart, Bernhard Kroener, and Heinz Stübig, eds., *Die preußische Armee* (Paderborn, 2008), pp. 45–71.

[67] Engelen, 'Garnisonsgesellschaft', p. 121.

[68] Ziekursch, *Städteverwaltung*, pp. 61–2. Andreas Nachama, *Ersatzbürger und Staatsbildung: zur Zerstörung des Bürgertums in Brandenburg-Preussen* (Frankfurt, 1984).

insulate themselves from the principal source of instability and limit the political consequences that could result from religious discord. Most states sought to achieve this by disentangling themselves from religious matters but only in a few cases was this withdrawal from the sphere of religious matters as far reaching as it was in Prussia. It was not accidental that Prussia became 'the first principality in the Empire where a limited religious toleration was not only proclaimed but actually practised'.[69] Religious toleration—in practice mainly of different Christian confessions—was a necessary ingredient in the rise of the Hohenzollern state and had a deep impact on the relationship between individuals and state. Developments in this area did not differ as much between town and country as in the evolution of military–fiscal institutions. Nonetheless, many conflicts over religious questions had their focus in the towns, and many of the implications this had for the spheres of sexuality and education were associated with the urban context.

From the point of view of religious politics, the most outstanding feature of the Hohenzollern polity was that it had a Reformed (Calvinist) dynasty and a largely Lutheran population. This peculiar situation was the outcome of two reformations: a first successful one in 1539 in which the spread of Lutheranism among the population led a reluctant ruler to introduce 'one of the most moderate, if not reactionary, Lutheran reforms in all of Germany'; and a second unsuccessful one in 1613 in which the Elector John Sigismund (1572–1619) converted to Calvinism but had to abandon his plans to 'Calvinize' Prussia in the face of widespread resistance from the population, the clergy, and the estates.[70] Historians have mainly been concerned with the consequences that the failed Second Reformation had for the Hohenzollern's ability to rule and for the wider process of state building.[71] We focus instead on the implications for the development of a religious culture in Prussia that was remarkably individualistic and free of state interference.

The failure of the Second Reformation was largely a triumph of the Lutheran estates over the Reformed ruler. Their power to withhold much-needed financial support meant that John Sigismund could not force them to accept his creed. Instead, he had to abandon his reformatory intentions and guarantee far-reaching religious freedoms. The first step was an edict of 1614 in which he ordered all pastors 'to cease, eschew, and avoid all berating and abuse of other churches'.[72] The end of the Second Reformation was sealed when he explicitly protected the religious rights of Lutherans and Reformed in 1615. In the same period, John Sigismund was also forced to accept increased rights for the Catholic community in the Duchy of Prussia as a concession to the king of Poland who was sovereign in

---

[69] Bodo Nischan, *Prince, people, and confession: the Second Reformation in Brandenburg* (Philadelphia, 1994), p. 235.

[70] Nischan, *Prince, people, and confession*, p. 1.

[71] Wolfgang Reinhard, 'Zwang zur Konfessionalisierung? Prolegomena einer Theorie des konfessionellen Zeitalters', *Zeitschrift für Historische Forschung*, 10 (1983), pp. 257–77.

[72] Cited in Nischan, *Prince, people, and confession*, p. 235.

this territory. Together these decisions made 'polyconfessionalism' a part of the constitutional structure of Prussia.[73]

Religious individualism was strengthened not only by the fact that the Second Reformation had failed, but also by the way in which it had happened. Public debates and popular unrest played a central role besides the resistance of the estates. The decision to introduce Reformed changes was criticized in dozens of publications and in many instances urban populations attacked Reformed pastors or violently resisted changes that were imposed by the new confession.[74] The most famous of these incidents was the *Kalvinistentumult* that resulted after iconoclasts removed a large crucifix and other items deemed incompatible with the Reformed faith from the cathedral in Berlin.[75] When officials appeared on the scene to disperse the mob they were shouted at: '"You damn black Calvinist...you have stolen our picture and destroyed our crucifixes; now we will get even with you and your Calvinist priests"'.[76] In the resulting tussle the representatives of authority were eventually forced to retreat. In the same way that such popular protest contributed to the failure of the Second Reformation, spontaneous expressions of Lutheran faith and disturbances of Catholic ceremonies had helped to bring about the First Reformation in Prussia.[77] In both reformations, the faithful made their voice heard and successfully defended their individual convictions against interference by the ruler.

Prussia's double reformation not only created a tolerant constitutional framework and a tradition of resistance against religious paternalism, but it also bequeathed a moral dilemma to Prussian society that would give rise to new forms of religious individualism. By the time of the failed Second Reformation, a widespread perception had emerged that the moral conduct of large parts of society was a far cry from the values and beliefs professed by the faithful and the clergy. At the same time, confessional difference between population and ruler, and recent conflicts over the attempted Second Reformation made it difficult for many to see in the state an institution that could set and uphold moral standards for the whole of society. Faced with this challenge, a growing number of reformers began to emphasize the responsibility of individual believers to discover true faith and uphold society's moral standards. The most visible result of this paradigm shift was the rise of Pietism as a religious movement that combined an emphasis on individual religious experience with a reformatory impetus for the betterment of individuals and society.[78]

The central role of the individual in Pietism is best illustrated through the so-called conventicles. Initiated by the movement's founding father Jacob Spener

---

[73] Nischan, *Prince, people, and confession*, pp. 212–36.

[74] Nischan, *Prince, people, and confession*, pp. 51, 88, 115, 161, 187, 193.

[75] Eberhard Faden, 'Der Berliner Tumult von 1615', *Jahrbuch für brandenburgische Landesgeschichte*, 5 (1954), pp. 27–44, at p. 27.

[76] Cited in Nischan, *Prince, people, and confession*, p. 187.

[77] Nischan, *Prince, people, and confession*, pp. 10–15.

[78] Richard Gawthrop, *Pietism and the making of eighteenth-century Prussia* (Cambridge, 1993), p. 106.

(1635–1705), these were small groups of faithful who, together with a pastor, studied and discussed the Bible with the ultimate goal to experience a religious 'rebirth'. With a focus on an individual access to the scripture these groups built explicitly on Luther's ideal of 'the priesthood of all believers'.[79] Finding religious truth was an inward-looking spiritual process for Pietists, but the betterment of society, to which they were equally committed, was to be achieved through an outward-looking activism. Armed with moral certainties and religious confidence, individuals tried to bring about concrete change in their communities and beyond. For Pietists faith signified also a potential for achievement and success in the earthly existence. Nobody has perhaps summed up the Pietist credo better than the Methodist John Wesley (1703–91), who exclaimed from the roof of the Pietist orphanage in Halle during a visit in 1738 that all things are possible for him who believes.[80]

The unshakeable belief in their aims and the eagerness to see them achieved meant that Pietists developed a unique sense of duty and discipline. The efficient focusing of all energies on the objective at hand was as much a defining trait as was a love for planning. In the early seventeenth century the Pietist institutions in Halle were the most impressive proof of the power of Pietist faith. The so-called Franckesche Stiftung (Francke's Foundation) included the orphanage that inspired Wesley, a school, and other institutions such as workshops and a pharmacy which were admired and copied in Prussia and beyond. The thriving institution was the result of a characteristic mix of Pietist tenancy and government patronage. The founder Hermann August Francke (1663–1727), a Pietist pastor and pupil of Spener, initially began his work in the desolate town of Glaucha near Halle. Frederick William I understood the potential of Francke's movement for the moral, economic, and educational improvement of the region and his whole realm, and he began to support it.[81] Pietism and state subsequently joined forces in different ways in a number of cases. Pietist pedagogy was used at the officers' school that was gradually built up in Berlin from 1716 and served as a blueprint for elementary schools that were founded in the period. From 1729 it became mandatory for all Lutheran clergy to complete at least two years of study at the largely Pietist university of Halle. The Pietist influence on the clergy was particularly important through the institution of the military chaplains. Through their work one of the central institutions of the Prussian state came to be thoroughly imbued with a Pietist spirit.[82]

---

[79] Gawthrop, *Pietism*, p. 106.

[80] Martin Schmidt, 'Der Pietismus und das moderne Denken', in Kurt Aland, ed., *Der Pietismus und die moderne Welt* (Witten, 1974), pp. 9–74, at p. 26.

[81] Mary Fulbrook, *Piety and politics: religion and the rise of absolutism in England, Württemberg, and Prussia* (Cambridge, 1983), pp. 165–71.

[82] Gawthrop, *Pietism*, pp. 218–52. On the military in particular see Benjamin Marschke, *Absolutely Pietist: patronage, fictionalism, and state-building in the early eighteenth-century Prussian army chaplaincy* (Tübingen, 2005). Michael Kaiser and Stefan Kroll, *Militär und Religiosität in der Frühen Neuzeit* (Münster, 2004).

The monarch's visit to Halle is often described as the beginning of a fateful friendship between Pietism and the Hohenzollern state in the course of which Prussia was fundamentally transformed. The 'futurologist' aspects of Pietism meshed well with the needs and aspirations of the ascendant Prussian state.[83] Along with the Wolffian tradition, Pietism provided Frederick William with a state ideology that made service and discipline central virtues permeating the military, administration, and eventually the whole of Prussian society.[84] In turn, cooperation with the state gave Pietists access to a sounding board that substantially magnified the resonance of their reformatory message. However, these striking affinities between Pietism and the Hohenzollern state have, to some extent, obscured other aspects of Pietism that had a different influence on Prussian society. In many respects Pietism was as much a force for strengthening individual autonomy as it was one for strengthening the state.[85] It is crucial to remember that the rapprochement between Pietism and state was above all a marriage of convenience, based on a shared preference for religious tolerance. For the Hohenzollern, religious tolerance had been the way out of the failed Second Reform and continued to be necessary for political stability. Moreover, the activist immigration policy of the Hohenzollern was only possible in an atmosphere of religious tolerance because many of those with attractive skills and strong motives to leave their home countries were members of the Reformed Church. The Hohenzollern had begun this policy on a larger scale as part of their attempts to promote economic recovery after the Thirty Years War but it remained a staple of economic policy well into the eighteenth century. Religious tolerance was thus politically and economically necessary. It became part of Prussia's *raison d'état*. In Pietism, the Hohenzollern saw a movement that could serve their interests as a 'fifth column' weakening the opposition of the Lutheran orthodoxy to religious toleration.[86] As a minority that was continuously under attack from the dominant church, Pietism stood equally to gain from tolerance. However, the ideal of religious freedom was embraced by Pietists not merely for opportunist reasons. It also derived from the theological content of their faith. This is not to say that Pietism embraced any form of relativism. Born-again Pietists harboured little doubt as to the superiority of their faith over that of others who had not been through a similar process. However, the individual and introspective manner in which true faith was to be achieved also meant that external pressure could not set individuals on the right path. The external imposition of doctrines could bring nothing but despicable hypocrisy. Whatever else may have resulted from the marriage between Pietism and the

---

[83] Schmidt, 'Pietismus', p. 12.

[84] On the influence of Christian Wolff and his relationship to Pietism see Eckart Hellmuth, *Naturrechtsphilosophie und bürokratischer Werthorizont. Studien zur preußischen Geistes- und Sozialgeschichte des 18. Jahrhunderts* (Göttingen, 1985). Fulbrook, *Piety and politics*, pp. 159–66. Gawthrop, *Pietism*, p. 213.

[85] James van Horn Melton, 'Pietism, politics and the public sphere in Germany', in James E. Bradley and Dale K. Van Kley, eds., *Religion and politics in enlightenment Europe* (Notre Dame, IN, 2001), pp. 294–333.

[86] Clark, *Iron kingdom*, p. 138.

Prussian state it was built on an accord to limit the power of the state in an important area.[87] The opportunistic nature of the alliance between Pietism and the Prussian state also becomes apparent when it is seen in a wider European context. Mary Fulbrook, in her study of European Pietisms and Puritanism, has shown convincingly that the relation between these movements and the respective states was largely determined by the specific religious and political contexts.[88] There was nothing inherent in Pietism that predestined it to become an ally or enemy of the state.

The visibility of the institutional cooperation between Pietism and the state has led many historians to draw a picture of Pietism that emphasized aspects of the movement that facilitated cooperation with the state at the expense of others that sat less comfortably with the notion of Pietism as Prussia's ideology of state.[89] Discipline, a zeal for social reform, and a forward-looking spirit were certainly part of Pietist ethics as well as being useful qualities for the civil servants of a nascent state. But the processes through which Pietists searched for the moral objectives that they as individuals, and the community as a whole, should pursue with the proverbial discipline were strictly individual and removed from the influence of the state. Pietism may have imbued its followers with qualities that prepared them to be loyal and efficient servants of the state, but it also equipped them with an ethos that originated from sources that were outside of the state's control and that formed a moral counterweight to state power.[90]

Recent scholarship on Pietism has therefore emphasized the movement's contribution to the construction of the modern self rather than its role in the creation of the modern state. Ulrike Gleixner has shown in her recent study of Pietism in Württemberg that the modern bourgeois concept of the self owes much to the heritage of Pietism and similar religious movements; James van Horn Melton has made similar points for the Prussian context.[91] Self-education, self-searching, and self-reflexion were the processes through which Pietists individually appropriated religious principles. The faithful were called upon to continuously reflect on their inner feelings and their relationship with God and the community. Much of this took place through written and printed works. Pietists—to the delight of historians—produced great volumes of diaries, letters, and other types of documents in which they reflected on the development of their faith in this three-way relationship.[92]

In the Pietist context the aim and effect of this process was not one of individualization in the sense of developing an individual distinctiveness or diversity. Rather it

---

[87] Klaus Deppermann, 'Pietismus und die moderne Welt', in Kurt Aland, ed., *Pietismus und die moderne Welt* (Witten, 1974), pp. 75–98, at pp. 84–5.

[88] Fulbrook, *Piety and politics*, p. 17.

[89] Most strongly in Gawthrop, *Pietism*, and Fulbrook, *Piety and politics*. In a more balanced form in Carl Hinrichs' classic work: *Preußentum und Pietismus* (Göttingen, 1971).

[90] Schmidt, 'Pietismus', pp. 25–39.

[91] Ulrike Gleixner, *Pietismus und Bürgertum: eine historische Anthropologie der Frömmigkeit, Württemberg 17.–19. Jahrhundert* (Göttingen, 2005), p. 404. Melton, 'Pietism, politics and the public sphere in Germany', pp. 294–333.

[92] Gleixner, *Pietismus und Bürgertum*, p. 26.

was a process of assimilation of religious values through an individualized process.[93] However, many of the techniques of Pietist devotion lost their religious content over time and as they spread through society and contributed to processes of secular individualization. Self-reflexion, self-reliance, and the emphasis on the improvement of the individual as a starting point for social progress contributed to the conceptualization of a stronger, more independent individual who became central to urban culture in the eighteenth century. In a similar manner, the practice of reflecting on moral questions and individual conduct in small groups of equals, and in writings that were partly private but also read by others, prepared the ground for the further development of forms of public debate.[94] The Pietist defence of freedom of assembly and expression and the direct dialogue with the public, which were central to the religious culture fostered by Pietism, contributed to create the communicative structures that fostered critical public debate. Primarily, Pietism contributed to changes in the religious public, but in a broader sense the tools and forums created by Pietism also contributed to the formation of an enlightened public who critically engaged with a wide range of subject matters.[95] As Nipperdey has pointed out, Pietist conventicles were precursors of the clubs, reading societies, and learned associations that were crucial elements of bourgeois sociability in the eighteenth and nineteenth centuries.[96] While contributing to the process of state building, Pietism also contributed to spreading the tools and techniques that were part of the constitution of the modern bourgeois self. This contradictory legacy of Pietism has led many historians to simply ignore parts of the movement's history and focus on its function in the context of state building. However, such a narrow approach not only misunderstands Pietism; it also fails to grasp the wider historical context of which the movement was a part and in which state power and individual autonomy developed jointly.

SEX AND THE PRUSSIAN TOWN

The religious individualism that resulted from the process of state building in Prussia also had a deep impact on the relation between individuals and the state in other areas, most importantly with regard to sexuality and education. In Prussia, as elsewhere in Europe, the sexual behaviour of individuals had traditionally been regulated by the moral prescriptions of the Catholic Church.[97] Indeed, sexual taboos and imperatives made up the bulk of Catholic morality and thus gave sexual behaviour an extraordinarily prominent position. Sexual pleasure was deeply suspect and abstinence in its different forms was exalted as a virtuous life style. The

---

[93] Gleixner, *Pietismus und Bürgertum*, p. 395.

[94] Schmidt, 'Pietismus'.

[95] Martin Gierl, *Pietismus und Aufklärung: theologische Polemik und die Kommunikationsreform der Wissenschaft am Ende des 17. Jahrhunderts* (Göttingen, 1997), p. 180.

[96] Nipperdey, 'Verein', p. 180.

[97] The following discussion of the state's role in the regulation of individual sexual behaviour is deeply indebted to the framework developed by Isabel Hull.

only permissible sexual relations were within 'monogamous, procreative, hetero-sexual marriage'.[98] Whether inside or outside marriage, individuals were told in great detail how to conduct themselves in all matters relating to their sexual behaviour. Nothing less than salvation or damnation in the afterlife was at stake. Where this distant outlook was insufficient to convince individuals to follow the right path the church developed a system to discipline and punish that was as elaborate as the catalogue of sins that underpinned it: confession, penance, and the ecclesiastical courts were the principal instruments.

Much of this changed with the Reformation. The perception that the Catholic Church had failed to uphold Christian values led its critics, in practice, to focus on reforming the everyday life of the faithful. For the regulation of sexual behaviour this meant a shift towards marriage as an organizing principle for the regulation of sexual behaviour. Reformers saw the union between man and woman as the foundation of a stable Christian society. Sex within marriage was seen as an element that fortified and supported this socially useful union. This view was in marked contrast to Catholicism's generalized distrust of all forms of sex no matter whether it took place inside or outside of marriage. The divergence from the Catholic tradition and the emphasis on the social utility of certain forms of sex also legitimized a far-reaching regulation of sexual behaviour in the name of social stability. As a consequence, sex outside of marriage, which was seen as potentially destabilizing to both marriage and society, became a primary target of regulation and repression. Protestant authorities were guided by these principles and nascent states inherited this utilitarian outlook on the regulation of sexual behaviour.[99]

In a parallel development states became more important in their role in enforcing rules regarding sexual conduct. As the state grew it undermined—as we have seen often quite consciously—the power of local and intermediary institutions, which were in many cases part of the systems that regulated moral conduct in general and sexual behaviour in particular. In the towns the corporations were among the most important institutions in this respect. The strict rules that they imposed on the conduct of their members and the criteria that had to be met by those who wished to join were powerful mechanisms that not only limited access to certain profes-sions, but also worked to control urban mores. Adulterous masters, for example, were expelled from the guilds, thus damaging their own and their family's liveli-hoods. Guild regulations were far-reaching in forbidding contact with individuals of questionable reputation and by excluding not only the offending master but also their legitimate offspring in case of moral transgressions. Corporative rules also governed the choice of marriage partners. Similarly strict guidelines applied to individuals hoping to join a corporation. A man's questionable reputation could prevent admission into the guild, as could similar doubts about the conduct of his wife: only virgins of legitimate birth were acceptable brides for guild masters. It is important to stress that these rules regulated sexual behaviour very effectively but that their objectives were not sexual in nature. Primarily they served to guarantee

---

[98] Hull, *Sexuality*, pp. 10–14.   [99] Hull, *Sexuality*, pp. 17–29.

legitimacy in the acquisition and transfer of economic privileges and to limit access to these privileges.[100] As the state tried to reduce the power of the guilds for fiscal and economic reasons it also undermined a crucial part of the system that regulated sexual behaviour and moral conduct in the towns. Other parts of this urban regulatory system, such as magistrates, were similarly weakened as a result of state building. The regulation of sexual behaviour thus increasingly became a responsibility of the state. This process occurred in similar ways in different parts of the empire. In Prussia, the role of the state was made even more prominent by the introduction of a degree of religious tolerance. Poly-confessionalism meant that in Prussia the ability of the Lutheran Church to function as a moral point of reference and disciplinary institution for the whole of society was severely impaired.

As the state began to assume its new role as regulator of sexual behaviour it also interpreted it according to its own priorities. Regulation grew much more relaxed. At first this happened in practice and then changes to the legal framework emerged. The looser practice of enforcement was in large part due to the limited resources of the state. Well into the eighteenth century, Prussia and other German states could not afford to devote much attention to any matters that were not part of their military–fiscal core functions. We encounter this factor again as a key determinant of the state's limited role in education.[101] However, in Prussia legal reform became eventually more important than scarce resources as a limiting factor. The origins of legal reform lay with the emphasis on the social utility of sexual regulation. The state inherited this outlook in part from the Reformation but it also reflected the state's own interest in the defence of marriage as a building block of a stable society. Closely related to this broader social and political motive was a more specific financial preoccupation. Authorities often feared that illegitimate children were more likely to become destitute, making it necessary for the community to support them in some way.[102]

Considerations of social utility thus led to the continuity of regulatory principles, and ultimately such considerations instigated the development of important changes. For what was useful or in the state's interest was liable to reinterpretation in a way that religious doctrines never were. Perhaps the most striking example of change in sexual regulation that was triggered by a redefinition of the state's interest can be found in the evolution of the laws against infanticide in Prussia. Infanticide and the regulation of sexual behaviour were closely linked in contemporary perception because of the widespread view that virtually all victims were illegitimately born children. The crucial legal reform occurred under Fredrick II. However, his father had already introduced changes as a reaction to an alleged dramatic increase in the number of cases of infanticide. Frederick William I reintroduced the previously abolished *Säcken* (drowning in a bag) as a punishment for those found guilty of infanticide. In addition to the harsher punishment his edicts contained elements of prevention. However, the guiding principle was that a harsher and

---

[100] Hull, *Sexuality*, pp. 41–4.
[101] Hull, *Sexuality*, pp. 97–106.
[102] Hull, *Sexuality*, pp. 24–9, 103–4.

more dishonouring punishment would work as a deterrent.[103] *Säcken* was abolished again when Frederick II ascended the throne in 1740. He also put an end to the so-called *Kirchenbußen*. These rituals of public penitence for fornicators—those guilty of extramarital sex—were in a wider sense part of the system of prevention and punishment of infanticide because of the contemporary view that linked the crime and illegitimacy.[104] The changes introduced by Frederick early on in his reign marked a shift in attitudes and foreshadowed further changes. Infanticide was no longer to be prevented by particularly shameful and cruel forms of punishment but by reducing the shame and ostracism that was associated with fornication. Like an increasing number of contemporaries, the king came to believe that less fear of being dishonoured by extramarital sex—and an illegitimate child as its most visible result—would be a more effective way to prevent infanticides.

This view informed subsequent legal reform. In 1765 a new edict marked a radical shift in the approach to infanticide. The logic of the new law was no longer to suppress fornication and thereby reduce the number of illegitimate children and therefore reduce the potential for infanticide. Rather, the focus shifted towards protecting the life of the children through the gradual decriminalization of fornication. The approach was two-pronged. On the one hand, the edict carefully avoided all derogatory comments on the moral conduct of illegitimately pregnant women and explicitly called for all shaming of such conduct to cease. It was thought that if the shame associated with an illegitimate child were reduced infanticide would become less likely. On the other hand, the edict placed emphasis on prevention: illegitimate pregnancies were decriminalized, while it became an independent criminal offence to secretly give birth to a child. However, to fulfil this requirement mothers no longer had to inform the authorities if they were pregnant with an illegitimate child. It was now enough that other mothers of good reputation were made aware of the pregnancies.[105]

The developments that culminated in the edict of 1765 thus limited the involvement of the state with the sexual behaviour and family life of individuals in two important ways. First, the state began to withdraw from the regulation and suppression of sexual acts between unmarried adults. This process was completed with the 'legalization' of fornication in the *Allgemeines Landrecht* of 1795.[106] Second, the prevention of infanticide was in large part handed over to private individuals. Rather than the authorities, other mothers were put in charge of 'supervising' pregnancies and protecting the life of the infant. The driving forces behind the 'deregulation' of sex that become apparent in the 1765 edict were in

---

[103] Hull, *Sexuality*, pp. 111–16, 280–5. Wilhelm Wächtershäuser, *Das Verbrechen des Kindesmordes im Zeitalter der Aufklärung* (Berlin, 1973), pp. 138–41.

[104] Hull, *Sexuality*, pp. 127–30.

[105] 'Preußisches Edikt v. 8 Febr. 1765 und dessen "Summaria"', in Wächtershäuser, *Verbrechen*, pp. 161–7.

[106] Under the Provision of the *Allgemeines Landrecht für die Preußischen Staaten* (ALR) it remained a criminal offence to promote or assist promiscuous behaviour of non-adults. However, the acts themselves were not considered to be crimes. ALR, Zwanzigster Teil, 'Von den Verbrechen und deren Strafen', §§ 992–98. See also Hull, *Sexuality*, p. 127.

part shifting moral attitudes. But at least as important was once again the state's single-minded pursuit of its own interest. For a long time, the preservation of marriage had been considered the primary objective of the state's regulation of sexual behaviour. However, in the aftermath of the devastations of the Thirty Years War another, potentially conflicting, objective became a priority of many administrators and monarchs. The power of the state, it was argued, depended crucially on the number of its citizens. 'Populationism' led the Hohenzollern to pursue an aggressive immigration policy, but the concern with demographics also contributed to changing attitudes towards illegitimate children. Fredrick II had already put forward arguments to this effect in 1749. In his discourse *On the reasons to introduce or abolish laws*, which was read out publicly in the Berlin academy, he pondered the question of whether abortion was not punished with excessive harshness in his lands. The young monarch asked: 'Does not the severity of the judge rob the state of two subjects, the aborted unborn child and the mother who could more than compensate the loss through legitimate births'.[107] When demographic questions acquired a new urgency after the Seven Years War, Fredrick decided to translate his academic musings into law in order to help the economic recovery of his realm.

Prosecution and regulation of infanticide are clearly only one aspect of the regulation of sex. However, their evolution provides us with a good indication of the direction of change in this area and it emerges clearly that official interference with individual sexual behaviour was continuously reduced in Prussia. This development was not the result of a concern for individual freedom but it led to an increased space for individual autonomy. Given the urban focus of this study it is necessary to consider whether this development was specific to the towns or whether it affected Prussian burghers in the same way as rural populations. Contemporary observers had a clear answer to this question. In the second half of the eighteenth century an intense debate developed over what the consequences of the newfound sexual freedom might be. In these exchanges the near-uniform opinion was that dangerous sexual excesses were associated with life in the cities. Masturbation—considered by many contemporaries as one of the most dangerous sexual practices for society—was even seen as an exclusively urban phenomenon. It was allegedly caused by 'the atmosphere of the city, the luxury [Pracht], the food, the privacy [Eingezogenheit], the idleness, the early efforts at education, the refined upbringing, the early gallantry, reading, the societies, [and] dancing'.[108] The greater sexual freedom in the cities interacted in a unique way with other forms of growing individualism and contributed to a perception of an unfettered pursuit of individual pleasure in the towns.

---

[107] 'Et la sévérité des juges ne prive-t-elle pas l'État de deux sujets à la fois, de l'avorton qui a péri, et de la mère, qui pourrait réparer abondamment cette perte par une propagation légitime?'. Frederick II, 'Dissertation sur les raisons d'établir ou d'abroger les lois', in Johann D. E. Preuss, ed., *Oeuvres de Frédéric le Grand* (30 vols., Berlin, 1848), vol. 9, pp. 9–37, at p. 30.
[108] Peter Villaume, cited in Hull, *Sexuality*, p. 268.

THE 'STATE-FREE' SCHOOLS OF PRUSSIA'S TOWNS

Education was another area where relations between individuals and the state were affected by religious change. Historians have argued that Frederick Wilhelm I, 'turned over' the 'school system' to Pietism and that it subsequently functioned as a powerful tool for the moulding of Prussians into obedient and hard working subjects of the state.[109] However, such arguments—quite apart from the one-sided picture that they paint of Pietism—do not sit easily with what we know about the reality of schooling in Prussia. As Wolfgang Neugebauer has shown, we can hardly speak of a coherent 'school system' in eighteenth-century Prussia. Even more importantly for the present purpose, the nascent Prussian state had little significant control over schools in this period.[110] Education was, without doubt, an important part of the modernizing and nation-building efforts of many nineteenth-century states. But in the early stages of state formation it was a task that was not central to the military–fiscal core functions of the state and was therefore largely ignored.[111] The experience of being a pupil in eighteenth-century Prussia—in particular in the towns—was only rarely one of interaction with the state. Instead, 'state-free private schooling' was the norm for most urban dwellers' educational experience.[112]

Education for Prussians varied greatly, but particularly in the towns the majority of pupils attended so-called *Winkelschulen* (niche schools), private schools that were either illegal or only loosely supervised by the state.[113] Since the time of the Thirty Years War the Hohenzollern had made efforts to promote schooling in the towns but the results on the ground remained limited and varied greatly.[114] Many ambitious-sounding edicts, for example the 1717 school edict of Frederick William I that nineteenth-century historians have described as the beginning of compulsory schooling in Europe, effectively only sanctioned already existing practices.[115] In our period the role of the Prussian state in schooling was characterized by far-reaching claims and a limited engagement in practice. While the importance of education was certainly understood, the Prussian state simply could not raise the money for schools, teacher salaries, and teacher training that would have been necessary to fully take charge of this sector. Even the oversight of non-state schools remained rudimentary for lack of resources. The result was a sort of 'salutary neglect' that allowed community initiatives to thrive.

---

[109] Gawthrop, *Pietism*, p. 222.

[110] Wolfgang Neugebauer, *Absolutistischer Staat und Schulwirklichkeit in Brandenburg-Preußen* (Berlin, 1985), p. 207.

[111] James van Horn Melton, *Absolutism and the eighteenth-century origins of compulsory schooling in Prussia and Austria* (Cambridge, 1988), p. 232. Neugebauer, *Schulwirklichkeit*, p. 627.

[112] Neugebauer, *Schulwirklichkeit*, p. 630.

[113] Neugebauer, *Schulwirklichkeit*, p. 601.

[114] Neugebauer, *Schulwirklichkeit*, p. 228.

[115] Melton, *Compulsory schooling*, p. 46. Wolfgang Neugebauer, 'Bemerkungen zum preußischen Schuledikt von 1717', *Jahrbuch für die Geschichte Mittel- und Ostdeutschlands*, 31 (1982), pp. 155–76. Ferdinand Vollmer, *Friedrich Wilhelm I und die Volksschule* (Göttingen, 1909), pp. 30–40.

In the period before 1740, Pietist schools were the most important examples of such initiatives. For despite the close relationship between Pietism and the Prussian state it is important to see these schools above all as an expression of the vitality and autonomy of local communities. The Pietist sympathies of Frederick William did play a role, but ultimately the majority of the individuals, ideas, and funds that brought these institutions into existence were associated with civil society rather than with the state.[116] Later, in the second half of the eighteenth century, the continued neglect of education by the state coincided with an enlightened urban culture in which education played a central role. The result of this combination was a fertile environment for initiatives that came out of local communities and that flourished above all in the towns.

Arguments that assume that schooling was part of the disciplinary apparatus of Prussian absolutism are also problematic on another level. Not only was the role of the state in school education limited, but schooling also produced more complex outcomes than simply instilling discipline. As Melton has pointed out, disciplining the population may have been among the objectives of absolutist school policy but in practice outcomes were varied and often contrary to such intentions. At school, pupils learned many of the skills necessary for autonomous thought and action. The most important of these skills was perhaps literacy. Its extent in Prussian towns is difficult to gauge for our period and improvements in schooling can certainly not be automatically equated with the spread of literacy. However, in the early eighteenth century literacy started to become a more prominent pedagogic pre-occupation. This is particularly true of the wave of improvements made to schooling in the wake of the Reformation. Initially, the imparting of religious education—either to further or counterbalance the Reformation—had been the main objective. In this context, reading was viewed with suspicion because it potentially exposed students to all sorts of 'heretic' texts, thus undermining the whole purpose of this type of education.[117] However, in the eighteenth century under the influence of Pietism, with its prioritization of Bible study, reading moved to a more prominent place in the curriculum of many Prussian schools. This converged with a similar tendency that originated mainly in some private schools where the teaching of useful skills such as reading, writing, and basic arithmetic was more important than religious education. Both influences were felt across Prussia but were particularly strong in the towns, where the main Pietist institutions were located and where private schooling was more widespread. In many cases the economic life of the towns also demanded an ability to deal with text and numbers, at least at a basic level.[118] Even where schooling was backed by the state and associated with the intention of instilling discipline and preserving the political and social status quo the result was often a strengthening of individual autonomy.

---

[116] Neugebauer, *Schulwirklichkeit*, pp. 55, 632. Carl Hinrichs, *Friedrich Wilhelm I* (Darmstadt, 1974), p. 567.
[117] Melton, *Compulsory schooling*, pp. 8–9.
[118] Melton, *Compulsory schooling*, p. 7.

In many ways the spread of reading, writing, and mathematical skills paved the way for a wider participation in public debates in Prussia's towns.

'WHERE INDIVIDUAL LIFE CARRIES ITS OWN CENTRE OF GRAVITY WITHIN ITSELF'

Paradoxically, the ruthless pursuit of dynastic and state interest that resulted from the traumatic experience of the Thirty Years War led to an increase in individual freedoms in several areas. The effects of this process could be felt everywhere in Prussia, but the different policies and administrative practices that the state pursued in town and country meant that urban societies experienced more significant change and offered more opportunities for the development of individual freedom. However, this process was neither a hard and fast retreat of the state nor did it establish stable lines of demarcation between state and civil society. It was a long and tortuous development that resulted in indistinct and shifting frontiers between state and civil society. The state never completely retreated from any area. As Skocpol has shown, the state continued to intervene in order to structure the way in which individuals interacted with it and among themselves, even in areas that it did not fully control.[119]

And yet, no matter how gradual and incomplete, the process of 'disentanglement' set state and non-state spheres on very different tracks of development. Tasks assumed by the state were typically carried out in a collective and coercive manner. Decentralized individual decisions, private interests, and their interaction became the principal forces guiding development outside the purview of the state. This newly emerging central role of the individual bound together otherwise fundamentally different aspects of human experience. The patchwork of economic, religious, and other freedoms came to be seen as part of a greater whole. This was in part because their opposite, the state, began to take a more sharply defined shape. But these disparate areas were also bound together by a shared characteristic: the paramount role that the interests and needs of individuals played within them. 'The fulfilment of the personality' had become, or was fast becoming, the guiding principle that they had in common.[120] Like many contemporaries, we use the term *bürgerliche Gesellschaft* ('civil society') in this study to describe the sum of those spheres in which the state played a lesser and individuals a greater role. In Chapter 2 we explore how urban Prussians used their growing freedom in everyday life and what they themselves thought about the chances and perils associated with the increasingly unfettered pursuit of private interests.

[119] Skocpol, 'Bringing the state back in', p. 7.
[120] Schumpeter, 'Crisis of the tax state', p. 109.

2

Urban Navel-Gazing

The exquisite delicacies that tempt the Prussians
Have turned them into Epicureans

Johann Georg Hamann, *To the Salomon of Prussia*, (1772).[1]

The burghers themselves can be trusted to create prosperity and industry.

Friedrich Gedike, *Berlinische Monatsschrift* (1783).[2]

From a structural point of view the history of civil society appears to a large extent as a history of state building turned on its head. It is, however, more than that. We must ask how contemporaries perceived the economic, religious, and other freedoms that they gradually acquired and whether they saw their era as one of growing individualism. This is not a secondary matter: thinking of oneself as an individual is a crucial part of being and acting as one. The rise of a more individualized society cannot simply be assumed based on the historical analysis of shifts in institutional structures. It makes sense to speak of a more individualized society only if the greater freedoms afforded by structural changes were also 'used' by individuals who saw themselves as increasingly autonomous and empowered. This chapter therefore explores contemporary commentary on urban life in the reign of Frederick II (1740–86) and argues that such commentary—written mostly by urban dwellers—reflects a perception of an increasing individualistic urban society. This is particularly true after the country was beginning to recover from the Seven Years War but similar comments can also be found earlier.[3] Among the main issues in these debates about the towns were population growth, the increase of manufacturing and trade, the rise of an urban consumer culture, and the different moral and social implications that these changes had for richer and poorer urban dwellers. We explore these interrelated debates in this order, reflecting causal relations seen by many contemporary commentators: urban population growth was largely seen

---

[1] 'Les mets exquis amorçant les Prussiens/Les ont changés en Epicuriens.' Johann Georg Hamann, 'Au Salomon de Prusse', in Josef Nadler, ed., *Sämtliche Werke/Johann Georg Hamann* (6 vols., Wien, 1951), vol. 3, pp. 55–60, at pp. 55.

[2] 'Bei Wohlstand und Industrie wird der Bürger sich schon selbst aufbauen.' Friedrich Gedike, 'Ueber Berlin, von einem Fremden (Briefe 1–3)', *Berlinische Monatschrift*, 1 (1783), pp. 439–65.

[3] Ludwig Beutin, 'Die Wirkungen des Siebenjährigen Krieges auf die Volkswirtschaft in Preußen', *Vierteljahrschrift für Wirtschafts- und Sozialgeschichte*, 26 (1933), pp. 209–43. Ingrid Mittenzwei, *Preußen nach dem Siebenjährigen Krieg: Auseinandersetzungen zwischen Bürgertum und Staat um die Wirtschaftspolitik* (Berlin, 1979), pp. 9–12.

as a consequence of the rise of commerce. The commercialization of urban societies was held responsible for an increase in luxury consumption which, in turn, was blamed for the erosion of traditional social bonds and increasing selfishness among urban dwellers. But great differences were seen in the ways in which the rise of commerce affected rich and poor. The rich were considered to be at risk of falling into a debauched and luxurious lifestyle, losing their moral judgement, and eschewing marriage in favour of the unfettered pursuit of sensual pleasures. This left them detached from family bonds; selfishness became the main motivation that governed their actions. The poor were exposed to the same temptations by the new consumer society, but because they did not have the means to enjoy them, they were likely to ruin themselves economically. Their poverty prevented them from marrying and meant that they remained without firm bonds attaching them to family and property, the bedrocks of stable societies. Rich and poor were put on different trajectories of degradation by the rise of commerce, but the outcomes for both groups were similarly associated with the decline of traditional social bonds and morality and the rise of greater individualism. Moreover, the poor were also seen as being exposed to a threat that could potentially undermine the established religious order: the monotony of factory work and their lack of education made them prone to influence by religious impostors and superstition. Increasing individualism in religious matters was likely to give rise to a more fractioned and instable religious landscape in the towns. How to respond to the challenges of greater individualism in economic and religious matters, resulting from the rise of urban commerce, was the subject of heated debates. However, the main insight that emerges from reading these debates is that contemporaries had very little doubt about the fact that urban societies were quickly becoming places primarily governed by the desires and interests of individuals. In short, Prussian urbanites not only enjoyed more freedoms but they also thought of themselves as living in an age of individualism.

Before delving into the Prussian debates, it should be said that many of the concerns and arguments on the minds of urban Prussians in this period will seem familiar to students of the European history of ideas. Praise and condemnation of luxuries couched in economic and moral terms, worries about religious stability, and spirited defences of toleration were all part of the great post-Renaissance debate about commerce and luxury. These exchanges are among the most exciting and best-studied chapters in the European history of ideas.[4] The purpose here is not mainly to add a new perspective to the understanding of this debate, but, rather, to show to what extent Prussia's intellectual life was a part of this wider European debate. Prussians knew many of the great contributions to this debate and borrowed, modified, and extended arguments from other parts of Europe for 'domestic consumption'. At the same time, they also formulated arguments that found their way into other national contexts. They could join in with this European

---

[4] See István Hont's magisterial survey of arguments and historiography in: István Hont, 'The early Enlightenment debate on commerce and luxury', in Mark Goldie and Robert Wokler, eds., *The Cambridge history of eighteenth-century political thought* (Cambridge, 2006), pp. 379–418.

conversation with ease because the questions and concerns posed by changing realities in Prussia were similar to the ones that many other European societies had confronted earlier or were facing at the same time. One of the objectives of this chapter is thus to put Prussia on the map of the great pan-European debate on luxury, which was also always a debate about the relation between states and individuals. However, it also seeks to use the Prussian case to emphasize a facet of this debate that is often overlooked. This is the extent to which contemporaries differentiated in their commentaries between rich and poor. The rise of commerce was seen as a challenge to everyone's way of life but the ways in which it did so and the nature of the advantages, dangers, and pitfalls were seen as differing greatly according to the social and economic conditions of individuals.

URBAN GROWTH

Looking at contemporary debates about Prussia's towns it seems that one of the most important questions on the minds of urban dwellers in this period was how many there were. Little was known about the size of Prussia's towns, their historical development, and how their size compared with that of the rural population. Despite this uncertainty, the assumption shared by most commentators was that the populations of their towns were growing rapidly. Of course this kind of impressionistic evidence was deeply unsatisfactory in an age in which precise measurement and statistics had become a 'universal fashion' in Prussia as much as elsewhere.[5] In Berlin, the lack of available information combined with a sense of dramatic change led a local pastor, Johann Süßmilch (1707–67), to systematically examine demographics. His curiosity was initially the result of local concerns but his comments quickly became part of an ongoing European debate about demographics.[6] Süßmilch commented on the principal British and Dutch authorities on the subject, and in his main work, *The divine order and the transformations of human kind* (1761–2), he presented a refutation of Montesquieu's argument that Europe's population had declined since Roman times, mainly as a result of the rise of Christianity.

However, Süßmilch's concerns were, at least initially, much narrower. The first result of his efforts was a report that he presented at the Royal Academy of Sciences—of which he was a member—reprinted as a small volume with the title *The rapid growth and building of the royal capital Berlin* (1752).[7] The rapid

---

[5] 'Ont pris une vogue générale.' Ewald Friedrich von Hertzberg, 'Réflexions sur la force des états et sur leur puissance relative et proportionnelle', in Académie Royale des Sciences et Belles Lettres, ed., *Nouveaux mémoires de l'Académie Royale des Sciences et Belles Lettres* (Berlin, 1782), pp. 475–86, at pp. 475–6.

[6] Süßmilch referred explicitly to the demographic works of John Graunt (1620–74), William Petty (1623–87), Gregory King (1648–1712), John Arbuthnot (1667–1735), and Bernard Nieuwentijt (1654–1718).

[7] Johann Peter Süßmilch, *Der königl. Residentz Berlin schneller Wachsthum und Erbauung in zweyen Abhandlungen erwiesen* (Berlin, 1752).

expansion of the capital, Süßmilch explained in the dedication, was a new phenomenon. In its current dramatic form it had only begun in the years immediately
preceding the publication of his tract, although substantial growth had been clearly
visible even before then. By the time of writing, 'flourishing growth' had made the
city one of the 'biggest, most populous and most beautiful cities of Germany, even
of Europe'. With the exceptions of London and Paris, not more than six cities in
Europe could boast a greater population than 'our fortunate Berlin'.[8] Süßmilch's
was primarily a description of a demographic phenomenon that had aroused his
scientific interest, but he could not avoid peppering his report with a strong dose of
civic pride. This may not be too surprising considering that he referred to himself
elsewhere in an almost Rousseauean fashion as an 'inhabitant and fellow citizen of
Berlin'.[9] After outlining a brightly optimistic picture in the introduction, Süßmilch
proceeded to a detailed discussion of Berlin's population and its historical development. In order to elucidate the current demographic situation he cited from two
censuses produced in 1747 on royal orders. Both put the civilian population at
roughly 85,000. A small difference of 265 inhabitants between the two reports was
taken by Süßmilch as proof of their veracity. Perfect similarity, he explained, would
have been 'suspicious'.[10]

Formulating innovative methods as he went along, Süßmilch used historical
mortality lists in order to reconstruct the demographic development of
Berlin over the last century. Again his findings were a cause of great pride.
Other European cities may still have been bigger at the time, but Berlin had
been growing at a speed that was 'beyond comprehension'. In the last sixty to
seventy years its population had increased sevenfold and was now much bigger
than that of Königsberg or Breslau, both of which had been bigger than Berlin as
little as fifty years earlier.[11] London, in comparison, had only grown fourfold
over a period of 130 years and many other European cities were even declining.[12]
Moreover, an end to this growth was not foreseeable. Süßmilch was
confident that the city had reached neither its 'highest level' nor its 'turning
point'.[13]

Exalted commentary on the development of Berlin was not uncommon at the
time, but there was also awareness of the diversity of the urban sector in Prussia.
Contemporaries lamented the lack of information about small and mid-sized towns
but went to considerable length to shed at least some light on their development.
The prevalence of this type of town, in Prussia, defined by Süßmilch as having
respectively one-twelfth and one-thirtieth of Berlin's population, was seen as a

---

[8] Süßmilch, *Der königl. Residentz Berlin*, p. 2.
[9] 'Einwohner und Mitbürger von Berlin.' Johann Peter Süßmilch, *Die göttliche Ordnung in den
Veränderungen des menschlichen Geschlechts, aus der Geburt, dem Tode der Fortpflanzung desselben
erwiesen* (2 vols., Berlin, 1765), vol. 2, p. 71.
[10] Süßmilch, *Der königl. Residentz Berlin*, p. 8.
[11] Süßmilch, *Der königl. Residentz Berlin*, not paginated. Johann Peter Süßmilch, *Die göttliche
Ordnung in den Veränderungen des menschlichen Geschlechts, aus der Geburt, dem Tode der Fortpflanzung
desselben erwiesen* (2 vols., Berlin, 1761), vol. 1, pp. 471–7.
[12] Süßmilch, *Der königl. Residentz Berlin*, pp. 25, 4.
[13] 'Wende-Punkt und höchste Stufe.' Süßmilch, *Der königl. Residentz Berlin*, p. 6.

strength, while the growth of larger cities caused preoccupation.[14] According to Süßmilch, from 1700 to 1750 Königsberg had grown by 38 per cent, reaching 56,000 inhabitants, and Halle had more than doubled its population in this period to 33,600. Breslau, in turn, had grown by 28 per cent since 1690, reaching a total of 44,800 inhabitants in 1730.[15] The problem with such 'considerable' cities was not so much the number of inhabitants in itself, but that they tended to have among other things 'extensive commerce', 'big factories', 'a sizeable court', 'a large garrison', and 'large and high schools'. These features, which came to define 'urbanity' for later generations, caused preoccupation among many contemporaries because they were associated with a type of town where 'much money circulates' and where 'splendour', 'opulence', and 'a voluptuous way of life' prevailed.[16]

Many observers were not only preoccupied with the growing number of larger towns, but also with the expansion of the urban sector as a whole. Perhaps most interesting in this context is the voice of a French observer who had taken up temporary residence in Prussia. Gabriel Riqueti, Comte de Mirabeau (1749–91) had arrived in Berlin in 1786 on an official mission for the French court. Despite his growing notoriety, the count had been given the task to report to Paris about the state of health of the ailing Frederick and the intentions of his successor. He discharged this task successfully: despite the gates of Berlin being closed, the count managed to dispatch the news of Frederick's death without delay to Paris using a carrier pigeon and a courier waiting outside the city walls.[17] However, Mirabeau was far too independent-minded to act merely as the 'eyes and ears' of the French foreign ministry in Berlin. As a committed physiocrat, he used his stay in Berlin to try and persuade Frederick and his successor to adopt the sect's teachings. His success was limited, but the count's missionary spirit led him to comment extensively on the situation of Prussia. In addition to short secret messages for the French court, Mirabeau wrote two long works about Prussia. One was the *Secret history of the court of Berlin* (1789) which caused considerable political scandal. The other was the four-volume *Of the Prussian monarchy under Frederick the Great* (1788) in which he and his co-author Jakob Mauvillon (1743–94) analysed Prussia's geography, population, and economy as well as its religious, military, and political institutions. Mirabeau examined the interplay of these different spheres and asked whether they came together as a harmonious whole. For the greater part, his verdict was damning and his criticism became part of a number of contemporary debates. Mirabeau's work was not only widely read inside and

---

[14] Süßmilch, *Göttliche Ordnung*, vol. 1, p. 116.

[15] Süßmilch, *Göttliche Ordnung*, vol. 2, pp. 471–7.

[16] 'Ansehnlichen Städte, in welchen grosse Handlung getrieben wird, wo grosse Fabricken, eine ansehnliche Hofstatt, viele Landes-Collegia, zahlreiche Garnison, grosse und hohe Schulen u.d.m. Kurtz alle die Städte, wo vieles Geld circuliret, wo daher Pracht, Ueberfluß und eine wollüstige Lebens-Art herrschet.' Johann Peter Süßmilch, *Die göttliche Ordnung in den Veränderungen des menschlichen Geschlechts, besonders im Tode durch einige neue Beweissthümer bestätigt u. gegen des Herrn von Justi Erinnerungen u. Muthmassungen in zweyen Sendschreiben an selbigen gerettet* (Berlin, 1756), p. 14.

[17] Honoré Gabriel de Riqueti Comte de Mirabeau, *Histoire secrète de la cour de Berlin. Avec des anecdotes plaisans et singulieres. Par le comte de Mirabeau.* (2 vols., London, 1792), vol. 1, pp. 88, 94.

outside Prussia, but it also stands out because it was in part based on a comprehensive reading of contemporary publications.

In the section about Prussia's population, Mirabeau relied heavily on the works of Süßmilch and Büsching. While Süßmilch's concern had been mainly with the increase of larger cities, Mirabeau was preoccupied with the growth of the urban sector as a whole. The excessive size of towns had long been a preoccupation of physiocratic authors in France because they were seen as draining labourers and resources from agrarian production.[18] To his disappointment, Mirabeau found similar problems in Prussia. In a country like Prussia, he wrote, the share of the urban population should not exceed one-fifth of the total population.[19] However, according to his calculations all provinces exceeded this threshold, some considerably so. The worst case was the Electoral Mark where towns had been growing steadily since the early seventeenth century. Even the Thirty Years War had not reversed this trend: urban population numbers rose roughly in line with the overall demographic trend, from 139,460 (1617) to 207,370 (1740), and 277,243 (1788). However, in reality the size of the urban sectors was even larger. Including the military population the towns had 334,300 inhabitants in 1779. Prussia's central provinces had a share of the urban population of nearly one half.[20] This 'very bad' ratio was caused mainly by the rapid growth of the capital and the large urban garrisons. The corruptive consequences of this imbalance were partly mitigated by the fact that towns were not just inhabited by members of what the physiocrats regarded as a 'sterile class', for example 'artisans', 'wage earners', 'capitalists', and 'merchants'.[21] In particular, the economies of the great number of smaller towns included an important agricultural element. However, this soothed Mirabeau's concerns only partially because even where urban dwellers were farmers he reckoned that they were ten times less productive than their rural counterparts. At any rate, the 'excessive' size of the 'sterile class' in this province was such that it was a burden for the whole of Prussia. The disproportionately large urban sector in the Electoral Mark could only be sustained through vast transfers from other Prussian provinces that already had to sustain their own excessively large towns. Of the regions for which Mirabeau gives numbers only East Prussia had a nearly 'healthy' share of urban population of 21 per cent, while it was 25 per cent in Pomerania and 26 per cent in the New Mark.[22]

Mirabeau would have found more reason for concern in a more comprehensive population statistic published subsequently by Büsching. Based on the results of an official census obtained by the author, his tables indicated slightly higher urban

---

[18] See, for example, the works of Mirabeau's father and François Quesnay's article 'Fermiers' and 'Grain' in Diderot's *Encyclopédie*.

[19] Honoré Gabriel de Riqueti Comte de Mirabeau, *De la monarchie prussienne, sous Frédéric le Grand: avec un appendice contenant des recherches sur la situation actuelle des principales contrées de l'Allemagne* (4 vols., London [Paris], 1788), vol. 1, p. 259.

[20] Mirabeau, *De la monarchie prussienne*, vol. 1, p. 378.

[21] 'Classe stérile', 'artisans', 'stipendiés', 'capitalistes', 'marchands'. Mirabeau, *De la monarchie prussienne*, vol. 1, p. 379.

[22] Mirabeau, *De la monarchie prussienne*, vol. 1, pp. 258, 283–5, 307–10.

shares for East Prussia (26 per cent) and the New Mark (29 per cent), and an only marginally lower share for Pomerania (24 per cent). The information provided by Büsching for the provinces for which Mirabeau did not have any data did not make the picture less worrying from a physiocratic point of view. The weighted average share of the urban population for all provinces included by Büsching was 28 per cent. This was below the percentage in the Electoral Mark but still substantially above the ideal postulated by Mirabeau.[23]

Mirabeau's concerns differed from Süßmilch's in that the former was more preoccupied with an excessive, but stable, relative size of the urban sector as a whole, while the latter emphasized the problems posed by the rapid growth of larger cities. They also differed in the way in which they collocated the Prussian demographic pattern in a European context. Süßmilch underlined the extraordinary character of Berlin's expansion and the way in which the capital's development was markedly different from the slow growth or decline of other German and European cities. Mirabeau, by contrast, saw the Prussian situation as structurally similar to those faced by France and many other European states. While Süßmilch was fascinated by the growth of Berlin, which he found to be 'beyond comprehension', Mirabeau did not consider the size of the capital's population 'extraordinary'. 'Many states', he added, 'have less well-proportioned [capitals] compared with the number of their inhabitants'.[24] However, it is important to note that despite certain disagreements, the principal concerns of contemporary commentators were with the excessive size or the rapid growth of Prussian towns rather than with their decline. It is no coincidence that Thomas Malthus (1766–1834) subsequently used Süßmilch's statistics to bolster his argument about the threats of rapid population growth.[25] Contemporary Prussian concerns with increasing urban demographics fit into a wider context of exchanges about urban growth and its social implications that dominated European debates well into the nineteenth century. However, modern historians have often described, and even more often tacitly implied, a markedly different image of the urban sector in Prussia as a small and stagnating part of society. It is crucial to fully acknowledge the different outlook of contemporaries in order to successfully eavesdrop on their conversations about life in Prussia's towns.

THE CAUSES OF URBAN GROWTH

There may have been disagreements about the distribution and volume of urban growth but there was wide agreement about its causes. Endogenous growth was generally dismissed as a possible cause. Living conditions in the towns were thought

---

[23] Anton Friedrich Büsching, *Zuverläßige Beyträge zu der Regierungs-Geschichte Königs Friedrich II. von Preußen: vornehmlich in Ansehung der Volksmenge, des Handels, der Finanzen und des Kriegsheers. Mit einem historischen Anhange* (Hamburg, 1790), pp. 153–9.

[24] Mirabeau, *De la monarchie prussienne*, vol. 1, p. 401.

[25] Thomas Malthus, *An essay on the principle of population* (London, 1798), pp. 36–44.

to be so unhealthy that death rates exceeded birth rates.[26] The increase in urban population was mostly seen as the result of immigration from the countryside and from abroad. The causes of population growth were considered to be twofold: new urban dwellers were either forced to take up residency in the city because they were soldiers or were attracted by the increase in trade and manufacturing.

'Crowds of soldiers' were described by Friedrich Gedike (1754–1803), the editor of *Berlinische Monatsschrift* (*Berlin Monthly*), as a distinctive feature of urban life.[27] According to Süßmilch, Berlin housed a 21,905-strong military population in addition to its 84,898 civilian inhabitants. Soldiers and their families thus made up more than 20 per cent of the total population.[28] In other towns the proportion of the military population could have been even higher. According to Mirabeau, Stettin and Magdeburg owed 36 and 27 per cent of their populations respectively to the garrisons.[29] But military service also contributed to urban population growth in other ways, as young men moved to certain towns like Berlin or Potsdam that were exempt from the draft, in order to avoid military service.[30]

Despite the substantial size of the military populations, the presence of soldiers did not provoke much critical comment. In his long article series on urban life in Berlin, Gedike only devoted a short passage to the question of whether the troops should be stationed elsewhere, and Mirabeau, normally highly critical of all aspects of Frederick's government, even expressed support for the distribution of the troops.[31] We can only speculate as to why the military presence did not provoke more of a reaction. It may well be that despite the far-reaching freedom of expression, public commentary on military and strategic decisions was still taboo. At the same time, recent historiography has described the cohabitation of civilians and soldiers in the towns as much more peaceful and symbiotic than earlier historical work had implied. It may have been the case that contemporaries did not comment much on the military presence simply because it did not cause much concern, or because patriotic pride in Prussia's military glory outweighed the daily inconvenience.

By contrast, commentary on the 'extraordinary number of factories' was abundant.[32] Their multiplication and the associated growth of commerce were widely considered the principal cause of urban population growth. Arguments about the causes and consequences of this phenomenon were central to debates about life in the towns. Süßmilch, like Mirabeau and others, attributed the growth of Berlin almost exclusively to the increase in trade and manufacturing brought by Huguenot immigrants, but he also saw economic development as decisive for the development

---

[26] Süßmilch, *Göttliche Ordnung*, vol. 1, pp. 80–97, 256. Gedike, 'Ueber Berlin (1–3)', p. 453. Süßmilch, *Gegen des Herrn von Justi Erinnerungen*, p. 14.

[27] 'Das Gedränge von Soldaten'. Gedike, 'Ueber Berlin (1–3)', p. 447.

[28] Süßmilch, *Der königl. Residentz Berlin*, pp. 7–8.

[29] Mirabeau, *De la monarchie prussienne*, vol. 1, pp. 245, 425.

[30] Gedike, 'Ueber Berlin (1–3)', p. 456.

[31] Gedike, 'Ueber Berlin (1–3)', p. 540. Mirabeau, *De la monarchie prussienne*, vol. 1, p. 405.

[32] 'Außerordentliche Menge Fabriken.' Gedike, 'Ueber Berlin (1–3)', p. 447.

of other towns with older commercial traditions, such as Königsberg.[33] Textiles were generally considered to be the most dynamic sector of manufacturing, and Süßmilch devoted considerable space to examining the number of people 'put to work and fed' by a single calico loom.[34] Cotton manufacturing was the latest addition to textile production in Prussia and was flourishing, particularly in Berlin. According to Süßmilch, a single loom gave employment to seven workers. In addition to the weaver, six other workers were needed: the production process required five spinners to produce the yarn and half the labour time of two other workers who finished the yarn. Still more workers were employed if the fabric was subsequently dyed or decorated with prints, according to the fashion of the day.[35] The 5,000 looms of Berlin thus gave direct employment to 37,000 workers. This was a substantial number relative to the total population of Berlin, although Süßmilch pointed out that not all of them were necessarily residents of the city, but lived within a radius of up to 24 miles. Still, the demand for labour in urban factories lured many country dwellers into the towns where they 'could work less hard and probably earn more'.[36] In addition, the factories also created further demand for labour in the towns because factory workers spent their wages there and the 'increased comfort of the middle class' caused by manufacturing led to the employment of 'more coachmen, footmen [and] maid servants'.[37]

The perceived importance of factories was such that long lists of the local establishments were included in many contemporary descriptions of towns and regions. In a description of his trip from Berlin to Reckahn near the town of Brandenburg, Büsching was careful to give statistical information about the number and type of factories in the different towns through which he passed. This information, he assumed, was important to readers and 'of service to politicians'.[38] In a similar way, Mirabeau filled a whole volume with descriptions and lists of makers of wool, linen, cotton, silk, leather, brandy, beer, and many other products in the various Prussian provinces.[39] The contemporary fascination with this bald statistical information can only be understood in the light of the crucial role attributed to manufacturing in the context of urban expansion.

Focus on the growth of manufacturing sometimes distracted from the agricultural character of many towns. Among the few authors to comment on this fact was Gedike in his letters about Berlin. There he described that, despite the 'extraordinary number of factories' in parts of Berlin, nothing but trees and farmland could be

---

[33] Süßmilch, *Der königl. Residentz Berlin*, pp. 27–8.

[34] 'In Arbeit setzt und ernähret.' Süßmilch, *Göttliche Ordnung*, vol. 2, p. 46.

[35] Süßmilch, *Göttliche Ordnung*, vol. 2, p. 48.

[36] 'Wobey er nicht so schwehr arbeiten darf, und auch wohl mehr verdienet.' Süßmilch, *Göttliche Ordnung*, vol. 2, p. 53.

[37] Süßmilch, *Göttliche Ordnung*, vol. 2, p. 52. 'Die reichen Familien, die grössere Bequemlichkeit des Mittel-Standes, die vermehrten Fabricken, erfordern mehr Kutscher, Laquayen, Mägde und Gesellen.' Süßmilch, *Der königl. Residentz Berlin*, p. 40.

[38] Anton Friedrich Büsching, *Anton Friderich Büschings Beschreibung seiner Reise von Berlin über Potsdam nach Rekahn unweit Brandenburg: welche er vom dritten bis achten Junius 1775 gethan hat* (Leipzig, 1775), p. 13.

[39] Mirabeau, *De la monarchie prussienne*, vol. 3.

seen and that government ministers in their offices might well be disturbed by peasants threshing and sheep bleating. Although his view of urban agriculture was broadly positive, he was still quick to point out that the Prussian capital was not unique in accommodating this kind of bucolic scene within its gates. Perhaps betraying a certain embarrassment at the lack of commercial sophistication, he added that other important European cities like Lyons and Nimes were, in this respect, similar.[40]

THE WEALTH OF TOWNS

In the eyes of many contemporaries, factories not only made Prussian towns bigger, but also more prosperous. In his chapter on urban textile manufacturing, Süßmilch discussed their demographic and also their economic impact. He calculated that only about one-seventh of the value of a piece of calico came from the imported raw material, while the remaining six-sevenths came from the fruit of local labour. The growing number of factory workers was seen as creating a bounty of increasing wealth, large amounts of which circulated in the towns.[41] Others pointed out that this effect was even more significant than was suggested by the increase in the number of workers. 'One should not believe it's possible', Friedrich Nicolai (1733–1811) exclaimed after visiting a piano-wire factory where he observed that the division of labour drastically increased productivity. Nicolai's exaltation about the wire factory may have been slightly affected. He was, at least theoretically, very familiar with the potential of what he called 'factory-like' production. Already in 1777, the translation of Adam Smith's (1723–90) *Wealth of Nations* (1776) had been reviewed in the *Allgemeine deutsche Bibliothek* (*Universal German Library*) of which Nicolai was editor. Smith's work, including his discussion of the division of labour, was widely read in Prussia at this time. German translations quickly went through several editions and in particular the university in the commercial city of Königsberg was instrumental in the diffusion of Smith's ideas among the intellectual and administrative elites of Prussia.[42]

However, Smith's argument was not universally accepted. His views about the origins of wealth were compatible, at least up to a point, with the views of Süßmilch and other more established writers, but they differed fundamentally from the physiocratic paradigm. Prussian readers were reminded of the differences by the Swiss physiocrat Isaak Iselin (1728–82), who reviewed the *Wealth of nations* in the *Allgemeine deutsche Bibliothek*. After heaping praise on the work, Iselin concluded his piece by pointing out that while Smith's theory was likely to explain the English situation well, it was doubtful whether all of it could be applied to

---

[40] Gedike, 'Ueber Berlin (1–3)', p. 447.

[41] Süßmilch, *Göttliche Ordnung*, vol. 2, p. 55.

[42] Wilhelm Treue, 'Adam Smith in Deutschland. Zum Problem des "Politischen Professors" zwischen 1776 und 1810', in Werner Conze, ed., *Deutschland und Europa* (Düsseldorf, 1951), pp. 101–35, at pp. 110–21.

Germany or other more 'extended' countries.[43] Similarly, Mauvillon and Mirabeau did not share the view that urban prosperity in Prussia—or anywhere else for that matter—was the fruit of manufacturing. Rather, they saw such wealth as the result of transfers from the country. In this view the monopolies of many urban factories siphoned wealth from the countryside to the towns. Rural populations thus supported the luxurious life of the cities with resources that would have been better used for the promotion of agriculture. Seen in this way, prosperous cities were not a sign of increasing wealth but the symptom of an unsustainable economic imbalance.[44]

EPICUREAN PRUSSIANS

Whatever its sources, increasing prosperity changed urban ways of life. In particular, consumption habits began to change rapidly from the first decades of the eighteenth century. In Königsberg the philosopher Johann Georg Hamann (1730–88) warned that the temptations of modern luxuries had turned Prussians into Epicurean pleasure-seekers, and in Berlin Süßmilch observed: 'State coaches and carriages, wine, silk, fashion and other similar things are now important items in all budgets. It would be easy to present a great number of witnesses who could confirm the marked changes that have happened in the last fifty, forty, even thirty years.'[45] These changes were also visible in the urban landscape. In Büsching's travel diary the first sight that the author found worthy of description was not a royal palace or a church, but the imposing buildings of Königliche General-Tabacks-Administration—the royal tobacco monopoly—which he passed in his carriage before leaving the city. 'It is impossible to see such a building without thinking of the enormous commerce that tobacco is now causing in Europe,' remarked the geographer who launched into a page-long diatribe about the increasing consumption of the fashionable drug.[46] So profitable had the sale of tobacco become in Prussia, he wrote, that the company could not only afford a splendid palace and warehouses in the city but it also paid its shareholders 10 per cent return on their investment. The king and his brothers were among the largest shareholders and Büsching estimated that the royal revenue from this investment exceeded that of his domains in the Electoral Mark by more than a half.[47] As Büsching continued on his way, he passed other monuments to the new consumerism, such as the royal porcelain factory

[43] 'Ausgedehnte.' Isaak Iselin, 'Smith, A.: Untersuchung der Natur und Ursachen von Nationalreichthümern. Bd. 1.: Rezension', *Allgemeine deutsche Bibliothek*, 31 (1777), pp. 586–9, at p. 589.

[44] Mirabeau, *De la monarchie prussienne*, vol. 1, pp. 412–17.

[45] 'Die Carossen und Wagen, der Wein, die Seide, die Moden und andre dergleichen Dinge, machen jetzt grosse Artickel in den Rechnungen aus. Es könte leicht eine grosse Anzahl Zeugen dargestellt werden, denen die starcke Veränderung seit 50, seit 40, ja seit 30 Jahren bewußt ist.' Süßmilch, *Der königl. Residentz Berlin*, p. 39.

[46] 'Man kann solche Gebäude nicht ansehen, ohne dabei an das ungeheuer große Gewerbe zu gedenken, welche der Taback jetzt in Europa verursacht.' Büsching, *Reise*, p. 4.

[47] Büsching, *Reise*, pp. 4–5.

which sold its sophisticated wares—far superior to the French competition, as the proud burgher did not fail to mention—directly from the site. To satisfy the demand in the provinces the factory also had branches in Königsberg, Marienwerder, Elbingen, Breslau, Magdeburg, Halberstadt, Stettin, and other towns. Clearly, Büsching expected his readers to take more than an academic interest in these establishments. As in the case of tobacco, he included extensive price lists in his book. Nine pages were devoted to coffee services alone, offered in various decorative schemes. These services came 'complete' with coffee, chocolate, and teacups as well as sugar bowls. As this assortment of specialized items suggests, exotic foodstuff was equally part of the changing consumption habits.[48] Tea and coffee were becoming increasingly common in Berlin and other larger Prussian towns. Süßmilch condemned this development unequivocally, but at the same time had to admit that certain 'luxuries' had already become so common that consumers, including himself, found it impossible to return to a more frugal lifestyle. 'How vexatious would it be for all of us even if we only had to renounce coffee,' he asked at the end of several pages of ranting about the pernicious effects of luxury.[49] Other commentators also included tea, tobacco, and sugar among the 'superfluities' that were now consumed so widely in Prussia that they had become 'necessities'.[50] Prussian urbanites were hardly original in their new tastes or in the terms in which they discussed them. The same beverages and other worldly pleasures inspired almost identical comments across Europe at the time.

Despite regional and social differences many contemporaries were convinced that urban populations, at least in the larger towns, were firmly in the grip of consumerism. 'The fashions are the tyrants of civil society,' Süßmilch warned. Even 'reasonable people' were 'forced' to bend to fashion's dictates for fear of not being 'ridiculed' and 'despised' as 'cranks'.[51] The 'tyranny of fashion' was seen to be strongest in Berlin, but from there it extended its reign to other Prussian towns. Together with foreign influences, in particular from France, the capital served as a model that was copied in the provinces.[52] Mutual observation and comparison among urban dwellers were seen as the primary mechanisms by which fashions were widely and rapidly spread.[53] Moreover, provincial towns were connected with the larger urban centres of Prussia and Europe by the flourishing print culture of the day. Michael North has shown how prominently new products and commentary on the phenomenon of fashion featured in many publications of the time. The leading *Journal des Luxus und der Moden* (*Journal of luxury and fashions*, published from 1786) had an important Prussian readership that extended deep into the

---

[48] Büsching, *Reise*, p. 28.

[49] 'Wie verdrießliche würde es uns allen fallen, wenn wir nur des Cafee entbehren sollten.' Süßmilch, *Göttliche Ordnung*, vol. 1, pp. 104, 85.

[50] 'Beynahe zum Bedürfniß gewordenen Ueberflussigkeiten.' Adrian Heinrich von Borcke, *Was ist für, und was ist gegen die General-Tabaks-Administration zu sagen* (n.p., 1786), p. 3. 'Le sucre s'est élevé . . . au rang des denrées de première nécessité . . . des matières dont l'usage est aussi universel que le sucre, le café, le thé, le tabac.' Mirabeau, *De la monarchie prussienne*, vol. 3, p. 283.

[51] Süßmilch, *Göttliche Ordnung*, vol. 1, p. 87.

[52] Süßmilch, *Göttliche Ordnung*, vol. 1, pp. 84, 97.

[53] Gedike, 'Ueber Berlin (1–3)', p. 421. Süßmilch, *Göttliche Ordnung*, vol. 2, pp. 87–8.

provinces. Berlin had by far the greatest number of subscribers of any city inside or outside Prussia, but towns like Königsberg, Stettin, Stendal, Magdeburg, Breslau, and others also had sizeable communities that followed the latest fashion news.[54]

'WEALTH IS A MOTHER OF POVERTY'

Urban prosperity was seen as leading to a greater diffusion of certain consumer goods and it also raised the frightening prospects of a life under the universal tyranny of 'unregulated appetites', 'voluptuousness', and 'debauched ways of life'.[55] However, contemporaries also had to come to grips with another paradox of urban life: growing prosperity engendered a seemingly universal 'tyranny of fashion', but at the same time increasing differences between rich and poor emerged. The same transformations that caused the siren calls of consumerism to be heard loud and clear by urban dwellers made it more difficult for many burghers to give in to the new temptations: in our towns, Süßmilch summarized the contradiction, 'wealth is a mother of poverty'.[56]

To some extent this was conceptualized as a nexus that existed at the level of perceptions. Contemporaries believed that wealth as a category of social distinction was reinforced by the growing importance of consumption. Mutual observation and increased awareness of different abilities to participate in consumption were seen as unavoidable and highly pernicious consequences of new lifestyles.[57] However, increasing inequality was also conceptualized as an economic problem. The growth of manufacturing had increased the overall prosperity of many towns, but it was also held responsible for an increasingly unequal distribution of wealth. This outcome was seen as inevitable because 'the production of wealth through commerce and factories is made possible by hands that almost never become rich'.[58] In Mirabeau's view, the unbalance was particularly strong in the case of the larger factories, which 'render one or two entrepreneurs prodigiously rich' but exclude the workers from the benefits of the factory, reducing them to the state of 'more or less well paid day labourers'. The physiocrats also preferred small-scale manufacturing to the more centralized production prevalent in the larger towns, which resulted in a growing number of economically disenfranchised workers.[59] In a similar vein, others warned of the plight of urban workers: these 'kinds of people are and remain

---

[54] Michael North, *Material delight and the joy of living* (Aldershot, 2008), p. 16.

[55] Süßmilch, *Göttliche Ordnung*, vol. 1, p. 108.

[56] 'Der Reichthum ist eine Mutter der Armuth.' Süßmilch, *Göttliche Ordnung*, vol. 1, p. 111.

[57] Süßmilch, *Göttliche Ordnung*, vol. 2, p. 88.

[58] 'Die Erwerbung des Reichthums durch Handlung und Fabricken geschieht durch Hände, die fast niemals reich werden.' Süßmilch, *Göttliche Ordnung*, vol. 1, p. 111.

[59] 'La fabrique réunie enrichira prodigieusement un ou deux entrpreneurs, mais les ouvriers ne seront que des journaliers plus ou moins payés.' Mirabeau, *De la monarchie prussienne*, vol. 3, p. 20.

poor'. They lived 'from hand to mouth' and illness always threatened to ruin their precarious livelihood.[60]

However, the main cause of the predicament of the 'poor who make us rich and our town flourishing' was not seen in low wages, but in rapidly increasing prices. Growing populations and greater wealth meant not only greater demand for exotic provisions but also for more ordinary foodstuffs. Supplies rarely grew proportionally and the cost of many products increased rapidly. Prices for 'necessary foodstuffs' were estimated to have doubled on average between 1712 and 1761. The price of grain increased by approximately 50 per cent, and even years with very good harvests did not reverse this powerful trend.[61] However, price inflation was not seen as having the same effects on everyone. It mainly impoverished urban wage earners and officials with fixed stipends or pensions, while agricultural producers and master artisans benefited from increasing prices and grew rich.[62] While the 'middle class' and 'rich families' enjoyed 'greater comforts', there seemed to be little hope that workers and servants would ever be able to participate in the material progress of the towns.[63]

THE PERILS OF WEALTH

An awareness of socio-economic differences meant that contemporaries conceptualized the consequences of the 'tyranny of fashion' in different terms for different groups in urban society. The moral and economic perils facing individuals who could indulge in various forms of hedonism were considered to be different from those encountered by urban dwellers whose poverty prevented them from participating in the new urban splendour. Belonging mostly to the former category the readers of the *Berlinische Monatsschrift* were warned, in the form of a moral tale, of the slippery slope on which they might find themselves. A satirical piece recounted the experience of a young couple recently arrived in Berlin. In the provincial town in the New Mark (Neumark) where they had previously lived, the upwardly mobile couple had found themselves with 'more income than we could spend and more time than we could use' and thus decided to move to the capital to turn their disposable income into enjoyment. Certainly, the couple were also intended to represent the many other provincial townspeople who followed the model of the capital's fashions without ever becoming its citizens.[64] In Berlin, the young wife's styles were scrutinized by her new metropolitan girlfriends. 'Once you are in the

---

[60] 'Diese Art Leute aber ist und sie bleibet auch arm. Der Lohn ist gering, und es geht wie man zu reden pflegt, aus der Hand in den Mund.' Süßmilch, *Der königl. Residentz Berlin*, p. 42.

[61] 'Diese Armen, die uns doch reich, und unsere Stadt blühed machen'. Süßmilch, *Der königl. Residentz Berlin*, p. 43. 'Die nöthigen Lebensmittel.' Süßmilch, *Göttliche Ordnung*, vol. 1, pp. 135, 143, 408, 432; vol. 2, p. 58.

[62] Süßmilch, *Der königl. Residentz Berlin*, p. 39.

[63] 'Die reichen Familien, die grössere Bequemlichkeit des Mittel-Standes, die vermehrten Fabricken.' Süßmilch, *Der königl. Residentz Berlin*, p. 40.

[64] 'Weil wir aber mehr Einkünfte haben, als wir dort verzehren konnten, und mehr Zeit, als anzuwenden wußten und weil wir soviel von den Wundern der großen Stadt Berlin hörten.' Friedrich

world, my dear,' was the advice to the newcomer, 'one has to follow the fashions.' No doubt she was aware that the friendly guidance on how to join the capital's elegant society came with a thinly veiled threat of exclusion. The young woman hurried to employ the 'fashionable hairdresser' recommended by her new friends, together with the services of other providers of urban styles.[65] However, her submission to the 'tyranny of fashion' came at a price. Soon, her husband found it difficult to tell whether the hairdressers, corset makers, tailors, and others who were regularly visiting the house in his absence were craftsmen or lovers. We are not told how the story ended but the message is clear: the marriage of the young couple was put at risk by the fashionable urban lifestyles of 'cursed Berlin!'[66]

Similar moral warnings were common at the time and could be encountered in different forms in contemporary publications. In 1774, the prominent print maker Daniel Chodowiecki (1726–1801) published a cycle of six etchings illustrating the pleasure-filled decline of an urban 'good-for-nothing' ('Lüderlicher'). (Fig. 2.1.) In a sometimes naïve fashion Chodowiecki's images show the slippery slope that led from sensual pleasure to sexual debauchery, and ultimately to economic and moral decay.

The consequences of luxury for the stability of marriage and demographic development were also a central question for Süßmilch. Luxury was seen as a threat to marriage because it was associated more broadly with an unfettered and egotistical pursuit of enjoyment that quickly extended beyond the consumption of luxurious goods to other sensuous pleasures, and ultimately to the pursuit of sexual gratification outside of marriage. 'Boozing and crapulence', Süßmilch contended, led directly to 'harlotry, adultery and bestiality'.[67] Luxury and the ensuing sexual misdemeanours thus undermined the elementary social bond of marriage which was seen as fundamental to the stability of society and morality. As Isabel Hull has shown, the most extreme form of this sexualized rejection of society and social bonds was seen in the pursuit of sexual pleasure without a partner. Unlike any other form of sexuality or pursuit of pleasure, masturbation epitomized an egotistical outlook and offered the prospect of a fragmented society.[68]

However, it was not just the pursuit of certain sexual pleasures that was seen as eroding the bonds of society. Ultimately all forms of luxury consumption had similar effects because they prevented the formation of new marriages. Couples would normally only marry and have children after showing they could sustain a family. Higher levels of consumption increased this barrier, causing more men and women to delay marriage or remain single.[69] The resulting negative effect on birth rates was a problem in itself from a populationist perspective, but this development

---

Gedike, 'Klage eines jungen Ehemannes in Berlin an einen Freund', *Berlinische Monatschrift*, 1 (1783), pp. 421–7, at p. 421.

[65] 'Modefriseur.' Gedike, 'Klage eines jungen Ehemannes', p. 423.

[66] 'Das verwünschte Berlin!' Gedike, 'Klage eines jungen Ehemannes', p. 427.

[67] 'Soff'; 'Völlerey'; 'Hurerey, Ehebruch und Bestialiät'. Süßmilch, *Der königl. Residentz Berlin*, p. 41.

[68] Isabel Hull, *Sexuality, state and civil society in Germany, 1700–1815* (Ithaca, NY, 1996), pp. 265–71.

[69] Süßmilch, *Göttliche Ordnung*, vol. 1, pp. 124, 146–54.

Fig. 2.1. 'Leben eines Lüderlichen' (Life of a good-for-nothing), one of six motifs in this series (Blatt 6), Daniel Nikolaus Chodowiecki, etching, 1773. Published in *Berlinischer genealogischer Calender*, 1774. Reproduced with permission from Klassik Stiftung Weimar, Museen, Inv. DK 416/84.

was also seen as a social and moral problem. The dictates of consumerism directly contributed to increasing the number of individuals eschewing the bonds of marriage and family. The resulting society of unattached individuals, rather than families, was bound to be more individualistic and selfish and therefore ultimately less stable.

Underpinning these arguments was the perception of an inherent nexus between enjoyment and selfishness which was formulated most radically by the mathematician Abraham Kästner (1719–1800), in a communication to the Royal Academy. He argued that all sentiments of pleasure in humans ultimately derived from sensations of self-perfection. This was true even where pleasant sentiments seemed to be caused by external objects, because ultimately it was not the perfection of the external object that caused enjoyment but the satisfaction felt by individuals that they had reached a level of perfection that allowed them to appreciate the excellence captured by their senses. The enjoyment of beauty in all its manifestations was thus a mere reflection of the self-congratulatory awareness of individuals that they possessed a sufficiently refined taste to appreciate perfection. Kästner contended that even the delight associated with man's humoristic disposition derived from the reverse effect. The humoristic joy experienced when humans perceive certain forms of imperfection in physical forms or behaviour was no less selfish. It derived from the satisfaction experienced by individuals when they noticed a distortion and congratulated themselves on their own refined sense of perfection.[70] Certain forms of the pursuit of pleasure might be particularly prone to undermining existing social structures and lead to a more individualized society, but in this view all pursuits of pleasure—even the enjoyment of humour—were ultimately selfish in nature. Consequently, a society in which the pursuit of sensual pleasure in various forms occupied a more central place was, by the same token, seen as a society that revolved to a greater extent around the preoccupations of individuals with themselves and their own perfection.

THE PERILS OF POVERTY

In this period excessive consumption was seen as a major threat to moral and economic welfare, but poverty did not offer any protection from the dangers of luxury either. The urban poor may have been to a large extent excluded from the more luxurious forms of consumption but their abstention had nothing in common with the salutary frugality of their rural cousins or of 'ancient Germans'.[71] In particular, the large number of textile workers were seen to be a 'fermentation' ('Sauerteig') breeding all sorts of moral evils and bound to infect

---

[70] Abraham Gotthelf Kästner, 'Réflexions sur l'origine du plaisir, où l'on tâche de prouver l'idée de Descartes: qu'il naît toujours du sentiment de perfection de nous-mêmes', *Histoire de l'Academie Royale des Sciences et des Belles Lettres* (Berlin, 1751), pp. 478–88, at pp. 484–5.
[71] 'Alten Deutschen'. Süßmilch, *Göttliche Ordnung*, vol. 1, pp. 443, 115.

the rest of urban societies.[72] The main problem associated with the condition of factory workers was that they became more unsettled in general, and less brave and reliable in warfare, because they had no family bonds and no bonds with their land or other property.[73] Society was thus at risk of a slow erosion of its foundations coupled with the possibility of becoming increasingly unable to withstand external attacks.

The uprooting of many workers was, in part, the result of tensions between limited means and excessive aspirations. Consumption of luxuries by those who could afford it was seen as dangerous, but the 'foolish imitation' of more prosperous lifestyles by the poor was considered to be even more perilous.[74] The 'haughty poor who want to do as the rich do' ruined themselves economically and lost all hope of accumulating some wealth of their own and reaching a level of prosperity that would allow them to marry and sustain a family. As a result, workers were increasingly likely to remain 'unattached' to family and property, thus posing a threat to social stability.

Moreover, commentators also considered the question of how firmly attached wage earners were to their employers and places of work. The political economist Johann Georg Büsch (1728–1800), for example, contrasted the freedom of wage earners with the more oppressive forms of bonded labour that had dominated Europe for centuries. This disciple of Smith argued that the economy of exchanges liberated men from the bonds that had previously tied them to the land or to a landlord and created incentives for free men to serve others.[75] For Büsch, who lived and published in Hamburg, this question was mainly a matter for historical consideration. However, in Prussia the contrast between urban workers and bonded agrarian labour was still a matter of relevance. Servile forms of labour persisted in the countryside and are often thought to have intensified in the eighteenth century. It is perhaps for this reason that Büsch's comments provoked a reply in the *Berlinische Monatsschrift*. The critic held that long-term employment, even under the auspices of a contract between free men, equally constituted a form of 'serfdom'. Population growth and inequalities in wealth inevitably produced hierarchical relations because the poor were always forced to seek employment. Commerce and the circulation of money merely changed appearances but did little to bring about greater individual freedom. Even if covered with gold or silver, he concluded, 'a chain remains a chain'.[76]

---

[72] Süßmilch, *Göttliche Ordnung*, vol. 2, p. 63.

[73] Süßmilch, *Göttliche Ordnung*, vol. 2, p. 67.

[74] 'Thörichten Nachahmung'; 'wenn der hochmüthige Arme es eben so machen will, wie der Reiche'. Süßmilch, *Der königl. Residentz Berlin*, p. 40.

[75] Johann Georg von Büsch, *Abhandlung von dem Geldumlauf in anhaltender Rücksicht auf die Staatswirtschaft und Handlung* (2 vols., Hamburg, 1800), vol. 1, not paginated.

[76] 'Die Kette bleibt Kette.' J. C. Schmohl, 'Von dem Ursprunge der Knechtschaft in der bürgerlichen Gesellschaft', *Berlinische Monatsschrift* 2 (1783), pp. 336–47, at pp. 346–7.

THE DANGERS OF RELIGIOUS INDIVIDUALISM

The economic and social changes of urban societies were also seen as impacting on the religiosity of individuals and hence on religious stability. In particular, doubts were also cast on the adherence of factory workers and their families to accepted forms of religiosity. Religious tolerance was a matter of great importance and pride to many enlightened commentators. However, the relative lack of state regulation and large degree of individual freedom in religious matters also led to fears among the intellectual elite. Journals of the time were filled with accounts of members of the public falling for religious impostors and charlatans promising miraculous cures. Whether the majority of the population was sufficiently 'enlightened' to distinguish between what the commentators considered legitimate forms of religiosity and superstition, was a question that was frequently asked. Such doubts were seen as particularly pertinent in the case of factory workers.

In 1781, the case of the so-called 'moon doctor' caused considerable discussion in Berlin. Such was the following of the *Monddoktor* that the healer and his unorthodox methods became a subject of Chodowiecki's etchings (Fig. 2.2.) and Marcus Herz (1747–1803), a prominent medic and former student of Kant, went personally to the tavern where the 'doctor' practised. In order to give the readership of the *Berlinische Monatsschrift* an authentic account, he disguised himself as an ordinary patient. This type of investigative journalism, he did not fail to mention to his readers, was not without dangers because of the risk of being exposed to the superstitious mob by the spies of the false doctor.[77] In the article the enlightened doctor mainly examined the dubious therapies of the *Monddoktor* from a scientific point of view. However, he also considered the question of what led to the appearance of such charlatans at regular intervals and what accounted for their large following among the urban populations. Differences in professional occupations were central to his argument. According to Herz, it was no coincidence that the *Monddoktor* was a stocking-maker. 'Simple chair-workers', like stocking-makers and weavers, were particularly prone to 'superstition, passing fancies, prophecies and miraculous powers'.[78] The cause was their monotonous work, which condemned them to mindlessly throwing the shuttle back and forth. The task required no skill or attention and thus led to the mind drifting off into the realm of imagination. The capacity of these professional groups to reason was further impaired by the position in which they worked. Bending over their loom impaired circulation of blood and digestion, causing flatulence that could not leave the body 'in the normal way' because of the posture of the workers but instead rose to their heads where it caused different forms of superstition depending on their diet.[79]

---

[77] Marcus Herz, 'Die Wallfahrt zum Monddoktor in Berlin', *Berlinische Monatsschrift*, 2 (1783), pp. 368–85, at p. 384.

[78] 'Es ist besonders wie häufig Aberglaube, Schwärmerei, prophetischer Geist und Wundermacht unter dieser von gemeinen Stuhlarbeitern sind.' Herz, 'Die Wallfahrt', p. 370.

[79] 'Anstatt den normale Weg zu nehmen.' Herz, 'Die Wallfahrt', p. 371.

Fig. 2.2. 'Der Mond Doctor' (The moon doctor), one of twelve motifs in the series 'Modethorheiten' ('The follies of fashion'), Daniel Nikolaus Chodowiecki, etching, 1788. Reproduced with permission from Kupferstich-Kabinett, Staatliche Kunstsammlungen Dresden, Photo: Herbert Boswank.

There may have been a certain amount of irony and polemic exaggeration in the last part of Herz's comments, but the underpinning notion of a link between monotonous work and intellectual decay was commonly accepted in Prussia. In Scotland similar concerns formed an important part of Smith's argument for publicly funded education.[80] In an article about yet another religious impostor who assembled a substantial following in the 1780s, the pastor and author Johan Moritz Schwager (1738–1804) recounted his experiences with religious dissenters in his own parish. When he took up his post in the provincial town of Jöllenbeck in 1768, he found that many of his parishioners had Pietist sympathies and gathered regularly in private conventicles where they prayed, studied the Bible, and discussed their faith without supervision by a member of the clergy. These groups of 'separatists', the pastor recalled, were entirely made up of people practising a 'sedentary lifestyle', in particular linen weavers, tailors, and shoemakers. In contrast, farmers and others who 'work hard' were 'free of this error'.[81] In the pastor's experience even worse consequences than sympathies for Pietism could result from monotonous work. Initially, his attempts to guide the 'separatists' back to the right path were thwarted by their 'prejudices against preachers'. Adopting a new tactic he chose to simply ignore their 'small conventicles', hoping to win them over in time.[82] However, after some time a member of one conventicle, unsurprisingly a shoemaker, began to pass himself off as Jesus Christ. The impostor led his own and another family into a life of laziness, excessive eating, drinking, and sexual promiscuity that quickly ruined them. In this case, only a small number of individuals were harmed, but the pastor's message was that the consequences of individuals who deviated from established religion posed a threat to the industriousness, morality, and general order of the whole state if they were not stopped.[83] The concerns associated with the circumstances of urban workers in manufacturing were different from those associated with excessive consumption, but both were seen to be equally threatening to social stability. The bonds that linked individuals to their families, religious communities, and to society as a whole were eroded in different ways among richer and poorer urban dwellers, but both developments were seen to contribute ultimately to a more individualistic and less firmly integrated society.

RECALIBRATING RELATIONS WITH THE STATE

Clearly the transformations of urban society caused great concern, but even the harshest critics did not think that they could or should be reversed. 'Towns are a

[80] Adam Smith, *An inquiry into the nature and causes of the wealth of nations* (2 vols., Oxford, 1976), vol. 2, pp. 758–87.

[81] 'Separatisten'; 'sitzende Lebensart'; 'die schwere Arbeit treiben'; 'frei von diesem Irrthume'. Johann Moritz Schwager, 'Noch ein neuer Messias', *Berlinische Monatsschrift* 2 (1783), pp. 266–76, at p. 267.

[82] 'Vorurtheile wider den Predigerstand'; 'kleinen Konventikeln'. Schwager, 'Noch ein neuer Messias', p. 268.

[83] Schwager, 'Noch ein neuer Messias', pp. 270–6.

true evil for the state,' a resigned Süßmilch wrote, 'but they are a necessary evil that cannot be helped.' The question was not whether to return to a more stable past, but how to recalibrate the relation between state and civil society so that the benefits of prosperity could be enjoyed while avoiding the dangers of excessive social fragmentation.[84]

The state's active promotion of trade and manufacturing was seen as causing at least some of the excessive circulation of wealth and population growth that were responsible for many of the problems afflicting urban society. Mauvillon and Mirabeau, in particular, were proponents of this view. Commenting on the progress of manufacturing in Königsberg, they explained that in the cold climates of Prussia workers would never acquire the skills necessary for a flourishing industry. Able workers would always prefer the milder climates of the south, thus destining the Prussian provinces for agriculture. By placing urban 'factories in a hothouse', the government disturbed the natural balance between country and town.[85] From the physiocratic point of view the monopolies enjoyed by many urban businesses were the main problem, but also other governmental attempts to support the towns were criticised. In a similar vein, Gedike denounced the royal subsidies given for the building of private houses in the towns because they promoted luxury. Instead, he called for a redirection of government efforts from the large towns to smaller ones and to the countryside.[86]

In the same spirit Süßmilch argued that government efforts to promote urban manufacturing were draining the rural population and creating morally decadent and demographically unsustainable large urban centres. Süßmilch's argument is particularly interesting because of the language he uses. One of his central theories was that, although demographic development was made up of a large number of seemingly unconnected events of births and deaths, it was still governed by divine harmony. This order was not easy to discern if one looks at the daily act of birth and death in thousands of households. However, using the power of statistical inquiry, Süßmilch rose above the chaos of these criss-crossing events and was able to see the balanced order that was created by the 'hidden hand of the creator'.[87] The use of this kind of language hardly makes Süßmilch a Prussian Smith.[88] The latter used the allegory to explain an orderly outcome in economic, rather than demographic, matters and the religious connotations of his version are more ambiguous. However, there are remarkable similarities in the political implications of both arguments. Süßmilch was adamant that the balance of the demographic system was offset by misguided policies for the promotion of manufacturing and that the imbalances were the cause of the moral and economic problems that afflicted society. Smith's attack on the 'mercantile system' was based on a similar outlook

---

[84] 'Städte sind daher ein würkliches Uebel für den Staat; sie sind aber ein nothwendig Uebel, dem sich nicht abhelfen lässet.' Süßmilch, *Göttliche Ordnung*, vol. 2, p. 115.

[85] 'En serre chaude'. Mirabeau, *De la monarchie prussienne*, vol. 3, p. 38.

[86] Gedike, 'Ueber Berlin (1–3)', pp. 457–62.

[87] 'Verborgene Hand des Schöpfers'. Süßmilch, *Göttliche Ordnung*, vol. 1, p. 58.

[88] For the use of the phrase before Smith see Peter Harrison, 'Adam Smith and the history of the invisible hand', *Journal of the history of ideas*, 72 (2011), pp. 29–49.

on socially costly imbalances caused, in large part, by government-sanctioned monopolies. The arguments were constructed in different ways, but in both cases the state was understood to disturb a potentially self-regulating system by overstepping boundaries to which the authors wished to see it confined.

Prussian commentators called on the state to limit itself to protecting and furthering liberties instead of artificially propping up urban commerce. 'I am against all rapid improvements coming from above,' declared Gedike, continuing, 'in matters of prosperity and industry burghers can be trusted to help themselves'.[89] Protecting the ability to 'help themselves' was also seen as crucial by Süßmilch and the physiocratic commentators. The former praised the merits of English government and its principles of 'Liberty and Property', and Mauvillon and Mirabeau saw 'freedom and peace' as the foundation of prosperity and progress.[90] In particular, they condemned guilds and similar restrictions, instead favouring complete freedom of enterprise. Crucially, this freedom also needed to extend to a freedom of commerce, allowing manufacturers to buy their supplies where they saw fit and consumers to make their own choices without governmental interference. Consumer sovereignty was seen as an essential part of economic freedom and Mauvillon and Mirabeau mounted an eloquent attack on the slogan 'We produce everything just as well domestically' that justified protectionism in Prussia and elsewhere. 'These words "just as well" are easily written and even more easily signed,' they replied, 'but how can [Frederick] and his ministers know? . . . Only the consumers can truly judge. Leave to them the task of choosing where they get their money's worth.'[91] Despite the widespread concerns with the moral consequences of luxury consumption, most commentators rejected a more significant role for the state in limiting the freedom of choice of consumers. Only Süßmilch called for a return of sumptuary laws, but he did so with reservations. His main advice was for the state to limit the promotion of urban manufacturing and favour agricultural development instead. However, in order to curb the consequences of urban luxury he also advocated limitations on the consumption of food and beverages, the use of clothing, tableware and furniture, and the number of servants and guests, but these restrictions were to be applied in light of social rank making them mainly an attempt to regulate the consumption habits of the lower orders. On the whole urban commentators therefore mounted a robust defence of economic individualism, blaming the interventions of an overzealous government rather than individual freedom for the excesses in urban development.

With regard to religious and moral matters, urban commentators appeared principled but far less convinced in their defence of individual freedom. Süßmilch

---

[89] 'Ich bin gegen alle schnelle, von oben kommende Verbesserung'; 'bei Wohlstand und Industrie wird der Bürger sich schon selbst aufbauen'. Gedike, 'Ueber Berlin (1–3)', pp. 462–3.

[90] Süßmilch, *Göttliche Ordnung*, vol. 2, p. 557. 'Paix et liberté'. Mirabeau, *De la monarchie prussienne*, vol. 3, p. 4.

[91] 'On fabrique tout aussi bien chez nous. Ces mots Tout aussi bien, s'écrivent facilement, et sont encore plus aisément signes; mais comment lui et ses ministeres pouvoient-ils le savoir?'; 'les vrais consomateurs peuvent seuls en juger à fond: laissez-leur donc le soin de se pourvoir où ils trouvent le mieux leur compte.' Mirabeau, *De la monarchie prussienne*, vol. 3, pp. 7–9.

openly regretted that 'the preservation of virtue was not an object of the attention of authorities' anymore and argued that this withdrawal of the state had opened up society to the dangers of instability.[92] Religiously inspired virtue was the only sound and consistent pattern of motivation for individuals that could provide the state with the citizens that it needed for a stable society. Attempts to build a solid social structure on philosophical virtues or the pursuit of honour were bound to fail. Therefore individual morality had to be brought back among the matters regulated by the state, ideally by means of religious education, but if necessary also by force.[93] However, Süßmilch's support for a closer cooperation between state and religion in the regulation of moral conduct did not mean that he called for an end to religious tolerance. To the contrary, like Mauvillon and Mirabeau, he explicitly linked the success of economic freedom to a broad range of rights, including freedom of thought and religion, and in a lengthy description he elaborated on the damage done by religious intolerance to the prosperity and population of both France and Spain.[94] However, the tolerance that Süßmilch had in mind was not a limitless freedom of religion. He argued that the tolerance of the state should not be one of 'indifference' but a 'well-ordered tolerance' that did not absolve the state from the duties imposed by 'truth'. Religious disorders could easily 'break the bonds of civil society' and the state therefore had an obligation not to 'take its eyes off' religious groups, mainly Catholics in Süßmilch's view, who were prone to disturbing social peace by their tendencies to violently suppressing dissent.[95] Süßmilch was not the only one to regret the far-reaching retreat of the state from the regulation of moral and religious matters. Some commentators like Schwager, the pastor of Jöllenbeck, seconded his view that the state's intervention was needed to prevent damage to social cohesion resulting from religious freedom. The pastor distinguished between 'sects that deserve tolerance' and cases 'where religion was only a cover for knavery'. False prophets ('two-legged hyenas') should be treated like common criminals because they were 'enemies of civil society' who threatened peace and the welfare of society.[96]

However, other commentators did not agree with such calls for a stronger role of the state. Gedike, for example, shared concerns about the derivations from religious freedom but believed they were a price worth paying for the freedom of conscious-ness that Prussians enjoyed. His description of the conventicles was no more flattering than Schwager's. For the editor of *Berlinische Monatsschrift* the Pietist groups were where a 'strange mix of superstition, freemasonry, beneficence and nonsense' thrived. He was equally preoccupied with the growing number of

---

[92] 'Das obrigkeitliche Ansehen hat die Erhaltung der Sitten garnicht zum Gegenstand.' Süßmilch, *Göttliche Ordnung*, vol. 1, p. 568.

[93] Süßmilch, *Göttliche Ordnung*, vol. 1, pp. 566–9.

[94] Süßmilch, *Göttliche Ordnung*, vol. 1, pp. 557–71.

[95] 'Gleichgültigkeit'; 'wohlgeordnete Toleranz'; 'Wahrheit'; 'Bänder der bürgerlichen Gesellschaft gar leicht können zerrissen werden'; 'nicht aus den Augen lassen'. Süßmilch, *Göttliche Ordnung*, vol. 1, pp. 560–5.

[96] 'Sekten die Toleranz verlangen'; 'ist aber die Religion vollends nur eine Dekmantel von Bubensücken'; 'zweibeinige Hyänen'; 'Feinde der bürgerlichen Gesellschaft'. Schwager, 'Noch ein neuer Messias', pp. 274–6.

'goldmakers', 'seers', 'moon doctors', 'arch-Jesuits', and other impostors who found a following in Berlin and elsewhere in Prussia.[97] Nonetheless, Gedike ardently defended freedom of thought, which formed the object of considerable civic pride. For Gedike, one of Berlin's most precious advantages was that 'frank remarks about Berlin can be printed in Berlin itself'.[98] In contrast to other German and European cities, in Berlin 'one thinks, speaks and writes freely'.[99] He cited the example of Guillaume Thomas Raynal (1713–96) whose writings were not banned in Berlin despite his harsh criticism of the Prussian king. Raynal had even stayed in the city without having to fear repression. Berlin was thus freer than Paris and while it could not claim to outdo London in this respect, Gedike still considered the Prussian brand of freedom to be superior, because its debates did not remain as 'sterile' as those in England.[100]

However, no amount of patriotism could completely dissolve the preoccupations that contemporaries associated with the freedom of consciousness and expression. Among the thriving urban businesses described in Büsching's writings were also the grocers who doubled as librarians for the lower orders. Their large offerings of 'nonsensical, tasteless, superstitious and dirty' writings deeply offended the geographer and preoccupied him, concerned as he was for the soul and intellect of current and future generations.[101] At times, he admitted to his readers, he dreamt of being a policeman, empowered to take away the 'nonsensical and pernicious' writings, burn them, and substitute them with more suitable reading.[102] It is perhaps noteworthy that Büsching's authoritarian daydreams remained limited to restrictions on the freedom of thought. He planned to fully reimburse the grocers for any material loss incurred as a result of the confiscations. This deeply rooted respect for the right to private property was also one of the main obstacles to the realization of his plans for a system of censorship that would be for the 'best of the common man'.[103] In Büsching's view, it was near impossible to separate the commerce of ideas and of goods. As an example, he cited the ill-fated attempt of the Berlin academy in 1779 to purge popular calendars of superstitious content, such as weather forecasts and indications of auspicious periods for seeding, planting, and cutting timber. However, when sales of the 'purged' edition remained sluggish the academy quickly consented to a return to the old ways.[104] The production of the calendar was outsourced to a publisher and the academy would have been liable for the losses incurred as a result of the revision. Büsching lamented the academy's lack of stamina in the face of the 'dumb and stubborn people' but acknowledged

---

[97] 'Ein seltsames Gemisch von Aberglaube, Freimäurerei, Wolthäthigkeit und Unsinn'. Friedrich Gedike, 'Ueber Berlin, von einem Fremden (Brief 4–6)', *Berlinische Monatsschrift*, 2 (1783), pp. 542–57, at p. 545.

[98] 'Freimüthige Bemerkungen über Berlin in Berlin selbst drucken lassen zu dürfen.' Gedike, 'Ueber Berlin (1–3)', p. 441.

[99] 'Man denkt, man spricht, man schreibt frei.' Gedike, 'Ueber Berlin (4–6)', p. 555.

[100] 'Fruchtlos'. Gedike, 'Ueber Berlin (4–6)', pp. 551–2, 556.

[101] 'Unsinnigen, abgeschmackten, abergläubischen und schmutzigen'. Büsching, *Reise*, p. 12.

[102] 'Unsinnigen und schädlichen'. Büsching, *Reise*, p. 13.

[103] 'Zum Besten des gemeinen Mannes'. Büsching, *Reise*, p. 13.

[104] 'Gereinigten'. Büsching, *Reise*, p. 13.

that the academy did not have a choice in the face of these economic impera-tives.[105] The commodification of ideas in the book trade led to a merging of mutually reinforcing discourses of consumer sovereignty and freedom of conscious-ness and expression. In this light, the practicality and legitimacy of more direct intervention by the authorities appeared questionable. Nonetheless, the potential consequences of granting freedom of thought to a 'dumb and stubborn' multitude remained a cause for concern. Education seemed to offer a solution to this dilemma. 'The public', Büsching argued, 'is a mighty beast which cannot be tamed violently and at once but needs to be made teachable and docile gradually and with intelligence.'[106] Ultimately, Büsching placed his faith more in the progress of education than in authoritarian measures. However, the ambiguity of his views in these matters was subsequently reflected by his actions. Despite his defence of the freedom of consciousness, Büsching later played a role in the removal from office of a dissenting clergyman during the time of the Woellner edicts.[107]

On the whole, Prussian burghers were clearly aware and proud of the liberties that they had acquired in many areas and the economic and cultural achievements that urban society had engendered. The freedom to take autonomous decisions in matters of consumption and other areas of material life occupied a central place in civic self-reflection. However, the rise of urban prosperity and changing consump-tion habits were not only a source of pride but also of preoccupation. Concerns about moral and religious fragmentation, largely seen as a consequence of economic change, were widely discussed. Contemporaries considered urban society to be increasingly individualistic, and the resulting challenges for that society were the object of extensive debates. But while many observers were concerned with aspects of this transformation, very few were prepared to renounce the degree of individual autonomy they were enjoying. Only a minority of commentators called for restrict-ive action by the state, while many others blamed excesses of state intervention for many urban evils. In this period, Prussia's urban dwellers had not only become more autonomous individuals as a result of the retreat of the state, but they also thought of themselves as such and, perhaps most importantly, were proud of their new position.

Stronger than the regret for attachments and bonds that were lost as a result of the process of individualization was a forward-looking sentiment, which led to the development of new forms of sociability. Just as state formation and the rise of individualism were complementary processes, so the rise of enlightened sociability in the form of clubs, learned societies, and cultural associations would have been impossible without the process of individualization. As Nipperdey has argued, the formation of associations of likeminded individuals who freely joined together in the pursuit of common goals was the result of the decline of traditional

---

[105] 'Dummen und eigensinnigen'. Büsching, *Reise*, p. 13.

[106] 'Das Publicum . . . ist ein großmächtiges Thier, welches sich nicht wohl durch Gewalt und auf einmal bändigen läßt, sondern durch Klugheit und nach und nach gelehrig und folgsam gemacht werden muß.' Büsching, *Reise*, p. 14.

[107] Michael Sauter, *Visions of the Enlightenment: the Edict on Religion of 1788 and the politics of the public sphere in eighteenth-century Prussia* (Leiden, 2009), pp. 49–78.

corporatist structures. The new associations, which were pivotal for the development of bourgeois culture in the eighteenth and nineteenth centuries, were based on the notion of autonomy and functioned as 'schools of bourgeois emancipation' (Nipperdey) where individualistic culture was developed further and the state's paternalistic claims were systematically challenged.[108] A rich historiographic literature has explored these structures and there is no need to investigate them here in more detail. It should, however, be pointed out that it is hardly a coincidence that many of the defences of individualism discussed in this chapter were fermented and discussed in such clubs and associations formed in this period in Prussia's cities. Paradoxically, greater individualism gave rise to new forms of collectivity in the guise of clubs and associations, prayer groups, and also in the shape of the new and elusive phenomenon of 'fashion'. The crucial difference was that these new forms of collectivity were devised by autonomous individuals in spheres that many now considered to lie outside of the purview of the state.

---

[108] Thomas Nipperdey, 'Verein als soziale Struktur in Deutschland im späten 18. und 19. Jahrhundert. Eine Fallstudie zur Modernisierung', in Thomas Nipperdey, ed., *Gesellschaft, Kultur, Theorie gesammelte Aufsätze zur neueren Geschichte* (Göttingen, 1976), pp. 176–205, at p. 196.

3

Official Perspectives on the Towns

And this is the states' very purpose. They seek prosperity and tranquility.
Wilhelm von Humboldt, *On the limits of state action* (1791–2).[1]

The active government, forcing the nature of things, placed the factories in hothouses.
Mirabeau, *Of the Prussian monarchy under Frederick the Great* (1788).[2]

Urban dwellers were not the only ones closely observing the transformations happening in Prussia's towns. Government officials were equally keen to gather information and make sense of the changes. Like urban commentators, they were preoccupied with correcting and steering the development, and in many ways their concerns with balance, and the languages of rationality and efficiency that they used, were the same as those that dominated public debates. However, official perspectives on the towns also differed in important respects from urban self-perceptions. While the needs and interests of individuals had become central to public debates in the towns, more traditional notions of the state as keeper of a holistic common interest continued to dominate official discourses. Like their urban counterparts, state officials did not see common and private interest as necessarily mutually exclusive or antagonistic. Both were concerned with creating balances between common and individual interests and other political and natural factors. However, compared with urban commentators, officials approached this quest for balance with different priorities and objectives in mind. Their debates did not centre on the fulfilment of individual needs, desires, or rights but on the conceptualization and pursuit of the mainly military–fiscal interests of the state. Officials were not necessarily opposed to individual autonomy and the Epicurean pursuit of individual pleasure that had become widespread in urban society, but for them it was only a means to achieving tranquillity in religious matters and economic prosperity. Where individualism resulted in other outcomes, in their view, it needed to be limited and guided. This chapter explores official perspectives

---

[1] 'Auch ist dies gerade die Absicht der Staaten. Sie wollen Wohlstand und Ruhe.' Wilhelm von Humboldt, *Ideen zu einem Versuch die Grenzen der Wirksamkeit des Staats zu bestimmen* (Stuttgart, 1967), p. 31. My translation deviates from J. Burrow's English edition: Wilhelm von Humboldt, *The limits of state action* (Cambridge, 1969), p. 24.

[2] 'Dont le gouvernement actif forcant la nature des choses, mettroit les manufactures en serre chaude.' Honoré Gabriel de Riqueti Comte de Mirabeau, *De la monarchie prussienne, sous Frédéric le Grand: avec un appendice contenant des recherches sur la situation actuelle des principales contrées de l'Allemagne* (4 vols., London [Paris], 1788), vol. 3, p. 38.

on the towns under Fredrick II, focusing first on official attempts to 'get to know the towns' and then on the terms in which administrators thought about urban development in the areas of political economy and religion. It reveals where official perspectives were similar compared with the self-perceptions of urban commentators, and where they differed. The differences of outlook that existed between state and non-state actors were at the origin of the conflicts between state and civil society that are at the centre of the following chapters.

KNOWING THE TOWNS

After the end of the Seven Years War, Frederick repeatedly ordered his officials to provide him with 'tables' about the urban population of his central provinces. However, the replies were apparently unsatisfactory and the king eventually began to make his own demographic calculations based on lists of births and deaths. This experience replicated earlier frustrations.[3] Already in 1752, Frederick had ordered the central administration of the *Generaldirektorium* to find out how many inhabitants the towns of the central Electoral Mark province had and, in particular, whether they had recovered from the population loss incurred during the Thirty Years War. After a prolonged delay a report came back indicating that the towns had recovered and even surpassed pre-war levels when urban population had represented almost half of the total population. Even the authors admitted that the information on which these numbers were based was extremely limited and, compared with other contemporary enquiries, it is clear that these numbers had most likely only a weak factual base. They were perhaps more the result of an attempt to please the monarch, than of a serious enquiry.[4]

These episodes reveal remarkable similarities between urban commentators and officials. Frederick asked for information about Prussia's urban demographics around the same time as Süßmilch began his enquiries. Officials and members of the public clearly shared the same curiosity about urban development. Also, on both sides there was a keen desire to replace unsystematic impressions and anecdotal evidence with 'solid' statistical facts, and some of the methods employed, such as the use of lists of births and deaths, were similar. The first servant of the state was no less gripped by the 'universal fashion' of statistics than private commentators. He shared the public's enlightened desire to capture complex realities by means of abstract categories and quantification and the hunger for empirical knowledge reflected common notions of the importance of evidence as a basis for rational discourses in matters of policy and elsewhere.

Moreover, the experiences of Frederick and Süßmilch also reflected the limited knowledge available to official actors and members of the public. The limitations of

---

[3] Instruction to Kurmärkischen Kammerdirector Siegroth, 29 October 1765; CO to Kurmärkische Kammer, 11 February 1766 in Ernst Posner, ed., *Die Behördenorganisation und allgemeine Staatsverwaltung Preußens im 18. Jahrhundert* (16 vols., Berlin, 1932), vol. 13, pp. 688, 751.

[4] Gustav von Schmoller, *Deutsches Städtewesen in älterer Zeit* (Aalen, 1964), p. 288.

Frederick's apparatus of state became clear when it failed to provide a satisfactory answer to a simple question about one of the fundamental factors of contemporary statecraft. In a similar way, Süßmilch could not rely on readily available information, but was forced to launch his own enquiry and even develop his own method of enquiry. The secrecy with which contemporary states treated many types of information should not lead to the misconception of a substantial disparity of information between public and state. The knowledge of both was extremely limited and in the case of the demographic development of Prussia's towns it may be argued that Süßmilch knew more sooner than the king.

The Prussian and other states of this period have rightly been described as *Ediktenstaat*: states that were much better at producing a flurry of new laws, often announcing far-reaching measures, than at making their decisions count. It has often been overlooked, however, that the flipside of impotence was ignorance. Not only were many of the acts of these states largely illusory but they also ruled to a large extent over imagined realms because reliable information was scarce. Efforts to improve the means of gathering knowledge were closely associated with the process of state building. Contemporary administrators were painfully aware that the lack of information severely limited their capability to act. 'Getting to know the realm' was a priority of many monarchs and administrations in this period, and Frederick II was perhaps one of the best examples of this official 'hunger for knowledge'.[5]

As a general Frederick was well aware that geography mattered. In his writings on warfare he made clear how crucial 'knowing the land' was to military success. He advised Prussian commanders to study the spaces in which battles, logistics, and manoeuvres would take place first on maps and then by visiting them repeatedly, preferably in the company of local mayors, hunters, shepherds, and butchers.[6] Frederick applied this approach also in his civilian role: annual inspection travels to the Prussian provinces were a fixture of his reign.[7] This type of 'government from the saddle' was effective in many ways but as a tool to gather knowledge it could hardly measure up to the increasingly refined epistemological standards of the time.

Frederick therefore also pursued more pioneering ways of knowing his realm by travelling not only through space but also through time. No other monarch, and few writers of his time, can claim to have been more engaged and innovative historians.[8] In his works about Prussia's history, he purposefully added to the narrow focus of more traditional historiographers by concerning himself in detail with what would today be termed social, economic, and cultural history. 'In order

---

[5] See the chapter 'Knowing France' in: Daniel Roche, *France in the Enlightenment* (Cambridge, MA, 1998), pp. 11–40.

[6] The text was published in translation in 1753 under the title 'Die General-Principia vom Kriege, applicirt auf die Tactique und auf die Disciplin derer preussischen Truppen'. The references here are to Preuss' edition of the original French text. Frederick II, 'Les principes géneraux de la guerre', in Johann D. E. Preuss, ed., *Oeuvres de Frédéric le Grand* (30 vols., Berlin, 1856), vol. 28, p. 26.

[7] Wolfgang Neugebauer, 'Zur neueren Deutung der preußischen Verwaltung im 17. und 18. Jahrhundert in vergleichender Sicht', in Otto Büsch and Wolfgang Neugebauer, eds., *Moderne preußische Geschichte* (Berlin, 1981), pp. 541–97, at p. 574.

[8] Christopher Clark, '"Le roi historien" zu Füßen von Clio', in Bernd Sösemann and Gregor Vogt-Spira, eds., *Friedrich der Große in Europa* (Stuttgart, 2012), pp. 155–78.

to acquire full knowledge of any state', the historian Frederick wrote, 'it is not sufficient to know its origins, wars, treaties, government, religion, or to know about the revenues of the sovereign.' Instead it was necessary to enquire also about the 'customs of the inhabitants . . . the birth of industry and the causes that led to its development, the causes that speeded or slowed the progress of the human mind and above all everything that characterised the spirit of the nation'.[9]

This approach to the writing of history was directly connected with Frederick's views on government. Where Frederick praised the 'utility' of the new ways of historical enquiry, he was speaking both as a historian and a monarch.[10] Already in the first year of his reign, Frederick argued in the *Antimachiavel* (1740) that knowledge of the past was an important tool in the hands of the prince. Much has been made of the work's moral critique of Machiavelli and the question of whether Frederick's subsequent record lived up to the standards that he had postulated in his critique.[11] This has overshadowed another line of criticism put forward by the young prince. Frederick accused Machiavelli of focusing too narrowly on the 'constitution of government', while ignoring the 'temperament of a state', specifically 'its location, its extension, the number and spirit of its people, its commerce, its customs, its laws, its strength, its weakness and its resources'.[12] In the same way in which medical cures did not work for all patients and illnesses, there could be no universal prescriptions on how to conduct the business of government. The crucial question, ignored by Machiavelli, was therefore whether a state's government and 'temperament' were in harmony.[13] This nexus remained central to all of Frederick's subsequent works on government. In his *Discourse on the reasons to introduce or abolish laws* (1751) Frederick emphasized the importance of sound knowledge for the legislator. Historically, the most successful lawmakers had been those 'who knew best the spirit of the people that they governed'.[14] It was therefore among a monarch's main duties to 'acquire a detailed and exact knowledge . . . of the nation that he has to govern'.[15] In particular, thorough study of a nation's history was necessary to procure the kind of knowledge that was

---

[9] 'Pour acquérir une connaissance parfaite d'un État, il ne suffit pas d'en savoir l'origine, les guerres, les traités, le gouvernement, la religion, d'être instruit des revenus du souverain', 'mœurs des habitants, comme l'origine des nouveaux usages, l'abolition des anciens, la naissance de l'industrie, les causes qui l'ont développée, les raisons de ce qui a hâté ou ralenti les progrès de l'esprit humain, et surtout ce qui caractérise le plus le génie de la nation dont on parle.' Frederick II, 'Des mœurs, des coutumes, de l'industrie, des progrès de l'esprit humain dans les arts et dans les sciences', in Johann D. E. Preuss, ed., *Oeuvres de Frédéric le Grand* (30 vols., Berlin, 1846), vol. 1, pp. 243–73, at p. 243.

[10] 'Utiles'. Frederick II, 'Des moeurs', vol. 1, p. 243.

[11] Theodor Schieder, *Friedrich der Große* (Berlin, 1983), pp. 102–26.

[12] 'Sa situation, son étendue, le nombre, le génie de ses peuples, son commerce, ses coutumes, ses lois, son fort, son faible, ses richesses et ses ressources.' Frederick II, 'L'antimachiavel, ou examen du prince de Machiavel', in Johann D. E. Preuss, ed., *Oeuvres de Frederic le Grand* (30 vols., Berlin, 1848), vol. 8, pp. 67–184, at p. 111.

[13] 'Le tempérament d'un État'. Frederick II, 'L'antimachiavel', vol. 8, p. 111.

[14] 'Qui ont le mieux connu le génie du peuple dont ils réglaient le gouvernement.' Frederick II, 'Dissertation sur les raisons d'établir ou d'abroger les lois', in Johann D. E. Preuss, ed., *Oeuvres de Frédéric le Grand* (30 vols., Berlin, 1848), vol. 9, pp. 9–37, at p. 11.

[15] 'Il doit se procurer une connaissance exacte et détaillée de la force et de la faiblesse . . . de la nation qu'il doit gouverner.' Frederick II, 'Essai sur les formes de gouvernement et sur les devoirs des

indispensable for a wise and successful legislator.[16] This view was also echoed by the king's officials. Isolated knowledge of single factors such as population numbers, argued the leading minister Ewald Friedrich von Hertzberg (1725–95), could never give full insight into a state's power. True strength resulted from the harmony between the 'character of government' and that of the nation.[17] As Frederick pointed out, establishing this kind of balance was a particularly assiduous task in the case of Prussia where studying the nation as a whole was not enough. Its provinces were so diverse that it was often impossible to govern them according to the same principles. Instead, the monarch had to acquire detailed knowledge of the local 'spirit'.[18] In many ways, these Prussian concerns mirrored wider French and European debates, explored masterfully by Paul Cheney, about the importance of a harmonious balance between geography, economy, and government for political stability.[19] But unlike Montesquieu and other writers who examined similar questions, Frederick was not merely concerned with satisfying an intellectual curiosity. For him and his administrators these questions were vital and directly linked with the practice of government. As Wolfram Fischer and Adelheid Simsch have argued, the concern with the adaptation of policies to different local conditions led to heterogeneity in the economic policies applied in Prussia's eastern and western provinces.[20] In a similar way, Prussia's split fiscal system represented partly an attempt to accommodate the different economic and social conditions of town and country.

The notion of a crucial link between empirical knowledge and successful government shaped not only Frederick's view that systematic study and enquiry were monarchical duties, but also his broader perspective on the apparatus of state. Historical enquiry was to provide the foundation for the great institutional decisions of the monarch, but it was equally important that the smaller decisions of day-to-day government should be based on solid factual knowledge. In the *Political Testament* of 1752, Frederick described the process by which the different branches of the administration produced a continuous stream of reports that placed the ruler in a position to make decisions 'provided that he takes the trouble to read the matters presented to him thoroughly and with reason'.[21] Perhaps as a result

souverains', in Johann D. E. Preuss, ed., *Oeuvres de Frederic le Grand* (30 vols., Berlin, 1848), vol. 9, pp. 221–40, at p. 229.

[16] Frederick II, 'Lois', p. 11.

[17] 'Le caractère de son Gouvernement'. Ewald Friedrich von Hertzberg, 'Réflexions sur la force des états et sur leur puissance relative et proportionnelle', in Académie Royale des Sciences et Belles Lettres, ed., *Nouveaux mémoires de l'Académie Royale des Sciences et Belles Lettres* (Berlin, 1782), pp. 475–86, at p. 476.

[18] Frederick II, 'Das politische Testament von 1752', in Gustav Volz, ed., *Die Werke Friedrichs des Großen* (10 vols., Berlin, 1912), vol. 7, pp. 115–94, at p. 143.

[19] Paul Cheney, *Revolutionary commerce: globalization and the French monarchy* (Cambridge, MA, 2010).

[20] Wolfram Fischer and Adelheid Simsch, 'Industrialisierung in Preussen. Eine staatliche Veranstaltung?', in Werner Süß, ed., *Übergänge—Zeitgeschichte zwischen Utopie und Machbarkeit* (Berlin, 1989), pp. 104–17.

[21] 'Vorausgesetzt, daß er sich die Mühe gibt, die vorgetragenen Sachen gründlich und mit Verständnis zu lesen.' Frederick II, 'Testament von 1752', p. 151.

of the disappointing experience with his own demographic enquiries, Frederick recommended in particular that his successors pay attention to the systematic collection of lists of births and deaths for population statistics.[22] In his view the gathering of information was not only a duty of the monarch but one of the principal purposes of the organs of the state. An intense, and increasingly systematic, curiosity thus became one of the defining features of government administration under Frederick II.

The official hunger for knowledge extended to all aspects of domestic policy, but the towns were in many ways the object of particular attention because of the importance for economic development that had been assigned to the prevalently urban sectors of trade and manufacturing. Frederick's predecessors had already established some of the structures that provided reports on urban development, such as the system of the *Steuerräte*. The most prominent example of new regulations was perhaps the *Fabrikkommisare* (factory inspectors) who were introduced towards the end of the reign of Frederick William. Like most administrative functions of the time their office developed out of the institution of the *Steuerrat*. In 1723, the latter were assigned assistant officers—*Fabrikinspektoren*—to help with quality control in wool manufacturing. The *Fabrikkommissare* collected statistical information about the number of artisans, factories, and their production, made sure that economic regulations were followed, and consulted with magistrates on economic development.[23] The reign of Frederick William also saw the introduction of other officers to work alongside the *Steuerräte*. *Polizeireuther* took over police functions and medical officers began to inspect local pharmacies.[24] Frederick's conception of government gave a new urgency to these endeavours. For example, the department for postal affairs, trade, industry, and urban colonization (often referred to as the 'fifth department') that Frederick created early in his reign, was in many respects as much a bureau for the collection of relevant information as it was an administrative tool for the promotion of urban development. In a similar way, Frederick's reform of the excise administration that we discuss in the next chapter was in part intended to create a more efficient mechanism for reporting information about the development of the towns.

Curiosity and ignorance were thus features that defined the ways in which officials and urban commentators looked at urban society. Officials needed systematically collected factual information as a basis for their decisions and commentators used similar types of knowledge to add credibility and legitimacy to the criticisms and proposals that they put to the public. The need for systematically collected empirical evidence as a basis of political judgements was thus transversely accepted. If we consider this to be a crucial part of what it meant to be enlightened, then there can be no doubt that the king and his administrators were no less enlightened than Prussia's civil society. With regard to their modes of reasoning, officials and commentators were clearly children of the same age. This intellectual affinity was

[22] Frederick II, 'Testament von 1752', p. 126.
[23] Schmoller, *Städtewesen*, pp. 405–6.
[24] Schmoller, *Städtewesen*, p. 406.

caused and maintained in part through the social vicinity and overlapping of both groups. However, as the similarities between the modes of thinking of the monarch and many members of the public illustrate, differences in status and class were not necessarily obstacles to a shared outlook.

FOR WHOSE BENEFIT?

However, if social milieus often overlapped, and rationality and empiricism were transversely shared values, what, if anything, differentiated public debates from official discourses? Much of the recent literature on the enlightened public in Prussia and elsewhere in Europe has taken such shared features as an indication that the distinction between the two spheres was far less clear-cut than previously assumed. In particular, the new emphasis on similarities and interconnectedness led to an intense questioning of the notion that public and state could be seen as antagonistic. The first part of this chapter offered some additional elements to support the revisionist view of public and state as deeply interconnected spheres by exploring similarities between the outlooks of private commentators and officials. However, there is also evidence that points in the opposite direction and that may have been neglected in recent historiographical debates. The remainder of this chapter explores some of the features that set official discourses about religious and economic matters apart from those of the public. Generally, it may be said that their locations and 'centres of gravity' were what distinguished the two. The first point may seem banal, but the primary difference between the two sets of debates lay clearly in the places where they occurred and in the limits to participation. In one case access was limited to state officials, while in the other debate was in theory completely open. Even if public debates never lived up to the professed ideal of open access, the restrictions imposed by education, gender, and other factors still meant that a broad section of urban dwellers could participate. The differences with regard to access had far-reaching consequences for the 'centre of gravity' of these debates. Government officials and urban commentators may have used the same language of rationality and held arguments to the same standards of empirical evidence, but the interests and ends to which they deployed these intellectual tools were different. The needs, desires, and interests of individuals had become central to urban debates, while holistic notions, variously conceptualized as state, common, or national interest, dominated official discourses. In practice these interests coincided mostly with the military–fiscal needs of the emerging Prussian state. A state, it should be remembered, that continued to lead a precarious existence in this period. The military genius ascribed to Frederick should not distract from the fact that he lost many battles and that his armies came close to complete defeat during the Seven Years War. Most likely, the consequences would have been severe territorial losses and permanent relegation of Prussia to the status of a second-rate power. The spectre that haunted Prussian monarchs and administrators after the Thirty Years War had not gone away and was as important as a motivation as the aspirations to increase Prussia's power and prestige. We will first explore the resulting official attitude to religion before turning our attention to Frederick's economic system.

TRANQUILLITY

As Humboldt pointed out, the main objective of states in this period was tranquillity and prosperity. The principal threat to the former was religious dissent and, as discussed in Chapter 1, religious tolerance became a part of Prussia's constitutional set-up in a bid to limit the destructive power of religious dissent. This basic nexus remained central to the state's attitudes towards religion during Frederick's reign. However, what became perhaps more apparent under the rule of a king who was himself a religious sceptic, was the extent to which official attitudes towards religious freedom differed from those held by private commentators. Urban Prussians were concerned with potentially negative consequences of religious freedom, but mostly they cherished and proudly defended their liberty in this area. The freedom to decide which theological convictions to adopt and which forms of worship to follow was seen as a crucial part of individual rights. And it was not only the Pietist tradition that saw the pursuit of a profoundly individualized religiosity as a precondition for the spread of true faith. This view was in sharp contrast with the official perspective, which saw religious tolerance mainly as a *means* to achieve social peace without associating any inherent value to it.

Frederick articulated the utilitarian underpinnings of the official stance towards religious tolerance more clearly than any of his predecessors. Early in his reign, he had already declared that in Prussia 'everyone must go to heaven in his own way'. Looking at this well-known phrase in its textual context illustrates the primary importance that considerations of the state's welfare had for the monarch. In the original text, one important caveat follows immediately after the assertion of religious freedom. Everyone was free in religious matters as long as they remained 'good citizens'. Religious freedom was limited to those individuals and forms of religiosity that did not harm social and political stability. Since this typology included most major sects, diversity was not a problem from the state's point of view. The major sects, Frederick argued, ultimately imbued their followers with rather similar moral codes, which were all conducive to maintaining order. Any attempt to impose religious uniformity was only bound to damage political and economic welfare: 'Mistaken [religious] zeal is a tyrant that empties the provinces: tolerance is a tender mother that nourishes them and makes them flourish'.[25] However, as Frederick explained elsewhere, emigration was 'the smallest' of the

---

[25] 'Toutes ces sectes vivent ici en paix, et contribuent également au bonheur de l'État. Il n'y a aucune religion qui, sur le sujet de la morale, s'écarte beaucoup des autres; ainsi elles peuvent être toutes égales au gouvernement, qui, conséquemment, laisse à un chacun la liberté d'aller au ciel par quel chemin il lui plaît: qu'il soit bon citoyen, c'est tout ce qu'on lui demande. Le faux zèle est un tyran qui dépeuple les provinces: la tolérance est une tendre mère qui les soigne et les fait fleurir.' Frederick II, 'De la superstition et de la religion', in Johann D. E. Preuss, ed., *Oeuvres de Frederic le Grand* (30 vols., Berlin, 1848), vol. 9, pp. 224–42, at p. 241–2.

negative consequences of religious persecution. Historically, 'the longest, bloodiest and most destructive civil wars' had been caused by intolerance. From the state's point of view the main advantage of religious freedom was therefore that 'everyone remains quiet'.[26] This pragmatic political approach was not the only justification that Frederick offered for religious tolerance. The king also explored rights-based arguments, which held that the original contract between ruler and subject could not conceivably have included religious matters. Therefore the monarch only had a right to interfere with individual religiosity when other areas were affected, such as the maintaining of law and order, where he was authorized by his subjects to rule.[27] However, in the Prussian case, the historical trajectory of the development of religious tolerance suggests that political expediency played a more significant role than versions of contract theory.

The differences between civic and official perspectives on religious liberty that become apparent here were not merely of theoretical importance. In practice, they meant that in the official view religious freedom could be curtailed when it did not achieve its objective, whereas many urban dwellers saw it as an absolute imperative. Diverging attitudes in these matters were at the root of the religious conflicts that dominated Prussian political culture in the 1780s and 1790s.

PROSPERITY

Similar differences existed between official and civic attitudes towards economic freedom. The changes in the state's role in the urban economy had endowed individuals with considerably greater autonomy in matters of consumption and production. However, as in the case of religiosity, individual autonomy was not seen as a value in itself. Rather, the free pursuit of economic self-interest was seen as a means to make society more prosperous and ensure higher tax revenue for the state. Again by this utilitarian logic the economic freedom of individuals could be guided and curtailed if necessary in order to ensure the desired outcome for the state. This was markedly different from urban self-perceptions, which put great emphasis on civic independence in economic matters.

In order to reconstruct the perspective of government officials on the transformations of urban society, it is crucial to understand the almost obsessive preoccupation with revenue that resulted from the permanent threat of war. This was not a specifically Prussian concern, as is illustrated by Edmund Burke's (1729–97) dictum 'revenue is the chief occupation of the state. Nay, more it is the state'.[28]

[26] 'Dès que tout culte est libre, tout le monde est tranquille; au lieu que la persécution a donné lieu aux guerres civiles les plus sanglantes, les plus longues et les plus destructives.' Frederick II, 'Essai sur les formes de gouvernement et sur les devoirs des souverains', in Johann D. E. Preuss, ed., *Oeuvres de Frederic le Grand* (30 vols., Berlin, 1848), vol. 9, pp. 221–40, at pp. 237–8.

[27] Frederick II, 'Essai sur les formes de gouvernement', vol. 9, pp 237–8.

[28] Cited in Patrick O'Brien, *Fiscal exceptionalism. Great Britain and its European rivals: from civil war to triumph at Trafalgar and Waterloo.* Working paper 65/1, Department of Economic History, London School of Economics (London, 2001), p. 25.

However, Prussia's small size, geography, and limited economic resources made the state of public finances a more vital preoccupation in Berlin than in other European capitals. Frederick discussed the paramount importance of the issue repeatedly in his writings. 'Finances are the nerve of a country', he wrote in his *Mirror of princes* of 1744, advising his peers that 'if you gain good knowledge of [finances] you will always be in control of everything else, too'.[29] He vigorously applied this maxim in his own reign, and while his primary preoccupation was certainly warfare, he knew that his capacity to act in matters of foreign and domestic policy depended entirely on the ability to secure sufficient revenue. 'Never has a poor government gained any respect,' he concluded in his *Political testament* after a lengthy discussion of the poor figures cut by impoverished monarchs throughout history.[30]

The towns played a central role in Frederick's plans to secure financial resources. They were centres of manufacturing which were seen as the main potential source of wealth for the country. Because Prussia lacked colonies, trade, and fertile soil, Frederick believed that the only significant resource was the hard work of its people. The king also clearly favoured the broad prosperity created by the 'nourishing mother' of industry over the elitism of commerce. 'One manufacturer can employ twelve hundred people,' he argued, 'while a merchant will hardly give a living to twelve.'[31] Besides economic considerations, this preference for industry most likely also had military motives. Long distance commerce, in particular, was vulnerable to disruptions by warfare, weather, and political conflicts, while industry in particular, when it was concentrated in towns, was easier to protect and could be relied upon as a source of military supplies.

Moreover, official attention also focused on the towns for fiscal reasons. Under the system that Frederick had inherited, the bulk of tax revenue came from the towns. The prominent fiscal role that they had acquired historically made them almost inevitably the focus of fiscal plans for the future. A much larger share of any increase in urban prosperity was bound to end up in the pockets of the state, compared with growth in the rural economy. Moreover, fundamentally different perspectives of officials on urban and rural taxation meant that the differentiation became even more marked. In the view of Frederick and his officials, the urban excise—at least in the form that it took after the Seven Years War—was essentially a voluntary payment because it was levied largely on luxuries. Taxpayers could avoid paying the tax by limiting themselves to 'necessary' forms of consumption. As a result, many officials believed that the tax could not be oppressive or

[29] 'Die Finanzen sind der Nerv eines Landes; wenn sie sich davon eine gute Kenntnis verschaffen, werden sie stets auch alles Übrige beherrschen.' Frederick II, 'Mirroir des princes ou instruction du roi pour le jeune Duc Charles-Eugène de Würtemberg', in Johann D. E. Preuss, ed., *Oeuvres de Frédéric le Grand*, (30 vols., Berlin, 1848), vol. 9, pp. 1–8, at p. 5.

[30] 'Noch nie hat sich eine arme Regierung Ansehen verschafft.' Frederick II, 'Testament von 1752', p. 120.

[31] 'Mere nourice', 'un seul fabricant peut employer douze cent personnes, tandis qu'un commerçant n'en feroit pas vivre douze'. Frederick II cited in Marc Antoine de la Haye de Launay, *Justification du système d'économie politique et financière de Frédéric II., roi de Prusse: pour servir de réfutation à tout ce que M. le Comte de Mirabeau a hazardé à ce sujet dans son ouvrage de la monarchie prussienne* (n.p., 1789), pp. 57, 59.

illegitimate because the consent of taxpayers was implicit in the decision to consume certain types of commodities. By the same token, there could be no excessive tax burden because the tax fell only on those wealthy enough to indulge in consumption of luxury goods. This view differed substantially from the ways in which urban taxpayers conceptualized their own consumption habits. Nonetheless, the official understanding of the excise as a 'voluntary tax' was crucial for fiscal development in this period because, as a result, rural taxation was seen in a fundamentally different light. As a land tax, the rural *Contribution* could not be avoided by taxpayers in the same way as the excise. Great care was therefore taken in order not to overburden 'nobles and peasants' fiscally.[32] Nobles were already exempt from most forms of taxation, but increasing taxes on non-noble inhabitants of the countryside could still hurt revenues of the rural elite indirectly. Excessive fiscal pressure on rural taxpayers potentially endangered their ability to meet the obligations to their noble landlords.

The fiscal restraint exercised with regard to the country was not only a question of fiscal legitimacy, but it was also associated with broader perspectives on political stability and military strength. Nobility and peasantry were seen as the foundations on which the Prussian state rested. In particular, the nobility formed the recruitment ground for officers and remained crucial for social and political stability as a result of its role in the administration of Prussia's rural provinces. As Frederick pointed out, the 'preservation' of the nobility and its economic basis was therefore always a crucial 'object of politics'.[33]

THE VISIBLE HAND OF THE PRUSSIAN STATE

The importance of the urban economy as a source of government revenue meant that, from the state's perspective, the prosperity of towns was not a private matter that could be left to the care of the urban dwellers themselves. Rather, the economic development of the towns was a matter of vital interest for the state. Consequently, government officials were more concerned with ensuring the functionality of the 'hothouses' under which urban economies prospered, than with tearing them down, as some members of the urban public demanded. In order to understand governmental attitudes to the towns, and the ensuing policies, we need to reconstruct the way in which officials conceptualized the inner workings of these 'hothouses' and in particular the associated assumptions about the relation between the state and private individuals. The most detailed discussions of the mechanics of governmental policies under Frederick II were produced in the later periods of his reign when his officials felt the need to defend the record of the state's policies,

---

[32] Frederick II, 'Testament von 1752', p. 122.

[33] Frederick II, 'Testament von 1752', p. 146. For the 'Adelspolitik' of the Hohenzollern see among others: Elsbeth Schwenke, *Friedrich der Große und der Adel* (Burg, 1911). Gerd Heinrich, 'Der Adel in Brandenburg-Preußen', in Hellmuth Rössler, ed., *Deutscher Adel, 1555–1740* (Darmstadt, 1965), pp. 308–10. Otto Hintze, 'Die Hohenzollern und der Adel', *Historische Zeitschrift*, 112 (1914), pp. 494–524.

sometimes along with their own record, in the face of growing public criticism. The most prominent defences of this type were offered by Frederick's minister von Hertzberg, who had started in 1778 to regularly present details about government policies in public lectures at the Royal Academy in Berlin.[34] These discourses were intended to administer a form of 'wise publicity' in carefully controlled doses to convince the public of royal policies. In the same way in which Jacques Necker's (1732–1804) publication of statistical information about state finances in 1781 was testament to the perceived power of the public in France, Hertzberg's decision to address policy questions in a public setting marked a significant shift in the relationship between state and public in Prussia. Contemporaries were well aware of the political significance of this step, and Hertzberg explicitly linked his discourses to Necker's publication and the speeches of the British monarch to parliament.[35]

The relationship between state and urban civil society was central to Hertzberg's arguments and he addressed it most concisely in a defence against the 'vulgar prejudice' that Prussia was a 'purely military state that cared little for its population'.[36] Interestingly, his defence did not focus on the protection offered by the military or the successes of Frederick's armies. Instead, he concentrated on the impact of the military on more mundane aspects of urban life. Rather than being a burden, he argued, urban garrisons contributed crucially to the prosperity of many burghers. In particular, the military was an important outlet for the products of urban manufacturing. This was not limited to the centrally purchased supplies, often sourced from monopoly providers in the towns. The location of the garrisons also meant that soldiers spent a large proportion of their pay in the towns thereby adding to circulation of money in urban economies. Hertzberg estimated that as a result of these arrangements two-thirds of the state's military budget—which represented the bulk of state expenditure—was spent in the towns, contributing substantially to their prosperity.[37] The magnitude of the transfers between country and town implicit in these claims becomes fully clear only when Hertzberg's arguments are read in conjunction with the Prussian budget. Most of the state's revenue was spent in the towns, but the urban contribution to the state's expenditure was proportionally much smaller. Urban taxes made up the bulk of tax revenues, but a large part of the budget was not supplied by taxes at all but by revenues from domains and other sources. Roughly 70 per cent of the Prussian budget was supplied by the country, either in the form of domain revenues or taxes.

[34] Ewald Friedrich von Hertzberg, 'Sur la population des états en général et sur celle des états prussiens en particulier. Dissertation qui a été lue dans l'assemblée publique de l'Academie des Sciences & des Belles-Lettres à Berlin, le 27. de Janvier 1785 pour le jour anniversaire du Roi', in Académie Royale des Sciences et Belles Lettres, ed., *Nouveaux mémoires de l'Académie Royale des Sciences et Belles Lettres* (Berlin, 1785), pp. 417–42, at p. 417.

[35] Ewald Friedrich von Hertzberg, 'Sur la véritable richesse des états, la balance du commerce et celle du pouvoir. Dissertation qui a été lue dans l'assemblée publique de l'Academie des Sciences & des Belles-Lettres à Berlin, le 26. de Janvier 1786 pour le jour anniversaire du Roi', *Nouveaux mémoires de l'Académie Royale des Sciences et Belles-Lettres* (Berlin, 1786), pp. 407–38, at pp. 407–9.

[36] Hertzberg, 'Sur la population', p. 428.

[37] Hertzberg, 'Sur la population', p. 431.

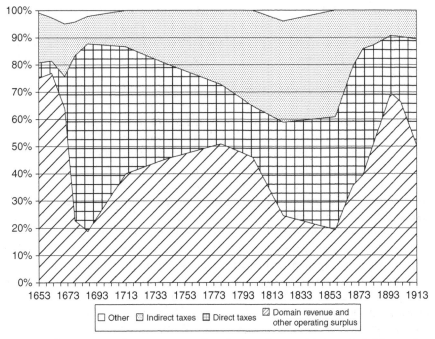

Fig. 3.1. The structure of state revenue in Brandenburg Prussia, 1653 to 1913. The graph is based on data kindly made available by Mark Spoerer. See Mark Spoerer, 'The revenue structures of Brandenburg-Prussia, Saxony and Bavaria (fifteenth to nineteenth centuries): are they compatible with the Bonney-Ormrod Model?', in Simonetta Cavaciocchi, ed., *La fiscalitá nell'economia europea secc. XII–XVIII* (Florence, 2008), pp. 781–91.

(See Fig. 3.1.) The towns thus contributed just over a third of the budget, while roughly two-thirds of it were spent there.[38]

Clearly, not all of the funds transferred from country to town in this way were spent on goods manufactured in the towns. A substantial part of a soldier's pay was used to buy food, which was grown partly in the towns but mostly in the surrounding countryside. Nonetheless, many types of food were prepared by urban artisans such as bakers, butchers, or distillers. If contemporaries are to be believed, the latter benefited in particular from the military presence, making the distilling of brandy a leading sector of urban economies in West Prussia and other provinces.[39] The manufactured goods consumed by soldiers were equally not exclusively produced in the towns themselves. Some came from the countryside or from abroad. However, where goods were not produced in the towns, urban merchants, shopkeepers, and other intermediaries still benefited from the

---

[38] Mark Spoerer, 'The revenue structures of Brandenburg-Prussia, Saxony and Bavaria (fifteenth to nineteenth centuries): are they compatible with the Bonney-Ormrod Model?', in Simonetta Cavaciocchi, ed., *La fiscalitá nell'economia europea secc. XII–XVIII* (Florence, 2008), pp. 781–91, at p. 788.

[39] Mirabeau, *De la monarchie prussienne*, vol. 3, p. 59.

additional demand. Even if detractions are taken into account, the effect of military transfers on urban economies discussed by Hertzberg must have been substantial. An important part of a soldier's pay and the budget for centrally purchased military supplies such as uniforms and weaponry were directly spent on goods produced in the towns.

Hertzberg also emphasized a second positive effect of the garrisons on urban economies. According to the minister, many soldiers were only occupied with their military duties for two days a week. During the rest of the time, they were free and looking for work 'which they can easily find in the great towns'.[40] The military thus not only increased the demand for urban products but also added to the supply of labour in the towns. This effect was multiplied by the fact that Prussian soldiers were allowed to marry and have families whose members became further additions to the urban labour market. According to Mirabeau, this practice was not merely tolerated but officially encouraged. The king himself advised soldiers to take on work in wool and linen manufacturing in order to top up their pay.[41]

The economic arguments put forward by Hertzberg were carefully calculated to respond to preoccupation and observations of the public. One of the central concerns of urban commentators was diverging trends of prices and wages. The perception was that since the early decades of the eighteenth century prices had increased, while nominal wages had stagnated. The increasing difference was cause for concern because falling real wages led to the impoverishment of workers, with negative consequences on marriage and birth rates. However, if the widening of the gap was seen as a problem, the possibility that it might be closed was even more worrisome. On a moral level, the handsome profits that urban merchants and manufacturers had made as a result of this diverging trend were condemned as excessive, but at the same time these takings were also seen as necessary. The main fear was that the pressure of rising prices and a limited supply of labour might in the future lead to increasing wages which would hinder further economic expansion in the towns. This danger was greatest in the larger cities where prices were higher and unhealthy living conditions made a continuous influx of workers particularly necessary. This danger was one of the principal motives behind the voices calling for manufacturing to be more evenly spread among smaller and medium-sized towns.[42]

Hertzberg responded to such concerns by claiming some of the credit for urban economic growth for the state and presenting the state as the structure that could also guarantee future prosperity. He argued that the funnelling of military expenditure to the towns had contributed to rising prices, while the urban population growth that resulted from the stationing of garrisons in towns helped to keep wages down. The state had thus engineered a profit inflation that accounted for much of

---

[40] Hertzberg, 'Sur la population', p. 431.

[41] Mirabeau, *De la monarchie prussienne*, vol. 3, p. 76.

[42] Johann Peter Süßmilch, *Der königl. Residentz Berlin schneller Wachsthum und Erbauung in zweyen Abhandlungen erwiesen* (Berlin, 1752), p. 39. Johann Peter Süßmilch, *Die göttliche Ordnung in den Veränderungen des menschlichen Geschlechts, aus der Geburt, dem Tode der Fortpflanzung desselben erwiesen* (2 vols., Berlin, 1765), vol. 2, p. 58.

the urban prosperity. The state, he suggested implicitly, should not only be credited with contributing substantially to the expansion of urban economies in the recent past, but also for offering an institutional framework that could guarantee the stability of economic growth in the future thanks to the deployment of the military's human and financial resources. In other words, the governmental 'hot-houses' under which the urban economies operated had worked well in the past and would continue to provide the towns with a microclimate in which commercial enterprises could thrive.

Such contemporary arguments about the flow of species and balances of trade have often been derided by modern economists as the childish confusions of 'mercantilists'. However, as John Maynard Keynes warned, contemporaries may have understood the dynamics of the early stages of capitalist development more clearly than some economic historians. In particular, Keynes argued that contemporaries were more clearly aware that the influx of 'Spanish treasure' was one of the main causes of the economic expansion of manufacturing and other sectors in parts of northern Europe in the sixteenth and seventeenth centuries.[43] Prussian manufacturing did not benefit from similar foreign demand, but contemporaries were keenly aware that the domestic transfers between town and country had an important impact on urban economies. The amounts involved were smaller by several orders of magnitude, compared with the gold and silver that had been channelled across the Atlantic, and the geographic spaces involved were minuscule by comparison, but the underlying economics were not dissimilar. Spanish elites spent much of the American bullion on goods that were either produced by English, Dutch, and French manufacturers or procured by merchants in these countries. At the same time, a variety of factors, including rigorous governmental regulation, meant that wages remained stagnant in these parts of Europe. The resulting dramatic increase in profits lured additional capital into commercial enterprises and provided the basis of the capital accumulation that resulted in the successful economic development of early capitalism in these regions. The constellation discussed by Prussian officials and commentators was in many ways a 'pocket-sized version' of the global transfers of the sixteenth and seventeenth centuries. Frederick was aware that Prussia did not have the mines of Peru at its disposal, but the government went to great lengths to emulate some of the effects that colonial transfers had in the past on the development of the then economically leading parts of Europe. The central aim of these efforts was to ensure that those willing to start a commercial enterprise in Prussia's towns stood a good chance to make a profit on their investment. Direct subsidies and monopolies for specific companies were a part of the arsenal of economic policies and Hertzberg does not fail to present the public with a list of the various royal subsidies that had been paid out in the Prussian provinces. The grand total for the year 1783 was of almost two

---

[43] John Maynard Keynes, *A treatise on money* (2 vols., London, 1950), vol. 1, pp. 148–63. For the origins of Keynes' argument see Earl Hamilton, 'American treasure and the rise of capitalism (1500–1700)', *Economica*, 9 (1929), pp. 338–57. For a critique see Pierre Vilar, 'Problems of the formation of capitalism', *Past and Present*, 10 (1956), pp. 15–38.

and a quarter million thaler. Substantial parts of these payments went to the towns in the form of subsidies for various businesses and for the construction of public and private buildings.[44] These payments injected additional funds into the urban economies and contributed substantially to the profitability of many urban businesses. Nonetheless, it is important to understand that creating a 'business-friendly climate' in the towns through the deployment of military personnel and resources was in many ways more important than specific interventions at the level of individual businesses. The disparity is well illustrated by the resources involved. The total amount of direct subsidies—only in part paid to recipients in the towns—was approximately a sixth of the 12–13 million thaler that made up the military budget in this period, which according to Hertzberg was largely spent in the towns.[45] Economic historians have commented extensively on the more 'dirigistic' aspects of Prussian economic policy, but despite the great number of privileges, monopolies, and subsidies accorded under Frederick's reign, none of these measures equalled the economic impact of the mostly overlooked strategic deployment of military resources that Hertzberg discussed.

GUIDED CONSUMERS

In addition to using the military as a conduit for the transfer of resources, Prussian officials also tried to guide private consumption in a way that would benefit economic growth in the towns. Taxes and customs duties were the most important tools in this context. Hertzberg also discussed the basic tenets of this dimension of fiscal policy but they were spelled out in more detail by Marc Antoine de la Haye de Launay (whose dates of birth and death are not known). The Frenchman was formally the head of Frederick's customs and excise administration, but de facto he was 'a kind of a finance minister' (Mirabeau) at a time when, formally, the office did not yet exist in Prussia.[46] Like Hertzberg, de Launay felt compelled by the rising tide of criticism against Fredrick's economic policies to explain and defend their logic publicly in his *Justification of the system of political economy of Frederick II* (1789).

   In his book, de Launay recalled the 'first lesson about fiscal policy' that the king gave him upon his arrival in Berlin: 'to protect the people because they were lacking the means to pay [taxes] and to protect industry because it gave work to the people and thus placed them in a position to pay [taxes] in the future'.[47] The generation of

---

[44] Hertzberg, 'Sur la population', pp. 436–40.

[45] Based on military expenditure for 1786. Eckart Schremmer, 'Taxation and public finance: Britain, France, and Germany', in Peter Mathias and Sidney Pollard, eds., *The Cambridge economic history of Europe* (Cambridge, 1989), pp. 315–494, at p. 415.

[46] 'Une espèce de contrôleur-général des finances'. Mirabeau, *De la monarchie prussienne*, vol. 3, p. 146.

[47] 'La premiere leçon qu'il m'ait donnée en arrivant, a été de ménager le peuple, parce qu'il n'avoit pas le moyen de payer; & de ménager l'industrie, parce qu'il falloit qu'elle occupât le peuple que l'on devoit faire gagner pour le metre en état de payer par la suite.' De Launay, *Justification*, p. 69.

revenue for the state always remained the ultimate objective, but the aim was not to achieve this through short-term fiscal measures. Besides effective tax collection the development of manufacturing industry and the formation of a tax base were the primary objectives of fiscal policy. In particular fiscal tools were to be used to procure 'sales' and 'customers' for Prussia's industry within and beyond its borders.[48] Domestic consumers, the king explained to de Launay, represented a great potential market because 'even the lowliest maid servant wants to wear a piece of silk nowadays'.[49] However, the problem was that Prussian consumers, if left to their own devices, were likely to turn to foreign wares to satisfy their desires. Imports were often of higher quality, more fashionable, or cheaper than Prussian equivalents. The king deplored such xenophile tastes and wanted to change them in order to ensure the profitability and expansion of Prussian manufacturing. The tools employed in Prussia were the same protectionist policies that many monarchs before Frederick had used. Manufactured goods from abroad were submitted to heavy import duties while domestic products were taxed lightly or not at all.[50] In cases where these gentler methods could not change consumer preferences, foreign goods were banned altogether. According to de Launay 490 products were removed from the market in this way. From the fiscal point of view, this caused considerable concerns because these goods were typically highly taxed and would have contributed substantially to the state's revenue. However, despite remonstrance from his most important tax official, Frederick remained adamant that the pernicious long-term effect outweighed the short-term benefits of abolishing import restrictions.[51] Besides redirecting consumers towards domestic products, the limitation of luxury consumption was also an objective of fiscal policy. De Launay recalled that he was instructed to 'constrain the unnecessary consumption by the people'.[52] Taken together with the king's orders to free the 'necessary' consumption of imposts, these fiscal policies may be seen as a further way to address concerns with the upward pressure on wages that resulted from price inflations and aspirations to consume 'above one's station'.

THE UTILITY OF SPECIE

In addition to reshaping the habits of domestic consumers, officials were also preoccupied with increasing urban exports as part of their strategy to ensure prosperity. Since restrictive measures such as product bans could not be applied to foreign consumers, efforts were concentrated on wooing them with competitive prices. Export duties were low or non-existent and subsidies were paid to reduce export prices further. In addition, several attempts were made to improve trade

---

[48] 'Procurer à l'industrie des debouches par l'assurance du débit.' De Launay, *Justification*, p. 40.
[49] De Launay, *Justification*, p. 57.
[50] De Launay, *Justification*, pp. 54–7.
[51] De Launay, *Justification*, pp. 53–61.
[52] 'Gêner le people sur les consommations non-nécessaires'. De Launay, *Justification*, p. 70.

channels through which Prussian goods could be sold to neighbouring countries and beyond. The creation of the Asiatic Trade Company in Emden in 1753 was an attempt to become independent of foreign traders and gain control over the lucrative long distance trade with Asia and America. At the same time, it was also to function as an outlet for Prussian manufactured products.[53] However, while the project had the full political and financial backing of the king, Prussia's 'oceanic moment' was cut short by the manoeuvres of Dutch and British competitors and by the outbreak of the Seven Years War. This first 'world war' made it clear to Frederick that trading companies required powerful navies to be successful and the project was subsequently abandoned.[54] Nonetheless, exports remained an important outlet for Prussian manufacturers. Hertzberg estimated that half of all manufacturing output was exported and that a substantial part of the 123,000 workers employed in manufacturing and their families owed their livelihoods to the 'very favourable balance of trade'.[55] Foreign trade was mainly with neighbouring countries, but also included more distant destinations such as Spain, Italy, and even China where Prussian textiles were exported via Russia. Towns like Königsberg, Memel, Elbing, and Stettin were the centres of this trade.[56]

A positive balance of trade was also central to the discussions between the king and de Launay about monetary matters.[57] Lacking 'Peruvian mines', there was a concern that the supply of specie might not keep up with the increasing circulation of goods and that shortages in the medium of payment could create a bottleneck for economic growth. In particular the consumption of foreign luxury goods threatened to exhaust available supplies of specie.[58] In a monetary system where the supply of money was not determined by economic necessities, but mainly by coincidences of geology and by trade flows, the balance of trade was one of the few ways in which governments could try to regulate the supply of money. Besides keeping a watchful eye on trade, Frederick tried to address this problem by also reforming the monetary system. The lack of financial expertise in Prussia led him to recruit the merchant turned administrator Johann Philipp Graumann (*c*.1690–1762) from Wolfenbüttel. As well as having gathered practical experience in the Netherlands, Graumann had studied the English and other European monetary systems in detail.[59] Frederick put him in charge of a reform that resulted in the introduction in 1750 of a uniform system of coins and exchange values in all Prussian provinces. The king's expectations were high and in 1752 he was still

[53] De Launay, *Justification*, p. 58.

[54] Florian Schui, 'Prussia's "Trans-oceanic moment": the creation of the Prussian Asiatic Trade Company in 1750', *Historical Journal*, 49 (2006), pp. 143–60. Writing in 1888 Schultze refers to the Seven Years War as the 'world war'. Walther Schultze, *Geschichte der preussischen Regieverwaltung von 1766 bis 1786, ein historisch-kritischer Versuch* (Leipzig, 1888), p. 18.

[55] 'Débit étranger'. Hertzberg, 'Sur la population', p. 427.

[56] Hertzberg, 'Sur la population', pp. 427–8.

[57] De Launay, *Justification*, p. 80.

[58] De Launay, *Justification*, p. 57.

[59] Johann Philip Graumann, *Gesammelte Briefe von dem Gelde; von dem Wechsel und dessen Cours, von der Proportion zwischen Gold und Silber; von dem Pari des Geldes und den Münzgesetzen verschiedener Völker; besonders aber von dem Englischen Münzwesen* (Berlin, 1762).

hoping for the reform to result in a huge influx of precious metals.[60] These ambitions were disappointed, but the reform made the Prussian monetary system more functional and stable and established it as a standard in the north of Germany.

AN ENGLISH BANK FOR PRUSSIA

Shortages in the money supply were also addressed through the creation of new financial institutions. Some of the more ambitious plans for a new bank hatched by the king and a financial adventurer from Italy failed because of the opposition of local businessmen, but nevertheless royal banks were created, first in Berlin and Breslau, in 1765.[61] Local merchants could obtain letters of exchange against their deposits from these banks, which also worked as clearing houses. When it became apparent to what extent these institutions contributed to increase the 'speedy circulation of money', the model was taken to other Prussian towns including Königsberg, Stettin, Kolberg, Memel, Frankfurt, Madgeburg, and Minden. Moreover, the remits of the banking activity were extended. Following the model of the 'English bank', the institutions issued 'banknotes' against deposits that were underwritten by the bank, convertible against specie, and guaranteed to be accepted by all royal 'cashier's offices'. These notes in denominations between four and a thousand *Bankopfunde* (bank pounds) were a widely accepted means of payment, not only to the state, but also in private commerce. In order to facilitate the circulation of money the banks also offered loans to creditors who could offer 'non-perishable' securities. Royal banks thereby increased the money supply by adding to the speed of circulation and the volume of money.[62]

The largely urban activities of the royal banks were complemented by the rural institution of the *Ritterschaftliche Kreditwerke* that existed in some provinces. These institutions issued bonds against the value of the landholdings of nobles. Participating nobles could receive up to half the value of their estate in such notes which were underwritten collectively and could circulate freely. The primary political intention of this institution was to support nobles who were struggling economically and prevent noble estates from being bought by wealthy commoners. However, a side effect of this financial innovation was the issuing of what resembled in many ways a land-backed paper currency. The large denominations of the bonds in values from 50 to 1,000 Reichsthaler meant that they were not suitable for smaller payments; nonetheless, they increased the volume of money in circulation substantially. Moreover, consumption patterns of nobles suggest that much of the rural

[60] Frederick II, 'Testament von 1752', pp. 124–5.

[61] Ingrid Mittenzwei, *Preußen nach dem Siebenjährigen Krieg: Auseinandersetzungen zwischen Bürgertum und Staat um die Wirtschaftspolitik* (Berlin, 1979), pp. 14–19. Marcus von Niebuhr, *Geschichte der Königlichen Bank in Berlin von d. Gründung derselben (1765) bis zum Ende d. Jahres 1845; nach amtl. Quellen* (Berlin, 1854).

[62] 'Den geschwinden Umlauf des Geldes', 'der englischen Bank', 'Banknoten', 'königlichen Kassen', 'unverderbliche Sachen'. Friedrich Nicolai, *Beschreibung der königlichen Residenzstädte Berlin und Potsdam und aller daselbst befindlicher Merkwürdigkeiten* (Berlin, 1779), pp. 337–9.

credit may have ended up in urban economies. Prussian observers attributed a substantial part of Berlin's exuberant luxury commerce to the consumption by nobles from the provinces who took up residence in the capital.[63]

Seen in conjunction, the discussions between Frederick and his officials about different areas of economic policy were focused on creating a framework that was conducive to commercial activity. The main concern was with luring private individuals into business by creating commercial opportunities that were too enticing not to be taken up. Individuals who acted out of selfish motives were crucial parts of this scheme, but they operated in a carefully constructed context that made sure that the state's desired outcomes were achieved. In this view, individual autonomy was therefore a potent force that needed to be carefully harnessed and channelled by strategic placing of incentives and disincentives. Frederick best summarized this outlook when he discussed the motives that led him to create the Asiatic Trade Company in Emden. At the top of the list was that 'it gives private individuals the opportunity to invest their capital with a profit of 20, or even 50 per cent'.[64] The objective was to shield and support the undertakings of private enterprise, rather than substitute them with direct government action. This does not mean that interventions did not take place, but they were conceptualized as a last resort when other stimuli to private enterprise failed. The king lamented that merchants and manufacturers sometimes failed to display entrepreneurial spirit even after the most favourable conditions had been created by the state 'to help them and to inspire them with courage'. 'It's in vain that I offer pecuniary incentives,' he complained to de Launay regarding the manufacturers of Berlin, 'they stick with what they have & they do not want to make any effort.'[65] Seen through the eyes of Prussian officials the local entrepreneurs did not appear as Schumpeterian heroes, held back by institutional constraints, but rather like fragile plants that struggled even in the protective atmosphere of a hothouse. Faced with this inertia, the king saw himself obliged to resort to direct orders on occasion. He recounts his efforts to get the merchants of Berlin to establish a new sugar refinery in Bromberg. Similar refineries already existed elsewhere and according to the king 'there was a margin' in the business. Nonetheless, the incentives offered failed to entice manufacturers to seize the opportunity and the king was eventually 'obliged to force them'. However, 'forcing' his subjects to 'earn' was only a fallback option for Frederick.[66] In many respects, the carrot rather than the stick characterized Prussian economic policy in this period.

[63] 'Pfandbriefe'. Nicolai, *Beschreibung*, pp. 286–9. See also Mirabeau, *De la monarchie prussienne*, vol. 1, p. 322.

[64] 'Weil das den Privatleuten die Möglichkeit verschafft, ihre Kapitalien mit 20, ja selbst mit 50 Prozent Gewinn anzulegen.' Frederick II, 'Testament von 1752', p. 135.

[65] 'Pour les seconder & leur inspirer du courage', 'j'offre en vain des secours pécuiaires, l'on se renferme dans ce que l'on a, & on ne veut pas augmenter ses peines'. De Launay, *Justification*, pp. 58, 60.

[66] 'Il y a de la marge', 'les forcer d'en [argent] gagner'. De Launay, *Justification*, pp. 60–1.

THE LONG SHADOW OF COLBERT

Perhaps the most striking feature of the way in which Frederick envisaged economic development in general, and in the towns in particular, was the lack of originality. Most of the tools deployed were in use and had been used in Prussia and elsewhere in Europe. Some particular features emerge when one looks in more detail at the implementation and the circumstances of these measures. However, Frederick mostly followed a path that was so well trodden that it is difficult to identify specific influences and inspirations. And yet it may well be argued that the history-conscious king saw in Louis XIV a model monarch whose reign was associated with a golden period for the arts and sciences as well as being one of military glory and political strength.[67] The admiration for Louis and his age was not extraordinary per se but few monarchs studied the past in general, and the great age of France in particular, with such zeal as Frederick. Voltaire's (1694–1778) project of writing the history of the *Age of Louis XIV* (1751) had captured the king's imagination since he first heard about it and the philosopher finished and first published the work in Berlin with the king's support. In the book Voltaire attributed much of the credit for France's golden age to Louis' minister Colbert and specifically to his promotion of commerce and industry. Roughly at the same time as Voltaire was exploring the causes of France's glorious age, and during a period in which both were in close contact, Frederick worked on his *Memoirs of the house of Brandenburg* (1747–9). Here, too, we find a particular emphasis on the connection between the periods of glory in the history of the dynasty and periods of progress in the arts, sciences, and industry. The nexus was important enough for Frederick to devote a separate volume under the title *Of the manners, customs, industry and progress of the human understanding in the arts and sciences* (1748) to the topic. Frederick's understanding of the historical link between the active promotion of commerce and industry and the rise of 'golden ages' of dynasties and countries, together with the sentiment that it might be Prussia's turn to be the place of such a great age, certainly reinforced tendencies to apply traditional economic recipes and made it more difficult for their critics to be heard.[68]

START-UP INDUSTRY PROTECTION

Frederick's economic policies were certainly rooted in the past, but he was not a reactionary or the 'last performer of a dying art'. Instead, the language and vision of Frederick's political economy were in many ways rather modern in the sense that they were part of theoretical and policy debates that extended beyond Frederick's

---

[67] Jochen Schlobach, 'Du siècle de Louis au siècle de Frédéric?' in Christiane Mervaud, ed., *Le siècle de Voltaire—hommage à René Pomeau* (2 vols., Oxford, 1987), vol. 2, pp. 831–46, at p. 832.

[68] For a more detailed treatment see Florian Schui, *Early debates about industry: Voltaire and his contemporaries* (Basingstoke, 2005), chs 2 and 3.

reign and beyond Prussia's borders. When de Launay suggested in 1779 that it might be time to collect the fruits of the careful nurturing of Prussia's industry by introducing higher levels of taxation, the king replied that the time was not yet ripe, since industry was still 'in the cradle' in many parts of the country.[69] As Friedrich List (1789–1846) reminds us, this was also the language of economic debates in the first half of the nineteenth century. In 1819 Jean-Antoine Chaptal (1756–1832) argued that it was necessary to 'protect infant arts by prohibitions, to save them from foreign competition until they shall have made that progress which enables them to withstand competition'. The language of infancy was equally common among economic liberals on the other side of the channel. In 1815 Lord Brougham (1778–1868), a prominent reformer and advocate of free trade with the continent, opined: 'England could afford to incur some loss on the export of English goods, for the purpose of destroying foreign manufactures in their cradle'.[70] Subsequently List himself perhaps did most to give currency to the language and content of what became known as the 'infant industry argument' in nineteenth-century Europe. List's views were in large part shaped by his exposure to debates and policies in the United States, but when he set out to popularize his arguments in Germany and the rest of Europe he relied on, among other things, examples from the successful industrial policies of Frederick's Prussia.[71] Given the subsequent importance of Frederick for the formation of Prussian and German identities, the association of 'infant industry protection' with the monarch contributed substantially to the continued vibrancy of this intellectual and political current in the modern period.

It is tempting to see Frederick's activist economic policies as inherently linked with his absolutistic government. However, transatlantic parallels between the conversations of the king of Prussia with his French financial advisor and exchanges between the first Secretary of the Treasury and the Congress of the United States show that such an association is misleading. In 1790, within a year of the publication of de Launay's *Justification*, Alexander Hamilton (1755/7–1804) presented his *Report on the subject of manufactures* to Congress. Hamilton used similar language to de Launay and Frederick, referring several times to 'manufactories . . . in their infancy'.[72] Equally inspired by the example of Colbert, Hamilton argued in favour of a whole catalogue of measures to protect and promote manufacturing in the face of superior foreign competition.[73] The specific policies envisaged included protective tariffs and import bans for manufactured goods, tax reductions for domestic industries, and various forms of subsidies for exports. These measures were to be complemented by improvements in the banking and transportation infrastructure, and government inspections to ensure quality standards in manufacturing.[74] The

---

[69] 'Au berceau'. De Launay, *Justification*, p. 58.

[70] Both cited in Friedrich List, *The national system of political economy* (Philadelphia, 1856), pp. 448, 157.

[71] List, *National system*, pp. 147–59.

[72] Alexander Hamilton, 'Report on manufactures', in Henry Cabot Lodge, ed., *The works of Alexander Hamilton* (12 vols., New York, 1886), vol. 4, pp. 193–285, at pp. 247, 261.

[73] Ron Chernow, *Alexander Hamilton* (New York, 2004), p. 170.

[74] Hamilton, 'Report on manufactures', pp. 244–57.

parallels to Prussian policies were obvious despite the unsurprising fact that Hamilton, unlike Prussian officials, failed to praise the economic advantages of the urban quartering of soldiers. Nonetheless, the development of manufacturing was in both cases connected with military objectives. In Berlin considerations focused mainly on the fiscal (and ultimately military) benefits of a strong manufacturing sector, while in Philadelphia the emphasis was more on the creation of an independent domestic supply of military equipment. This dimension was also present in Prussian debates, but the well-developed weapons manufacture and geographical and political differences meant that the issue had become less urgent.

Perhaps even more important than the similarities in the language of debate and the specific measures proposed, were the parallels in the underpinning visions of the state's economic role. Hamilton concluded his report by remarking that 'in countries where there is great private wealth, much may be effected by the voluntary contributions of patriotic individuals; but in a community situated like that of the United States, the public purse must supply the deficiency of private resource'.[75] Not much earlier Frederick had instructed de Launay: 'know that when there are things that are above the forces of my subjects in my realm, it is my duty to shoulder the expenses and for them to collect the fruits'.[76] These passages reflect not only similar visions about the relation between the state and private economic activity, but more deeply rooted affinities with regard to the conceptualization of the relation between national and private interests. In 1820 the American economist Daniel Raymond analysed the economic policies pursued by Hamilton and others with the aim of formulating the underpinning economic principles. In particular, he defended the expediency and rationality of protecting tariffs against the Smithian critique. Against Smith's 'admitted dogma' according to which 'national and individual interests are never opposed', Raymond argued that such conflicts occurred systematically and that common interest had to take precedent over narrow individual ones.[77] 'In military tactics', he wrote, 'it is a fundamental principle that the army is ONE, and the general the head; no soldier is permitted to have a right, or an interest, to the general good of the army.'[78] In a similar way, citizens could not be permitted to pursue individual interests separate from those of the nation in matters of political economy. In this case the legislature took on the role of the general in deciding the limits to individual freedom that were compatible with the 'public interests'. The legislator, in particular, had a right to interfere with individual property rights. Since private property was always, to some extent, a bounty bestowed on the individual by the community, property rights were never absolute but always 'conventional or conditional subject to any such regulation as may be made respecting it, with a view to the general interests of the whole nation'.[79] In the

---

[75] Hamilton, 'Report on manufactures', p. 285.

[76] 'Apprenez, que lorsqu'il y a dans mes Etats des choses qui sonst au-dessus de la force de mes Sujets, c'est à moi à en faire les frais, & à eux à en ramasser les fruits.' De Launay, *Justification*, p. 72.

[77] Daniel Raymond, *Thoughts on political economy* (Baltimore, 1820), p. 355.

[78] Raymond, *Thoughts*, p. 347.

[79] Raymond, *Thoughts*, p. 349.

same way in which God could legitimately take the health and life of a person because he had given them, the legislator was allowed to take a person's property that the community had helped them acquire.

This line of argument is also familiar from the Prussian context where Hertzberg and others held that the prosperity enjoyed by private individuals was, at least in part, owed to the state's policies. It was the state, Hertzberg argued, that put 'Prussian subjects' in a position to pay their taxes 'without great difficulty'. This type of argument supported specifically the legitimacy of the state's seizure of parts of private property mainly through taxation and its right to interfere with the use of private property.[80] Underlying Hertzberg's argument was a broader vision of the role of the legislator identified by Frederick in 1751. In similar terms to those of Raymond, the king described the legislator as an arbiter who established a balance between 'the power of government' and the 'freedom of citizens' in order to achieve the common good which remained the supreme objective of legislation.[81] In this endeavour the legislator could not hope to rely on the virtuosity of the citizens. The main motivation of men was always 'self-love'. The legislator could not change the nature of man but he could more or less successfully attempt to 'regulate', 'direct', and 'manage' their selfishness and passions so as to 'show them that it is in their interest to be virtuous'.[82] Selfishness was not to be repressed or reformed but rather 'harnessed'.[83] As illustrated by Frederick's economic policies, it was the task of the legislator to construct a context in which individuals, guided by self-love, would gravitate in a seemingly natural way towards behaving in a manner that served the common good. Defining the latter, and directing selfish individuals towards it with 'carrots and sticks', remained the central tasks of the legislator.

The trajectory of the economic development of Prussia and the United States may be seen as confirmation of the validity of the economic arguments put forward in this period. However, irrespective of the economic merits, this vision was likely to give rise to political tensions in situations where notions of what constituted national interests, and how they were related to the interest of individuals, developed in different ways within the state and civil society. Such a divergence is clearly visible in Prussia in the second half of the eighteenth century when the official emphasis on holistic notions of national, common, and state interest stood in contrast with public discourses that turned increasingly to the needs, desires, and interests of individuals. Officials, including the monarch, were not unaware of these concerns. Frederick discussed urban life in very similar terms to those of the

---

[80] Hertzberg, 'Sur la population', p. 431.

[81] 'Un juste équilibre entre le pouvoir du gouvernement et la liberté des citoyens', 'bonheur public'. Frederick II, 'Lois', pp. 25, 11.

[82] 'Réglerait l'amour-propre, il le dirigerait au bien, il saurait opposer les passions aux passions, et, en démontrant aux hommes que leur intérêt est d'être vertueux, il les rendrait tels', 'manier leur passions'. Frederick II, 'Essai sur l'amour-propre envisagé comme principe de morale', in Johann D. E. Preuss, ed., *Oeuvres de Frederic le Grand* (30 vols., Berlin, 1848), vol. 9, pp. 99–114, at pp. 105, 111.

[83] Albert Hirschman, *The passions and the interests: political arguments for capitalism before its triumph* (Princeton, NJ, 1997), pp. 14–19.

commentators that we encountered in Chapter 2. Like many of his urban subjects, he saw a close link between urban life and the development of vice and criminality. The 'tyranny of fashion' was as much part of his vocabulary as were ironic comments about the faithfulness of the female inhabitants of Berlin and their infatuation with consumption of luxury goods.[84] However, from an official perspective, concerns of this type were secondary compared with the fiscal–military objectives that the state had to protect. The spread of new patterns of consumption and their moral, economic, and demographic consequences for urban society were, from an official point of view, mainly of interest to the extent that they affected longer-term economic and military development and, in particular, the growth of the tax base. Like urban commentators, officials were concerned with balancing different interests in order to create harmonious order, but their conception of the state as the keeper of common interest meant that interference and limitation of the ability of individuals to pursue their interests was legitimate and often necessary. However, it would be simplistic to describe the difference in terms of a state eager to regulate as much as possible and burghers who sought freedom of interference. Policies that officials considered to be conducive to the common interest often led to less interference in private affairs. Conflicts between the perspectives of officials and the growing urban individualism were not generalized, but occurred with regard to specific matters where the understanding of what constituted common and private interests, and how the two categories were interrelated, developed in different ways between officials and urban dwellers. During the reign of Frederick II such differences emerged most clearly with regard to the material culture of urban societies. Burghers were increasingly claiming the right to choose what to consume and, closely related, what and how to produce. In addition, the growing importance of consumption also meant that individuals sought to protect and maximize their economic resources. State officials, in contrast, believed that it was legitimate and even necessary to limit consumer choice, direct and control the production of goods, and secure a substantial part of private revenues for common, mainly military, purposes.

Paradoxically, the adoption of an enlightened mindset by urban commentators and officials did not help to reconcile such differences, but rather contributed to exacerbate conflicts. To the extent that officials formulated policies increasingly based on rational enquiry and systematically collected empirical evidence, there seemed to be little necessity for formal or informal consultation, compromise, and negotiation. Armed with universal and unassailable truths, produced by enlightened tools of knowledge, officials felt little need to take seriously what they saw as the narrow-minded concerns and parochial interests of urban dwellers.

Perhaps no one has described this problem more clearly than John Quincy Adams (1767–1848) in his *Letters on Silesia* (1804). As an ambassador to Berlin the future president of the United States travelled to the province in 1800–1. In his

---

[84] Frederick II, 'Lois', p. 12. 'Tyrannie de la mode'. Frederick II, 'Des moeurs', p. 250.

letters he praised the fiscal policies that Frederick introduced after the annexation of the province from Austria as a 'luminous proof of the difference between a good and bad administration'. However, while the policy was 'to the real advantage of the people', it was still highly problematic according to Adams because there was little more than a 'shadow of . . . the subject's consent for the levying of taxes'.[85]

[85] John Quincy Adams, *Letters on Silesia, written during a tour through that country in the years 1800, 1801* (London, 1804), pp. 317–19.

4

Taxation and its Discontents

To tax and to please, no more than to love and to be wise, is not given to men.
Edmund Burke, *First speech on conciliation with America* (1774).[1]

The different outlooks of urban dwellers and government officials did not, a priori, make conflict inevitable. After all, it had been the single-minded prioritization of state interests that had opened up many of the spaces in which a more individualistic urban society developed. And even in areas where the state attempted to interfere with individual freedoms, its capability to translate paternalistic ambitions into administrative practice remained limited. As a result, where the differences between public and official visions were substantial in theory they did not necessarily lead to much friction in the daily interaction between state officials and burghers. This benign parallelism could have continued during the reign of Frederick II and beyond, if the almost uninterrupted warfare of the first sixteen years of the king's reign had not made it necessary to raise additional revenue for the state. Already in the first year of his reign Frederick had decided to invade and annex the Habsburg province of Silesia. The successful outcome (from the Prussian perspective) of this first Silesian War (1740–2) resulted in two further conflicts in 1744–5 and 1756–63. Known as the three Silesian Wars in Prussian history, these conflicts were part of two larger European conflicts, the War of Austrian Succession (1740–8) and the Seven Years War, which involved all major European powers in changing constellations. The globally fought Seven Years War, in particular, proved to be enormously costly for winners and losers alike. In the decades after the war most European states struggled to regain financial stability and sought in various ways to increase revenues. In Prussia the state turned mainly to the towns in order to satisfy its financial appetite because the other main sources of state revenue could not be utilized in the same way. Proceeds from the domains could not be increased quickly and, for the reasons discussed earlier, greater fiscal pressure on the country was not considered to be a politically viable option. As a result, the ambitious military agenda of Frederick's early reign was mirrored by a domestic 'fiscal campaign' that was mainly directed against the towns. Central to these endeavours

---

[1] Edmund Burke, 'First speech on conciliation with America: American Taxation (19 April 1774, House of Commons, London)', in Paul Langford, ed., *The writings and speeches of Edmund Burke* (12 vols., London, 1981), vol. 2, pp. 406–63, at p. 454. This chapter is an extensively revised version of the article Florian Schui, 'Tax payer opposition and fiscal reform in Prussia, c.1766–87', *Historical Journal*, 54 (2011), pp. 371–99. Copyright © Cambridge University Press 2011, reproduced with permission.

were attempts to increase the administrative reach of the state in the towns in order to collect existing duties more effectively and ensure that tax increases did not remain mute edicts, but resulted in tangible financial flows. However, administrative reforms also meant that differences between urban individualism and the state's paternalism became more difficult to ignore. Edicts and academic writings of their king may have meant little to many urbanites, but the result of the new financial imperatives meant that such musings were now translated into administrative practice more stringently, which led to changes that were felt in the daily lives of many urban dwellers. This chapter reconstructs the transformation of the practices of urban fiscal administration under Frederick II and the forms of resistance put up by urban dwellers, eventually leading to the repeal of substantial parts of the fiscal changes.

MEMBRANES MADE OF STONE

Before the beginning of Frederick's reign the state had already made increasingly forceful claims for a more effective collection of urban taxes. These attempts manifested themselves most visibly in the excise walls that surrounded most Prussian towns.[2] These barriers—often mere palisades or ridges—were in many cases older than the excise and also served other purposes including urban defence and the prevention of desertion of soldiers. However, since the introduction of the excise the barriers were systematically improved in order to prevent contraband. The excise wall of Berlin, for example, was completed in 1736 and all traffic was now supposed to pass through the city's gates where the excise was collected.[3] Gates such as the Brandenburg Gate in Berlin were thus among the most important points of tax collection in the towns and locations of regular interaction between burghers and tax officials (see Fig. 4.1). As Mintzker points out, town gates were 'spatially peripheral but economically and socially central'.[4] This made them the focal points of fiscal frictions and conflicts in this period. In many ways the semipermeable urban walls embodied the complex relationship between urban society and state. On the one hand, the walls were traditionally symbols of the pride, independence, and special legal status that distinguished towns from the surrounding countryside.[5] On the other hand, during Frederick's reign the walls increasingly became physical symbols and tools of a patronizing and often unwanted presence of the apparatus of the military–fiscal state in the towns. Not only

---

[2] It should be noted that not all settlements that were subject to the excise were towns. However, the categories overlapped to a large extent and we use them here interchangeably. Anton Friedrich Büsching, *Topographie der Mark Brandenburg* (Berlin, 1775), pp. 18–63.

[3] Helmut Zschocke, *Die Berliner Akzisemauer. Die vorletzte Mauer der Hauptstadt* (Berlin, 2007), p. 25.

[4] Yair Mintzker, 'What is defortification? Military functions, police roles, and symbolism in the demolition of German city walls in the eighteenth and nineteenth centuries', *Bulletin of the German Historical Institute*, 48 (2011), pp. 33–58, at p. 49.

[5] Büsching, *Topographie*, p. 57.

Fig. 4.1. 'Das Brandenburger Thor in Berlin' (The Brandenburg Gate in Berlin), Daniel Nikolaus Chodowiecki, etching, 1764. Reproduced with permission from Klassik Stiftung Weimar, Museen, Inv. DK 208/84.

in a political but also in a spatial sense Prussia's excise walls and gates were, at the same time, zones of separation and interaction between civil society and state organs. As a result they often became the locus of frictions between the two spheres.

During the reign of Frederick II the experience of those passing through the gates of their own or other towns changed substantially. The presence of excise walls may have seemed imposing but in practice the controls carried out at the gates were often lax. The reality at the lower end of Prussia's fiscal administration has been well captured in the memoirs of the educational reformer and geographer Karl Friedrich Klöden (1786–1856) who was the son of an excise official in Märkisch-Friedland. His father, a former army officer, was often too drunk to fulfil his duties and as a ten-year-old Klöden substituted for him, filling in forms and carrying out controls as well as he could. Klöden recalled that corruption was rampant: 'On none of these excise posts can a man live without additional income if he did not want to starve, and the additional incomes were hardly ever legal'.[6] Officials often lacked essential administrative skills, were corrupt, or colluded with merchants and consumers; in short, they were anything but loyal servants of the state.[7] From the state's point of

---

[6] 'Auf keinem dieser Akziseposten ein Mensch ohne Nebeneinkünfte bestehen konnte, wenn er nicht Hungers sterben wollte, und diese Nebeneinkünfte waren fast nie erlaubte.' Karl Friedrich von Klöden, *Jugenderinnerungen* (Leipzig, 1911), p. 95.

[7] Schmoller sees the excise administration as the origin of Prussia's loyal civil servants ('pflichttreue Beamten'). Gustav von Schmoller, 'Die Epochen der preußischen Finanzpolitik', *Jahrbuch für Gesetzgebung, Verwaltung und Volkswirtschaft im Deutschen Reich*, 1 (1877), pp. 32–114, at p. 63. For the problem of corruption as a systemic problem of the *ancien régime* see Jacob van Klaveren, 'Die historische Erscheinung der Korruption in ihrem Zusammenhang mit der Staats- und Gesellsch-

view this situation was hardly satisfactory and in Frederick's view any attempt to increase excise revenues had to focus on 'the lack of able men . . . and of precision in the execution'.[8] 'Careful selection' and 'military subordination' of officials were thus the central tenets of his reform plans.[9]

MAKING AN ADMINISTRATION ONE
OFFICIAL AT A TIME

The practical implications of this approach emerge from a handbook with instructions for fiscal administrators that was produced for the province of Pomerania in 1749. Under headings such as 'Of the office of the excise inspector in general' the instructions contained guidelines for the conduct of officials, but also details about the proper way to carry out administrative procedures and instructions for the interaction with other officials and taxpayers.[10] The handbook replaced the last comprehensive general instructions which dated back to 1699. Many rules had been changed since that time and, above all, the instructions were often not applied by the employees. Many excise officers did not even possess a copy of the instructions. This situation was to be remedied by the new guidelines. Published in the form of a pocket-sized booklet with an index, the instructions were intended to be a universal reference manual that officers could take with them at all times. In order to increase further the loyalty of the officials and instil a heightened sense of duty in them the manual also included an oath which inspectors were supposed to take.[11]

While the focus of the manual was on the conduct of officials, it also contained guidelines for recruitment. In matters of the excise, the instructions state, much depended on the appointment of good inspectors and cashiers. They ought to be accurate, awake, fearless, cunning, and hard-working, but not lazy, negligent, brutal, or drunkards. Ideally the officers were also obliged to leave a deposit but exemption from this rule could be granted. In addition to these qualities, the

aftsstruktur betrachtet', *Vierteljahrschrift für Sozial- und Wirtschaftsgeschichte*, 44 (1957), pp. 289–324. Jacob van Klaveren, 'Fiskalismus—Merkantilismus—Korruption. Drei Aspekte der Finanz- und Wirtschaftspolitik während des Ancien Régime', *Vierteljahrschrift für Sozial- und Wirtschaftsgeschichte*, 47 (1960), pp. 333–53.

   [8] 'C'est défaut de sujets assez habiles . . . et d'exactitude dans exécution'. *Cabinett-Order* (CO) to De la Haye de Launay, 7 January 1767, in Hugo von Rachel, ed., *Die Handels-, Zoll- und Akzisepolitik Preußens* (Berlin, 1928), p. 166.

   [9] 'Sorgsam ausgewählt', 'in militärischer Unterordnung'. Frederick II, 'Das politische Testament von 1752', in Gustav Volz, ed., *Die Werke Friedrichs des Großen* (10 vols., Berlin, 1912), vol. 7, pp. 115–94, at p. 141.

   [10] 'Vom Amte des Accise-Inspectoris insgemein'. 'Seiner königl. Majestät in Preußen Allergnädigst neu approbirtes Reglement und Verfassung des ganzen Accise-Wesens, dero Vor- und Hinter-Pommerschen Städten wie auch Fürstenthum Cammin, imgleichen der Herrschaften Lauenburg und Bütow, wornach (!) die sämmtliche Accise-Bediente ihre Arbeit zu bestellen, die Accisanten abzufertigen, die dabey vorkommende Fälle zu entscheiden, und sich überhaupt allerunterthänigst zu achten haben. De dato Berlin, den 28. Febr. 1749.' Geheimes Staatsarchiv Preußischer Kulturbesitz (GStAPK), HA II, Abt. 12 Pommern Materien, General Accise Sachen, Nr. 20a, folio 3.

   [11] GStAPK, HA II, Abt. 12 Pommern Materien, General Accise Sachen, Nr. 20a, folio 104.

instructions required prospective officers to be able to calculate and write in a legible hand.[12] These skills were not very sophisticated but in Frederick's view they were sufficient for the lower ranking officers of the excise.

With regard to the conduct of the officers, the principal concern was with a clear separation of the operations that they carried out in their official function from other aspects of their life.[13] This distinction was in part associated with physical spaces: the excise was always to be collected in the same '*loco publico*'. In small towns where no office was available the officers were instructed to choose a 'specially designated room' in their house for this purpose. Official acts had to be carried out by the employee himself. His wife and children had to leave the excise room when the employee was carrying out official business. Within the specially designated room the officials were ordered to keep official documents exclusively in a special cabinet thus creating an even more limited space; this contained the essence of their official activities. Temporal constraints were associated with the spatial delimitations. Excise hours were from 8 to 11 a.m. and 1 to 4 p.m. in winter, and 7 to 11 a.m. and 2 to 5 p.m. in summer, and were to be followed strictly. Exceptions to this timetable were only possible with the approval of superiors and in clearly defined circumstances. Hours could be reduced in cases of sickness and holidays, while extensions were possible for special markets and in order to meet the needs of merchants. The measures were aimed at a clear spatial and temporal distinction between the official and personal spheres which was required of the officers. The two spheres also had to be kept separate at the level of financial flows. It was explicitly forbidden to accept or ask for any payments in cash or kind other than the ones prescribed by the excise tariff or to collect less than the full amount of taxes due. In the same way, great care was taken to ensure that officers kept private and official finances separate and did not use tax money for personal purposes. These instructions were associated with punishments and rewards. When the officers exceeded the limits proscribed by the instructions, they were threatened with punishment; when they remained within the limits, they were promised the support of all others branches of government, including the use of physical force by the army.[14]

In addition to the limits that separated private and official acts of the excise officers, another set of rules dealt with the delimitation of their sphere of authority in their interaction with taxpayers. They had the right to search baggage, vehicles, workshops, shops, houses, barns, basements, attics, and rooms of those who were suspected of tax fraud. These rights explicitly extended to all individuals without distinction of rank. However, the exercise of this power was also curtailed in important ways. A sufficient reason for the suspicion was needed, and all searches had to be carried out with great care so as not to damage or inconvenience

[12] GStAPK, HA II, Abt. 12 Pommern Materien, General Accise Sachen, Nr. 20a, folios 3, 10–12.

[13] For the central importance of similar processes for the formation of bureaucracy see Max Weber, *Economy and society* (2 vols., Berkeley, 1978), vol. 2, p. 957.

[14] '*Loco publico*', 'in einer besonders dazu gewidmeten Stube'. GStAPK, HA II, Abt. 12 Pommern Materien, General Accise Sachen, Nr. 20a, folios 3–10.

taxpayers. In particular, delays at the gates were to be avoided. Officers who undertook controls in an arbitrary manner or for effect, or who treated taxpayers impolitely, were threatened with severe punishment. Employees who interacted in unacceptable ways with the taxpayers could be dismissed, but employees who were insulted by taxpayers while they were properly carrying out their duties were assured of adequate punishment of the offender. With these rules the monarch sought to ensure that the authority that he conferred on the tax officers was only used for implementation of their orders and rules.[15]

In many respects the system of routines, controls, and disciplinary measures that was deployed to produce loyal and efficient tax administrators resembled the techniques used in the military for similar purposes. The perception that loyalty and precision in the execution of orders were the principal skills required was also in part responsible for the practice of assigning veterans to the fiscal administration. They were used to routines and the precise execution of orders, and their loyalty was further increased by the lack of alternative employment.[16] The recruitment of former army officers was thus considered an ideal way to ensure the welfare of veterans and to supply the excise administration with officials who had proved their ability to leave their private identities behind and become loyal parts of the organs of state when on duty.

Central to the fiscal reforms of Frederick was thus the division between the sphere belonging to the state and that of individual privacy.[17] A distinction was drawn both between taxpayers and tax officials and between the private life and the official functions of individuals in the state's employ. It was acknowledged that an excise official was also a private individual, but when he wore his 'official hat' he ceased to be a private man, just as he reversed into a private individual when he left his office or when his office hours ended. Clarification of the boundaries between the individual private sphere and that of the state was crucial for increasing the administrative reach and effectiveness of the state. Just as war could only be waged successfully if soldiers executed orders with precision, setting aside any individual concerns, so Frederick believed that a sharp separation of fiscal officials from the public would lead to a more effective fiscal administration. However, the instructions also show an awareness of the dangers associated with this increased effectiveness and separation. Increasing the ability of tax officials to intrude and interfere with the private affairs of taxpayers was the purpose of the reform efforts but this ability also bore the danger of vexing and offending private individuals. The cautions and limitations that the administrative instructions included in this regard reflected the concerns that we have seen in official discourses about balancing

---

[15] GStAPK, HA II, Abt. 12 Pommern Materien, General Accise Sachen, Nr. 20a, folios 7, 11, 62.

[16] Frederick William I cited in Zschocke, *Akzisemauer*, p. 35. Edgar Kiser and Joachim Schneider, 'Bureaucracy and efficiency: an analysis of taxation in early modern Prussia', *American Sociological Review*, 59 (1994), pp. 187–204.

[17] I have discussed this aspect of the excise reform previously in Florian Schui, 'French figures of authority and state building in Prussia', in Peter Becker and Rüdiger von Krosigk, eds., *Figures of authority: contributions towards a cultural history of governance from 17th to 19th century* (Oxford, 2008), pp. 153–76.

private and public interests. While more effective intrusion and controls were considered to be legitimate and necessary in order to meet the financial needs of the state, it was clearly understood that a distinctly private sphere of urban individuals had developed and that any interference by the state constituted a transgression that had to be limited and contained in order to remain acceptable. However, no matter how much officials were aware of this problem and sought to avoid it, administrative reform, as it was envisaged, inevitably meant greater interference with private affairs and a higher financial burden on urban dwellers.

THE CREATION OF THE RÉGIE

After the Seven Years War, it became apparent that Frederick's attempts to make the excise administration a more efficient and loyal instrument of the Prussian state remained largely unsuccessful. The war had brought Prussia to the brink of financial collapse. New revenue needed to be raised, but foreign occupation and the war effort had placed considerable strain on Prussia's towns which had suffered occupation and looting. In this difficult climate, Frederick asked the leaders of his administration to explore ways of raising additional revenue for the state. In a remarkable move of open rebellion the officials refused to carry out the orders, deeming the new charges to be too onerous on the population.[18]

Frederick refused to compromise and decided to create a completely new excise administration to be staffed by foreigners. About 350 Frenchmen filled the higher ranks of the administration which was officially established in 1766 under the name of *Administration générale des accises et de péages* and which came to be popularly known as the Régie (see Fig. 4.2).[19]

The new institution was led by de Launay, who quickly became one of the most important officials of Frederick's reign. His biography remains sketchy but we know that he was part of the French tax administration in Languedoc as a *sous fermier* and that he was related to two families whose members had been among the *fermiers généraux*, the consortium of tax farmers that ran much of the French fiscal system for the crown. Mirabeau claimed that it was Claude Adrien Helvetius (1715–71), himself a tax farmer, who recruited de Launay and his associates for Frederick but the exact circumstance remains unclear.[20] De Launay's business ventures had earlier taken him to Germany where he had invested in a company that provided military hospitals for the French army in Germany during the Seven

---

[18] Walther Schultze, *Geschichte der preussischen Regieverwaltung von 1766 bis 1786, ein historisch-kritischer Versuch* (Leipzig, 1888), pp. 25–7. Heinrich von Beguelin, *Historisch kritische Darstellung der Accise- und Zollverfassung in den preussischen Staaten* (Berlin, 1797), p. 111. Honoré Gabriel Riquetti Comte de Mirabeau, *De la monarchie Prussienne, sous Frédéric le Grand: avec un appendice contenant des recherches sur la situation actuelle des principales contrées de l'Allemagne* (4 vols., Paris, 1788), vol. 4, p. 403.

[19] Schultze, *Regieverwaltung*, p. 46.

[20] For a more detailed discussion see Florian Schui 'Learning from French experience: the Prussian Régie tax administration, 1766–86', in Holger Nehring and Florian Schui, eds., *Global debates about taxation* (London, 2007), pp. 36–60.

Fig. 4.2. 'Die Einwanderung der Franzosen zur Errichtung der Regie' (The arrival of the French for the creation of the Régie), Daniel Nikolaus Chodowiecki, etching, 1771. Reproduced with permission from Klassik Stiftung Weimar, Museen, Inv. DK 293/84.

Years War.[21] The company failed and de Launay nonchalantly switched sides after the end of the war, becoming a loyal servant of the monarch whose armies he had helped to fight. In what is most likely the only surviving depiction of de Launay we see him with his family in his lodgings in Berlin with a prominently displayed painting of Frederick in the background.[22]

In some respects the recruitment of French officials was not an unusual step for, on many occasions, the Hohenzollern had employed foreigners with skills that could not be found in Prussia, and towns such as Berlin had a substantial French population.[23] Skilled immigrants may not have been new in Prussia, but it was a bold step to entrust an administration as sensitive as the excise to officials who were not members of local hierarchies. Despite Frederick's efforts, in some Prussian provinces all officials were still recruited from the ranks of local nobility.[24] By recruiting French officials, Frederick took an important step towards creating a loyal body of civil servants. The process of drawing a sharp distinction between the sphere of the state and the private spheres of taxpayers was expedited by their recruitment in a way that could not have been achieved by new administrative guidelines. The new excise administration was more professional and loyal than any of its predecessors. From a fiscal viewpoint these qualities made the institution a success story. Compared with the fiscal year 1765–6, annual gross revenues

---

[21] Marc Antoine de la Haye de Launay and others, *Mémoire à consulter et consultation pour le Sr. De la Haye de Launay, Conseiller Intime des Finances de Sa Majesté le Roi de Prusse, & Régisseuer Général de ses Droits; l'un des Associés dans l'Entreprise des Hôpitaux militaires des Armées Françoises en Allemagne, pendant les années 1758, 1759 & 1760. Contre les S.rs Ménage, Chardon, Fauveau & autres. Aussie Associes en la même Entreprise* (Paris, 1785).

[22] The painting is *Marc Antoine de la Haye de Launay im Kreis der Familie unter einem Portrait Friedrichs des Großen* by Heinrich Franke (oil on canvas, Berlin, 1774). It is in the collection of the Deutsches Historische Museum, Berlin.

[23] Frederick regarded the French fiscal system as one of the most sophisticated and well administered. In retrospect, his opinion may appear surprising, although it has to be remembered that administrative inefficiency was perhaps the least problematic aspect of the French system.

[24] Gustav von Schmoller, *Preußische Verfassungs-, Verwaltungs- und Finanzgeschichte* (Berlin, 1921), p. 144.

increased by between 7 and 57 per cent in the twenty years during which the Régie operated. The additional net revenue generated was equally large and contributed substantially to the increasing importance of indirect taxes in the Prussian budget.[25] (See Chapter 3, Fig. 3.1.) The latter were the Prussian state's fastest growing source of revenue and became the most important form of taxation in this period. Revenues from excise and customs accounted for 35 per cent of tax revenue in 1740; in 1786 this share had nearly doubled to 60 per cent. This was not as high as in Britain where customs and excises comprised more than 80 per cent of tax revenue, but it was higher than in France where they represented roughly half.[26] However, along with the dramatic increase in revenue from the excise one can also observe a disproportionate increase in the cost of collection associated with the excise. The rising marginal cost of collecting additional revenue through the Régie points to the political costs associated with the new tax administration. Every additional thaler extracted from Prussia's taxpayers required more controls and sanctions. The Régie could deliver the necessary pressure, and hence the additional revenue, but this ability to carry out the king's orders also created political problems, which ultimately led to the administration's abolition in the face of public pressure.

The new administration's immediate objective was to raise additional revenue by making the excise collection and administration more efficient, primarily by fighting smuggling and corruption. In practice this amounted to an increase of taxation in particular on the most smuggled goods, among them luxury goods such as coffee and sugar. But Frederick's intentions also extended to developing new excise tariffs. Among the principal changes was the abolition of most forms of grain excise, which was compensated by increased taxation of wine, beer, and meat intended to shift the tax burden towards wealthier consumers. In the case of meat a distinction was made between pork ('the common food of the poor') and

[25] Schultze, *Regieverwaltung*, pp. 140–1. Schultze's numbers need to be read with great caution for two reasons. First, it is impossible to distinguish to what extent fluctuations of revenue are attributable to the creation of the Régie. Changes in economic growth and patterns of trade and consumption had a significant impact. For example, harsh winters and wars disrupted trade significantly and consequently lowered certain types of fiscal revenues administered by the Régie. Second, the source of this statistical information is sketchy. See Schultze's comprehensive discussion of the sources at pp. 141–70 and 383–93. No attempt will be made here to critically re-evaluate Schultze's numbers for two reasons: first, it is even more difficult today to distil firm data from the sources than it was in Schultze's time because of the losses of archival material in the meantime. Second, and more importantly, the focus on the fiscal performance of the Régie has obscured rather than helped our understanding of the institution's failure. While we cannot know the numbers with precision, it is clear that a substantial increase of revenue occurred under the Régie. We therefore need to shed light on the paradox of an institution that failed despite the fact that it successfully fulfilled the task for which it was designed. The answer, it is suggested here, cannot be found in the account books of the Régie but in the way contemporaries perceived the institution.

[26] Mark Spoerer, 'The revenue structures of Brandenburg-Prussia, Saxony and Bavaria (fifteenth to nineteenth centuries): are they compatible with the Bonney-Ormrod Model?', in Simonetta Cavaciocchi, ed., *La fiscalità nell'economia european secc. XII–XVIII* (Florence, 2008), pp. 781–91, at p. 789. Eckart Schremmer, 'Taxation and public finance: Britain, France and Germany', in Peter Mathias and Sidney Pollard, eds., *The Cambridge economic history of Europe* (8 vols., Cambridge, 1966–89), vol. 8, pp. 315–494, at pp. 316, 326, 370, 415.

other types of meat. The former was free of the additional imposts while other meat was subject to an increased excise.[27] This shift in the tax burden reflected in part concerns with fiscal justice, but it was also a way to address the widespread concern that increasing food prices and resulting wage inflation could threaten urban economic growth.[28] In order to ensure that merchants did not use the excise reform as an opportunity to hide price increases the edict included a mechanism of price control that limited price increases to the amount of additional taxes.[29] Moreover, the important task of directing and promoting urban economic activity through protective tariffs and subsidies was, in large part, entrusted to the Régie. Protective tariffs and bans of certain imports were not new, but henceforth the Régie was to enforce such policies more effectively. The new administration also sought to change consumer habits for non-economic motives. As we have seen, many of the newly developing urban consumer habits were regarded with suspicion by officials and public commentators alike. Whilst the consumption of coffee, to-bacco, brandy, and other products helped to fill royal coffers, it was also associated with moral and health concerns.[30]

The Régie was also intended to gather and compile urgently needed information about the economic situation of Prussia's towns. As discussed, the lack of infor-mation hampered the ambitious paternalism of the Prussian state to no small extent. The limits of the state's knowledge were made clear to Frederick not only when his administration was unable to provide him with reliable population statistics. When he enquired about the consumption of coffee in his lands his administration was equally unable to answer his question.[31] One important task of the Régie was therefore to compile and report statistical information. Finally, among the tasks assigned to the Régie was also that of quality control. This was partly in order to prevent tax evasion by means of cutting and diluting products, and partly in order to protect consumers from the practices of fraudulent traders and merchants. In particular, the amounts of grain used to brew certain types of beer were stipulated and shops that sold brandy were subject to frequent controls.[32] Frederick thus pursued multiple objectives with the new administration. But while the objectives were diverse, the means to achieve them had one important

---

[27] 'Gewöhnliche Nahrung der Armen'. Frederick II, 'Vorläufiges Declarations-Patent wegen einer für sämtliche königliche preußische Provizien, wo bishero die Accise eingeführt gewesen, vom 1ten Juni 1766 an, allergnädigst gut gefundenen neuen Einrichtung der Accise- und Zoll-Sachen. De dato Berlin, den 14ten April 1766', *Novum Corpus Constitutionum Prussico-Brandenburgensium Praecipue Marchicarum (NCC)* (12 vols., Berlin, 1766), vol. 8, pp. 293-308, at 298. CO to Horst, 21 March 1766 in Rachel, *Handels-, Zoll- und Akzisepolitik*, p. 144.

[28] Frederick II, 'Essai sur les formes de gouvernement et sur les devoirs des souverains', in Johann D. E. Preuss, ed., *Oeuvres de Frederic le Grand* (30 vols., Berlin, 1848), vol. 9, pp. 221–40, at p. 234.

[29] Frederick II, 'Declarations-Patent', p. 301.

[30] See, for example, Frederick II cited in Marc Antoine de la Haye de Launay, *Justification du système d'économie politique et financière de Frédéric II., roi de Prusse: pour servir de réfutation à tout ce que M. le Comte de Mirabeau a hazardé à ce sujet dans son ouvrage de la monarchie prussienne* (n.p., 1789), pp. 57–9. Adrian Heinrich von Borcke, *Was ist für, und was ist gegen die General-Tabaks-Administration zu sagen* (n.p., 1786), pp. 7, 11.

[31] Schultze, *Regieverwaltung*, p. 28.

[32] Schultze, *Regieverwaltung*, pp. 193–5.

characteristic in common: greater interference with the ways in which urban Prussians produced and consumed goods. Paradoxically, the creation of the Régie resulted at the same time in better-defined boundaries between the spheres of the state and those of private individuals, and in more frequent and more intrusive transgressions of that boundary by the state.

TAXPAYER OPPOSITION

Although taxpayers' opposition to the new regime did not immediately take the form of public protest, from the onset the conflict contained elements of collaboration and collective resistance which must have included forms of public debate among taxpayers, although such debates are often difficult to reconstruct. Until the last moment, towns tried to avoid the creation of the new centralized administration. Merchants in the western town of Minden collectively offered to pay the excise revenue quarterly in advance if they were allowed to organize tax collection themselves.[33] Frederick initially replied that placing merchants in charge of the excise would be like 'setting a fox to keep the geese'.[34] Soon, however, he was forced to change his mind. The merchants in the commercially more developed western provinces of Kleve, Moers, and Mark vigorously resisted the increased interference with their businesses associated with the Régie. Already in the first months of its existence the Régie had to request military support to inspect the accounting books of local merchants in Krefeld. Faced with strong opposition and on the advice of his ministers Frederick grudgingly decided to abolish the Régie in the western provinces only a year after its introduction and to replace it with the payment of a fixed sum which was collected by local authorities without central state control. The Régie's early failure did not mean the end of fiscal conflicts there, but it set the western provinces on a different path of fiscal development from the rest of Prussia. For this reason, and also because fiscal conflicts in the western provinces have been studied elsewhere by Ingrid Mittenzwei, we concentrate on developments in the other Prussian provinces.[35] However, it is important to point out that ultimately the development in the western and eastern provinces was not fundamentally different. The conflicts that led to the failure of the Régie were similar in all parts of Prussia and the development in the western provinces was different from the rest of Prussia mainly in that urban dwellers prevailed more quickly. This outcome may in part be attributed to the greater prosperity and strength of the urban sector in these provinces, but at the same time early failure of the Régie in the west also reflects the lesser importance that the central state attributed to these distant and isolated provinces. Where attempts to abolish the Régie were not immediately

---

[33] Hagen, Immediatbericht, 28 Feb. 1766, in Rachel, *Handels-, Zoll- und Akzisepolitik*, p. 143.

[34] 'Den Wolf zum Schäfer bestellen'. CO to General Direktorium, 1 March 1766, in Rachel, *Handels-, Zoll- und Akzisepolitik*, p. 143.

[35] Ingrid Mittenzwei, *Preußen nach dem Siebenjährigen Krieg: Auseinandersetzungen zwischen Bürgertum und Staat um die Wirtschaftspolitik* (Berlin, 1979), pp. 51–70.

successful, urban taxpayers began to resist the new administration mainly through petitioning, smuggling, and violent attacks, as confirmed in reports of the Kammern (the administrative bodies in charge of the royal domains and other matters) to the king, and through his replies and the Régie's reactions.[36]

Discontent was mainly provoked by the new administrative procedures and the more rigorous enforcement of existing ones that resulted in delays and intrusive controls. The controls and administrative procedures for anyone entering a town could indeed be lengthy and vexatious. The first control occurred at the town gates. Travellers with small items of luggage were checked there and paid any dues immediately before continuing. Merchants and private individuals who carried greater volumes were escorted by a guard to the central packing and storage place, the *Packhof.* There a bookkeeper checked the waybill, noted the inspection on the papers, and entered the details in his register. There were then two different forms and procedures for goods remaining in the town and for those in transit. (For the sake of brevity we only describe the procedure for imports into the towns here.) With a form issued by the bookkeeper the excise payer now had to go to the *estimateur* (estimator) in order to have the value of his cargo assessed. These officials then filled in a form, registered the declared value in their own documents, and sent the taxpayer with the form back to the bookkeeper who entered the additional details in his register and noted this on the form. A new form was then issued which was to be taken to the *visitateur* (inspector) The goods were unpacked in a special location and inspected jointly by the *visitateur* and *estimateur.* Their exact value was now entered on the form and, depending on the type of cargo, the taxpayer now had to go to one or more of the four different cashier offices for beverages, meat, victuals, and other goods. There his payments were entered on the form, which then had to be taken back to the *estimateur* who entered the details into his register and signed the form. Finally, the owner could collect his goods by presenting the completed paperwork to the *visitateur.* Other processes applied to goods that were in transit or that were kept in the storage of the Régie for longer periods. Also, there was a separate procedure administered by the military for the control and registration of individuals entering a city, which had to be completed in addition to the excise process.[37] Even a description of the excise controls is lengthy and complicated, and in practice it was confusing and vexing, in particular for anyone who was

---

[36] Reports reflected taxpayers' mood, but were also instrumental in the power struggle between established branches of administration and the Régie. Conflicts over areas of competence and administrative hierarchies were as much at stake as the merchants' and consumers' concerns. The alliance of local administrations and taxpayers against the Régie was, however, not purely opportunistic. The Kammern and other local administrative bodies were often largely composed of members of local elites where loyalties lay more with private or local interests than with the king's. Frederick was well aware of this 'connection' and repeatedly warned the Kammern not to plead 'en faveur' of local merchants. The Kammern were to refrain altogether from commenting on matters about which they were unable to judge, but no royal rebuke could prevent local administrators and taxpayers from voicing criticism. Schmoller, *Preußische Verfassungs-, Verwaltungs- und Finanzgeschichte,* pp. 145–51. CO to Dachroeden, 17 July 1766; CO to Auer, 11 August 1766; CO to Horst, 3 January 1767; CO to Domhardt, 8 June 1767, all in Rachel, *Handels-, Zoll- und Akzisepolitik,* pp. 156, 180.

[37] Friedrich Nicolai, *Beschreibung der königlichen Residenzstädte Berlin und Potsdam und aller daselbst befindlicher Merkwürdigkeiten* (Berlin, 1779), pp. 293–5, 318–20.

not used to the workings of administrative machinery. This was not merely a short-term control of goods and individuals; for at least several hours both were entirely in the hands of excise officials who had taxpayers running back and forth across the *Packhof.* In addition, delays occurred frequently in times of increased traffic.

Unsurprisingly, the drudgery of the controls quickly became the subject of complaints. In a lengthy pro memoria, the *Kammerpräsident* of Königsberg described the various vexations in detail. He complained about the numerous new forms ('*Zettel*') that had been introduced by the administration and the multiplicity of registers and lists that were kept. Despite additional officers at the gates, many of those subject to excise controls in Königsberg had to wait long hours. During a recent fair some merchants had been kept waiting at the gates from 3 a.m. to midday. In particular, those with fresh produce had 'suffered very much'.[38] In addition to the 'running to and fro' necessary to complete all procedures, delays also resulted from more thorough searches and the application of seals to merchandise.[39] Goods were opened and unpacked according to the procedure just described, which led to further delays, intrusions, and vexations. In some cases, merchants had apparently preferred to return home rather than submit to the procedures.[40]

Elsewhere, wine merchants, brewers, and distillers in the towns complained about lengthy administrative procedures and daily visitations of their shops by Régie officials. The journal of an excise inspector in Glatz gives an insight into the frequency of such searches. In ten days in January 1778 the inspector and his officers carried out extraordinary searches at ten distilleries, two breweries, two mills, and a herring merchant.[41] Officials demanded the right to inspect books and inventories as well as physical access to the workshops where they interfered directly with production processes, frequently disrupting them. The majority of the many complaints from producers and merchants about the Régie concentrated on perceived drudgery, 'ill-treatments', 'despotism', and 'arbitrariness'.[42]

Besides producers and merchants, consumers and other private individuals were also subjected to intrusions. The vivid description by Johanna Schopenhauer

---

[38] 'Sehr gelitten'. Domhardt, Pro Memoria, 22 August 1766, in Rachel, *Handels-, Zoll- und Akzisepolitik,* p. 160.

[39] 'Vielfältigen Hin- und Herlaufens'. Report of Kriegsrat Gossler, September 1786, in Rachel, *Handels-, Zoll- und Akzisepolitik,* p. 172.

[40] CO an Horst, 27 June 1770, in Rachel, *Handels-, Zoll- und Akzisepolitik,* p. 227.

[41] 'Circulair Verfügungen der Regie bereffend das Zoll und Transitowesen (in frz Sprache). Bd. I 1768–1772', GStAPK, HA II, Gen.Akzise/Zolldept., A Titel XLVII, Sect. 1, Nr. 2, folio 35.

[42] 'Harte Verfahren', 'despotisch', 'willkürlich'. Relation der Königsberger Kammer, 6 Feb. 1767; Klagen der Ostpreußischen Kammer, Aug. 1767; CO to Hoym, 3 August 1770; Circular de General-Administration, 12 January 1779, all in Rachel, *Handels-, Zoll- und Akzisepolitik,* pp. 168, 182, 229, 273. Reports also frequently include warnings that commerce would inevitably suffer or be destroyed if the vexations and the increased tax burden did not cease; 'merchants and professionals ("professionisten") suffer extraordinarily', said one report. Domhardt, Pro Memoria, 22 August 1766; Relation der Königsberger Kammer, 6 Feb. 1767; Instruction, 2 March 1767; CO, 29 July 1767; General-Direktion and General-Administration, 17 January 1770, in Rachel, *Handels-, Zoll- und Akzisepolitik,* pp. 161, 168, 172, 174, 221.

(1766–1838)—daughter and wife of prominent Danzig merchants and mother of Arthur Schopenhauer—of the Régie's controls deserves to be quoted at length:

> Neither rented coaches and equipages nor wagoner's and peasant's coaches were spared detailed searches. Ladies and children sometimes had to alight from their coaches in a torrential downpour and wait patiently without a roof over their heads and under the scornful laughter of their tormentors until the latter had completed their slow inspection of even the most hidden spaces in the coach. After that, began the search of the individuals. . . . A type of light hoop skirt that was in fashion at the time which had roomy pockets of which the contents could not be seen easily from the outside was a major object of suspicion for the French riff-raff. No lady could refuse to empty her pockets in front of them if she did not want to expose herself to the most insulting treatment. . . . House searches which no one could refuse without exposing himself to the threat of a heavy punishment happened every day and coffee-snoopers . . . searched in courtyards, homes and kitchens for the smell of freshly roasted coffee which could only be bought ready-roasted within the Prussian borders.[43]

In particular, the intrusions into private homes and the interference with the consumption of coffee in this private setting was a source of resentment and earned the Régie officials their popular nickname of 'snoopers'.[44] The ritual coffee drinking at home was the apogee of bourgeois culture in Prussia and elsewhere in Europe, and the nickname given to the state's agents who disturbed it expressed all the indignation of righteous burghers at an intrusion into the intimacy of the home.

Schopenhauer also described another way in which the controls of the Régie intruded into the intimacy of bourgeois families in Danzig by disturbing the cherished annual ritual of the summer retreat or *villegiatura*. The families of the local patricians were in the habit of spending the warmer summer months in holiday homes outside the city. The arrival of the Régie meant that travel to and from the holiday homes was now perceived as a punishing expedition and suspended until a lump sum payment had been negotiated that allowed Danzig's burghers free access to their holiday homes.[45]

---

[43] 'Mietkutschen und Equipagen wurden ebensowenig als Fuhrmanns- und Bauernwagen mit genauester Durchsuchung verschont. Damen und Kinder mußten zuweilen im heftigsten Platzregen aus ihrem Wagen steigen und unter dem Hohngelächter ihrer Peiniger geduldig unter freiem Himmel es abwarten, bis es jenen gefiel, die Visitation auch der verborgensten kleinsten Räume im Wagen langsam zu vollenden. Dann began noch die Durchsuchung der Personen; die damals Mode [gewordene] . . . Art leichterer Reifröcke, die freilich aus sehr geräumigen Taschen bestanden, denen man ihren Inhalt von außen durchaus nicht ansehen konnte, waren dem französischen Gesindel ein Hauptgegenstand des Argwohns; keine Dame durfte sich weigern, ihre Poschen vor den Augen desselben auszuleeren, wenn sie nicht der beleidigendsten Behandlung sich aussetzen wollte. . . . Haussuchungen nach Kontrebande, denen niemand bei schwerer Strafe sich widersetzen durfte, fielen täglich vor, und Kaffeeriecher . . . spürten in Höfen, Häusern und Küchen dem Geruch des frischgebrannten Kaffee nach, der innerhalb der preußischen Grenze nicht anders als schon gebrannt verkauft werden durfte.' Johanna Schopenhauer, *Im Wechsel der Zeiten, im Gedränge der Welt* (Munich, 1986), p. 86. Danzig became part of Prussia only in 1793 but from 1772 the city had been surrounded by Prussian territory. Schopenhauer wrote her memoirs after the Prussian annexation of the city and the Napoleonic wars; changed attitudes towards Prussia and France may have affected her memories.

[44] 'Schniffler'. Mirabeau, *De la monarchie prussienne*, vol. 3, p. 310.

[45] Schopenhauer, *Wechsel der Zeiten*, pp. 86–90.

Frederick was well aware of the complaints about the Régie and the conflicts it had been causing since its inception, but at this stage he clearly did not expect public discontent to become a serious obstacle to his policies. In 1766 he joked in a poem to a clergyman:

> Leave to each his domain
>
> . . .
>
> To my Régisseurs généraux to steal from me
>
> . . .
>
> To my subjects the frivolous advantage
> Of complaining about customs
> (They are very wrong but in good faith)
> But if you wish to please me
> Shout from the height of your pulpit
> Christians, fear hell and pay the king![46]

Six years later, in 1772, the king noted with sorrow that complaints about the Régie had not subsided.[47] Undeterred, he vigorously defended the institution, insisting that although vexations had to be avoided, tighter controls were necessary to achieve 'my interests and those of the public'.[48] The king's steadfastness resulted in the increase in another form of resistance: reports about smuggling grew dramatically. This was partly because stricter controls revealed more illicit trade, and partly because controls and higher tariffs rendered smuggling more lucrative. Coffee and other luxury goods were among the most commonly smuggled wares. According to Mirabeau's estimates, Prussians consumed every year 4–5 million thaler worth of illicitly traded sugar and drank more than twice as much smuggled coffee than was legally acquired. Mirabeau suggested that the extent of tax evasion was such that certain tax revenues were reduced by half.[49] It is always difficult to gauge the extent of illegal economic activity and Mirabeau certainly had an interest in inflating his estimates in order to support his argument about the oppressive

---

[46] Laissez à chacun son domaine,

> . . .
>
> Laissez de me voler la peine
> A mes régisseurs généraux,
>
> . . .
>
> A mes sujets le frivole avantage
> De murmurer de leur péage;
> (Ils ont grand tort, en bonne foi.)
> Mais si vous cherchez à me plaire,
> Criez-leur du haut de la chaire:
> Voilà, chrétiens, l'enfer; payez le Roi!
> Et ne rimez jamais sur mon anniversaire.

Frederick II, 'Vers envoyés par Frédéric a un curé qui s'était avisé de célébrer le jour de sa naissance par une ode', in Johann D. E. Preuss, ed., *Oeuvres des Frédéric le Grand* (30 vols., Berlin, 1846–56), vol. 14, p. 170.

[47] CO, 16 June 1772, in Rachel, *Handels-, Zoll- und Akzisepolitik*, p. 250.

[48] 'Mes interests et ceux du Public.' CO, 19 June 1769, in Rachel, *Handels-, Zoll- und Akzisepolitik*, p. 216.

[49] Mirabeau, *De la monarchie prussienne*, vol. 3, pp. 295–305.

nature of the tax regime. Nonetheless, there was widespread agreement among commentators and officials that smuggling was rampant. This development was by no means a Prussian peculiarity. Attempts to fiscalize consumption led to similar results in Britain, where a 'vast world of pilfering and smuggling' developed, and in France which saw the rise of a 'vast web of illicit trade'.[50]

However, the ways in which smuggling was perceived by officials and consumers differed greatly, reflecting in many ways their different perspectives on the state's right to interfere with individual choices of consumption. Officials who regarded luxury goods as superfluous and high taxes on them as legitimate saw contraband merely as a form of disrespect for the law and consumers and smugglers as common criminals who deserved harsh punishment. The outlook of urban consumers was different. They often regarded the laws interfering with their consumption habits as illegitimate and consequently saw smugglers as 'martyrs'.[51] 'A smuggler', commented even the admirer of Frederick II, Christian Dohm (1751–1820), 'encounters sympathetic hearts everywhere.... One talks about amusing inventions to circumvent the excise and nobody thinks it wrong when they handle smuggled goods. Denouncing it to the authorities is even considered a disgrace among the people.'[52] The view that the trade in coffee and other luxury goods was fundamentally a legitimate activity that was criminalized by unjust laws was widely held at the time.[53] 'It is not the thing in itself that is evil', argued the citizen and historian of Breslau Samuel Benjamin Klose (1730–98) in 1783 in the *Berlinische Monatsschrift* with regard to smuggling, 'but our laws'.[54] Echoing widespread contemporary concerns Klose discussed the problem of contraband in terms of a dissonance between the state's policies and nature. Specifically, he considered high imposts to be not only obstacles to commerce but also to be in conflict with natural rights that government should respect. Arguing in the same vein Mirabeau described the increase in smuggling as one of the 'strange disorders' through which 'public opinion' ('opinion public') about the excise expressed itself, thus placing the blame for contraband squarely on the inappropriate fiscal structure while absolving the public and even adding political legitimacy to its attempts to evade the tax.[55]

---

[50] William Ashworth, *Customs and excise: trade, production and consumption in England, 1640–1845* (Oxford, 2003), p. 9. Michael Kwass, 'Court capitalism, illicit markets, and political legitimacy in eighteenth-century France: the salt and tobacco monopolies', in D. Coffman et al., eds., *Questioning 'credible commitment': rethinking the origins of financial capitalism* (Cambridge, forthcoming).

[51] Beguelin, *Accise- und Zollverfassung*, p. 135.

[52] 'Ein Accisebetrüger trifft überall sympathisierende Herzen an.... Man erzählt mit wohlgefallen lustige Erfindungen, durch welche die Akzise betrogen wurde, und niemand glaubt Unrecht zu thun, wenn er Kontrebande verhehlen hilft. Sie zu verrathen, wird unter dem Volk sogar für Schande gehalten.' Christian Dohm, 'Ueber die Kaffeegesetzgebung', *Deutsches Museum*, 2 (1777), pp. 123–45, at p. 129.

[53] For another example of the explosive implications of shortages of 'luxury goods' in the eighteenth century, see Colin Jones and Rebecca Spang, 'Sans-culottes, sans café, sans tabac: shifting realms of necessity in luxury in eighteenth-century France', in M. Berg and H. Clifford, eds., *Consumers and luxury. Consumer culture in Europe, 1650–1850* (Manchester, 1999), 37–62.

[54] 'Die Sache ist an sich nicht böse nur unsere Gesetze sind es'. Samuel Benjamin Klose, 'Bemerkungen auf einer Reise durch die Lausitz und Sachsen', *Berlinische Monatsschrift*, 1 (1783), pp. 115–52, at p. 117.

[55] Mirabeau, *De la monarchie prussienne*, vol. 4, p. 142.

Similar defences of contraband were common elsewhere in Europe. Most prominently it was Smith who, in the *Wealth of nations*, placed the blame on the unjust laws regulating commerce rather than on the smugglers. However, in 1776 his views were merely echoing what had become a received view among public commentators and political economists across Europe.[56]

The radically different outlooks on whether smuggling was mere criminality or an assertion of 'natural rights' against a misguided and oppressive government contributed to escalating the conflict, eventually leading to violent episodes. As controls and punishments successively increased in reaction to the high volume of contraband, complaints about ill-treatment by Régie officials also rose, together with more violent incidents. By 1776 Frederick observed that smugglers were becoming bolder and even dared to fire at royal hussars.[57] Cases of violent resistance against the Régie, such as that of Berlin victualler Schulze who shot an official, were not isolated. Harsh punishments meted out—Schulze was to be broken on the wheel—escalated the conflict further.[58] Violent resistance also assumed collective forms. Smugglers might 'band together' and violently threaten excise officers, while confrontations with the Régie led to 'riots' among the urban population.[59] Schopenhauer gives this description of a lynching of Régie officials in Danzig:

> The two vile creatures . . . were instantly surrounded by an angry mob. Roaring like waves lashed by the storm more people were arriving from all sides; armed with stones and sticks thousands of menacing fists were raised, under wild threats and curses the death sentence of the two hated creatures was pronounced. Only immediate flight could save them. Bleeding from many wounds the faster of the two saved himself in the guard house. . . . In the meantime his comrade—under a hailstorm of stones—was driven through half of the city's streets and alleys like a deer hunted by a couple of dogs. . . . Shouting and howling in fear of death, covered with blood and with the remains of his torn clothes I saw the pitiful presence with the raging mob behind him chase past our house. He fell from exhaustion but rose quickly enough and only in the next street the fate which he sought to escape caught up with him.[60]

---

[56] Ashworth, *Customs and excise*, p. 165. Kwass, 'Court capitalism', pp. 14–21.

[57] CO, 18 March 1776, in Rachel, *Handels-, Zoll- und Akzisepolitik*, p. 266.

[58] CO, 22 March 1784, in Rachel, *Handels-, Zoll- und Akzisepolitik*, p. 306.

[59] 'Aufruhr', 'Zusammenrottirens der Contrabandiers'. CO, 27 February 1768; CO, 18 January 1784, in Rachel, *Handels-, Zoll- und Akzisepolitik*, pp. 195, 305. In such instances the Régie could not always count on the loyalty of other organs of the state. In more than one case, soldiers and officers sided with the 'contrebandiers' and even arrested tax officials. CO, 2 October 1767; CO 15 June 1771, in Rachel, *Handels-, Zoll- und Akzisepolitik*, pp. 182, 235. For a discussion of other cases of collective and violent resistance against the state in early modern Germany, see the discussion of conflicts over military drafts and soldiers' pay in Peter Wilson, *War, state and society in Württemberg, 1677–1798* (Cambridge, 1995).

[60] 'Zwei dieser Elenden . . . waren im Nu vom wüthenden Pöbel umringt. Brüllend wie die vom Sturm gepeitschten Meereswogen strömte von allen Seiten das Volk herbei; mit Pflastersteinen und Stöcken bewaffnet, erhoben sich tausend drohende Fäuste, unter wilden Flüchen und Schmähungen erscholl aus tausend Kehlen das Todesurtheil der verhaßten. Nur schleunige Flucht konnte sie retten. Aus vielen Wunden blutend gelang es endlich dem Leichtfüßigsten unter den Beiden, sich in die Hauptwache zu werfen, wo seine Verfolger von ihm abließen. Wie ein gehetzter von einer Koppel Hunde gejagter Hirsch wurde indessen sein Begleiter durch die halbe Stadt, durch Gassen und Gäßchen im angestrengtesten Lauf unter einem Hagel von Steinwürfen erbarmungslos fortgetrieben;

Again, such events were not peculiarly Prussian. Verbal defences of smugglers went hand in hand with more physical ways of preventing the persecution of illicit traders in Britain also, where brutal attacks on customs officers were not uncommon, and in France, where smugglers like Louis Mandrin acquired the status of popular heroes.[61]

Rioting, smuggling, and petition writing were probably associated with elements of oral debate, which are now impossible to reconstruct. Long-distance trade and smuggling networks may have created greater pan-Prussian connections but, at this stage, opposition remained ultimately regionally fragmented and drew on a rudimentary public. Even a fragmented public nevertheless constituted a substantial challenge to royal authority associated with direct and violent attacks on state representatives and intended to limit the state's ability to act. Seen from the state's perspective the additional revenue raised by the Régie thus came at a high price because unrest—irrespective of the form it took—was perceived to be dangerous by the weak states of the period. The state was also challenged by such developments on another level. While Frederick rejected 'comments' on his fiscal policies by anyone 'not appointed to be a judge' in such matters, his view that these policies protected 'my interests and those of the public' was questioned by the acts of rioters, smugglers, and petitioners who implicitly claimed to know their own interests better than the state.[62] Likewise, those purchasing contraband challenged the state's attempts to determine what they should consume. Hence, the state's authority to take or influence decisions in matters of commerce, production, and consumption was challenged through various forms of anti-excise resistance.

THE POWER OF THE WRITTEN WORD

A Prussian, and even European, network of public debates developed only gradually from these local conflicts. The rich source material bequeathed by the philosopher and tax official Hamann supplies an insight into the connection between personal experience and public reasoning in this context. Hamann was well known to a Prussian and European public despite living in peripheral Königsberg. He was also, however, notoriously short of money and it was thus that the 'veteran of Apollo' eventually accepted a position as a customs official with the

---

nur die mit jedem Schritt sich mehrende Anzahl seiner Verfolger, die endlich in den engen Straßen eine dicht zusammengedrängte Masse bildeten, verhinderte sie ihn zu ergreifen. Brüllend, heulend vor Todesangst und Schmerz, mit Blut bedeckt, die Ueberreste seiner Kleider in Fetzen um ihn herumflatternd, sah ich das Jammerbild, ganz nahe hinter ihm drein der tobende Haufen, an unserm Hause vorüberjagen; er stürzte vor Entkräftung, raffte sich aber schnell genug wieder auf, und erst in der nächsten Straße ereilte ihn endlich das Schicksal, dem er vergeblich zu entfliehen strebte.' Schopenhauer, *Wechsel der Zeiten*, pp. 100–2.

[61] Ashworth, *Customs and excise*, pp. 165–6. Kwass, 'Court capitalism', p. 14.

[62] 'Remarques', 'als worüber Ihr und die Kammern nicht zu Richtern bestellet seid'. CO, 17 July 1766, in Rachel, *Handels-, Zoll- und Akzisepolitik*, p. 156. CO 19 June 1769, in Rachel, *Handels-, Zoll- und Akzisepolitik*, p. 216.

Régie in 1767.[63] Hamann's mentor Kant had been instrumental in securing the post. Despite initial reluctance, Hamann pursued his administrative career with considerable energy and success, and rose from translator to 'Licent Pack Hofmeister', a position where he was in charge of the local *Packhof* and several officials.[64] Paradoxically, Hamann became simultaneously one of the most vocal critics of the excise administration. His criticism was informed by first-hand experience, as well as by a long-standing interest in political economy and a critical stance towards Frederick II's modernizing state.

From 1767, much of Hamann's correspondence with Johann Gottfried Herder (1744–1803), Friedrich Hartknoch (1740–89), Nicolai, and other members of the Prussian intelligentsia became a running and often harshly critical commentary on the Régie.[65] In his letters, fellow administrators were described as 'thieves', 'bastards', and 'vagabonds'; his employer and king was described ironically as 'Salomon'.[66] Initially, Hamann's letters were primarily concerned with his own interests and career within the Régie. For example, he spent much time quarrelling with his employer as to whether a certain type of payments made by merchants to officials in Hamann's position was a 'royal or a private revenue'.[67] Very quickly, however, such concerns to delineate Hamann the private individual from Hamann the royal tax official merged with a broader critique of the Régie's political and commercial implications. Hamann accused the Régie of oppressing the people's initiative to 'wheel and deal' and even of robbing Prussians of their 'will to live'.[68] Royal efforts to end corruption in the Régie were hypocritical since the whole administration had been created to steal for the king.[69] Consequently, commerce in Königsberg was 'consumptive' and 'on its last legs', whilst the Régie was as popular with the people as 'Moses' horns'.[70] This allegory doubtless supplied an ironic comment on Prussia's enlightened government: according to some Bible translations Moses had acquired the 'horns', which frightened the Israelites, after he had received the

---

[63] 'Invalides des Apolls'. Johann Georg Hamann to Friedrich Carl von Moser, 11 September 1763, in Johann Georg Hamann, *Briefwechsel*, eds. Walther Ziesemer and Arthur Henkel (7 vols., Wiesbaden, 1955), vol. 3, p. 19.

[64] Arthur Henkel, 'Vorwort', in Hamann, *Briefwechsel*, vol., 6, pp. 1–14, at p. 12.

[65] On the importance of networks of correspondence for contemporary debate in Germany see Hans Bödeker, 'Lessings Briefwechsel', in Hans Bödeker and Ulrich Herrmann, eds., *Über den Prozess der Aufklärung in Deutschland im 18. Jahrhundert* (Göttingen, 1987), pp. 113–38.

[66] 'Dieb', 'Lumpenhundes', 'vagabonds', 'Salomo'. Hamann to Johann Friedrich Reichardt, 2 January 1778, in Hamann, *Briefwechsel*, vol. 4, p. 2. Hamann to Johann Friedrich Reichardt, 11 November 1782, in Hamann, *Briefwechsel*, vol. 4, p. 448.

[67] 'Eine königl. oder Privat Einnahme'. Hamann to Johann Friedrich Hartknoch, 12 November 1782, in Hamann, *Briefwechsel*, vol. 4, p. 450.

[68] 'Die Lust zu leben, geschweige zu handeln und zu wandeln'. Hamann to Johann Friedrich Reichardt, 1777 (probably March), in Hamann, *Briefwechsel*, vol. 3, p. 356.

[69] Hamann to Johann Friedrich Reichardt, 11 November 1782, in Hamann, *Briefwechsel*, vol. 3, p. 447.

[70] 'Des schwindsüchtigen, in letzten Zügen liegenden Handels'. 'Moses Hörner'. Hamann to Johann Gottfried von Herder, 12 April 1780, in Hamann, *Briefwechsel*, vol. 4, p. 183. Hamann to Johann Friedrich Reichardt, 1777 (probably March), in Hamann, *Briefwechsel*, vol. 3, p. 356. In some versions, Exodus 36:29. Hamann to Johann Friedrich Reichardt, 1777 (probably March), in Hamann, *Briefwechsel*, vol. 3, p. 356.

divine law during his encounter with God on Mount Sinai. According to Hamann Prussians were equally afraid of encounters with the Régie because the administration was one of the excesses of a state that considered itself in possession of absolute enlightened truth.

As Hamann's frustration with the Régie increased, he started to articulate it to a larger public, although his first attempt at publishing a short piece entitled *To the Salomon of Prussia* failed in 1772. Initially he could not find a publisher and subsequently his friend Herder prevented publication of the text, presumably fearing that Hamann might be taking too great a risk by attacking the king and the 'political arithmeticians' of his tax administration.[71] Curiously, however, it was an official request, perhaps from within the administration, to comment on Guillaume Raynal's (1713–96) *History of the two Indies* (1770) that facilitated Hamann's most comprehensive public criticism.[72] In the two editions of *To a financier in Pe-Kim* (1773), Hamann merged theoretical criticism of Raynal's work with attacks on Prussian fiscal practice.[73] Hamann attacked Raynal as one of the 'ragoutistes de l'Encyclopédie' who were exercising excessive influence on Frederick's government. He feared this 'most modern of enthusiasts for humanity' and his associates who armed governments with coolly rational, radical, and allegedly universal truths.[74] Ensuing modernizing reforms replaced moral responsibilities of government with 'political arithmetic' and threatened to eclipse traditional customs and livelihoods and individual religiosity and morals.[75] Hamann gloomily predicted that 'this is only the dawn of an aurora that is the sign of a golden age when the Fredericks d'Or will shine brighter than the stars of the most brilliant winter night'.[76] Previously Hamann had warned that governments excessively concerned with finance thereby neglected ethics as the core of the art of governance.[77] For Hamann, the Régie was the concrete expression of this modern obsession with finance. He blamed 'languishing' commerce and the prospect of an epidemic of 'mortalité mercantile' on the government's fiscal modernization, warning that commerce, if subjected to excessive pressure, would suddenly break and hurt the 'hand that oppresses it'.[78] Faced with this type of enlightened reform,

[71] 'Arithmeticiens politiques'. Johann Georg Hamann, 'Au Salomon de Prusse', in Josef Nadler, ed., *Sämtliche Werke/Johann Georg Hamann* (6 vols., Vienna, 1951), vol. 3, pp. 60, 423.

[72] Hamann's notes refer to the following edition: Guillaume Thomas François Raynal, *Histoire philosophique et politique, des établissemens & du commerce des Européens dans les deux Indes* (6 vols., Amsterdam, 1772).

[73] The 'financier de Pe-Kim' of the title is the high-ranking excise official de Lattre who, needless to say, was not in Beijing but in Berlin. See the editorial notes in Johann Georg Hamann, 'Lettre à un financier de Pe-Kim', in Josef Nadler, ed., *Sämtliche Werke/Johann Georg Hamann* (6 vols., Vienna, 1951), vol. 3, pp. 299–305.

[74] 'L'enthousiaste le plus moderne de l'humanité'. Hamann, 'Financier', p. 302.

[75] 'Arithmetique politique'. Hamann, 'Salomon', pp. 60, 423.

[76] 'Ce n'est que le crépuscule d'une aurore boréale, messagère du Siècle d'or, où les Fredrics d'or défieront le numeraire de la plus brillante nuit d'hiver.' Hamann, 'Financier', p. 303.

[77] Hamann to Baron von W., 22 September 1958, Johann Georg Hamann, *Schriften*, ed. Friedrich Roth (8 vols, Berlin, 1821–43), vol. 1, p. 304.

[78] ' "Dechire la main qui le comprime" '. Hamann uses a modified citation from Raynal to express his views. Hamann, 'Financier', p. 303.

Hamann wrote, the 'Prussian eskimos' petitioned their king to introduce the Jesuits to exterminate such 'modern paganism' to save the kingdom's 'fabrics' and 'commerce'.[79]

Although Hamann was not the only critic to express his concerns in print his case stands out in several respects. His writings reveal how individual frustration with fiscal practice led to the articulation of public criticism in letters and pamphlets that extended beyond the local. Hamann told a Prussian, German, and potentially a European public about his grievances. His commentary was in every respect part of a broader continental debate about political economy. Hamann's reply to Raynal was not only informed by personal experience, but also confirmed him as an avid reader of contemporary financial and political literature. He even tried to obtain a copy of Jean-Louis Moreau de Beaumont's (1715–85) survey of European fiscal systems, which was a much-coveted work since it contained the most comprehensive and reliable information about the subject.[80] Pondering fiscal questions in another northern commercial hub in the same period, Smith used a copy of Beaumont, sent to him by Anne Robert Jacques Turgot (1727–81), as the main source for the chapters on taxation in his *Wealth of nations*.[81] To support his argument against the imported French political arithmetic Hamann also translated substantial parts of Ferdinando Galiani's (1728–87) *Discourse on the commerce of grain* (1770) and published extracts in a local paper.[82] While Hamann's criticism of the Régie was rooted in local experience, his comments thus formed part of a politicized and reform-minded European public.

Hamman's criticism was clearly public and politicized but was it part of a *bourgeois* public sphere? He was, by birth, part of the Königsberg middle class since his father was a barber-surgeon, and his later career was typical in confirming how the state's employ was often the only possible option for young educated bourgeois.[83] Hamann's experience casts doubts on the view that the state employment of many public commentators meant that the Prussian public was a state-led affair. Paradoxically, Hamann put considerable distance between himself and his employer when writing, but identified with the state when inspecting merchants. He was thus a loyal civil servant when he refused a merchant's bribe in the morning and a critically minded member of the public sphere when writing his pamphlets in

---

[79] 'Tous les Esquimaux de la Prusse', 'paganisme moderne', 'fabriques', 'Commerce'. Hamann, 'Financier', pp. 304–5.

[80] Jean-Louis Moreau de Beaumont, *Mémoires concernant les impositions et droits en Europe* (Paris, 1768).

[81] Florian Schui, 'Observing the neighbours: fiscal reform and transnational debates in France after the Seven Years' War', in Gabriel Paquette, ed., *Enlightened reform in southern Europe and its Atlantic colonies, c. 1750–1830* (Farnham, 2009), pp. 271–86.

[82] Johann Georg Hamann, 'Beylage zum 77., 78., 80., 87. Stück, 25, 28 Sept. and 5, 30 Oct. 1775' (Hamann's translation of excerpts from *Discours sur le commerce des bleds*), in Josef Nadler, ed., *Sämtliche Werke/Johann Georg Hamann* (6 vols., Vienna, 1952), vol. 4, pp. 389–404.

[83] Rudolf Vierhaus, 'Die aufgeklärten Schriftsteller. Zur sozialen Charakteristik einer selbsternannten Elite', in Hans Erich Bödecker and Ulrich Herrmann, eds., *Über den Prozess der Aufklärung in Deutschland im 18. Jahrhundert* (Göttingen, 1987), pp. 53–65, at p. 60.

the evening.[84] Hamman was certainly not a cynic and he was certainly not the only contemporary example of a customs officer who publicly criticized the institution that he served. Generations of scholars of economic thought have tried to come to grips with the fact that Smith was not only a lucid critic of British mercantilism but also a loyal and motivated employee of the Scottish customs service who was responsible for carrying out many of the policies that he attacked.[85] The 'double lives' of Hamann and Smith reflected the separation of private individual and state official that both the manuals of the Prussian administration and the ethos of the bourgeois public demanded. Excise officers were drilled to keep their private lives separate from their roles as public officials. In the same vein, members of the Republic of Letters and of Enlightenment societies were invited to leave worldly rank, hierarchy, and profession behind and to encounter each other as private men in the public sphere.

In the self-perception of members of this public, it was not hypocritical to act in one way as an official and to think in another as a citizen. Kant used the terms 'private use of reason' and 'public use of reason' to clarify this distinction. The 'public use of reason', which must, for Kant, remain completely free was the use that a 'learned person' made 'before the reading public'. By contrast, the 'private use of reason' occurred in the context of 'a civic post or office'. 'Here', Kant continued, 'one certainly must not argue, instead one must obey' because the individual was part of a 'machine' which would not function with independently minded parts. It was, however, perfectly possible for the same person to make use of his or her reason in private and in public in different ways without contradiction: 'It would be disastrous if an officer on duty who was given a command by his superior were to question the appropriateness or utility of the order. He must obey. But as a scholar he cannot be justly constrained from making comments about errors in military service.' Applied to matters of taxation, this meant that 'the citizen cannot refuse to pay the taxes imposed on him' but 'the same person does not act contrary to civic duty when, as a scholar, he publicly expresses his thoughts regarding the impropriety or even injustice of such taxes'.[86] As seen, Kant underestimated the extent to which limits between public reasoning and civic disobedience were blurred. Nevertheless, it is anachronistic to regard state employment of public commentators as an indication of a significant role of the state's hand in the process of the development of public debates. For Kant and his contemporaries, Hamann's situation was not only rather common, but also not deemed to imply any limits on the independent use of reason in a public context.[87]

---

[84] Hamann to Johann Friedrich Reichardt, 1777 (probably March), in Hamann, *Briefwechsel*, vol. 3, p. 356.

[85] Gary Anderson, William Shughart II, Robert Tollison, 'Adam Smith in the customhouse', *Journal of Political Economy*, 93 (1985), pp. 740–59.

[86] Note that Kant uses the term 'bürgerlicher Posten, oder Amt' in the original; evidently the holding of a public office did not exclude 'Bürgerlichkeit' in his view. Immanuel Kant, 'What is Enlightenment?', in Lewis White Beck, ed., *Foundations of the metaphysics of morals* (Chicago, 1950), pp. 286–92, at pp. 287–9.

[87] On the same issue see Michael Sauter, 'The enlightenment on trial: state service and social discipline in eighteenth-century Germany's public sphere', *Modern Intellectual History*, 5 (2008),

Just as the public sphere was not state-led because of the state employment of some authors, so it was not primarily bourgeois because of the way in which such authors derived their livelihoods. Despite his social origin, Hamann was not a bourgeois in the narrow sense of someone mainly engaged in commercial activity through ownership of capital, although he—like most urban Prussians—was still part of the commercial sphere as a consumer and as someone who made a living partly from selling his articles and books. However, the conflicts on which he commented would not have arisen had it not been for the development of a private bourgeois sphere of 'wheeling and dealing' which found itself in conflict with the interference of an overreaching state that armed itself with the universal truths of an age of enlightenment.

By the early 1780s, not only men of letters, merchants, artisans, and consumers had begun to oppose the Régie, but even Frederick II was increasingly frustrated with the institution. This is all the more remarkable because the king categorically rejected all criticism of his fiscal policies from within the administration. One of the earliest and most striking examples of his unwillingness to put up with internal opposition was certainly the case of the official Erhard Ursinus, whose criticism of Frederick's economic and fiscal policies in the wake of the Seven Years War landed him in prison for a year.[88] Subsequently critiques of the Régie from subordinate administrators were normally countered by the monarch with orders to refrain from all commentary on matters that were none of their business.[89] Nonetheless by the 1780s the king himself had become preoccupied with the rampant contraband, which reduced fiscal revenue and rendered protective tariffs ineffective.[90]

Paradoxically, the disaffection of the monarch was in part the result of the successes of the Régie in fulfilling the tasks assigned to it. Among other developments, the tighter controls contributed to the 'making' of smugglers because tax evasion became more lucrative and the likelihood of being caught increased. At the same time, the systematic and centralized collection of statistical information begun by the Régie meant that Frederick had a much more complete picture about the economic situation in the towns of his realm. This had been one of the principal tasks of the Régie since the beginning and some news received in this way was positive. In 1772 de Launay presented the king with a comprehensive report about different forms of excise revenues from the different provinces. De Launay also reported directly about the volumes and types of trade in specific provinces and the whole country. Before the Régie started to procure this kind of information, he later recalled, the king did not know how much the nation's 'industry and commerce' produced every year.[91] The Régie also informed the king about commerce in specific cities. The fair at Frankfurt on Oder, for example, was one of the most

pp. 195–223. Ian Hunter, 'The history of philosophy and the persona of the philosopher', *Modern Intellectual History*, 4 (2007), pp. 571–600.

[88] Mittenzwei, *Preußen*, pp. 39–50.
[89] CO to Domhardt, 8 Juni 1767, in Rachel, *Handels-, Zoll- und Akzisepolitik*, p. 180.
[90] CO to de Launay, 30 March 1783, in Rachel, *Handels-, Zoll- und Akzisepolitik*, p. 296.
[91] 'L'industrie & commerce national'. De Launay, *Justification*, p. 36.

important commercial hubs in Prussia but, as in many other matters, the king only had a rudimentary notion of the volume and nature of trade there. After establishing more effective controls and surveys de Launay reported that the turnover was much higher than the estimated 600,000 ecus and that it amounted to a total of over 5 million ecus. The king was also informed about the principal products traded and about the share of commerce that was made up from imports, exports, and domestic trade.[92] In part the king was undoubtedly pleased that the previous estimates of the volume of trade were too low by a factor of nine. However, the finding that commerce was in fact much greater than had been assumed also shone a new light on tax receipts and hence on the volume of smuggling. Moreover, the Régie did not only catch more contrabandists but it also compiled information about them more thoroughly and systematically. Frederick may have been keen to get to know his realm but not everything that he learned about it pleased him. Just as the Régie's greater effectiveness in collecting taxes made it unpopular with taxpayers, so its superior system of collecting and reporting information contributed to undermining its position with the king.

As we have seen, Frederick did not interpret the widespread contraband as implying the public's verdict on the institution. For the monarch, the problem of the Régie was not a lack of legitimacy, but of loyalty and honesty on the part of many officials. In particular his opinion of the French administrators had changed dramatically.[93] In the early 1780s, responding to a request from an official to leave Prussia for a visit to France the king gave permission, adding: 'There is no need for him to return because we do not need him here. He is like most of these Frenchmen: . . . they come here, obtain leading positions in the Régie, plunder the provinces and when they have made their profit they return to France.' In the future, he instructed de Launay: 'I no longer want you to employ Frenchmen in such positions but good officers [Quartiers Maitres] of our regiments who could work some time at the Régie in order to learn the skills required before their appointments.'[94]

These comments of the king represent one of the rare instances where the problems of the Régie were conceptualized in terms of nationality by contemporaries. Hardly any of the other public or privately made comments on the Régie from this period associated the problems of legitimacy with the fact that the fiscal administrators were foreigners. There were instances where authors like Gedike expressed concerns about the immigration of foreigners to Prussian cities and the number of foreign officials that were present in all provinces. In particular he

---

[92] De Launay, *Justification*, pp. 34–44.

[93] Schultze, *Regieverwaltung*, pp. 105–28.

[94] 'Il peut rester où il voudra, étant inutile qu'il revienne, puisque nous n'avons pas besoin de lui. C'est ainsi que sont la plupart des ces François: . . . ils débarquent ici, obtiennent les premieres places dans la Regie, pillent les provinces, et quand ils on fait leur bourse, ils retournent en France. Je ne veux plus par consequent que vous preniez de François pour des places pareilles, mais de bons Quartiers Maitres de nos Regimens, qui avant d'etre places pourront travailler quelque temps à la Regie pour s'instruire et se mettre au fait de l'employ qui leur sera destiné'. CO to de Launay, 28 February 1783, in Rachel, *Handels-, Zoll- und Akzisepolitik*, pp. 292–3.

singled out the Académie and the Régie as institutions that were likely to tarnish the gratitude of Berliners for the positive things brought to the city by French immigrants.[95] However, unlike in the king's comments, there were no suggestions in Gedike's writings that a replacement of French officials with Prussians could have solved the problems associated with the institution. Even Mirabeau, who later criticized the Régie in much more outspoken terms and openly attacked his countrymen in the Régie, did not make the issue of nationality a focus of his critique. In his view nothing short of the abolition of the tax could solve these problems, certainly not a change of personnel. The issue of nationalism was emphasized much more strongly by authors who wrote about the conflict after it had ended. Heinrich von Beguelin (1765–1818), who occupied a leading role in the excise administration after the abolition of the Régie, included the fact that the institution employed 'foreigners who could never be nationalized and who did not even bother to learn German' among the causes of its failure.[96] Nonetheless he saw this only as one of many causes that also included the oppressive tax burden and the vexatious methods of collection. It was only in the late nineteenth century that historians began to see national identities as the principal cause of the Régie's failure.[97] Those directly involved in the conflict over the Régie were mostly oblivious to the issue of nationalism and mainly took issue with the nature of the tax and the methods of collection. This lack of a significant nationalistic element in the debate (at least to the extent that we can reconstruct it) may be surprising. The recruitment of officials from among their own nationals is a central part of the identity of modern national states and today one would certainly expect strong resistance to the suggestion that the higher ranks of the tax administration in Germany or elsewhere should be filled with foreigners, quite independently of the fiscal agenda that they might be pursuing. However, the world that urban dwellers of eighteenth-century Prussia inhabited was not that of modern national states. Loyalties and identities were still local to a large extent and it was only in this period that a sense of unity among the Prussian provinces began to emerge. As we have seen, the spirits of nations formed by geography and nature were important parts of political considerations, but in a territory as fragmented and spread out as that of Prussia, regional spirits were often considered to be as heterogeneous as those of territories that belonged to different rulers. Moreover, the status of some Prussian territories as part of the empire further complicated the formation of shared identities. The common and victorious experience of the Seven Years War, the strong persona of the monarch, and the administrative reforms discussed here did much to foster a common Prussian identity, but at the same time Prussians were also used to a strong tradition of both civilian and military immigration in the towns. Also, cultural and economic influences from abroad, in particular from

---

[95] Friedrich Gedike, 'Ueber Berlin, von einem Fremden (Briefe 1–3)', *Berlinische Monatsschrift*, 1 (1783), pp. 439–65, at pp. 455–6.

[96] 'Fremde, die nie nationalisiert werden konnten und die sich nicht einmal die Mühe gaben Deutsche zu lernen'. Heinrich von Beguelin, *Historisch kritische Darstellung der Accise- und Zollverfassung in den preussischen Staaten* (Berlin, 1797), p. 162.

[97] Schultze, *Regieverwaltung*, pp. 105–27.

France, were significant and generally seen in a positive light. Finally, it should also be remembered that in the case of the Régie most of the daily interaction that Prussians had was with Prussian officials. Only the leading officials of the Régie were French and the fact that they were foreigners remained largely inconsequential for most taxpayers. Only the king and higher-ranking administrators had direct contact with the French officials. Together with the fact that the notion of a national identity was not diffused among ordinary Prussians at the time, the comparably high ranks of the French immigrants contributed to limit the importance of nationalities in this context to an elite audience of administrators and commentators.

In the years before Frederick's death in 1786, we can thus observe a growing disaffection with the Régie that extended not only to taxpayers, administrators, and men of letters, but also to the king himself. However, the different actors thought about the nature and causes of these problems in very different terms. For the king the problem was mainly one of disloyalty and incompetent officials, and he introduced certain reforms to ensure a more effective execution of his orders.[98] With these measures, the king continued to pursue an objective central to his fiscal policy since the beginning of his reign: the creation of a loyal and professional administration. The changes did little, however, to solve the contraband and other problems of the Régie. From the perspective of many taxpayers the real problem was not officials who could be convinced with a small bribe to bend the rules, but rather those who followed instructions to the letter. As Hamann had pointed out, the problem was not that some officers stole but that an institution had been set up to steal for the king. We can only speculate, however, as to whether Frederick's growing frustration with aspects of the Régie would eventually have led him to abolish the whole institution, or where his steadfastness in the face of growing public discontent may have led.

THE FALL OF THE RÉGIE

After Frederick's death, the conflict over the Régie inspired a rapidly increasing quantity of printed declarations, pamphlets, and multi-volume treatises that started to influence political change in fiscal matters. Public debate unfolded alongside the confidential hearings and deliberations of a commission for reform of the excise established in 1786 by Frederick William II which concluded its work in the following June. At the public trial that accompanied the commission's work, ideas already 'widespread in many agitated and ambitious heads' during the previous king's reign were now expressed publicly. The clamour of 'learned hucksters' and 'political quacks' became ubiquitous, and defenders of the late king, such as his personal physician Johann Zimmermann (1728–95), were indignant that public commentators dared to 'put themselves in the place' of a great

---

[98] Schultze, *Regieverwaltung*, pp. 119–21.

monarch and thereby claim superior knowledge of the business of governing.[99] Much of the public criticism of Frederick focused on his fiscal policies. 'The voices of the discontented who loudly called for free trade were ubiquitous', Carl von Struensee (1735–1804), a member of Berlin's most prominent debating society, the Mittwochsgesellschaft, and later finance minister, pointed out. Struensee was himself part of this growing chorus of commentators calling for free trade, whilst also reflecting on the increasing power of the public. An article by Struensee in *Berlinische Monatsschrift* about Frederick's trade policies, together with those of his successor Frederick William II, began and ended with the exclamation 'How kings have to suffer to be judged!' The 'clamour' of the public, Struensee noted, had become so powerful that it was influencing commercial policies under the new king.[100] Another commentator feared that the 'clamours of the public' had become so agitated that the public in Berlin might turn violent and that 'people may be beaten up unnecessarily'.[101] The 'people' in question were the king's leading excise officers.

Besides the escalation of the fiscal conflict and the dynastic transition, two other factors contributed to the debate's resurgence: revolutionary and pre-revolutionary events in America and France, and the spread of statistical information about fiscal matters. In 1783, for example, Biester published a portrait of Benjamin Franklin (1706–90) together with a lengthy article about the life and achievements of the American revolutionary, including his role in the successful struggle against tyrannical and oppressive taxation of the Stamp Act. The article also included extensive quotes from Franklin's attacks on greedy and troublesome tax collectors. Considering the ongoing fiscal conflict in Prussia and the well-known consequences of Franklin's agitation in America, the article was certainly testing the limits of the famed Prussian freedom of expression.[102] The publication of Jacques Necker's *Compte rendue* (1781) in France and subsequent fiscal debates associated with the Revolution were equally followed eagerly in Prussia. Between 1788 and 1790, Struensee contributed 16 pieces entitled 'On the latest financial condition of France' to *Berlinische Monatsschrift*.[103] Increasing availability of information

---

[99] 'In sehr vielen unruhigen und ehrgeizigen Köpfen verbreitet.... Sie wollten alle an die Stelle Friedrichs des Großen treten.... Überall erscholl das Geschrey gelehrter Marktschreyer und politischer Quacksalber.' Johann Georg von Zimmermann, *Fragmente über Friedrich den Grossen zur Geschichte seines Lebens, seiner Regierung, und seines Charakters* (3 vols., Leipzig, 1790), vol. 3, p. 227. Former barriers that the respect of the great monarch had imposed on public opinion during his lifetime were no more; his successor, who later earned the popular nickname 'the fat good-for-nothing' ('der dicke Lüderjahn'), was not as awe-inspiring as his uncle.

[100] 'Allgemein war die Stimme der Misvergnügten, die laut nach freiem Handel schrien', 'wie sich doch die Könige müssen beurteilen lassen!'. Carl August von Struensee, 'Über den freien Getreidehandel in den preußischen Staaten', *Berlinische Monatsschrift*, 1 (1787), pp. 414–25, at pp. 414, 425.

[101] 'Clameurs publiques', 'qu'on ne frappât inutilement sur les personnes'. Mirabeau, *De la monarchie prussienne*, vol. 4, p. 145.

[102] Johann Biester, 'Etwas über Benjamin Franklin', *Berlinische Monatsschrift* 2 (1783), pp. 11–38, at pp. 26–33.

[103] The first piece in this series was Carl August von Struensee, 'Über den neuesten Finanzzustand Frankreichs', *Berlinische Monatsschrift*, 2 (Berlin, 1788), pp. 399–427.

about France's financial condition stimulated curiosity about Prussia's finances that had been 'covered in the most profound secrecy' during Frederick's reign.[104] In Prussia, however, this veil of secrecy had already begun to be lifted through the spread of statistical information, before news about the imminent financial collapse of the Bourbon monarchy reached the country. As early as 1775 Büsching published substantial amounts of statistical information and details about state finances, subsequently used by other authors in this debate.[105] Information about fiscal matters was not, however, only provided by private authors. From 1780, the minister of Hertzberg presented items of information about fiscal and other state affairs in annual discourses at public meetings of the Berlin Academy. We have already discussed some of these interventions in Chapter 3. To the extent that the intention was to convince the public of Frederick's fiscal policies, they must be considered a failure.[106] Instead, increasing availability of information about the state finances of Prussia and other European countries from different sources contributed substantially to the formation of networks of critical public debate about fiscal matters that extended beyond local contexts.

Within the far-reaching fiscal debate that unfolded after Frederick's death, we focus on an issue central to contemporary commentators: the relationship between the interests of private individuals and the common interest represented by the state. One of the first surviving contributions to this debate was a pamphlet defending the Régie's coffee and tobacco monopoly by Heinrich Adrian Graf von Borcke (1715–88), an officer who had been chosen by Frederick II as a mentor for his young nephew, the later Frederick William II. Borcke had remained close to both kings, but at the time of writing had retired to his country estate where he had turned his attention to matters of political economy. As public pressure for the abolition of monopolies increased after Frederick's death, Borcke wrote a small book summarizing and refuting public criticism against the monopolies.[107] Interestingly, although Borcke might have hoped to receive a sympathetic reception had he tried to convey his advice to his former pupil, or to the members of the commission in private, he nevertheless chose to express his views publicly. His

---

[104] Mirabeau, *De la monarchie prussienne*, vol. 4, p. 1.

[105] Anton Friedrich Büsching, *Anton Friderich Büschings Beschreibung seiner Reise von Berlin über Potsdam nach Rekahn unweit Brandenburg: welche er vom dritten bis achten Junius 1775 gethan hat* (Leipzig, 1775). See Mirabeau's comments in Mirabeau, *De la monarchie prussienne*, pp. 106, 191. In 1790 Büsching complemented his statistical travel narrative with a statistical handbook about Frederick II's reign. Anton Friedrich Büsching, *Zuverläßige Beyträge zu der Regierungs-Geschichte Königs Friedrich II. von Preußen: vornehmlich in Ansehung der Volksmenge, des Handels, der Finanzen und des Kriegsheers. Mit einem historischen Anhange* (Hamburg, 1790).

[106] Ewald Friedrich von Hertzberg, 'Sur la véritable richesse des états, la balance du commerce et celle du pouvoir. Dissertation qui a été lue dans l'assemblée publique de l'Académie des Sciences & des Belles-Lettres à Berlin, le 26. de Janvier 1786 pour le jour anniversaire du Roi', in *Nouveaux mémoires de l'Académie Royale des Sciences et Belles-Lettres* (Berlin, 1786), pp. 407–38.

[107] It is difficult to establish whether Borcke wrote before or after the edict. The title of his book gives 1786 as the date of publication and the edict abolishing the monopoly was dated January 1787. In his last chapter, however, Borcke mentioned that abolition of the monopoly had already been signed into effect, meaning that he was either writing in the period between signature and publication of the edict, or that he began his work before the edict and completed it only after the king had made his decision.

audience was the reading public who started to lead the king's hand in such policy decisions.

Borcke's pamphlet appeared shortly before publication of the edict abolishing the monopoly in January 1787. In the edict, Frederick William explicitly identified the objective of his new policy as being to 'move everything out of the way that . . . serves to constrain commerce and trade' and thereby revive 'all branches of bourgeois business' through the application of 'fair and equitable freedom'.[108] This argument also featured prominently in Borcke's opening summary of public criticism: the monopoly was denounced for the 'hard' and 'oppressive' operations of customs and excise that limited the freedom of trade and compromised 'natural freedom' and 'property rights'.[109] Since Borcke believed that the Régie's excessively intrusive and vexatious methods were the principal cause of public criticism, he suggested immediately ending searches of private homes.[110] Nevertheless, he defended in principle the necessity of state interference in commercial matters. Ending the monopoly and the resulting 'suffocation' of domestic factories was certainly in the 'interest' of merchants who could anticipate a flourishing business with the foreign tobacco trade, but the effect of free trade on domestic manufacturing in a country such as Prussia experiencing 'visible physical and moral growth' would be devastating.[111]

The king and vocal members of the public were, however, unconvinced by Borcke's arguments. His tract provoked two anonymous replies that took issue with his arguments in a remarkably similar tenor. Both welcomed abolition of the monopoly, whilst one thanked the king for liberating the country of the 'devils', 'barbarians', and 'mob of demons' that had been the Régie.[112] Subtle differences distinguished the two refutations of Borcke. The first author defended the private citizen's economic freedom as an inalienable right. As much as Borcke deserved esteem as a 'defender of the common interest', he should be condemned for trying to prove 'with sophistry and contradictions' to the 'citizen . . . that his liberation will make him a slave'. The Régie's abuses were inevitable consequences of the monopoly and no legitimate case could be made for such oppressive interference with the liberty of manufacturers, merchants, and consumers.[113] The second author took a

---

[108] 'Alles dasjenige . . . möglichst aus dem Weg zu räumen was nur irgend zur Einschränkung des Handels und Verkehrs . . . gereichen kann', 'alle Zweige des bürgerlichen Gewerbes', 'billige Freyheit'. Frederick William II, 'Declarations-Patent wegen Aufhebung der General-Tabacks-Administration und Caffeebrennerey-Anstalt auch Heruntersetzung der Cafee-Accise. De Dato Berlin den 6 Januarri 1787', in *Novum Corpus Constitutionum Prussico-Brandenburgensium Praecipue Marchicarum* (12 vols., Berlin, 1787), vol. 8, pp. 243–50, at p. 243.

[109] 'Harte und preßhafte Einrichtungen', 'natürliche Freyheit, und die Eigenthums-Rechte'. Borcke, *General-Tabaks-Administration*, p. 20.

[110] Borcke, *General-Tabaks-Administration*, p. 66.

[111] 'Ersticken', 'Interesse', 'sichtbaren physischen und moralischen Wachstum' Borcke, *General-Tabaks-Administration*, pp. 46–57.

[112] 'Unholden', 'Barbaren', 'Legion Teufel'. Anon., *Beantwortung und Widerlegung der Schrift, Was ist für und was ist gegen die General-Tobaks-Administration zu sagen* (Berlin, 1787), pp. 23, 25, 62.

[113] 'Verfechter des gemeinsamen Interesses', 'mit Sophismen und Widersprüchen dem Bürger beweisen wolte, er werde dadurch zum Sklaven, daß man ihn frey macht'. Anon., *Beantwortung und Wiederlegung*, pp. 1–2, 20.

slightly different approach. He denounced Borcke's 'nasty' depiction of merchants and opposed the very notion of a contradiction between the private interests of merchants and the common interest; a free coffee and tobacco trade was equally in the interest of all involved.[114] However, the common ground among the three authors is perhaps more revealing than their differences. All agreed that the state and the private activities of consumption and production formed separate, but interacting, spheres. Interference in private matters was inevitable, but the questions were how it should be carried out, whether it could be done in an acceptable manner, where limits should be drawn, and to what extent interests of state and private individuals diverged.

The debate about monopolies contributed to a larger, related, public controversy over reform of the Régie's other operations. Like the exchanges about the monopolies, this debate began with a pamphlet commenting publicly on matters being put before the reform commission. In this case, however, the author Mirabeau did not write to slow the reformatory zeal, but to expedite it. Unsurprisingly, the Régie was an anathema to the count. It sinned against the physiocratic maxims of laissez-faire and of a single tax on agricultural surplus. Mirabeau therefore seized the opportunity to contribute to the end of the institution and to encourage the new monarch to implement a wide range of reforms by publishing a small pamphlet entitled *Letter sent to Frederick William II reigning king of Prussia on the day of his ascent to the throne*.[115] This tract unleashed a public controversy about the Régie that invoked familiar arguments, but became more intense and more widespread than preceding exchanges. Once Mirabeau had publicly attacked Frederick's fiscal policy, Zimmermann responded by defending the Régie.[116] Meanwhile, Mirabeau had completed a more substantial and well-informed critique of Frederick's policies: the monumental four-volume study of state, society, and economy in Prussia, an entire volume of which was devoted to a detailed critique of the tax administration, including commentary on Borcke and his critics.[117] This attack attracted contributions from Zimmermann, de Launay, and the von Hertzberg,[118] in turn provoking

---

[114] This was, however, no dogmatic defence of free trade. In other cases, the author argued, protectionist measures might be in the common interest of state and merchants. 'Gehäßige'. Anon., *Gedanken eines Patrioten über die Schrift: Was ist für und was ist wider die General-Tobacks-Administration zu sagen* (Berlin, 1787), pp. 20–46, 50.

[115] Honoré Gabriel de Riqueti Comte de Mirabeau, *Lettre remise à Fréderic Guillaume II, roi régnant de Prusse, le jour de son avènement au trône* (n.p., 1787). Also published in German as Honoré Gabriel Riqueti Comte de Mirabeau, *Schreiben an Friedrich Wilhelm II. itzt regierenden König von Preussen, am Tage seiner Thronbesteigung* (Paris, 1787).

[116] Other matters played a role in this debate, but as Zimmermann pointed out, 'the greatest part of the accusations that have been levelled against Frederick relate to the French Régie'. Johann Georg von Zimmermann, *Vertheidigung Friedrichs des Grossen gegen den Grafen von Mirabeau: Nebst einigen Anmerkungen über andere Gegenstände* (Hannover, 1788), p. 34.

[117] Mirabeau, *De la monarchie prussienne*, vol. 4, p. 113. Zimmermann saw Mirabeau's work as a joint effort of the 'clique' of the 'Berlin enlightenment synagogue' which had very quickly adopted Mirabeau and made him its spokesman; Zimmermann, *Fragmente*, vol. 3, p. 258.

[118] Zimmermann, *Vertheidigung Friedrichs des Grossen*. De Launay, *Justification*. Also published in German as Marc Antoine de la Haye de Launay, *Friedrichs des Zweyten, Königs von Preussen, ökonomisch-politisches Finanzsystem gerechtfertigt: Eine Widerlegung der falschen Behauptungen des Grafen von Mirabeau, in seiner Schrift: über die preuss. Monarchie (Nebst Anhang)* (Berlin, 1789).

a number of counter-attacks including one by the standard-bearer of the Berlin enlightenment, Nicolai.[119] Only in 1791, after the Régie's critics had triumphed, did the debate subside.

In his initial public letter, Mirabeau fiercely attacked the 'fiscal robbery' and urged Frederick William to lower or abolish indirect taxes. In particular the king was urged to 'relegate to hell' the oppressive powers granted to the Régie to pursue and punish smugglers.[120] As Mirabeau later explained, it was less the excise's financial burden than its 'manners' and 'humiliating vexations' that disgusted merchants and rendered commerce near impossible.[121] 'We would have paid voluntarily the sum that this hated administration collected'— Mirabeau cited 'thousands' of nameless Prussian taxpayers—'if only commerce had been free'.[122] This argument was countered by de Launay who emphasized the care taken in drafting the Régie's operative rules and the many instances in which disciplinary action had been taken against officials guilty of abuses. De Launay also maintained, however, that where officials had acted within the rules, no abuse could have taken place by definition. Formalities, he argued, were the 'natural consequences' of the law and therefore 'vex no one when they are followed'.[123] Mirabeau made a similar connection, insisting that intrusive searches and draconian punishments were not accidental, but inevitably associated with the excise. The only remedy was therefore for the monarch to fix the amount of revenue required by the state and to leave tax collection to taxpayers themselves.[124] The controversy was clearly not about the excesses of the Régie's personnel which could be remedied by better discipline or by introducing gentler tax collectors. What was at stake was the legitimacy of laws that allowed the state to collect the tax and thereby to intrude deeply into the private spheres of thousands of urban Prussians.

The Régie's defenders therefore concentrated on demonstrating the necessity of intrusions, not only in terms of the royal prerogative but also as a means of

Ewald Friedrich von Hertzberg, 'Discours qui a été lu dans l'assemblée publique de l'Académie des Sciences de Berlin le 26 Septembre 1788, Au jour de naissance du roi par le Comte de Hertzberg, Ministre d'État, Curateur & Membre de L'Academie', *Nouveux mémoires de l'Académie Royale des Sciences et Belles-Lettres* (Berlin, 1788), pp. 307–11.

[119] Friedrich Nicolai, *Freymüthige Anmerkungen über des Ritters von Zimmermann Fragmente über Friedrich den Großen von einigen brandenburg. Patrioten* (Berlin, 1791). Johann Heinrich Friedrich Quittenbaum, *Zimmermann der I, und Fridrich der II* (n.p., 1790). Carl Friedrich Bahrdt, *Mit dem Herrn [von] Zimmermann Ritter des St. Wladimir-Ordens von der dritten Klasse deutsch gesprochen* (n.p., 1790).

[120] 'Brigandage fiscal', 'rélégué dans les enfers'. Mirabeau, *Lettre*, pp. 45–53.

[121] 'Des formes de la Régie, de ses vexations humiliantes'. Mirabeau, *De la monarchie prussienne*, vol. 4, p. 142.

[122] 'On auroit volontiers payé, nous a-t-on dit mille fois, la somme que rapportoit cette administration odieuse, pourvue qu'à cette condition le commerce eût été libre.' Mirabeau, *De la monarchie prussienne*, vol. 4, p. 142. This central point is already familiar from earlier parts of the controversy over the Régie and is later repeated by Nicolai and Beguelin.

[123] 'Des conséquences naturelles, qui ne vexent . . . personne.' Marc Antoine de la Haye de Launay, 'Compte rendu au roi', edited in Mirabeau, *De la monarchie Prussienne*, vol. 6, p. 284.

[124] Mirabeau, *De la monarchie Prussienne*, vol. 6, pp. 51–6.

safeguarding the common good against narrow private interests.[125] Replying to Mirabeau, de Launay explained that Frederick's intentions had primarily been to promote industry, which was a view supposed by Zimmermann in 1790: 'No other wish and purpose did the king have with the Régie besides... helping domestic factories'.[126] According to de Launay, fiscal motives and commercial growth were subordinate to this objective because only industry could provide employment and prosperity to the people.[127] To 'manage industry' ('ménager l'industrie') in this way, it was necessary to collect statistical information, introduce protective tariffs, ban certain foreign products, and to encourage and, on occasion even to force, Prussian entrepreneurs to open new factories.[128] Whilst such policies might hurt individual interests, Zimmermann categorically rejected any broader criticism:

> Forty or fifty thousand merchants of all classes must not believe that the welfare of the whole Prussian monarchy only depends on their living in happiness; on their right to bring foreign cloth, silken, woollen and cotton factory goods freely into the country even if this ruins the factories that are the livelihood of more than two million men in Prussia. Frederick the Great was more than right not to want what the merchants wanted.[129]

Their opponents countered this defence by arguing that Frederick's policies had not actually helped Prussia's industry but had ruined it; indeed, much of the dispute between Hertzberg and Mirabeau concerned statistical evidence.[130] Mirabeau also, however, rejected the alleged incompatibility of common or state interest and private interests. Having already warned the king against 'governing too much', he argued that the citizens if left to 'pursue their own business and their own greatest interest... will achieve their own interests and yours.'[131] In contrast to Frederick's opinions about the loyalties of merchants, Mirabeau even advised Frederick William to employ merchants to take care of his affairs wherever possible.[132]

---

[125] See discussion of older political theories on the issue in Eckhart Hellmuth, *Naturrechtsphilosophie und bürokratischer Werthorizont: Studien zur preußischen Geistes- und Sozialgeschichte des 18. Jahrhunderts* (Göttingen, 1985).

[126] De Launay, *Justification*, p. 58. 'Keinen andern Wunsch und Zweck hatte der König bey der Regie, als... die einländischen Fabriken menschenmöglichst in die Höhe zu bringen.' Zimmermann, *Fragmente*, vol. 2, p. 72.

[127] De Launay, *Justification*, pp. 43, 48, 59–60, and *passim*.

[128] De Launay, *Justification*, pp. 69, 36, 40, 51–69, 36, 75, 60.

[129] 'Also müssen allerhöchstens vierzig bis fünfzig tausend Kaufleute von allen Classen, nicht glauben: die Wohlfahrt der ganzen preussischen Monarchie hänge bloß daran, dass sie in Freuden leben; dass ihnen erlaubt sey ausländische Tücher, seidene, wollene, baumwollene und andere Fabrikwaaren, frey ins Land zu bringen, wenn auch dabey die Fabrieken zu Grunde giengen, wovon doch in Preussen über zwey Millionen Menschen leben. Friedrich der Grosse wollten also mit dem größten Recht, nicht was die Kafuleute wollten.' Zimmermann, *Fragmente*, p. 75.

[130] Mirabeau, *De la monarchie prussienne*, vol. 6, p. 172. Hertzberg, 'Discours... 26 Septembre 1788'.

[131] 'Ses citoyens... en faisant leurs affaires sous votre protection pour leur plus grand intérêt, font celles de l'Etat & les vôtres.' Mirabeau, *Lettre*, p. 15.

[132] Mirabeau, *Lettre*, p. 59.

AFTER THE END

In 1787 the Régie was abolished. De Launay and most other French officials were removed and the collection of the excise became part of a new department that was created by merging the fourth department responsible for customs and excise and the fifth department for factories and commerce.[133] The critics had prevailed fully: not only were most of their demands met but Frederick's successor even adopted their language in his reform edicts. In the opening paragraph of the principal edict Frederick William acknowledged the view that the reforms that his uncle had introduced twenty-one years earlier had damaged the 'moral' and economic condition of his subjects. In the language of the edicts, it was the way in which the administration carried on in its 'daily practice' ('Dienst-Verwaltung') with 'incessant house searches' and 'terrible punishments' that led Prussians to turn to contraband. That smuggling turned into a lucrative and widespread activity was explicitly blamed on the unjust tax laws that had turned honest Prussian consumers into criminals and led merchants astray from their legitimate businesses. But the Régie had not only been responsible for moral decline. The 'prosperity of our towns' was undermined by the 'nasty formalities' and 'vexations' that made the 'mistreated citizens' 'despondent' and closed all 'sources of prosperity'. 'Merchant', 'cartwright', and 'mariner' suffered from 'time-consuming circuitousness and formalities', 'unnecessary searches of their goods', 'rude encounters', and 'costly and unjust punishments'.[134] The new king was resolved to end these vexations and remove everything that 'limits commerce and circulation'. Instead, the new tax regime was to 'revive bourgeois business' through the establishment of a 'legitimate freedom'.[135]

The specific measures announced in the edicts reflected the new fiscal spirit. The king ordered an end to time-consuming controls for merchants and wagoners, and intrusive inspections of shops and workshops were to be limited.[136] Equally important were the alterations to the tariff structure. Frederick's intention, however incompletely implemented, had been to 'de-tax the poor' and introduce a significant progressive element into the excise through higher imposts on luxury goods. In

---

[133] Frederick William II, 'Rescript an das Cammer-Gericht, wegen Etablirung eines eigenen General-Fabriken- und Commerzial-, wie auch Accise- und Zoll-Departements des General-Directorii. De dato Berlin, den 2 Februar 1787', *Novum Corpus Constitutionum Prussico-Brandenburgensium Preacipue Marchicarum* (12 vols., Berlin, 1787), vol. 8, p. 294.

[134] 'Wohlstand unserer Städte', 'gehässige Formalitäten', 'Haussuchungen' and 'Plackereyen', 'gemißhandelten Bürger', 'muthlos', 'Quellen des Wohstands', 'der Commerciant, der Fuhrmann, der Schiffer', 'zeitverderbende Weiläufigkeiten und Foralitäten', 'unnöthige Durchsuchungen ihrer Waaren', 'unanständige Begegnung', 'kostbare und unbillige Strafen'. Frederick William II, 'Verordnung für sämmtliche Provinzen diesseits der Weser, wegen einer neuen Einrichtung des Accise- und Zoll-Wesens. De Dato Berlin, den 25sten Jan. 1787', *Novum Corpus Constitutionum Prussico-Brandenburgensium Praecipue Marchicarum* (12 vols., Berlin, 1787), vol. 8, pp. 256–8.

[135] 'All dasjenige . . . möglichst aus dem Weg zu räumen, was nur irgendwie zur Einschränkung des Handels und Verkehrs . . . gereichen kann', 'durch eine billige Freyheit alle Zweyge des bürgerlichen Gewerbes mehr zu beleben'. Frederick William II, 'Verordnung für sämmtliche Provinzen', p. 243.

[136] Frederick William II, 'Verordnung für sämmtliche Provinzen', p. 266.

practice, the most important step in this direction had been the abolition of most taxes on grain and a reduction in the taxation on pork and brandy, all of which were seen as commodities of primary necessity. Wealthier consumers of luxury goods contributed more to the state's income through higher excise tariffs on these products and through the inflated prices of coffee and tobacco provided by state-run monopolies. The abolition of these monopolies was among the first reform acts of Frederick William. Limitations on growing, trading, and processing both commodities were lifted and the excise duties on imports were reduced.[137] To compensate for these losses the *Mahlaccise*, a tax on the milling of grain which had been abolished by Frederick II, was reintroduced along with an increase of imposts on a number of other widely consumed commodities.[138]

REAPING THE BENEFITS

The reforms led to a series of changes, some of which benefited all urban dwellers, while others were mainly in the interest of groups within urban society. On a political level the urban public as a whole, or at least those who had in one way or another expressed their discontent with the Régie, could affirm their political power against that of the state. Writers, smugglers, and those who petitioned the authorities had made it clear that their views could not be ignored in decisions about economic policy. The state had to renounce some of its universalist ambitions of control against a civil society that affirmed its distinctiveness and self-reliance in this context. The conflict over the Régie stands out because of the importance of the institution for the state and because of the extent to which the public prevailed. However, this type of conflict over economic and fiscal questions was not a one-off in this period and the Régie was not the only ambitious project of Frederick II that failed because of urban opposition. Mittenzwei has painstakingly reconstructed similar conflicts that pitted urban merchants and producers against the state in the period after the Seven Years War. These conflicts and debates were less significant than those regarding the Régie, and pressure on the state was mostly exercised by means of petitions to the king or subordinate administrative levels and by forms of passive resistance. In the case of a controversial insurance scheme, for example, merchants in Königsberg simply refused to take out contracts, and opposition against a trade monopoly in cotton led cotton producers to collectively avoid purchases from the company that were priced above a certain level. In ways similar to the behaviour of Prussian consumers who avoided the monopoly coffee and tobacco of the Régie, businessmen sought to avoid cooperation with the state-sponsored institutions they opposed. In several cases documented by Mittenzwei they did so successfully and were able to obtain modifications and concessions. For example, Frederick had to significantly modify his plans for the royal bank and an

---

[137] Frederick William II, 'Declarations-Patent wegen Aufhebung', pp. 243–50.
[138] Frederick William II, 'Verordnung wegen einer neuen Einrichtung des Accise- und Zoll-Wesens', p. 258.

associated trading company in light of opposition. Similarly, urban opposition led to a modification to the Levant Trading Company with its cotton monopoly.[139] The regulation of manufacturing through urban guilds equally came under attack in this period. From the late 1760s Johann Albrecht Philippi (1721–91)—another official who doubled as a publicist—began to attack the guild system by petitions and publishing his views in print. The debate gathered some momentum when Prussians began to comment on Turgot's attempt to abolish guilds in France in 1776.[140] However, whereas the resistance against the Régie had found almost universal support in urban society, substantial portions of the urban population benefited from guild regulations and were therefore unlikely to oppose them.

Nonetheless, in the case of the Régie resistance was also not supported uniformly across all segments of society. Some elements of urban society clearly played a more important role in exercising pressure on the state, and the political successes achieved may be seen as being more closely associated with them. Historians are able to reconstruct much more fully the resistance put up by economic and intellectual elites, while the contours of the participation of the broader urban population, for example in the form of smuggling, and the participation in oral debates remain less clear. However, even if the movement against the Régie was spearheaded by an elite of educated and wealthier burghers, the political results benefited, at least to some extent, virtually all urban dwellers. This universal appeal contributed in no small way to add legitimacy and political strength to demands that were championed by a minority. Only one political outcome of the abolition of the Régie clearly only benefited a small elite segment of urban society. The dismissal of the French administrators opened up a substantial number of lucrative and powerful administrative positions that were certainly not filled from the ranks of the urban poor, but by highly educated starvelings like Hamann or by other administrators who could thus further their careers. Rosenberg has emphasized this factor in the history of the Régie and interpreted the conflict associated with the institution mainly as the outcome of a rivalry with the established Prussian administration that was, at least in part, driven by the individual ambitions of Prussian administrators.[141] In this context it is worth reiterating that the nationalistic element in the debate remained weak, but where it appeared it was proposed by exponents of the administrative and intellectual elite whose personal ambitions Ernest Gellner saw as being among the driving forces behind the rise of modern nationalism.[142] Nonetheless, the fact that the end of the Régie not only brought a replacement of the French administrators with Prussian equivalents but also a far-reaching reform of tariffs and administrative practices also shows the limitations of an interpretation of the conflict over the Régie in terms of nationalistic rejection or as the expression of an administrative rivalry. The removal from office of the French

---

[139] Mittenzwei, *Preußen*, pp. 13–38.

[140] Mittenzwei, *Preußen*, pp. 135–46.

[141] Hans Rosenberg, *Bureaucracy, aristocracy and autocracy. The Prussian experience, 1660–1815* (Cambridge, MA, 1958), p. 168, 173.

[142] Ernest Gellner, *Nations and Nationalism* (Oxford, 1983), p. 61.

administrators would have been sufficient to appease the opposition that originated from these sources, but the end of the Régie also brought far-reaching change in the substance of the tax regime.

The attribution of the economic benefits associated with the demise of the Régie is much clearer than that of the political advantages. Most of the economic benefits of the reform were accrued by economic elites, while the economic interests of poorer consumers were often harmed by the abolition of the Régie. This is most clearly visible in the revision of the tax structure. The imposts on coffee and tobacco were substantially lowered. The consumption of both commodities had become more widespread in the period but was far from universal, and the volume of consumption varied substantially with wealth and income. Wealthier consumers clearly benefited to a much larger extent from this change. In order to compensate for the loss of income the state reintroduced the milling excise. Given that the consumption of flour can be assumed to be similar across all levels of urban society, or at least not significantly higher among the upper echelons, this tax represented a proportionally higher burden on lower incomes. The attempt of Frederick II to create a more progressive fiscal structure was reversed and the new tariff structure was strongly regressive.

The unequal effects on rich and poor were almost certainly even stronger in practice than the change of the tariff structure suggests because of two separate effects. The first was associated with the phenomenon of 'fiscal overshifting'. It is normally assumed that indirect taxes paid by merchants are shifted on to the consumer: consumer prices are increased in proportion to the amount of tax paid by the merchant or producer. However, it can be shown that frequently prices increase by more than the additional cost represented by the tax.[143] There are a number of economic theories that explain this phenomenon but perhaps the most convincing is the simplest: tax increases, just like currency reforms, offer an opportunity to hide price increases and pass on the blame to the political authorities. Clearly this must have been a problem in Prussia in our period otherwise Frederick would not have included a price control provision in his edict of 1766. The second effect that most likely alleviated the tax burden on wealthier burghers beyond the effects of the nominal tariff changes was associated with the behaviour of contrabandists. A priori, laxer controls make the smuggling of all commodities easier and therefore it could be assumed to result in lower average prices of all products that were subject to the excise. However, the fact that all forms of smuggling were 'equally illegal' and carried similar levels of punishment led to a concentration on certain goods.[144] Given that the risks were similar, smugglers likely opted for smuggling commodities with high imposts in order to maximize the reward and their ability to sell the contraband. The efforts of smugglers were thus most likely focused on luxury items with high excise tariffs. This effect was

---

[143] See the summary of economic arguments on overshifting in Mark Spoerer, 'The Laspeyres-Paradox: tax overshifting in nineteenth century Prussia', *Cliometrica*, 2 (2008), pp. 173–6.

[144] See the discussion of smuggling in nineteenth-century Prussia in Spoerer, 'Tax overshifting', p. 12.

reinforced further by the fact that it was easier to smuggle small and light items than bulkier ones, and that this distinction often coincided with the distinction between luxury items and goods for everyday consumption. There is of course no direct evidence for this but smugglers' concentration on coffee and tobacco under the Régie would suggest that those engaging in illicit commerce were susceptible to this way of reasoning. If then the existing contraband networks continued to operate after the abolition of the Régie, taking advantage of the laxer regime of controls, their concentration on luxury goods disproportionally reduced the tax burden on the wealthy who were the principal consumers of such goods. Overshifting thus worked against the poor while lax controls disproportionally favoured the rich. Together both factors further exacerbated the regressive effects of the tariff reform.

The reforms also resulted in other advantages for merchants and businessmen who, as privileged consumers, already benefited in other ways. As Büsching pointed out, the tobacco trade had become one of the most lucrative and the sale of coffee was equally profitable. With the demise of the Régie two attractive fields of commerce were thus opened up to enterprising Prussian merchants who were poised to collect at least a part of the profits that had until now filled the coffers of the Prussian state. In addition, merchants and to some extent producers also benefited from the reduction in the excise controls. The thorough checks and inspections of the Régie not only violated the private sphere of many Prussian businessmen but they also incurred substantial additional costs as a result.[145] As the *Kammerpräsident* of Königsberg had reported, delays at the gates caused fresh produce to spoil thereby creating losses for the merchants. Producers whose production processes were disturbed by the inspectors probably faced similar additional costs. Such delays could also result in additional wage costs and opportunity costs because capital remained bound up in commodities that were lying idly in the *Packhof* instead of producing a return for their owners. The additional costs caused not by the excise itself but by the circumstances of its collection were all the more annoying for merchants and producers because they could not be shifted on to consumers because of the price controls introduced by Frederick II. The same was true for merchants specializing in the transit trade. They incurred substantial costs as a result of controls and inspection but found it difficult to shift them to consumers because they may have been competing with merchants who were using different trade routes—avoiding Prussian territories and the Régie's controls—where they did not incur similar costs. The abolition of the Régie thus significantly benefited larger merchants and manufacturers, two often overlapping segments of urban society that, according to Straubel's research, was much more significant in Prussia's towns and cities than often assumed.[146] Considering the outcome of this

---

[145] For discussion of incurred costs in a similar context see Spoerer, 'Tax overshifting', pp. 16–17.

[146] See, among others, Rolf Straubel, *Kaufleute und Manufakturunternehmer: eine empirische Untersuchung über die sozialen Träger von Handel und Großgewerbe in den mittleren preußischen Provinzen (1763 bis 1815)* (Stuttgart, 1995). Rolf Straubel, *Frankfurt (Oder) und Potsdam am Ende des Alten Reiches Studien zur städtischen Wirtschafts- und Sozialstruktur* (Potsdam, 1995). Rolf Straubel, *Die Handelsstädte Königsberg und Memel in friderizianischer Zeit ein Beitrag zur Geschichte des ost- und gesamtpreußischen 'Commerciums' sowie seiner sozialen Träger (1763–1806/15)* (Berlin, 2003).

fiscal conflict it may be added that the mercantile element of urban society had not only acquired economic importance but was also able to successfully defend its political interests.

LONG-TERM OUTCOMES

In this instance urban elites were able to shape a central part of policy and impose their agenda on the Prussian state. This success was neither isolated nor was it short-lived. Rather it was the beginning of a structural shift in fiscal and economic policy that lasted well into the nineteenth century. The excise as it was established in 1787 continued to exist in essence until 1820 when it was abolished in the context of the Stein-Hardenberg reforms as part of a comprehensive fiscal reform. The existing taxes, most importantly the rural land tax and the urban excise, were substituted with a class tax in the countryside and some mostly smaller towns, and a milling and slaughter tax that was levied mainly in the larger cities. The class tax was a graduated tax that combined elements of a primitive income tax and of a poll tax.[147]

The excise was thus substituted in the larger cities with what effectively amounted to an excise that was levied only on meat and flour. The introduction of this tax continued a trend in fiscal policy that had its origins in the conflict over the Régie. The excise had become more regressive after 1787, in particular through the detaxing of luxury goods and the reintroduction of the milling excise. The milling and slaughter tax took this development to an extreme by taxing only two basic foodstuffs. The result was that the urban poor bore the brunt of the new tax while the contribution of wealthier taxpayers was negligible. Contemporaries were well aware of this distributional effect. Until the abolition of the tax in 1875 socialist agitators such as Ferdinand Lassalle railed against the tax, while the rich lobbied for its continuation and tried to move their residences where possible to towns that were subject to the milling tax to avoid the less favourable class tax.[148]

---

[147] Spoerer, 'Tax overshifting', p. 5. See also the literature cited there: M. von Henckel, 'Schlacht- und Mahlsteuer', in Johannes Conrad, ed., *Handwörterbuch der Staatswissenschaft* (Jena, 1893), pp. 571–6. Carl Kries, 'Über die Mahl- und Schlacht-Steuer, die Einkommen- und Klassen-Steuer in Preußen', *Archiv der politischen Oekonomie und Polizeiwissenschaft*, 8 (1849), pp. 179–224, 227–324. Friedrich Schimmelpfennig, *Die preussischen indirekten Steuern oder die auf Produktion, Fabrikation und Konsumtion ruhenden Abgaben im Innern der preussischen Staaten. Eine systematisch geordnete Zusammenstellung der darauf Bezug habenden Gesetze und Verordnungen bis zum Schlusse des Jahres 1835* (Potsdam, 1840). Otto Wolff, 'Die Mahl- und Schlachtsteuer', *Vierteljahrschrift für Volkswirtschaft Politik und Kulturgeschichte*, 2 (1864), pp. 168–96.

[148] Spoerer, 'Tax overshifting', p. 1. Mark Spoerer, 'Wann begannen Fiskal- und Steuerwettbewerb? Eine Spurensuche in Preussen, anderen Deutschen Staaten und der Schweiz', *Jahrbuch für Wirtschaftsgeschichte*, 2 (2002), pp. 11–35. See also D. Born, *Denkschrift über den Einfluß der Mahl- und Schlachtsteuer auf die gewerblichen Verhältnisse Berlins, besonders in Bezug auf die Arbeitslöhne und auf die Konkurrenzfähigkeit anderen Städten gegenüber* (Berlin, 1850). Ernst Engel, 'Die Ergebnisse der Classensteuer, der classificirten Einkommensteuer und der Mahl- und Schlachtsteuer im Preussischen Staate', *Zeitschrift des königlich preussischen statistischen Bureaus*, 8 (1868), pp. 25–84. A. Reinicke, 'Resultate der Mahl- und Schlachtsteuer in der Periode von 1838 bis 1861', *Zeitschrift des königlich preussischen statistischen Bureaus*, 3, 4 (1863), pp. 160–7, 217–35.

The milling and slaughter tax corresponded also in other respects to interests that had already shaped the changes to the excises after the abolition of the Régie. The limitation of the tax to meat and flour meant that it lost the qualities of an economic steering and planning tool that was prominent in the Frederickian excise. The milling tax was a purely fiscal tool, rather than being a part of artfully constructed 'green houses' for urban economies. This was partly because customs collection at Prussia's external borders was becoming more effective and began to fulfil protective functions. In the context of Hardenberg's reforms the limitations on the establishment of industries in the countryside were lifted and duties levied at the external borders of Prussia could now be used to protect urban and rural industries alike.[149] However, the 'blunting' of urban taxation as an economic planning tool was also the result of the efforts of merchants and manufacturers to free themselves from the intrusion into their affairs that had played a central role in the conflict over the Régie. Thanks to the Hardenberg fiscal and economic reforms, a much more liberal economic policy emerged in Prussia in the early nineteenth century. The first steps in this direction had been taken with the abolition of the Régie.

It is noteworthy that a similarly regressive fiscal system remained in place until the late nineteenth century despite strong agitation against it by working-class groups. This outcome was mainly the result of the Prussian electoral system which gave disproportionate political power to the urban rich who dominated city councils and the lower house of parliament.[150] However, even more remarkable than the persistence of this fiscal structure were its origins. Contrary to a received view of Prussian history, this transformation was not a gift bequeathed on urban elites by a lucky combination of an inferior Prussian military defeated by Napoleon and a superior corps of liberally minded administrators who were put in charge of rebuilding the country. Instead, Prussian burghers wrung this success from the hands of an unwilling Prussian state. They pressured one of the most stubborn and autocratic absolutist monarchs of the time and his admittedly less imposing successor into adopting their fiscal and political agenda long before a historic caesura was forced on Prussia from the outside.

A SOFT LANDING FOR THE PRUSSIAN STATE

The flipside of the political success that urban dwellers could celebrate in 1787 was a political defeat of the Prussian state. However, compared with the kind of earth-shattering consequences that fiscal conflicts had elsewhere at the time the Prussian state got off lightly. In France attempts to repair the fiscal consequences of the Seven Years War contributed significantly to fermenting a revolution that destroyed the whole Bourbon state, and British attempts to recover the war costs in part by increasing taxes in North America were similarly ill-fated although in this case

---

[149] Schmoller, *Preußische Verfassungs-, Verwaltungs- und Finanzgeschichte*, pp. 180–4, 190–6.
[150] Spoerer, 'Tax overshifting', p. 19.

revolution happened in a peripheral part of the colonial empire rather than in the metropolis. Clearly, these developments cannot be solely explained as the outcome of a fiscal dynamic. However, fiscal conflicts did play an important role and this creates the question of why the conflict over the Régie did not escalate in the same way.

In the Hohenzollern polity a number of factors contributed to limiting the extent and consequences of the conflict. In part, chance played a role. As dissatisfaction with the institution began to reach its apogee Frederick II was replaced by an inexperienced successor who, unlike his predecessor, could not capitalize politically on his military record. Frederick William's weakness as a ruler may well have spared Prussia an escalation of the conflict although this character trait should not be emphasized excessively considering that we later see the same monarch enacting aggressive and unpopular religious policies with great tenacity. Other factors that were more material than the character of the ruler and closely related to the fiscal and political structure of Prussia were more important in preventing a further escalation of the conflict.

Frederick William may have been a comparably weak monarch, but more importantly he was a monarch who could afford to compromise in fiscal matters. By abolishing the Régie the Prussian state renounced—at least in the short run—a significant portion of its income. However, because Prussia had no significant debt and a substantial treasury at this stage it was under much less pressure than other countries, France in particular, to raise more revenue despite the associated political perils.[151] This advantageous position was reinforced by the diversified revenue structure of the Prussian state (see Fig. 3.1). While the indirect taxes were an important and also the most rapidly growing part of the state's revenues, income from direct taxes and domains was equally significant. In particular the latter was a politically non-contentious form of revenue because it derived from the exploitation of economic assets of the state rather than from the appropriation of funds from private incomes. Frederick's decision to develop the excise as a source of revenue rather than expanding the domains as his father had done may have been far-sighted from a fiscal point of view. Unlike most incomes from the domains, excise revenues grew with commercial development and thus enabled the state to harvest the fruits of economic progress. However, in the short term the political advantages of large domains were significant because they made the Prussian state far less dependent on tax revenues than, for example, France or Britain where domain revenues had become insignificant in this period.[152]

Moreover, the opposition to the Régie never radicalized in the way that other fiscal protest movements did. This was partly due to the fact that despite all the shortcomings of the Régie the excise in itself was still seen as a fundamentally

---

[151] Wolfgang Neugebauer, 'Epochen der preußischen Geschichte', in Wolfgang Neugebauer, ed., *Handbuch der preußischen Geschichte. Das 17. und 18. Jahrhundert und große Themen der preußischen Geschichte* (Berlin, 2009), pp. 113–410, at p. 365. Reinhold Koser, 'Die preußischen Finanzen von 1763–86', *Forschungen zur brandenburgischen und preussischen Geschichte*, 16 (1903), pp. 445–76.

[152] Schremmer, *Taxation*, pp. 316, 326, 370, 415.

equitable and 'benign' form of taxation. Montesquieu had described indirect taxes in the *Spirit of the laws* (1748) as the form of fiscality most appropriate to free political systems.[153] Nicolai echoed this judgement in the Prussian context as late as 1783, when the conflict over the Régie was already well under way. Despite his outspoken criticism of the Régie, he described the fiscal and political conditions in the towns before the introduction of the excise in the seventeenth century in very negative terms and identified the introduction of the tax as one of the main factors that led to a resurgence of the urban sector in Prussia.[154]

To contemporaries indirect taxes thus appeared as less fraught with political dangers. However, the political benefits of this perception should not be overstated. The Prussian Régie was not the only case were political conflict was triggered by the excise. In the 1730s, the Excise Crisis had deeply shaken the British political system and forced Walpole to withdraw a fiscal reform that was seen by many urban dwellers as illegitimate. Protests were partly provoked by the increase of the tax burden on the towns, but as in the Prussian case urban dwellers rejected, above all, intrusive controls of their businesses and homes. Paul Langford summarizes the core of the conflict: 'Excise duties involved giving extensive powers of search to revenue officers, and a wide jurisdiction to magistrates and excise commissioners. The Englishman's right to privacy on his own property, and also to trial by jury, were put at risk. An entire genre of horror stories, retailed in the press and depicted in broadsheets and prints, exploited such fears.'[155] The consequences of the Excise Crisis in Britain were not as far-reaching as the crisis in Prussia. The reform proposals were withdrawn before they were implemented and the crisis was resolved in a much shorter time span. Nonetheless, the crisis marked a watershed in Walpole's government and the impact on British politics was significant. As Ashworth points out, few taxes, if any, had the same impact as the excise on British politics in the long eighteenth century.[156] In both Britain and Prussia, eighteenth-century conflicts over the excise did not lead to revolutionary unrest, but they played a much more incendiary role in North America. The most iconic act of resistance in the American Revolution, the Boston Tea Party, was directed against customs duties on tea and, as in the Prussian case, the interference with the freedom of consumption brought by indirect taxes and customs was a central part of this conflict.[157]

Paradoxically, the transnational nature of the Régie itself may also have contributed to reducing the explosiveness of this conflict. Some historians have seen the French origin of the Régie officials as one of the main causes of the public's discontent. However, apart from the limited evidence for this argument, it also

---

[153] See Charles Louis Secondat Baron de Montesquieu, 'Of the relation which the levying of taxes and the greatness of the public revenues bear to liberty', in *The spirit of the laws* (London, 1914), book XIII.

[154] Nicolai, *Beschreibung*, p. 180.

[155] Paul Langford, *A polite and commercial people: England, 1727–1783* (Oxford, 1989), p. 29.

[156] Ashworth, *Customs and excise*, p. 8.

[157] T. H. Breen, *The marketplace of revolution: how consumer politics shaped American independence* (Oxford, 2004).

overlooks an important way in which the French origin of the administrators contributed to mitigating conflicts. When Frederick II appointed the Frenchmen he was looking to farm out the collection of the excise on the model of the French *ferme générale*, which bought the right to collect a certain number of taxes for a fixed period for an up-front lump sum payment from the crown. It was not uncommon at the time for French tax officials to sell their services in this way outside France.[158] However, when de Launay arrived in Berlin he strongly advised the Prussian monarch against this type of arrangement. According to de Launay it gave the tax farmers 'interêt au pressoir': it created a strong incentive to maximize the amount of taxes collected in order to increase profits.[159] De Launay's concerns were not unfounded. The draconian methods of tax collection and the enormous fortunes amassed by the tax farmers caused much of the discontent in the period leading up to the French Revolution and it is hardly a coincidence that tax farmers were among the most represented professional groups on the scaffolds of the revolution.[160] Whether de Launay advised Frederick against tax farming out of altruistic motives or because he could not raise the necessary funds cannot be said with certainty. However, he had been a *sous fermier* and was related to members of the financial elite of France. Even while he was in Prussia his relationship with this environment must have continued since one of his daughters married the French *Fermier Général* Mangin de Bionval. His own background and his close connections to the world of French financiers suggest that he could probably have raised the necessary funds for the creation of a tax farming operation in Prussia and that he insisted on different arrangements because he had first-hand experience of the political dangers that were associated with the French model. In this way de Launay not only gave the Régie its popular name, which referred to the fact that the operation was run in the *régie* of the state rather than being farmed out, but he also prevented the Prussian monarch from adopting a fiscal system that contributed significantly to the downfall of monarchies elsewhere, most notably in France.[161] In a way the Hohenzollern state thus learned from the French experience more effectively than the French monarchy itself and avoided some of the outcomes that led to revolution in France.[162]

Finally, the extent of the conflict was also limited by the geography of the opposition movement. This was mainly the result of Prussia's peculiar fiscal structure with its sharp division between town and country. Urban dwellers in most Prussian provinces were confronted with similar fiscal arrangements in this period and, as we have argued, this contributed much to the creation of unified urban opposition to the state. However, the Régie was never introduced in the countryside and was quickly abolished in some towns. Therefore only a part of Prussia's population, roughly one third, was subjected to the tax and could serve as

[158] Jean-Claude Waquet, 'Les Fermes Générales dans l'Europe des lumières', *Mélanges de l'École Française de Rome*, 8 (1977), pp. 983–1027.

[159] De Launay, *Justification*, p. 17.

[160] Colin Jones, *The great nation: France from Louis XV to Napoleon 1715–99* (London, 2002), pp. 266, 554.

[161] Kwass, 'Court capitalism', p. 6.

[162] For a fuller discussion of this issue see Schui, 'Learning from French experience'.

a recruitment ground for the fiscal opposition. Regional and other differences among taxpayers also existed elsewhere, but hardly anywhere was the public as clearly split as in Prussia. One of the principal causes of Prussia's political stability in this revolutionary period may thus be summed up as 'divide and tax'. Related to this issue is also the question of the size of the urban sector. The notion that the urban sector in Prussia was small by Western European standards has been an implicit or explicit assumption by much of the existing historiography. While it is possible that this was the case, there is little evidence to support this view. Population statistics are incomplete and difficult to compare because contemporary definitions of what constituted a town varied between countries. In order to make meaningful international comparison possible, historical demographers are avoiding contemporary definitions of towns and measure urbanization in terms of the share of the population that lived in towns of a certain size. However, the scarcity of population data for Prussia means that comparisons based on this approach are only available from the early nineteenth century. For the nineteenth century comparative research sees Prussia as the second most urbanized society in Europe, second only to Britain. While eighteenth-century conditions cannot be directly inferred from this, the statistical work on the early nineteenth century casts doubts on the assumption that in the eighteenth century the urban sector was small by European standards. It is of course possible that Prussia went directly from last to second rank in matters of urbanization in a short time span around 1800. However, Schmoller estimated that the relative size of the urban sector in Prussia was no smaller in the eighteenth century than it was in the late nineteenth century.[163] Further research that goes beyond compiling contemporary statistics is urgently needed and is likely to revise current views substantially. It seems likely that the urban development of Prussia was not quite as retarded as has been assumed and contemporary perceptions of urban growth in the second half of the eighteenth century must be taken seriously when explaining Prussia's advanced level of urbanization in the early nineteenth century. However, until more detailed knowledge about the comparative levels of urbanization in the eighteenth century become available, it seems prudent to exclude this factor from considerations about the strength of social protest in Prussia in this period.

---

[163] Gustav von Schmoller, *Deutsches Städtewesen in älterer Zeit* (Aalen, 1964), p. 289. Richard Lawton and Robert Lee, 'Introduction: the framework of comparative urban population studies in Western Europe, *c.*1750–1920', in Richard Lawton and Robert Lee, eds., *Urban population development in Western Europe from the late eighteenth century to the early twentieth century* (Liverpool, 1989), pp. 1–18, at p. 12.

5

Religion and the State

'Or do you think that the burghers and peasants here and elsewhere cannot
read for themselves or that only the learned know what God's will is?'

Samuel Lobegott Apitzsch, *We have now all read it* (1781).[1]

In the same period in which urban dwellers clashed with the Prussian state over
fiscal and economic questions, similar conflicts also developed in matters of religion
and education. In 1781, an attempt by Frederick II to impose a new hymnal on
parishes and schools across Prussia failed after sustained public opposition, and in
1788 Frederick William II's influential minister Woellner tried to curtail the
freedom of religion and expression with two notorious edicts that eventually had
to be abandoned in the face of public resistance. Far-reaching religious freedom had
become part of the constitutional structure of the Hohenzollern polity as a result of
the turmoil of the Thirty Years War and Prussia's 'double reformation'. Nonetheless, in the 1780s Frederick II and Frederick William II both intervened heavy-
handedly in religious matters. Motives and means differed, but the outcomes were
similar. In both cases, the state's overreaching led to controversial public debates
and acts of resistance that eventually forced the state to limit its ambitions in an area
in which individuals guarded their autonomy as jealously as in economic and fiscal
matters.

These conflicts not only occurred in the same period as the conflict over the
Régie, but they also developed along the same lines of confrontation, included
some of the same means and actors, and took place in the same urban setting.
However, while the conflict over the Régie was clearly delineated as a strictly
urban affair, this was much less clear in the case of the conflicts that will
be explored in this chapter. Religious controversy erupted earlier and was more
significant in the towns but it also affected Prussia's rural regions. This chapter
focuses on the conflicts as they related to urban society and its interaction with
the state, but this should not be taken as an indication that they were limited
to the urban setting. In what follows, the discussion will roughly follow the
chronology of events.

---

[1] 'Oder denken Sie, dass die Bürger und Bauern hier und anderswo nicht lesen können, oder dass
nur Studierte allein wissen was der Wille Gottes sei?', Samuel Lobegott Apitzsch, *Wir haben's nun alle
gelesen eine Vertheidigungsschrift* (n.p. [Berlin], 1781), p. 13.

A NEW HYMNAL FOR PRUSSIA

In October 1780, Frederick II decided that Lutheran parishes and schools across Prussia were to adopt a new hymnal over the following two to three years. Yet only four months later the monarch repealed the order and confirmed the right of the faithful to freely choose their hymnals. The cause of this remarkable volte-face was public pressure led by ordinary members of four parishes in Berlin. We will first explore the nature and context of the proposed changes in order to understand the motivations behind Frederick's decision, before turning to the forms and causes of the opposition to the new hymnal.

The decision to introduce a new hymnal in Prussia was part of a wider trend that swept the Protestant territories of the empire, where over a hundred new hymnals were published in the second half of the eighteenth century.[2] These revised editions often reflected views of neologic theologians, who were influenced by the wider context of Enlightenment thought. Also, the new Prussian hymnal, the *Hymnal for the use in worship in the royal Prussian lands*, commonly known as the *Mylius Hymnal*, after its publisher, was edited by three exponents of the reformist religious tendency led by the Berlin pastor Johann Samuel Diterich (1721–97).[3] Already in 1765 Diterich had been the principal editor of a supplement to the existing Pietist hymnal that had been in use since 1713. The *Mylius* represented a further revised version of this supplement, which was not only much shorter than its predecessor but was also substantially different from a theological and aesthetic point of view.

The principal concern of enlightened religious reformers was to create a version of Christianity that was compatible with rationality. Miracles and other supernatural elements of Christian tradition stood in the way of this reform project and so their importance was systematically diminished. It was impossible to deny that such mystical elements were apparent in the Bible itself, but reformers argued that they were remnants of past periods when they had been necessary to convey the message of Christianity to primitive audiences. However, in an age of enlightenment more rational approaches to religion were increasingly to take the place of obsolete irrational elements.[4] The revision of the Prussian hymnal in this spirit led to some important changes that provoked an immediate and radical public response.

---

[2] Paul Graff, *Geschichte der Auflösung der alten gottesdienstlichen Formen in der Evangelischen Kirche Deutschlands* (2 vols., Göttingen, 1937), vol. 2, pp. 193–5.

[3] *Gesangbuch zum gottesdienstlichen Gebrauch in den königlich preussischen Landen*. Christina Rathgeber, 'The reception of Brandenburg-Prussia's new Lutheran hymnal of 1781', *Historical Journal*, 36 (1993), p. 120.

[4] Rathgeber, 'Hymnal', p. 116. Rathgeber summarizes an extensive historiography including Karl Aner, *Die Theologie der Lessingzeit* (Halle/Saale, 1929). Karl von Barth, *Die protestantische Theologie im 19. Jahrhundert ihre Vorgeschichte und ihre Geschichte* (Zollikon, 1947). Friedrich Wilhelm Kantzenbach, 'Die Spätaufklärung: Entwicklung und Stand der Forschung', *Theologische Literaturzeitung*, 102 (1977), pp. 337–48. Anthony Dyson, 'Theological legacies of the enlightenment: England and Germany', in Stephen Sykes, ed., *England and Germany: Studies in theological diplomacy* (Frankfurt, 1982), pp. 45–63.

The first 'improvement' on which critics focused was the absence of the concept of 'original sin' from the new hymnal. The opponents of the new edition denounced Diterich and his colleagues for not explaining the wickedness of men in traditional terms and for attributing human flaws to negative earthly influences that corrupted an allegedly existing original 'pagan virtue'.[5] The notion that man was essentially good, or could at least be made good if protected from corrupting influences and exposed to the right education, was a central tenet of the religious enlightenment and wider enlightened thought of the period.[6] However, critics radically rejected such ideas as euphemistic and contrary to scripture.

In a closely related criticism, the almost complete absence of the figure of the devil from the new hymnal was denounced. The emphasis on the goodness and improvability of man led enlightened theologians to give lesser importance to the destructive work of the force of evil in human existence. In the eyes of the critics this distortion was directly linked to the omission of original sin and was a dangerous tendency. Reducing the importance of evil, the critics argued, would eventually lead to the elimination of the need for salvation. Upon reading the *Mylius*, they feared, the faithful were left wondering why Jesus should redeem them.[7]

Consonant with this elimination of evil from the hymnal, but equally objectionable from the point of view of traditionalists, was a proposed reinterpretation of Christ's divinity. 'It contains far too little about the majesty and the divine dignity of our Lord Jesus Christ', complained the critics, adding that this omission resulted directly from the lack of emphasis on man's 'natural miserable condition'.[8] The Christ of the *Mylius* was not a divine redeemer who changed the prospects of humanity through his self-sacrifice. Instead, he was a much more human figure who made men 'wiser' and helped them to lead an 'honest life as good worldlings', thus becoming a prophet of enlightened politeness and earthly progress, rather than a figure of religious redemption.[9]

Diterich stood accused of wanting to substitute 'religious revelation' ('Erleuchtung') with 'enlightenment' ('Aufklärung'), thus transforming the ideal of a deeply individual and mystical relationship of the faithful to God into a mainly rational and intellectual experience.[10] Moreover, critics not only denounced that the prospect of divine redemption was missing, they also condemned the absence from the hymnal of a punishing God whose judgement men had to fear. The prospects of 'eternal pain', 'damnation', and 'punishment in hell' had been largely substituted by milder and temporary sanctions, meted out by a deity that was far too forgiving and understanding in the view of many Prussian Christians.[11]

---

[5] 'Heidnische Tugend'. Apitzsch, *Vertheidigungsschrift*, pp. 18–19.

[6] Rathgeber, 'Hymnal', p. 117.

[7] Apitzsch, *Vertheidigungsschrift*, p. 19.

[8] 'Es enthält viel zu wenig Lehren von der Majestät und der göttlichen Würde unsers Herrn Jesus Christus', 'natürlichen elenden Zustandes'. Apitzsch, *Vertheidigungsschrift*, p. 20.

[9] 'Weiser'; 'ein honettes Leben als gute Weltbürger'. Apitzsch, *Vertheidigungsschrift*, pp. 19–20.

[10] Apitzsch, *Vertheidigungsschrift*, p. 21.

[11] 'Ewige Pain'; 'Verdammniß'; 'Höllenstrafe'. Apitzsch, *Vertheidigungsschrift*, p. 24.

However, in addition to introducing a different theological perspective, the new hymnals also used new language and artistic form. Many sophisticated urban 'worldlings' found the rustic language and imagery of some of the older hymns embarrassing and inappropriate for an age of enlightenment.[12] The content of the new hymnal, its advocates argued, could be understood more easily by the faithful and thus open up a more rational and reflected way of engaging with religion.[13] Moreover, some of the older hymns were considered to be 'tasteless songs' because of references to bodily love and eroticism, including descriptions of 'the most beautiful girl's breasts' and of 'a navel surrounded by roses'.[14]

It seems likely that the rationality and enlightened aesthetics of the new hymnal appealed to Frederick and led to his decision to make the work mandatory in the Mark-Brandenburg. The exact circumstances of the decision are not known, and the fact that the monarch's signature was absent from the original order has led to speculation about the extent to which Frederick was involved or even aware of the decision. However, as Christina Rathgeber has convincingly argued, the style of Frederick's government makes it highly improbable that a decision of this importance should have been taken without the monarch's direct involvement.[15] It seems likely, instead, that Frederick saw this as an opportunity to impress upon a wider public forms of religiosity that had his sympathy but that had not been received to any significant extent beyond the reified environment of urban literary circles.[16]

FORMS OF RESISTANCE

Congregations reacted with various forms of protest and resistance against the introduction of the new hymnal. Most commonly, the order to use the revised edition was simply ignored, often pointing to the fact that neighbouring parishes had not yet followed the instructions either.[17] Where the use of the new hymnal was forced on the faithful by reform-minded or obedient clergy, congregations resorted to other forms of resistance. Church services were boycotted or the new hymns were drowned out by the loud singing of the old hymns. Where conflicts escalated, threats and acts of violence were equally part of the strategies employed. In Charlottenburg, a certain pastor Dressler found his church empty after he had insisted on the introduction of the new hymnal. When the faithful began to return

---

[12] 'Weltleute'. August Cranz, *Supplement zum ersten Stück der Chronika von Berlin, in einem Sendschreiben an den Weltmann in Berlin, wohmeritirten Tantenbelehrer und Verfasser der Briefe an einem (sic) Landgeistlichen das neue Gesangbuch betreffend von dem Verfasser der Bokiade* (Berlin, 1781), p. 6.

[13] Wilhelm Teller, *Drey Predigten bey Bekanntmachung und Einführung des neuen Gesangbuchs in der Peterskirche zu Berlin* (Berlin, 1781), pp. 36–44.

[14] 'Geschmacklose Lieder'. Johann D. E. Preuss, ed., *Friedrich der Große: eine Lebensgeschichte. Urkundenbuch zu der Lebensgeschichte Friedrichs des Grossen* (Berlin, 1833–4), p. 233. 'Den schönsten Mädchenbrüsten, von einem runden Bauch und rosenumsteckten Nabel'. Cranz, *Supplement*, p. 30.

[15] Rathgeber, 'Hymnal', pp. 121–2.

[16] Rathgeber, 'Hymnal', pp. 122–3.

[17] Rathgeber, 'Hymnal', pp. 125–6.

over the following days he did not alter his stance and castigated them for their behaviour. The response was an attack on his house during the following night, in the course of which his windows were smashed. Violence was also threatened against the preacher's servant who was intercepted by a parishioner when he was on his way to buy a new batch of hymnals in Berlin. A concerned citizen offered the messenger a good thrashing and forced him off the coach on which he was travelling.[18] Even preachers themselves were not safe from violent attacks on their person, as one clergyman in Altena experienced when an enraged mob of parishioners dragged him from the pulpit and threatened to stone him.[19]

However, as with the resistance against the Régie, the most effective forms of opposition revolved around the public use of the written word. The government's decision to impose the new hymnal led to a number of publications attacking and defending the decision,[20] whether defences of the new hymnal, moderate rejection or stinging attacks.[21] Perhaps the most incendiary rhetoric can be found in a pamphlet that circulated in Berlin attacking Diterich and his fellow authors as 'apostles of the devil'. Accused of 'distorting, dismembering [and] hashing the beautiful old songs' the authors surmised that the three reformers were taking their orders from Satan directly. The pamphlet detailed some of the main theological errors of the three 'beasts', before moving on to attack a pastor Stork who had been using the new satanic hymnal. In the course of the text, Stork went from 'stupid man' to 'damned dog', before the pamphlet culminated in a general attack on the 'damned clergy' and its 'ungodly' conduct.[22] Together with the acts of violence that took place, this rhetoric was certainly a cause for concern, not only among the loyal clergy but also among the authorities.

FREDERICK THE GREAT FLEES FROM A FLOCK OF BURGHERS

Ultimately it was in response to more moderate appeals that the decision about the hymnal was repealed. However, the persuasive power of more supplicant texts needs to be understood in the context of the more aggressive pamphlets and acts that conjured up the possibility of a further escalation of the conflict. A petition to Frederick II signed by 130 members of the Berlin parishes of Dreifaltigs-, St. Gertraud-, Kölnische Vorstadt-, and Neuen und Jerusalemer Kirche led to the reversal of the king's position.[23]

---

[18] Apitzsch, *Vertheidigungsschrift*, pp. 10–11.   [19] Rathgeber, 'Hymnal', p. 125.

[20] For an overview of the publications see Walter Delius, 'Zur Geschichte des berliner Gesangbuchs', *Theologia Viatorum. Jahrbuch der kirchlichen Hochschulen Berlin*, 9 (1964), pp. 16–19.

[21] Johann Spalding, *Predigt von dem, was erbaulich ist. Mit einer Anwendung auf das Gesangbuch zum gottesdienstlichen Gebrauch in den königl. preußl. Landen* (Berlin, 1781). Teller, *Drey Predigten*. Cranz, *Supplement*.

[22] 'Verdrehen, zerstümmeln, zerhacken die alten schönen Lieder'; 'des Teufels Apostel'; 'dumme Mensch'; 'verfluchte Hund'; 'so gottlos handeln unsre verfluchten Geistlichen'. Anonymous untitled pamphlet cited in Delius, 'Zur Geschichte', p. 19.

[23] Apitzsch, *Vertheidigungsschrift*, p. 50. Preuss, *Urkundenbuch*, p. 224.

Fig. 5.1. Anonymous, 'Samuel Lobegott Apitzsch, Kaufmann zu Berlin', 1781 (Samuel Lobegott Apitzsch, merchant in Berlin), 1781, etching, 1781. Reproduced with permission from LWL-Landesmuseum für Kunst und Kulturgeschichte Münster (Westfälisches Landesmuseum) / Porträtarchiv Diepenbroick.

The petitioners were led by Samuel Lobegott Apitzsch (?–1786) who also published a pamphlet in which he shed light on the circumstances in which the petition was written and the concerns that motivated the authors. Not much is known about Apitzsch's biography, but, according to his own account, he was a novice to public debates. He descried himself as an honest merchant who had no debts, never missed a payment, and ran a sound commercial enterprise.[24] This association with Berlin's commercial classes is also emphasized in a contemporary etching (see Fig. 5.1). Apitzsch is shown with various religious writings connected with his rebellion. For example, clearly visible in the foreground is a copy of the 'Porstsche Gesangbuch', the traditional Pietist hymnal that he and his friends

---

[24] Apitzsch, *Vertheidigungsschrift*, pp. 3–6.

wanted to keep. There is also a clearly legible extract from the hymn 'Upon the cross extended' and an extract from the New Testament's 'Epistle to the Romans'. Both texts were central to the theological content of Apitzsch's argument. The hymn speaks of the suffering of Christ, a central theme that set Pietism and other traditional currents apart from the new 'painless' neologic theology. Even more important was the biblical verse, which was seen by Apitzsch and others as evidence that Jesus was explicitly called 'God' in the New Testament, clearly contradicting enlightened tendencies that emphasized the human qualities of the Messiah. However, despite the religious attributes that dominate the picture, Apitzsch is also clearly identified in the caption as a 'merchant from Berlin'. Clearly, contemporaries set great store by the combination of his religious and social identities and by the fact that he was an urban dweller. Being a bona fide member of Berlin's commercial bourgeoisie Apitzsch had experienced a religious rebirth five years earlier and had since organised conventicles in his home.[25] Apitzsch described the participants as coming from all parts of society, although virtually everyone who is mentioned individually was an artisan.[26]

It was at one of these conventicles that the idea of the petition was born and the text collectively written. Resistance against the imposition of the hymnal thus emerges as driven by the type of religious grassroots movements that thrived as a result of the confluence of religious freedom and Pietist traditions. Urban dwellers used the religious freedom afforded to them under the 'constitutional settlement' of the Hohenzollern polity to form and express their own individual forms of religiosity. Apitzsch described Bible study, singing, and praying as part of the activities in the conventicle, but emphasized that all of this was undertaken without the direction of a preacher. The sense of a gathering of like-minded individuals in a private bourgeois home that was free of hierarchies was further underlined by the process of collaboration that gave rise to the petition. If religious tolerance provided the wider social context for this phenomenon, Pietism provided the model for this form of sociability and served as the blueprint of its individualistic approach to religiosity. Evidently Pietist traditions were part of a context in which individual autonomy and direct opposition to the state were kindled. It is impossible to reconcile this historical reality with a simplistic view of Pietism as a purveyor of an authoritarian ideology to a repressive Prussian state.

The social context in which resistance to the official imposition of the hymnal emerged is noteworthy in another respect, too. Merchants such as Apitzsch, along with artisans and other urban dwellers, belonged also to the social networks that led to resistance against the Régie. Merchants were among the urban dwellers who suffered most from long delays and intrusive controls at the hands of excise officers. Apitzsch most likely interacted on a regular basis with these officers and may well have shared the indignation of many of his colleagues about the way in which they carried on. Whether or not he ever resisted the fiscal policies of the Prussian state in similar ways to his opposition of Frederick's religious policies is impossible to know.

---

[25] Rathgeber, 'Hymnal', p. 127.
[26] Apitzsch, *Vertheidigungsschrift*, p. 44. See also Rathgeber, 'Hymnal', pp. 127–8.

In their pamphlet, Apitzsch and other members of the conventicle claimed that the king was free to take their blood and possessions if he only left their soul to God. However, this may have been more a rhetorical device than a blanket agreement to fiscal demands.[27]

THE CAUSES OF REBELLION

The way in which the authors of the petition lived their religion provides us with important cues that explain the speed and intensity of their response to the new hymnal. For contemporaries such as Apitzsch, religion was a deeply individual matter that was closely linked to the privacy of the home. Hymnals formed an important part of this domestic piety and were interwoven with the private life of the faithful on several levels. 'It was in the home', Rathgeber points out, 'that not only passages from the Bible but also verses from hymns were learned from parents and then preserved through repeated singing at work and in church.'[28] As contemporary commentators themselves emphasized, traditional hymns were deeply woven into all parts of private life including, most importantly, the intimacy of the family home and the economic sphere.[29] The guilds of Breslau, for example, opposed the new hymnal on the grounds that, unlike the widely known traditional hymns, those of the *Mylius* could not be sung together at work.[30] Moreover, the importance of the hymnals for the private sphere went beyond religious practices. Many lines from the hymns that had been in use for generations were universally known and were widely used as proverbs among artisans and peasants. By rearranging and contextualizing these linguistic building blocs, individuals expressed themselves in a language understood by their peers. Deviation from tradition meant a dissolution and possibly fragmentation of this universal medium of expression. A new hymnal potentially deprived individuals of a way of expressing themselves while at the same time identifying them as part of a wider community.[31]

The consequences of the imposition of the new hymnal by the state thus went far beyond a modification of public religious functions such as Sunday prayer in church. Instead, they reached deep into the private sphere of individuals and interfered with the some of the most intimate aspects of religious, family, and community life. The outrage felt at this paternalistic intrusion is clear from Apitzsch's comments. Freeing themselves from the oppressive 'rule of the improvers of religion' was the protesters' main objective.[32] They considered their own judgement in religious matters to be as good as that of the learned men of the Prussian enlightenment, and this kind of imposition was therefore utterly unacceptable. 'Or do you think', Apitzsch exclaimed, 'that the burghers and peasants

---

[27] Apitzsch, *Vertheidigungsschrift*, pp. 45–6.
[28] Rathgeber, 'Hymnal', p. 124.
[29] See also the comments in Cranz, *Supplement*, p. 22.
[30] Rathgeber, 'Hymnal', p. 124, note 53.
[31] Rathgeber, 'Hymnal', pp. 124–5.
[32] 'Herrschaft der Religionsverbesserung'. Apitzsch, *Vertheidigungsschrift*, p. 32.

here and elsewhere cannot read for themselves or that only the learned know what God's will is?'[33] Another pamphlet against the new hymnal argued in very similar terms. In his *Message to a worldling in Berlin* (1781) August Friedrich Cranz (1737–1801) warned the religious reformers that their tutelage was not welcome. 'The public', he wrote, 'has its own head and power to examine everything and keep the best'.[34] In Apitzsch's view, it was impossible that the imposition of religious dogma from above could ever have a benign effect. 'Jesus', they pointed out true to the spirit of Pietism, 'does not want forced [followers] but only volunteers'.[35] If anything, preachers were to adapt to the religious principles of their congregations or move on to 'go hunting or another profession'.[36] In an outpouring of republican sentiment Apitztsch exclaimed: 'Neither is the people there for a preacher! No, the preacher is there for a congregation.'[37]

The question of who should have the last word in religious matters, the public or religious leaders, was central to this conflict. This also can be seen clearly in the arguments of the defenders of the new hymnal. It is hardly a coincidence that the first of Teller's *Three sermons on the announcement and introduction of the new hymnal* was a critical examination of the phrase 'The voice of the people is the voice of God'. Unsurprisingly, Teller came to the conclusion that this maxim applied only in matters that could be judged on 'impressions of the senses'. But when 'the high teachings of God's wisdom' were at stake, the populace could hardly be taken to express God's will. Instead, the people required guidance in such matters.[38]

In contrast to this view, Apitzsch and his companions asked in their petition not merely for permission to use the old hymnal, but also for a reiteration of Frederick's policy of religious tolerance.[39] This call for the protection of diversity was not merely opportunistic. Individual freedom was central to the protesters' religion. The ways in which they experienced religion in their lives were closely associated with a sociability of free and equal individuals, which could only exist where government and other forms of coercion were absent. Similarly, the theology that had developed in this context emphasized individual freedom because freely chosen and truly felt religious sentiments were a precondition for spiritual awakening, whereas all imposed religion necessarily remained superficial and formulaic. The authors of the petition also explicitly linked this argument to the issue of social and political stability. If the imposition of the unwanted hymnal persisted, they warned, their children would quickly become 'wicked and disloyal subjects'. The first

[33] 'Oder denken Sie, dass die Bürger und Bauern hier und anderswo nicht lesen können, oder dass nur Studierte allein wissen was der Wille Gottes sei?' Ibid., p. 13.

[34] 'Das Publikum selbst Kopf und Kraft hat alles zu prüfen und das beste zu behalten'. Cranz, *Supplement*, p. 32.

[35] 'Christus will keine gezwungene sondern nur freywillige haben.' Apitzsch, *Vertheidigungsschrift*, p. 39.

[36] 'Auf die Jagd oder andere Profession gehen'. Apitzsch, *Vertheidigungsschrift*, p. 32.

[37] 'Das Volk ist auch nicht fuer einen Priester da! Nein, der Priester ist fuer eine Gemeinde da.' Apitzsch, *Vertheidigungsschrift*, p. 32.

[38] 'Bloß sinnlicher Eindruck'; 'die hohen Lehren göttlicher Weisheit'. Teller, *Drey Predigten*, pp. 16–17.

[39] Petition edited in Preuss, *Urkundenbuch*, p. 226.

manifestations of these subversive effects, they added, could already be observed.[40] Whether or not this should be seen as a veiled threat must remain open. However, this remark connected the theological and religious arguments that were presented in a humble and supplicant fashion in the petition with a wider context of political and social stability. From the point of view of the state any prospect of civil unrest fuelled by religious conflict was highly sensitive not only in the light of Prussia's historical experience but also because of the tense atmosphere spreading across parishes throughout Prussia.

RELIGIOUS *REALPOLITIK*

The king's response was swift. The petition had been submitted in January 1780 and within days Frederick replied confirming that the petitioners and all other Prussian subjects were 'completely free' to 'believe and sing' what they wanted.[41] Despite its shortness the *Cabinetts-Resolution* contained some hints that make it possible to understand why Frederick the Great allowed himself to be overruled by a flock of burghers. Both in the official text and in a postscript, Frederick made it clear that he continued to prefer the new hymnal. 'Probably', he formulated cautiously but unequivocally, 'the . . . new hymnal is clearer, more reasonable and more appropriate for true worship'.[42] In this passage he clearly embraced the spirit of the religious enlightenment that had underpinned the revision of the hymnal. However, no matter how far his sympathies for enlightened religion extended, other concerns were more important. This becomes clear from the qualifications associated with the confirmation of religious freedom in the *Resolution*. In the conclusion, the four parishes in Berlin were ordered to calm down, now that their demands had been met. Earlier in the text, the religious freedom of everyone in Prussia had been confirmed 'as long as his dogmas and religious practice were not detrimental to the peace of the state and good morality'.[43] Frederick was clearly sympathetic to the diffusion of enlightened religious ideas, but he was not prepared to jeopardize political stability and risk public unrest. Even the vague shadow of a trade-off between the pursuit of enlightened ideals and the preservation of state power was enough to lead to Frederick's immediate and unequivocal return to the principle of religious tolerance that had been one of the cornerstones on which the edifice of the Prussian state had been constructed.

---

[40] 'Lasterhaften und untreuen Unterthanen'. Petition edited in Preuss, *Urkundenbuch*, p. 225.

[41] 'Ganz frei steht, zu glauben und zu singen, was er will.' 'Cabinets-Resolution für den Kaufmann Apitzsch als Deputirten der evangelischen Gemeinden der Dreifaltigkeits-, Jerusalemer-, Gertrauden- und Kölnischen Vorstadt Kirche. Berlin 18 Januar 1781.' Edited in Max Lehmann, *Preussen, und die katholische Kirche seit 1640* (Leipzig, 1885), p. 410.

[42] 'Vermuthlich ist der neue Katechismus sowie das neue Gesangbuch verständlicher, vernünftiger und dem wahren Gottesdienst angemessener'. Cabinetts-Resolution edited in Lehmann, *Preussen*, p. 411.

[43] 'Nur dass seine Lehrsätze und Religions Übungen weder die Ruhe des Staates noch den guten Sitten nachtheilig sein müsssen.' Cabinetts-Resolution edited in Lehmann, *Preussen*.

Frederick's reaction reminds us of the utilitarian foundations on which religious tolerance rested in Prussia. As discussed in Chapter 3, Frederick, even more explicitly than his predecessors, embraced tolerance as a *means* to prevent religious discord. Religious freedom was not endorsed as an individual right but because it was seen to guarantee social order more effectively than religious restriction. This is clear from Frederick's behaviour in 1780. After all, a rights-based approach to religious toleration should have categorically prevented attempts to impose a new hymnal in the first place. It seems more likely that Frederick misjudged the likelihood of protest that could result from this intervention and back-tracked when such protest became apparent. Political realism also explains why a comparably limited extent of resistance persuaded Frederick to change his mind in this case, while twenty years of sustained resistance against the Régie caused him to doubt the institution, but did not lead him to abolish it. As a religious sceptic Frederick was clearly not willing to risk political instability in order to save Prussian souls; but he was prepared to take political risks in areas where the rewards for the state were more tangible.

Irrespective of the motives that led Frederick to give up his religious reform project, the outcome of the conflict showed that an urban public was able to impose itself politically in religious as well as other matters. This was true in Berlin, but the introduction of the hymnal was also opposed successfully elsewhere in Prussia, and urban congregations often played a leading role in resisting the decision.[44] The extent of the public's power may be illustrated by further development of the conflict over the hymnal in two parishes in Berlin. After Apitzsch and his associates had extracted the repeal of Frederick's decision for their parishes in January 1781, petitioners from Dorotheenstadt and Friedrichswerderstadt asked for a similar concession in March of the same year. The monarch granted their request in May, but overturned his decision again in 1782, when he was presented with a petition in favour of the new hymnal that was supported by larger numbers of faithful.[45] In this case the power of public pressure made Frederick the Great change his opinion and back again in just over a year. Even by the standards of today's political culture, the speed and ease of his 'flip flopping' in the face of a perceived change in public opinion must count as extraordinary and does not sit easily with some of the historical perceptions associated with Frederick the Great.

Frederick's vacillations in this matter show not only the power that the public had acquired in this period; they also warn us against any interpretation that associates these conflicts with political or theological tendencies. This was not a case of an enlightened public taking on a reactionary monarch or vice versa. The conflict arose because members of civil society rejected the paternalistic overreaching of the state in matters that they considered to be their own private affairs. As is evident, public controversy could result from the rejection of governmental intervention that favoured enlightened ideas just as much as from intervention that

[44] Rathgeber, 'Hymnal', pp. 126–7, 128–30.
[45] Preuss, *Urkundenbuch*, pp. 132–3.

opposed it. It was not the content of the state's intervention that was incendiary, but the fact that it trod on individual autonomy.

It has been argued that the public as a whole could hardly be seen as subversive in respect of state power because public debates were only ever in part composed of critics of the state. Clearly, in the conflict over the hymnal both critics and supporters of official policies publicly expressed their opinions. However, to see this as proof of the political innocuousness of the public is to misunderstand the concerns of contemporary states, in particular in regard to religion. The challenge for the states of the period did not lie in the spread or decline of specific religious opinions, but in religious controversy itself. The memories of the destructive power that incontrollable conflict over often arcane questions of religious dogma could unleash were still present in Prussia and elsewhere. Frederick may have had sympathies for the religious enlightenment and he certainly had strong views on religion himself, but his principal objective in religious matters was not to help the triumph of this or that doctrine or sect. For Frederick there was only one good type of religion—a quiet one that did not pose a threat to political stability. Public religious controversy, no matter whether dominated by 'friends' or 'foes', was in itself a threat to the state. The main reason why Frederick so fervently defended religious tolerance was that he saw it as the best way to prevent the eruption of religious controversies that had the power to weaken and even destroy entire states.

WOELLNER'S MACHINATIONS

Urban Prussians, together with their rural cousins, were soon confronted with an even more far-reaching intrusion into their autonomy in matters of religion and education. In 1788, the newly appointed head of the Department of Religious Affairs, Woellner, introduced the two notorious edicts that are associated with his name. The first required the clergy of the principal confessions, Lutherans and Reformed in particular, not to stray from accepted religious dogma in their sermons and in teaching. The second edict was released five months after the first and tightened the rules of censorship, in particular with regard to religious publications in order to quell the public debate that was triggered by the first edict. Much of the historiographical debate about the edicts has focused on the nature and motives of Woellner's policies, but little attention has been paid to the fact that his project ultimately failed. After the mid-1790s his efforts had already 'run out of steam', and the disgraced Woellner was eventually dismissed only months after the death of Frederick William II in 1797.[46] In this case Prussian civil society once again affirmed its political power and independence against the state by sustaining a prolonged conflict in which it eventually prevailed. The means employed to resist the state in many ways resembled those encountered in the other conflicts

---

[46] Christopher Clark, *Iron kingdom: the rise and downfall of Prussia, 1600–1947* (London, 2007), p. 273.

examined in this book. Public criticism, often in printed form, played by far the most important role, but acts of civil disobedience and violence or threats of violence were equally part of the conflict.

As Michael Sauter has shown, the conflict was not provoked by a simple clash between reactionary obscurantist policies and a progressive enlightened public. Rather, Woellner's policies were rooted in currents of political and religious thought that were closely linked to contemporary public debates and to the traditions that had informed Prussia's reason of state since the Thirty Years War. What led to the conflict between parts of Prussia's civil society and Woellner were not so much differing degrees of 'enlightenment' but contrary interests of a state eager to preserve stability and individuals defending their autonomy. Like many members of the public, Woellner believed that an excessive religious individualism was spreading and that the increasing fragmentation of religious beliefs would lead to political and social instability. He therefore thought that it was necessary to abandon religious tolerance. In his view tolerance did not work anymore as a means to prevent conflicts between different religious groups. Rather, tolerance had led to an increasing and dangerous level of fragmentation of society in religious matters. Instead of relying on tolerance to prevent religious strife, he sought to impose stability on the religious sphere by limiting individual freedom of interpretation. Although his approach turned out to be counter-productive, there was per se nothing sinister or irrational about his intentions. They were deeply rooted in both public discourse and governmental thinking of the time. Like generations of Hohenzollern rulers and their administrators, he sought to protect the state's interests by preventing religious strife, and, like many contemporary commentators, he was worried about religious individualism. Nonetheless, large parts of Prussia's civil society opposed his policies because they interfered with individual autonomy in an area of life that had come to be considered an integral part of the private sphere. The perception of an overreaching state was central to the ensuing controversy and triggered a broad public debate. At stake were not contrasts between different modes of thinking, but the question who—state or private individual—should wield ultimate authority in religious matters. In a way, the conflict was not over the question how to think but about who should do the thinking and who should have the power to decide in religious matters. It soon became clear that Woellner was unable to implement his plans in the face of widespread resistance. Moreover, he had achieved the opposite of what he intended. Rather than ensuring stability, he had lit a firestorm of religious controversy at a time when monarchical states across Europe feared nothing more than a replication of the public controversies and disorder that had proven so corrosive to the Bourbon state in France.

Before going on to expound this argument in more detail, a word should be said about the geography of this conflict. Like the *Gesangbuchstreit*, the conflict over Woellner's edicts was not limited to the towns. However, several factors meant that urban dwellers played a particularly prominent role in the confrontation. The limited depth of the state's reach meant that Woellner was able to take his project further in the larger towns of the central provinces than in the countryside and in more peripheral parts of Prussia, which in turn led to stronger public reactions in urban centres. Moreover, many urban dwellers resented Woellner's authoritarian policies because of the widespread diffusion of individualistic values in the urban society. Urban society was also better equipped to express criticism publicly, partly because of higher literacy rates and a flourishing publication scene, and partly because of the easier access to forums of enlightened sociability that facilitated the fermentation of ideas and criticism.

THE INTELLECTUAL ORIGINS OF THE EDICTS

Woellner's edict of July 1788 began by confirming the religious freedom not only of the three major Christian denominations but also of the Jews and some of the smaller Christian sects that existed in Prussia. However, the Lutheran and Reformed preachers in particular were ordered to conform to the traditional dogmatic framework of their confessions and to desist from teaching or preaching anything else. Specifically, they were required to exclude any ideas from their sermons or classes that were circulating under the 'misused label of enlightenment'.[47] In the cases of the Lutheran and Reformed confessions, the state's department of religious affairs would henceforth enforce compliance in their regard with a 'watchful eye' and under threat of 'Cassation and harsher punishments'.[48] These provisions, however, applied only to preaching and teaching. The individual freedom of consciousness of clergymen was explicitly confirmed. In essence preachers were allowed to hold any views they chose but were barred from 'laying them out before the people'. Matters became even more complex with the second edict of December 1788. The first edict had provoked widespread public criticism and, in order to limit this debate, the second reiterated and tightened the existing rules of censorship. The second edict argued that increased 'control and guidance by the state' had become necessary in this area to prevent public commentary that attacked the 'foundations of religion' or the 'state' and 'moral and civic order' in general.[49]

The complexity of the edicts' provisions has led historians to interpret their historical significance in different ways. In the late nineteenth century, Hintze famously described the edict on religion as an 'edict of toleration', but the majority of modern historians including most notably Paul Schwartz and Dirk Kemper have

---

[47] 'Gemißbrauchten Namen Aufklärung'. Frederick William II, 'Circulare an alle Inspectoren der Churmark, nebst Edict vom 9ten July, die Religions-Verfassung in den Preußischen Staaten betreffend.', *Novum Corpus Constitutionum Prussico-Brandenburgensium Praecipue Marchicarum (NCC)* (12 vols., Berlin, 1788), vol. 9, p. 2179.

[48] 'Offenes Auge'; 'Cassation und noch härteren Strafen'. Frederick William II, 'Edict die Religions-Verfassung betreffend', p. 2182.

[49] 'Aufsicht und Leitung des Staates'; 'Grundsätze der Religion'; 'Staat'; 'moralischer oder bürgerlicher Ordnung'. Frederick William II, 'Erneuertes Censur-Edict für die preußischen Staaten. Nebst Begleitungs-Rescript an das Cammer-Gericht vom 25. December. De Dato Berlin, den 19. December 1788', *Novum Corpus Constitutionum Prussico-Brandenburgensium Praecipue Marchicarum (NCC)* (12 vols., Berlin, 1788), vol. 9, pp. 2339–40.

interpreted Woellner's project as an obscurantist attempt to roll back the budding Prussian enlightenment.[50] Recently, Sauter has proposed a revision of the established view by arguing that Woellner's politics were not a manifestation of intellectual currents of counter-enlightenment but a product of authoritarian tendencies within the Prussian enlightenment itself, which were attempting to limit the religious freedom mainly of the uneducated majority, while preserving a greater degree of liberty for the intellectual elites.[51] Paradoxically, all these varied interpretations bring insight to our understanding of Woellner's policies that were far too complex to be captured under a simple heading.

In the traditional view of Woellner as an exponent of the counter-enlightenment, the resistance of Prussia's civil society was explained as the outcry of an enlightened public that saw some of its most cherished values, freedom of religion and speech, attacked and that rose to the defence of these ideals. However, as Sauter convincingly shows, Woellner was in his habitus and ideas close to the mainstream of contemporary civil society. In particular, sympathies for the regulation of religious matters and the freedom of speech were not peculiar to Woellner and his circle, but rather common also among many members of the wider public. However, if there was no clear line of demarcation that separated an obscurantist Woellner on one side from an enlightened public on the other, this forces us also to re-examine the causes of the political conflict that surrounded the edicts. If this was not a conflict over freedom of consciousness and expression as an ideal, then what caused members of civil society to contest Woellner's policies with such intensity that they had eventually to be abandoned?

It will be argued here that the backlash of large elements of civil society was caused in large part by Woellner's intrusive interventions into matters that many Prussians had come to regard as belonging to the private sphere of individuals and had previously been treated as such by the state. Most importantly, his edicts affected individual autonomy in religious matters, and through the second edict also the freedom of expression in a broader sense. Woellner was not guided by a single motive. He pursued a mixture of objectives that may seem contradictory to modern historians but they were not so to him and his associates. Imposing 'literalist' religiosity on the population was a part of this policy, but the promotion of this reactionary theology was not driven exclusively by his own 'obscurantist'

---

[50] Otto Hintze, *Die Hohenzollern und ihr Werk* (Berlin, 1915), p. 411. For the interpretation of Woellner as an exponent of the counter-enlightenment see among others Paul Schwartz, *Der erste Kulturkampf in Preussen um Kirche und Schule 1788–1798* (Berlin, 1925). Dirk Kemper, 'Obskurantismus als Mittel der Politik. Johann Christoph Wöllners Politik der Gegenaufklärung am Vorabend der Französischen Revolution', in Christoph Weiß, ed., *Von 'Obscuranten' und 'Eudämonisten'. Gegenaufklärerische, konservative und antirevolutionäre Publizisten im späten 18. Jahrhundert* (St Ingbert, 1997), pp. 193–220. Christina Stange-Fayos, *Lumières et obscurantisme en Prusse* (Bern, 2003). Uta Wiggermann, *Woellner und das Religionsedikt Kirchenpolitik und kirchliche Wirklichkeit im Preußen des späten 18. Jahrhunderts* (Tübingen, 2010).

[51] Michael Sauter, 'The enlightenment on trial: state service and social discipline in eighteenth-century Germany's public sphere', *Modern Intellectual History*, 5 (2008), pp. 195–223. Michael Sauter, *Visions of the Enlightenment: the Edict on Religion of 1788 and the politics of the Public Sphere in eighteenth-century Prussia* (Leiden, 2009).

religious convictions, but by a combination of the pursuit of political objectives that had been part of Prussia's reason of state for generations with an understanding of contemporary trends in religiosity that was widespread among the public at the time. The traditional Hohenzollern policy in matters of religion was one of far-reaching tolerance. However, as discussed, this policy was never mainly motivated by a principled commitment to tolerance as an ethical imperative. Rather, religious toleration was embraced for opportunistic reasons in order to shield the Prussian polity from the destabilizing effects of religious controversy. Woellner appropriated this political objective and fully understood the crucial relation between religious peace and political stability. Yet, like many of his contemporaries he was at the same time concerned that the individualism that had developed, above all in the towns, would undermine the effectiveness of the traditional policy of toleration as a means to achieve this end. Religious toleration had prevented strife between different sects in the past, but Woellner and many contemporaries believed that religious peace was facing new challenges in their time. As discussed in Chapter 2, the 'religious landscape' was seen as increasingly fragmented as a result of the religious individualism that thrived under the umbrella of toleration. For many contemporaries this fragmentation raised a political and social problem: if an increasing number of individuals embraced their own form of religiosity how could religion continue to provide the ethical 'glue' that held Prussia's society together? Religious toleration worked because different sects all helped to uphold morality and respect for political authority. They did so in different ways but they all contributed to this objective. However, if the faithful were no longer loyal to these large and ultimately rather similar religious groups, but began to adhere to their own individual forms of religiosity there would be no guarantee that their beliefs would uphold religious peace and political stability. Religious individualism taken to the extreme could potentially mean that no two Prussians continued to share the same moral and religious values and, perhaps even more frighteningly, there was no telling what kind of morality and ethics individuals would embrace if they were left completely unguided. Sauter has suggested that the divide between tolerated and repressed forms of religiosity under Woellner's regime was delineated by their medium of transmission. The orally transmitted religiosity for the masses was to be regulated, while the written commentary of the elite on religious matters was to remain free. This dichotomy coincided to some extent with the one that we are proposing here because the established sects had a substantial number of well-educated clergymen while religious individualism thrived in conventicles and appealed often to less educated citizens. However, we suggest that the targets of Woellner's authoritarianism were all forms of religiosity that deviated from traditional and consolidated religious form, irrespectively of the medium of expression.

For Woellner, the rise of religious individualism was the central problem. The threat of religious fragmentation meant that toleration alone was no longer an efficient means to achieve political stability, but a cover under which morally subversive subcultures thrived. As a result, a new policy in religious matters was now required to protect political stability. Religious toleration still had a role to play in preventing conflict between the major sects, but it had to be limited to these.

Additional measures had to be taken to prevent religious individualism and fragmentation on the 'edges' of established religiosity. The relation of these seemingly contradictory elements of toleration and regulation present in Woellner's policies can only be fully understood if we look at these policies with their principal objective—securing political stability—in mind.

The objective of Woellner's policies was thus specifically to reduce individual autonomy in religious matters. This thrust of his policies was to a large extent responsible for the opposition against the edicts. The delimitation of state power and individual freedom was a central theme in the public debate that was triggered by Woellner's legislation. The remainder of this chapter first examines Woellner's own comments on the objectives of his religious policies, then locates this position in the wider context of contemporary debates and preceding government policies, before turning to the role that Woellner's attempt at limiting individual autonomy played in resistance against these policies.

THE DANGERS OF 'SELF-THINKING'

In the first edict two justifications are offered for the new policies to protect the Christian religion in Prussia. One was associated with the salvation of Prussian souls. Efforts to limit religious teaching to the fundamental texts were to guarantee that Prussians could find happiness in life and consolation on their deathbed.[52] The other objective, mentioned far more frequently in the texts, was the upholding of the realm's moral and social order. The 'alteration of the fundamental truths', 'faithlessness', and 'superstition' inevitably led to 'licentiousness of morals'.[53] However, this was a problem for state as well as for the individual or civil society because a 'conscienceless and bad man' could never be 'a good subject and even less a loyal servant of the state'.[54] For the state it was therefore important to ensure the purity of religious teaching in order to uphold the application of laws in the ways that they had been intended. In the same way that judges were not allowed to 'fiddle around' ('klügeln') with the law and interpret it in their own way, preachers had to be forced to adhere to the letter of the fundamental religious texts. The central passage of the edict bears quoting at length:

> For in the same way in which for the welfare of the state and the happiness of our subjects we have to uphold the full respect for civil laws and cannot permit to any judge or executor of these laws to fiddle with their content or change them as they please; as little and even less we can permit that a clergyman acts in matters of religion following

---

[52] Frederick William II, 'Edict die Religions-Verfassung betreffend', p. 2180.
[53] 'Der Verfälschung der Grundwahrheiten des Glaubens'; 'Unglauben'; 'Aberglauben'; 'Zügellosigkeit der Sitten'. Frederick William II, 'Edict die Religions-Verfassung betreffend', p. 2180.
[54] 'Gewissenloser und böser Mensch'; 'guter Unterthan, und noch weniger ein treuer Diener des Staates'. Frederick William II, 'Edict die Religions-Verfassung betreffend', p. 2183.

his own head as he thinks best or that he could be free to teach the basic truths of Christianity in one way or another as he pleases.[55]

Woellner's comparison is telling because it clearly shows not only that political objectives occupied a crucial place among the motives of his policies, but also that he believed a fundamental reorganization of the relation between politics and religion was necessary for the protection of stability and order. Rather than continuing on the path of separating the two spheres, Woellner argued for closer integration of politics and religion. Upholding political and social order was simply not possible without a religiously based morality that pervaded society. Therefore the state needed to ensure that there was a clear and fixed 'norm', 'precept', and 'rule' according to which the populace was to be 'guided' and 'taught' by the clergy.[56]

Religious homogeneity was not only threatened by preachers who 'followed their own head', but potentially even more by those faithful who eschewed guidance altogether and refused to be taught by anyone. The conventicles, notorious to many members of the public as breeding places of religious autonomy, were mentioned explicitly in the edict. They constituted an 'abuse of tolerance' and needed to be suppressed because their effects were clearly 'corruptive for the state'. In particular, they offered a forum for 'new teachers' and 'all sorts of men who were dangerous for tranquillity'.[57] The edict formulated a political response to these potentially subversive developments in the religious sphere by guaranteeing the religious liberties 'innocuous to the state'—those of the established sects—while resolutely restricting the liberty to deviate from the canon of accepted religiosity.[58]

The notions underpinning the edict were not new to Woellner or to the wider public. Already in 1782, Woellner had expressed his views about religious freedom in a public defence of the Rosicrucians. Woellner had become a member of the secret order in the late 1770s after a disappointing involvement with the Masonic movement. The novice quickly rose to prominent positions as a result of his tireless engagement for the order, and he was most likely the driving force and author of large parts of the programmatic treaty *The duties of the Gold- and Rosicrucians of the old system*.[59] One of the themes that occupied a prominent place in the work was the

---

[55] 'Denn so wie Wir zur Wohlfahrt des Staates und zur Glückseligkeit Unserer Unterthanen die bürgerlichen Gesetze in ihrem ganzen Ansehen aufrecht erhalten müssen, und keinem Richter oder Handhaber dieser Gesetze erlauben können, an dem Inhalt derselben zu klügeln, und selbigen nach seinem Gefallen abzuändern; eben so wenig und noch viel weniger dürfen Wir zugeben, daß ein jeder Geistlicher in Religionssachen nach seinen Kopf und Gutdünken handele, und es ihm freystehen könne, die einmal in der Kirche angenommenen Grundwahrheiten des Chrsitenthums das Volk so oder anders zu lehren . . .' Frederick William II, 'Edict die Religions-Verfassung betreffend', pp. 2180–1.

[56] 'Allgemeine Richtschnur'; 'Norma'; 'Regel'; 'geführet'; 'unterrichtet'. Frederick William II, 'Edict die Religions-Verfassung betreffend', p. 2181.

[57] 'Dem Staate schädliche Conventicula'; 'allerley der Ruhe gefährliche Menschen und neue Lehrer'. Frederick William II, 'Edict die Religions-Verfassung betreffend', p. 2177.

[58] 'Diese dem Staat unschädliche Freyheit'. Frederick William II, 'Edict die Religions-Verfassung betreffend'.

[59] The book was published under the name used by Woellner as member of the order, but the extent of the authorship is not certain. It is, however, likely that the text was written entirely or in large

dangers associated with 'schisms and unloving animosity' among Christians. Such conflicts were seen as the fruit of the 'satanic haughtiness and self-importance' that were caused by the 'illusion of wisdom and learnedness'. The result of such 'self-thinking' was 'idle sophistry, bickering over words, hatred, revenge and persecution' that damaged true Christianity and helped to expand 'Lucifer's kingdom'.[60] Such evils thrived where 'everyone teaches and no one learns' and the only remedy was a reaffirmation of religious and worldly authority. Matters of faith were seen as fundamentally different from those areas where the light of reason and critical enquiry could be fruitfully employed by individuals. This argument is familiar from the controversy over the hymnal. Faith was a 'great gift from above' that had to be accepted without questioning. Only one year before the publication of Woellner's tract the theologian Teller had used this argument to defend the right of the clergy to impose the new hymnal on the faithful. Woellner shared this authoritarian outlook. 'Fear God, honour the king' was one of the most important imperatives that Woellner recommended to his readers. 'That we have to obey to worldly and religious authorities' was seen as crucial for 'the welfare of men' and questioning either form of authority was a direct affront to divine will. Religious and worldly hierarchies were thus seen as inexorably linked: 'there is no authority without God; but where there is authority it is prescribed by God'.[61]

The central notions underpinning Woellner's thought and legislation were familiar to anyone who had been following public debates in Prussia attentively. Süßmilch had already argued in the 1760s that the tide of moral decay and selfishness that was rising in the towns could only be stemmed if the state and religion renewed their ties that had been progressively loosened in the past. Toleration, he argued, was important to prevent religious strife and served also to attract useful immigrants to the country. However, toleration was not to be confused with 'indifference' to religious matters or even 'irreligiosity' of the state.[62] Indifference was perilous because the forces of fanaticism and intolerance—in his view most importantly the Catholic Church and the Jesuits in particular—were likely to abuse any leeway given to them in order to proselytize and persecute. Therefore, protestant countries like Prussia in particular needed to accompany toleration with 'wise oversight' rather than being simply indifferent

parts by Woellner with the cooperation of other authors who were close to him in their views. Chrysophiron, *Die Pflichten der G. und R. C. alten Sistems* (n.p., 1782). Kemper, 'Obskurantismus', p. 207.

[60] 'Spaltungen und lieblose Animmositäten'; 'satanischen Hoffart und jenes Eigendünkels'; 'eingebildete Weisheit und Gelehrsamkeit'; 'Selbstdenkerei'; 'eitle Spitzfindigkeiten, Worzänkereien, Haß, Rache, und Verfolgung'. Kemper, 'Obskurantismus', pp. 126–7.

[61] 'Wo alle lehren und niemand lernen'; 'eine grosse Gabe von oben'; 'Fürchte Gott, ehre den König'; 'daß wir der weltlich- und geistlichen Obrigkeit gehorchen müssen'; 'Denn es ist keine Obrigkeit, ohne von Gott; wo aber Obrigkeit ist, die ist von Gott verordnet'. Kemper, 'Obskurantismus', pp. 125, 128–9.

[62] 'Gleichgültigkeit'; 'irreligiösität'. Johann Peter Süßmilch, *Die göttliche Ordnung in den Veränderungen des menschlichen Geschlechts, aus der Geburt, dem Tode der Fortpflanzung desselben erwiesen* (2 vols., Berlin, 1761), vol. 1, p. 560.

to religious matters.[63] Potentially even worse were the consequences of irreligiosity. It was an illusion to believe that social stability could be ensured by civil laws alone. Using the same language as Woellner's edict, Süßmilch argued that judges, officers, and other servants of the state would become unable to carry out their tasks if their sense of religious morality was corrupted. The loyalty and trustworthiness of the king's common subjects would be equally undermined if they lost their Christian faith. None of the worldly substitutes that were discussed at the time could replace religion as a way to ensure moral behaviour. Neither the teachings of the *philosophes* nor the principle of honour that Montesquieu saw at the heart of the monarchical system could exercise sufficient power and influence to ensure social stability. The state, by withdrawing from the regulation of moral behaviour and by trampling on religion, was undermining its own foundations. As Süßmilch pointed out, the state resembled a great machine but no matter how artfully it was constructed it could not work if those who operated it were not governed by religious virtue.[64] To support his position he included a lengthy quote from an anonymous French tract, *The interests of France misunderstood* (1756), which enjoyed a certain popularity in Paris at the time. In it the author deplored the withdrawal of the French state from the regulation of moral issues and predicted that this neglect would eventually lead to the collapse of the whole political order.[65] Pastor Süßmilch may have omitted the references to the work had he known that the author, Ange Goudar (1708–*c*.91) was not only a prolific political writer but also a notorious adventurer, gambler, fraudster, and womanizer.[66]

Süßmilch still identified Catholicism as the main threat to religious peace under an excessively tolerant politically regime, but other writers were already more concerned with the effects of small fringe groups and religious impostors. As we have seen, weavers and other urban textile workers were considered to be particularly vulnerable to the lure of religious impostors, and conventicles were perceived as dangerous breeding grounds for deviating forms of religiosity. Calls for increased state intervention to prevent this fragmentation of the religious spectrum were equally part of the debates that appeared in some of the principal publications of Prussia's urban elites. To this context also belong the authoritarian fantasies, already discussed, that the otherwise measured theologian and geographer Büsching experienced when he walked past bookstalls in Berlin bulging with what he saw as misleading religious teachings.

The conflict over the hymnal had confirmed many of these preoccupations. In response to the new hymnal various factions had formed among the faithful and these groups had conducted themselves in an independent and disorderly way. They were not led by members of the clergy and bypassed clerical authority by appealing directly to the king or by using public criticism, acts of passive resistance,

---

[63] 'Kluge Aufsicht'. Kemper, 'Obskurantismus', p. 561.

[64] Kemper, 'Obskurantismus', pp. 567–8.

[65] Kemper, 'Obskurantismus', pp. 569–71.

[66] Ange Goudar, *Les intérêts de la France mal entendus dans les branches de l'agriculture, de la population, des finances, du commerce, de la marine, et de l'industrie* (Amsterdam, 1756). Jean-Claude Hauc, *Ange Goudar: un aventurier des Lumières* (Paris, 2004).

and violence. Anyone harbouring suspicion against the diffusion of conventicles would have seen their views confirmed by the central role of Apitzsch's group in this controversy. Moreover, Frederick's political response had shown the limitations of traditional religious policies. If tolerance meant—as Frederick's decisions in this context suggested—to agree to all demands of all groups if they were presented with sufficient force, then a breakdown of religious authority and an unstoppable process of fragmentation seemed a likely outcome.

It was against this backdrop that Woellner first formulated the need for firmer spiritual guidance, but he was by no means alone in arguing in this direction at the time. Cranz, one of the more moderate contributors to the debate about the hymnal—so moderate in fact that historians have varyingly classified him as a supporter and opponent of the new hymnal—attributed the causes of the conflict to a collapse of spiritual leadership.[67] He saw 'the sole cause of the great division that is driving our congregations crazy in our new clergy'.[68] Preachers had become keen to show their 'theological cleverness' to their congregations by preaching their own views and attacking those of their colleagues. This intellectual profligacy had led to fragmentation and there was no longer 'one shepherd and one flock' but 'many shepherds and many flocks'.[69] The credibility of preachers also suffered from their public disputes and dogmatic innovativeness. As a result, Cranz suggested, their teachings were by now received with the same defiance that the public normally reserved for the wares of the least trusted merchants, such as wine merchants who were notorious for cheating the consumer with adulterated produce. Just as consumers resorted to trusting their own tongue, rather than the claims of the wine seller, the reaction of the faithful to the lack of unity of religious teachers was to 'follow their own convictions'.[70] The roots of 'self-thinking' among the faithful thus lay in the heterogeneity of messages that they received from their spiritual leaders.

The notions that underpinned the turn in religious policies led by Woellner were also widely held outside the immediate entourage of the minister. Many commentators who were not necessarily associated with 'obscurantist' tendencies shared the belief that the traditional policy of religious toleration needed to be modified and amended in the face of new challenges to political stability emanating from recent religious developments. Political expediency was at least as important as religious obscurantism in shaping Prussia's religious policies after the death of Frederick II. In this sense the policies of Frederick William II were also much more part of a political continuity than is often argued. The means of religious policies changed in the face of a perceived change of conditions but the political objectives remained the same as

[67] Delius, 'Zur Geschichte', p. 18. Johann Friedrich Bachmann, *Zur Geschichte der berliner Gesangbücher ein hymnologischer Beitrag* (Hildesheim, 1970), p. 213.

[68] 'Wenn ich von der großen Spaltung, wodurch die hiesigen Gemeinden irre gemacht werden, den alleinigen Grund in der Spaltung zwischen der neuern Geistlichkeit selbst suche.' Cranz, *Supplement*, p. 37.

[69] 'Theologische Klugheit'; 'ein Hirte und eine Heerde, sondern es sind viel Hirten und viel Heerden'. Cranz, *Supplement*, pp. 39, 43.

[70] 'Seiner eigenen Ueberzeugung folgt'. Cranz, *Supplement*, p. 43.

those Hohenzollern rulers had pursued since the Thirty Years War. This is not to deny that Woellner also had genuine sympathies with the 'fundamentalist' theology that he was promoting, but if we reduce his policies to the political outflow of his personal religious convictions we overlook an important part of the larger political context in which they emerged. Considering Woellner's policy from a political point of view, it becomes clear that his objective was not merely to repress certain theological orientations, but that individual religious autonomy per se was the target. For the purposes of ensuring political stability it mattered little what the outcome of 'self-thinking' was from a theological point of view. The political challenge lay in the fact that as long as individuals thought for themselves in religious matters, continued fragmentation seemed inevitable.

OPPOSITION TO THE EDICTS

Woellner's edicts marked not only a substantial deviation from well-established political approaches to religion, but they were also at odds with the direction in which Prussia's society had developed, particularly in the urban setting. As one of the earliest critics of the edict pointed out, Prussians had turned into a people of 'self-thinkers' who could never accept the minister's religious paternalism.[71] Consequently, much of the public debate that was triggered by the policy shift focused on the question of the legitimacy and expediency of Woellner's policies, rather than on the theological content of the dogmas that were imposed or the dangers and advantages of the 'Enlightenment'. The prominence of this issue in the earlier parts of the debate, that is, before the publication of the edict on censorship in 1788, is particularly important. Opposition against the limitation of religious autonomy was an important part of the debates since the first edict of July 1788, when Woellner was still mainly concerned with the content of oral communication in preaching and teaching and had not yet begun to interfere with the freedom of expression in print. Protest against Woellner's policies was thus clearly not limited to his interference with print culture. The examination of this strand of the debate suggests that the critical response of civil society was in large part a reaction to the extension of the remits of state power in religious matters at the expense of individual autonomy. The focus will be on these aspects of the debate, bearing in mind that it was only one strand, albeit a central and insufficiently studied one, of a vast debate, that was triggered by the opposition against Woellner. After examining these aspects of the debate we turn to other forms of resistance and the increasing difficulties encountered by Woellner in implementing his policies that preceded his dismissal in 1798.

The tone of the early debate was in large part set by Peter Villaume's (1746–1825) treatise *Honest considerations about the edict of 9 July 1788* (1788).

---

[71] 'Selbsdenkern'. Degenhard Pott, *Commentar über das königlich preuß. Religionsedikt vom 9. Julius 1788* (Amsterdam [Halle or Leipzig], 1788), p. 3.

Villaume, a publicist and teacher in Berlin, structured his pamphlet around three questions: 'Can the dogmatic aspect of religion be the object of laws? Does the state have the right to rule over religion; and how far does his power extend?' and 'Can a faltering religious system be saved successfully with edicts and laws?'[72] What is perhaps most striking about this critique is that it did not engage with the specific content of Woellner's policies. Rather than criticizing the dogmas that the edict imposed or defending 'enlightened' positions, Villaume questioned the inner logic, legitimacy, and expediency of this type of state intervention. In his answer to the first question he evoked two arguments. The first related to the problem that true belief could not be imposed and that a merely superficially accepted religiosity was ultimately nothing more than hypocrisy. Like the Pietist tradition that rejected all imposition in religious matters because of the emphasis of honestly and individually felt piousness, Villaume argued that the moral consequences of imposed religiosity were potentially worse than a lack of religious beliefs. Dogmatic impositions accustomed individuals and society to live in duplicity and falsehood. Attempts to impose religiosity, such as Woellner's edict, could therefore not contribute much to upholding moral order in society and were likely to undermine it.[73] In a second but related argument Villaume pointed to the uncertainty associated with the search for religious truth. Since no one could ultimately know with certainty which religious dogmas were true no one could legitimately impose them. The limitations on the human ability to gain certainty in religious matters also imposed limitations on the legitimacy of coercion in this domain. Restrictions such as the ones imposed by Woellner on the content of sermons could only be imposed if the people or at least the majority of the congregation supported them. The power of the state to intervene in religious matters, Villaume wrote with respect to his second question, was narrowly circumscribed to the maintainance of public order. When-ever the state went further, it overstepped its 'limits' ('Schranken').[74] In the answer to the third question, he added reservations about the practicality of the edict. Attempts to stem the tide of ideas, he argued, were mostly futile and the dams constructed to hold them back only increased the power of the ideas they were supposed to contain when the barriers eventually and inevitably gave way.[75] The overreaching of the Prussian state in religious matters was thus not only illegitimate but also poised to fail.

In the context of this study it is significant that some critics of the edicts began to link their concerns about the containment of state power in religious matters to questions about the role of the state in economic and fiscal matters. One pamphlet likened the attempts of Frederick William II to impose certain dogmatic views to

---

[72] 'Kann das Dogmatische in der Religion ein Gegenstand von Verordnungen werden? Hat der Staat ein Recht, über Religion zu gebieten; und wie weit geht hierin seine Macht? Kann einem schwankenden Religionssystem durch Edicte und Verordnungen mit gutem Erfolge zu Hülfe kommen?' Peter Villaume, Freimüthige Betrachtungen über das Edict vom 9. Julius 1788 die Religionsverfassung in den preußischen Staaten betreffend (Frankfurt, 1788), p. 10.

[73] Villaume, *Freimüthige Betrachtungen*, pp. 11–15, 44.

[74] Villaume, *Freimüthige Betrachtungen*, pp. 16–17, 20–2, 23.

[75] Villaume, *Freimüthige Betrachtungen*, p. 27.

the efforts of an imaginary oriental tyrant who banned the production and sale of pork meat because he found it difficult to digest. The citizens of the imaginary country were outraged at this interference with their freedom to decide for themselves what food they found tasty and digestible. However, their resistance proved futile and farmers, merchants, and consumers suffered under the vexatious rule that ruined their businesses and limited their freedom of choice in matters of consumption.[76] The connection between the defences of individual autonomy in religious and economic matters was made even more explicitly by another commentator who discussed Woellner's edict in the context of the recent conflict over the Régie and other ongoing excesses in the area of taxation. The state, he argued, was clearly overstepping the limits of its power with the recent edicts just as the burden caused by the excise under the Régie had been excessive. But even after the abolition of the hated institution, taxes on many consumer goods like coffee and sugar remained too high and procedures vexatious. The anonymous author therefore pleaded with the monarch for more governmental restraint in a broad range of areas including religious, economic, fiscal, and other matters.[77]

The defenders of the edict saw Villaume and other authors who called for limitations on the state's authority as subversive.[78] However, while a variety of counter-arguments were presented, Villaume's original questions were rarely altered. His questions about the extent of the state's authority in religious matters were central to the arguments of defenders and opponents of the edict. One common response to Villaume's critique was that there was no need to demonstrate the truth of the religious dogmas that the edict imposed and or the right of the monarch to do so. Both were established by religious revelation and by laws that might have fallen into disuse but had never been repealed.[79] On this basis, commentators such as the Saxonian jurist Karl Heinrich von Römer (1760–98) argued that the welfare of a Christian state ultimately depended on its close association with Christian religion. The question of where the limits of state power in religious matters should be drawn was therefore seen as inherently misleading. Individual freedom of consciousness in a narrow sense was to be guaranteed, but, like Woellner, many commentators saw a rapprochement between state and religion and a far-reaching reversal of the separation of political and religious spheres as essential for political and moral stability.[80]

---

[76] Pott, *Commentar*, pp. 68–70.

[77] Anonymous, *Schreiben eines preußischen Patrioten, am sechs und vierzigsten Geburtstage seines Königs. Den 25sten September 1788* (Philadelphia [Berlin], n.d.), pp. 23–5.

[78] Anonymous, *Was ist Gewissensfreyheit? Und wie weit erstreckt sich die Macht des Monarchen in Religionssachen? Eine Antwort auf die Freymüthige Betrachtung über das Edict com 9. Julius 1788 die Religionsverfassung in den preußischen Staaten betreffend. Von einem Auswärtigen Wahrheitsfreund* (Berlin, 1788), p. 37.

[79] Anonymous, *Das Blendwerk der neumodischen Aufklärung in der Religion* (Frankfurt, 1788), p. 16. Karl Heinrich von Römer, *Vertheidigung des neuesten preuß. Religions-Edikts gegen die Beschuldigungen und Besorgnisse des Verfassers der freimüthigen Betrachtungen über dasselbe* (Berlin, 1788), p. 31. Anonymous, *Apologie der unumschränkten Gewalt eines Monarchen in öffentlichen Glaubenssachen* (Rom [Weißenfels or Leipzig], 1795).

[80] Römer, *Vertheidigung*, p. 13.

Many saw Villaume's ideas as the beginning of a slippery slope. Once the power of the state was curtailed and once the notion that popular consent was the only legitimate basis for religious regulation was accepted, the next step was the abdication of state power and ultimately the handing over of government to the people.[81] In 1788, with political agitation in France nearing its peak, such possibilities were more than hypothetical threats, and for many commentators the limitation of state power and a continuation of its separation from religion were dangerous steps in the wrong direction. They agreed with Woellner that only a strengthening of worldly and religious authorities as well as their closer association could preserve stability.

Besides the publications discussed here, Woellner's edicts triggered a flood of public commentary in pamphlets and newspapers of which more than a hundred independent publications survive.[82] Hardly any other event in the history of the period triggered a comparable public debate in Prussia. The fact that the opinions expressed in the debate were inevitably heterogeneous and that careful analysis shows that a majority of the publications were in favour of the edict has led historians to question whether the debate should be seen as an oppositional force against Woellner's policies. Many of those who published their views, according to this perspective, were keen to rally to the support of the minister rather than trying to stop him.[83] Clearly it is difficult to substantiate claims about the relative strength of opinions in historical debates. The sheer number of publications, classified as belonging to one side or the other, does not say much about their actual diffusion because the number of copies printed and the readership of each remain in the dark. Moreover, there is no way of knowing in what relation the sample of surviving publications stands to the whole body of printed commentary produced at the time. But even if this information were available fully and processed by eager statisticians, the outcome would not tell us anything about the persuasive power and political influence associated with the ideas and arguments put forward in each publication. We may simply have to acknowledge that statistical methods can contribute only narrowly to our understanding of past debates. However, what remains is a more basic but not less important question: can the public response to Woellner's edicts be seen as a force of opposition given that only a part of the public opposed the minister's policies?

From the state's point of view not only public opponents but also public supporters created a problem. The principal objective of the edict on religion was to ensure quiet, stability, and unity in religious matters. The outcome, however, was controversy, division, and unrest. Woellner tried to address this problem with the second edict, but this move only made matters worse by creating even more controversy. The weak states of this period feared nothing more than unrest, and

---

[81] Johann Salomo Semler, *D. Joh. salom. Semlers Vertheidigung des Königl. Edikts vom 9ten Jul. 1788 wider die freimüthigen Betrachtungen eines Ungenannten* (Halle, 1788), p. 40.

[82] See Dirk Kemper's edition 'Mißbrauchte Aufklärung?' and the editorial comments in Dirk Kemper, *Mißbrauchte Aufklärung? Schriften zum Religionsedikt vom 9. Juli 1788. 118 Schriften auf 202 Mikrofiches. Begleitband* (Hildesheim, 1996). For subsequently discovered titles and periodicals see Sauter, *Visions*, pp. 201–12.

[83] Sauter, *Visions*, pp. 141–67.

this was particularly true of the context in which Woellner acted. His policies were motivated in the first place by a perceived weakness of the authority and stability of the state, but as Kemper has emphasized any broad public debate about a decision of the government was in itself subversive and illegal from the state's perspective.[84] Long before the Woellner controversy Büsching had pointed out that the public was a 'mighty beast' and anyone contributing to public debates made it more powerful and more dangerous no matter what his opinions were.[85] Paradoxically, the interventions of Woellner's defenders did not help to silence his critics but instead fanned the flames of the controversy started by the minister's enemies. To the extent that quelling religious debate and dissent were the objectives of Woellner's policies, the sheer existence of an unremitting stream of publications about religious matters signalled the limited success of his policies from their inception.

Woellner and his allies were well aware of their limited success. In 1791 a report of the *Immediatexaminationskommission*—the new administrative organ created by Woellner for the implementations of the edict's provisions—described the slow progress that had been made in the two years since the promulgation of the edict on religion: the commission had not been able to place most of its preferred candidates for the posts of preachers, university professors were still not toeing the line, Prussian and foreign journals were publishing material that was worse than what was circulating in revolutionary France, and teaching in schools had still not improved. 'In this way', the authors of the report concluded, 'it is impossible to form loyal subjects for the king of kings and consequently also for the monarchs that he places on their thrones.'[86] Even if one accepts that the slowness of progress may have been exaggerated in order to convince the king to grant additional powers to the commission—which it received subsequently—the self-assessment was still sobering.[87]

Despite these frustrations Woellner could also point to successes in which he was able to silence more or less prominent contemporaries and periodicals. The most prominent of these cases was certainly that of Kant, who was banned from expressing his views on religion after the publication of *Religion within the bounds of bare reason* (1793/4). In another high-profile case, Nicolai was forced in 1792 to sell the journal *Allgemeine deutsche Bibliothek* to a publisher in Hamburg. The publication continued under a new title but was eventually banned from circulation in Prussia in 1794. Measures like these were certainly important successes for Woellner, but it should not be overlooked that they were only temporary victories. As a result of mounting pressure from other parts of the government administration, Frederick William repealed the ban of Nicolai's journal in 1795 and Kant

---

[84] Kemper, 'Obskurantismus', p. 212.

[85] 'Großmächtiges Thier'. Anton Friedrich Büsching, *Anton Friderich Büschings. Beschreibung seiner Reise von Berlin über Potsdam nach Rekahn unweit Brandenburg: welche er vom dritten bis achten Junius 1775 gethan hat* (Leipzig, 1775), p. 14.

[86] 'Auf die Art können keine wahren Untertanen des Königs aller Könige, mithin auch nicht der Monarchen, die er auf ihre Throne setzte, gebildet werden.' Cited in Schwartz, *Kulturkampf*, p. 258.

[87] Schwartz, *Kulturkampf*, p. 261.

continued his commentary on religious matters after the political career of Woellner had ended in 1798.[88]

In other cases Woellner could not achieve even temporary victories. The most dramatic defeat was inflicted on him by the professors and students of the University of Halle. In 1794, two of Woellner's closest associates, Herman Daniel Hermes (1731–1807) and Gottlob Friedrich Hillmer (1756–1835), were dispatched to Halle to inspect the university. The institution had provoked Woellner's ire on a number of occasions. Rumours about students plotting the assassination of the minister had reached Berlin together with accounts of professorial clubs where the taint of 'Jacobinism' could be detected.[89] Finally, in 1791, a textbook written by a Reformed theology professor from Halle, August Herrmann Niemeyer (1724–1828), was banned, substituted with one that was more to the liking of Woellner, and the theological faculty was reprimanded. When it became subsequently known that the professor was commenting on these policies in his seminars, Woellner threatened further actions. However, a punitive expedition of Hermes and Hillmer did not quite bring the expected outcome. An earlier inspection of similar type at the University of Königsberg had resulted in the silencing of Kant. However, when the two emissaries reached Halle on 29 May 1794, they were greeted by shouts from passing students. In the evening of the same day a mob of students—some wearing masks—gathered outside the inn where the officials were staying. The crowd dispersed, but on the following evening an even larger gathering congregated and, after a student's rousing speech, the inn was pelted with bricks and tiles. Perhaps in view of the fact that the local regiment was absent from the city at the time, Hermes and Hillmer decided to leave Halle early the next morning, without having completed their mission.[90] Not only did this visit turn out to be a failure, but Hermes is also said to have expressed to Niemeyer his frustration about the ineffectiveness of his own policies in this context: 'What is our power? We have not deposed a single neologic preacher. Everywhere people are against us.'[91] These comments may be apocryphal, but their thrust is certainly confirmed by the outcome of the conflict between Woellner and the University of Halle. In the exchanges that ensued after the visit of Hermes and Hillmer the university held its own and when the matter was brought before the privy council Woellner could not impose himself and had to abandon his hostile position.[92]

However, Woellner's efforts were not only slowed down by resistance from an insuppressible public and rebellious students against the extension of state power, but also by the inherent weakness of that power. This is perhaps most visible in his

---

[88] Kemper, *Mißbrauchte Aufklärung*, pp. 103–6. Schwartz, *Kulturkampf*, pp. 348–54. Ludger Lüdtkeaus, 'Karl Friedrich Bahrdt, Immanuel Kant und die Gegenaufklärung in Preußen', *Jahrbuch des Instituts für deutsche Geschichte der Universität Tel Aviv*, 9 (1980), pp. 83–106.

[89] Schwartz, *Kulturkampf*, pp. 242–3.

[90] Schwartz, *Kulturkampf*, pp. 369–79.

[91] 'Was ist denn unsere Macht? Noch nicht einen neologischen Prediger haben wir absetzen können. Man ist uns überall zugegen.' Cited in Wilhelm von Schrader, *Geschichte der Friedrichs-Universität zu Halle* (2 vols., Berlin, 1894), vol. 1, p. 521.

[92] Schwartz, *Kulturkampf*, pp. 379–84.

policies regarding schools. Visitations of schools often revealed a shocking state of ignorance and heterodoxy among teachers and pupils, but open resistance against the inspectors was rare. Yet Woellner and his associates became quickly aware that the state lacked the resources to implement far-reaching change. The number of inspections had to be curtailed because travel expenses could not be covered and even less money was available to fund school reform. Considering the reality of schooling in Prussia at the time, the limited impact of Woellner's efforts can hardly surprise us. Neugebauer concluded that throughout the eighteenth century 'the "state" was not at all able to control schools' and this did not change under Woellner. The minister's policies did not result in 'a dictatorial or even gradually stronger control of the state over schools' and remained 'purely at the level of plans'.[93]

The structural weakness of the Prussian *Ediktenstaat* and the resistance of civil society meant that, long before Woellner's political career ended, his political project had lost its impetus. It had become clear that his policies could not achieve the objectives that had been grandly announced in the edicts. Instead of a heightened sense of religiosity as well as religious unity and stability, the edicts resulted mainly in discord and acrimony. Although Woellner's edicts were never formally repealed, the newly crowned Frederick William III made it immediately clear in a Cabinet Order of 1797 order that he shared much of the public criticism. Before the edict on religion, he wrote, 'there was certainly more religion and less hypocrisy in the country'. The edict had failed with regards to its religious objectives, but even more importantly, Frederick William pointed to its political failures: 'I honour religion, follow gladly her uplifting commandments and would not like to rule over a people without religion. However, I also know that it must be and remain a matter of heart, sentiment and of individual convictions and must not be degraded by the use of systematic force to meaningless chatter if it is to advance virtue and honesty.' For the king, disagreement over 'dogmatic subtleties' mattered little. The ultimate test for any policy in religious matters was whether it contributed to upholding 'happiness' and 'morality' among 'all classes of the people' and thus helped to preserve political stability.[94] By the time that Frederick William III was crowned, it had become clear that Woellner's approach had failed this test. His policies were abandoned and he was swiftly dismissed.

[93] Wolfgang Neugebauer, *Absolutistischer Staat und Schulwirklichkeit in Brandenburg-Preußen* (Berlin, 1985), pp. 200, 207, 630.

[94] 'Aber gewiß mehr Religion und weniger Heuchelei als jetzt'; 'Ich selbst ehre die Religion, folge gern ihren beglückenden Vorschriften und möchte um vieles nicht über ein Volk herrschen, welches keine Religion hätte. Aber ich weiß auch, dass sie Sachen des Herzens, des Gefühls und der eigenen Überzeugung sein und bleiben muß und nicht durch methodischen Zwang zu einem gedankenlosen Plapperwerke herabgewürdigt werden darf, wenn sie Tugend und Rechtschaffenheit befördern soll'; 'dogmatischen Subtilitaeten'; 'Glueck und die Moralitaet aller Volksklaessen'. Kabinettsorder of Frederick William III of 1797, cited in Schwartz, *Kulturkampf*, pp. 459–60.

A PEOPLE OF 'SELF-THINKERS'

Perhaps the most striking feature of the religious conflicts examined was the ecumenical nature of the state's failures. Public resistance thwarted all attempts to extend the power of the state in religious matters, irrespective of whether the state claimed to act in the name of enlightened or traditionalist theology. The defence of individual autonomy itself was at the heart of these conflicts and the public successfully defended its right to think for itself in religious matters. The means used to push back the state's attempts to extend its power in this domain were similar to those that we have encountered in conflicts over economic freedoms. They included petitions, controversial public debates partly laced with violent rhetoric, acts of passive resistance such as boycotts of religious services and unwanted hymns, and acts or threats of direct violence directed at preachers and officials who were charged with enforcing intrusive policies on the ground. The degrees to which members of civil society resorted to these different forms of response varied between religious and fiscal conflicts. The volume and intensity of public debate triggered by Woellner's edicts was significantly greater than the comparable reactions to the Régie despite the latter's much longer existence. In religious conflicts passive resistance took on different forms and yet was clearly identifiable as political. Publicly singing from an outlawed hymnal was certainly a form of 'religious contraband' comparable in many ways to the symbolic political value of collectively drinking smuggled coffee. However, the economic benefits associated with the contraband of worldly commodities meant that the lines separating political resistance and the pursuit of economic advantages were fuzzier than in the area of religion. Still, there were important similarities: in both cases individuals put their own judgement and interests before the impositions of the state, and violence was present in both sets of conflicts as a possibility and a concrete reality. Yet the level of violence exercised by the defenders and challengers of state authority in the context of the fiscal conflicts far exceeded the occasional stone-throwing encountered in this chapter.

Compared with fiscal conflicts, tamer forms of opposition led to quicker defeats of the state in matters of religion. It took Frederick only weeks to repeal the new hymnal and even the nine years of Woellner's ministry constituted a short period compared with the two decades that the Régie lasted. This outcome was in part the result of the breadth and speed with which civil society reacted in the case of challenges of religious autonomy. Historically the Prussian public had played a decisive role in shaping the religious developments in the country in opposition to the will of the ruler. The Lutheran Reformation was partly forced on a reluctant ruler by the faithful and a second Calvinist Reformation from above was aborted in the face of widespread popular resistance. This background gave the public not only confidence but also established traditions of public religious debate on which the protesters of the 1780s and 1790s could draw. In particular, Prussia's Pietist traditions played an important role here because it provided forums, institutions, and religious convictions that helped to form and publicly express dissenting views.

It is hardly a coincidence that the nucleus of the resistance against the new hymnal was a Pietist conventicle and that Woellner's most clamorous defeat was in a conflict with a Reformed theologian (incidentally a great-grandson of the Pietist founding father, Francke) at the largely Pietist University of Halle. Far from instilling discipline, the Pietist tradition provided the fertile soil on which rebellion against the state thrived in the late eighteenth century. Public debates on fiscal matters could not be replicated in a similar tradition. There had been a limited public debate about the introduction of the excise towards the end of the seventeenth century, but fiscal matters had been largely the subject of institutional conflicts between estates and monarch and were much less the subject of public exchange.[95] A religious public existed already and consequently public responses to the new hymnal or Woellner's edicts were published within weeks, whereas it took years for the first public commentaries on the Régie to emerge.

The long history of religious conflict in Prussia also contributed to weakening the state's resolve to insist on religious policies in the face of opposition. The near catastrophic consequences of the Thirty Years War for Prussia, and in particular the political precariousness that resulted from the fact that in Prussia a Reformed monarch ruled over mostly Lutheran subjects, made the dynasty cautious. Moreover, the geography of religious conflict implied greater political risks. Urban society often led religious opposition, but friction was not limited to this setting in the same way that opposition to the excise was bound to remain a strictly urban phenomenon. The potential of religious conflict to unite town and country in opposition to the state levered the power of political resistance.

Moreover, in religious matters the state's lack of political resolve was complemented by a lack of resources. The state's means were limited and scarce resources needed to be concentrated on core military and fiscal functions. And while the political risks and economic costs associated with the Régie could be justified by a substantial increase in state revenue, there was no comparable premium for greater resolve in controversial religious policies. A religious sceptic, Frederick looked at these matters with greater detachment than his nephew, but even the latter monarch, who was willing to lend extraordinary political support and legal powers to Woellner, could not ignore the limitations of the state's resources and left the minister's project in many respects without sufficient administrative and economic support.

Comparison between the conflicts over excise and religious edicts is complicated by the radical change in the wider historical context brought about by the French Revolution. French fiscal troubles prior to the revolution were 'present' in the Prussian context in different forms, but this was quite different from the openly revolutionary situation that unfolded soon after Woellner had begun his political project. Woellner's reactionary domestic policies were closely linked to Prussia's anti-French foreign policy, and French events may also have influenced the

---

[95] Karl Theodor von Inama-Sternegg, 'Der Accisestreit deutscher Finanztheoretiker im 17. und 18. Jahrhundert', *Zeitschrift für die gesamte Staatswissenschaft*, 21 (1865), pp. 515–34.

response to Woellner's policies.[96] It has been argued that many civil society actors in Germany were at pains to distinguish themselves from revolutionary Frenchmen, and this may also have contributed to limit the forms of the resistance in a way that did not apply to earlier fiscal conflicts.[97] It seems clear that the French context played an important role in the conflict over Woellner's edicts. However, the precise nature and effect of this connection are more difficult to establish than the 'French dimension' of the conflict over the Régie.

WOELLNER, VOLTAIRE, AND SUBVERSIVENESS

Some historians have taken the limited nature of the conflict over Woellner's edicts compared with the escalation in France as a starting point for arguing that the Prussian public was structurally less subversive and closer to the state than its French equivalent.[98] The argument focuses on the fact that Woellner and substantial parts of the Prussian public that supported him sought to promote popular religiosity with authoritarian means, while reserving more free-spirited ways of thinking to the intellectual elite. This is seen as an indication of an authoritarian strand in the Prussian enlightenment that was allegedly absent in the French case. However, this view may not sufficiently take into account similar tendencies among exponents of the French public. Perhaps no French author is more closely associated with the corrosive effect that the French public had on state and religion than Voltaire (1694–1778). Yet his views on the political and moral effects of religion were in many respects not substantially different from those that led Woellner and other Prussians to argue for the necessity of popular religiosity. Many biographers have now debunked the myth of Voltaire's atheism and as early as 1959 Peter Gay showed that the *philosophe* saw a clear link between social and political stability and the popular diffusion of religious values. The famous line 'if God did not exist one would have to invent him' was not an expression of cynicism but of the view that morality rested and would continue to do so for the foreseeable future on religious foundations.[99] Gay explicitly contrasted Voltaire's genuinely held belief 'that it is absolutely necessary for prince and people that the idea of a Supreme Being, creator, governor, rewarder and avenger, be profoundly graven in all minds' with the unsentimental perspective of Frederick the Great who looked at religious matters mainly in terms of political expediency.[100] Voltaire clearly rejected dogmatic impositions, but he shared preoccupations that were also widespread among the Prussian public and that gave rise to much of the support for Woellner's policies.

---

[96] Kemper, 'Obskurantismus', p. 213.

[97] Thomas Saine, *Black bread—white bread: German intellectuals and the French Revolution* (Rochester, NY, 1988).

[98] Tim Blanning, *The culture of power and the power of culture: old regime Europe, 1660–1789* (Oxford, 2006), p. 13. Sauter, *Visions*, p. 82.

[99] Voltaire cited in Peter Gay, *Voltaire's politics, the poet as realist* (New York, 1965), p. 265.

[100] Voltaire cited in Gay, *Voltaire's politics*, p. 264.

Like many Prussians, the philosopher-king was concerned that a breakdown of religion would ultimately undermine all social and political stability.[101]

In a similar way, the notion that exponents of the French public were more distant from the state overlooks many close links. The attempts of Mirabeau to convert Frederick II and Frederick William II to physiocracy have been discussed earlier. And Voltaire, like other *philosophes*, frequently consorted with the powerful and vied for offices at the French and other European courts. Moreover, Voltaire was an admirer of strong officials and monarchs of the past and in his own time. Among his historical heroes were Louis XIV and the minister Colbert, whose authoritarian policies he praised with only very few caveats. He also lavished praise on Turgot, his fellow *philosophe* and minister of Louis XVI, and his reform agenda. When the latter imposed a liberalization of the grain trade against substantial popular opposition Voltaire applauded him. Even the deployment of the military and execution of substantial numbers of opponents did not trouble either Voltaire or Turgot.[102] Compared with the Flour wars fought by Turgot, the political campaign of Woellner was a rather peaceful affair. A simple juxtaposition of a subversive French public and an authoritarian Prussian variant with close ties to the state clearly does not stand up to scrutiny. A more systematic comparison and examination of the numerous connections between both publics is likely to yield a far more nuanced picture of an interrelated development that displays many similarities.

Perhaps more important than differences between the French and Prussian publics were the diverging ways in which the Bourbon and Hohenzollern dynasties had sought stability after the turmoil of the Thirty Years War. While the Hohenzollern had embraced religious toleration as a way to insulate themselves from the dangers of religious controversy, Louis XIV sought to achieve the same end by abolishing toleration and attempting to create a religiously homogeneous society. While religious toleration became a part of the constitutional basis of Prussia, much more repressive and exclusionary policies took root in France. When religious conflicts escalated in the eighteenth century, the French monarchy did not fall back on a tradition of religious toleration in the way that Prussian monarchs did. An examination of the different political responses to religious dissent in France and Prussia seems to be a more promising approach to our understanding the diverging ways in which the conflicts between state public developed in this period. In Prussia, the repeal of controversial religious policies in the face of public opposition meant that the religious conflicts between state and urban civil society ended—much like the previous fiscal conflicts—with political success for Prussia's urban dwellers.

---

[101] Gay, *Voltaire's politics*, pp. 265–7.
[102] See the chapter about Voltaire and Turgot and the literature cited in Florian Schui, *Early debates about industry: Voltaire and his contemporaries* (Basingstoke, 2005), pp. 161–73.

6

A Prussian on Liberty

Few persons, out of Germany, even comprehend the meaning of the doctrine which Wilhelm von Humboldt . . . made the text of a treatise—that 'the end of man . . . towards which every human being must ceaselessly direct his efforts, and on which especially those who design to influence their fellow-men must ever keep their eyes, is the individuality of power and development.'

John Stuart Mill, *On liberty* (1859).[1]

The conflicts that we have been concerned with here were also relevant beyond their immediate chronological and spatial context. Political realities created at the time and views about the limits of state action that had been formed in these late eighteenth-century debates played an important role in the reconstruction of Prussia after the end of the Napoleonic wars as well as in the development of wider European discourses on individual liberty in the nineteenth century and beyond.

The unlikely connections between the rebellious brewers, merchants, coffee drinkers, and churchgoers of late eighteenth-century Prussia, the politics of post-Napoleonic reconstruction, and the intellectual world of nineteenth-century liberalism were associated with some of the first attempts at political writing by a still very young W. von Humboldt. He was only in his early twenties when the Régie was abolished and Woellner took office, but, as we argue in this chapter, the controversies surrounding both developments were the context in which the central notions of his tract *On the limits of state action* were formed. The work was only published in its entirety in 1850, but he began writing it in 1788–9, completed it in 1791–2, and published some of the most important parts in the form of articles in 1792. Most historians of Humboldt have either professed puzzlement about the motives that led the young man to address a similarly bald subject in a period that coincided with his honeymoon, or have pointed to the French Revolution as the event that triggered Humboldt's interest in the matter.[2] This chapter argues that French events and political commentary influenced Humboldt, but that the Prussian context is just as relevant for the understanding of his arguments.

---

[1] John Stuart Mill, *On liberty* (Cambridge, 2006), p. 58.
[2] Lothar Gall, *Wilhelm von Humboldt ein Preuße von Welt* (Berlin, 2011), pp. 64–75. Paul Sweet, 'Young Wilhelm von Humboldt's writings (1789–93) reconsidered', *Journal of the History of Ideas*, 34 (1973), pp. 469–82, p. 474.

The importance of the Prussian political and intellectual environment becomes more apparent when we reconstruct the way in which contemporaries would have encountered and read Humboldt's work. Only a small number of friends of Humboldt saw the complete manuscripts of *Limits*. Instead, most contemporary readers encountered Humboldt's ideas in the form of four chapters that were published as articles at the time. These articles focused on the effect of state interventions on individual development in general, and on the limits of the state's power in matters of education, consumption, and military affairs. From the perspective of most contemporary readers the articles appeared as contributions to important public debates of the time, including those that had been triggered by the Régie and Woellner's edicts, and not as parts of a more comprehensive treatise on political theory. The only central chapter of *Limits* that was not published at the time was that on religion. Humboldt had written it first and it was in many ways the central piece of the treatise. Nonetheless, Humboldt insisted on not publishing it in the form of an article. This was most likely because he was worried that it would be censored under the more restrictive rule that Woellner's second edict had established. His fear of censorship was probably warranted and belies his own claim that his arguments were purely theoretical considerations 'entirely apart from the details of actual practice'.[3] Clearly, the text of *Limits* was, on many levels, part of contemporary debates and this chapter proposes a perspective that places Humboldt's arguments in their original historical context.

Although Humboldt's arguments were much more deeply rooted in a Prussian context than has often been assumed, their influence extended far beyond that.[4] Tracing the influences of political writings is a notoriously difficult task, but there can be little doubt that Humboldt and his ideas played an important role during the reconstruction of Prussia after 1806, in which he participated as a high-ranking official, and for the development of liberal ideas in the nineteenth century. The complete text of *Limits* was published in 1851 in German and was subsequently translated into French and English. In France, Humboldt's work inspired Édouard Laboulaye (1811–83)—the liberal commentator and energetic proponent of the idea to give a statue of 'Liberty enlightening the world' to the United States—in his work on the book *The state and its limits* (1863).[5] In Britain, Mill used a phrase from Humboldt's *Limits* as an epigraph for *On liberty* (1859) and wrote about the intellectual debt to the tract and wider German debates in his autobiography.[6] This connection establishes a proximity between the ideas of the most prominent exponent of English liberalism in the nineteenth century and the intellectual and political world of Prussian absolutism in the eighteenth century that raises questions about historiographical traditions and constructions of national identity on both sides of the North Sea. However, besides the similarities

---

[3] Wilhelm von Humboldt, *The limits of state action* (Cambridge, 1969), p. 36.

[4] Sweet, 'Humboldt's writings', p. 474.

[5] Robert Leroux, 'Guillaume de Humboldt et J.S. Mill', *Etudes Germaniques*, 6–7 (1951–2), pp. 262–74, 81–7.

[6] John Stuart Mill, *Autobiography* (London, 1989), p. 191.

between the views of Mill and Humboldt, the two writers were also separated by substantial differences which this chapter explores and which suggest that Humboldt's ideas should be seen as more closely connected with traditions of liberal thought that were different from that of Mill.

This chapter reconstructs the original intellectual and political context of *Limits* by focusing on the chapters that Humboldt regarded as the 'more important' parts of his tract, most of which were published shortly after they had been written.[7] Rather than looking at the work as whole, in the way that a handful of eighteenth-century readers and most readers after 1851 read it, each of the chapters will be placed in their specific context, which was formed by major contemporary debates about policies in religious, educational, and economic and fiscal matters that we have discussed in previous chapters. Along with the original context, we also discuss the role that Humboldt's views played in the nineteenth century in a Prussian and European context.

ON RELIGION

The first aspect of the limits of state action that Humboldt wrote about was the extent of the power of the state in religious matters. Like most of the manuscript, the part on religion was written between January and August of 1792. However, this chapter is in large part based on an earlier unpublished text entitled 'On religion' that Humboldt wrote in 1788/9 before he travelled to France in the summer of that year.[8] The timing alone of Humboldt's decision to write about the relation between religion and state suggests a connection with Woellner's edict on religion of July 1788. Hardly any politically interested Prussian or even German was unaware of the edict. The extent to which the issue gripped public debates in general, and Humboldt's interest in particular, is evident from a diary that he kept to record the events of a journey that took him through several western states of the Reich in the months between September and November 1788. For almost every stop of his trip Humboldt recorded discussions about Woellner's policies. In the diary he mostly referred simply to 'the edict'; further qualification or explanation was clearly unnecessary, given the importance that he attributed to it. Where interlocutors did not volunteer an opinion Humboldt quizzed them about their views and none of his often scathing comments about the intelligence of those he encountered was more damning than the observation 'he had not even read the edict'.[9] However, he did not have to use this epithet very often and his eagerness to find occasions to discuss the edict almost eclipsed the other principal interest that he pursued during the trip, which consisted in trying to meet the most attractive

---

[7] Humboldt, *Limits*, p. 82.

[8] Editorial notes in Wilhelm von Humboldt, 'Tagebuch der Reise nach dem Reich 1788', in Albert Leitzmann, ed., *Wilhelm von Humboldt's gesammelte Schriften*, (20 vols., Berlin, 1916), vol. 14, pp. 430–2.

[9] 'Das Edikt hatte er nicht einmal gelesen'. Humboldt, 'Tagebuch der Reise', p. 23.

women at every station he passed through. In a curious mixture Humboldt's travel diary thus recorded the graces of the female inhabitants of several provincial German towns, along with the views on Woellner's edict held by the usually male members of the local elite. On occasion both interests converged as in Arolsen, where he visited a leading doctor because he had heard about his beautiful daughters. Upon his arrival he found that of the three daughters only the two less attractive ones were present. In an attempt to make the best of his bad luck, he turned to discussing the edict with the father but despite this quick-witted reaction he remained disappointed and noted in the diary that the visit was a failure.[10] Although Humboldt limited himself to recording the views of his interlocutors and mostly remained silent about his own judgement on the edict, it is still possible to glean some insights about his views from his diary. He systematically classified the opinions about the edict that he encountered as 'reasonable' or 'unreasonable'.[11] Unfortunately he did not always refer to the content of the comments that he classified, but where he did approvals of the edict clearly fell in the latter category.[12] Humboldt was also well aware of the potential for political conflict that the new policies entailed. At one point during his travels, there seem to have been rumours that the edict had been repealed, a possibility that led Humboldt to enquire eagerly about news from Prussia and speculate that the turnabout could only have been triggered by a 'revolution in Berlin'.[13]

His awareness of the charged political atmosphere and the tightened censorship rules of the second edict may well have been the reason why in both his early text 'On religion' and the corresponding chapter in *Limits* he did not repeat the direct references to Woellner that can be found in his private diary. The arguments presented, however, were clearly responding to the minister's policies. The chapter on religion in *Limits* ended with the conclusion that 'all that concerns religion lies beyond the sphere of the State's activity; and that the choice of ministers, as well as all that relates to religious worship in general, should be left to the free judgement of the communities concerned, without any special supervision'.[14] It is difficult not to see this as a rejection of Woellner's regulation of religious freedom in general and his attempt to interfere specifically with the content of sermons and the appointment of preachers.

The arguments that led Humboldt to this conclusion bore many similarities with the views of other critics of Woellner who were writing at the time. Early on in Humboldt's article we encounter an objection that is familiar from the writings of Villaume, among others. Any direct intervention of the state in religious matters could not be limited to furthering religiosity in general, but was bound to promote a specific form of religion. And even if the furthering of religiosity in general was the objective, this required the state to adopt a 'norm' ('Richtschnur') that defined what

---

[10] Humboldt, 'Tagebuch der Reise', p. 11.
[11] Humboldt, 'Tagebuch der Reise', pp. 3, 6, 19, 37.
[12] Humboldt, 'Tagebuch der Reise', p. 3.
[13] 'Revolution in Berlin'. Humboldt, 'Tagebuch der Reise', p. 35.
[14] Humboldt, *Limits*, p. 70.

forms of religiosity were acceptable and worthy of promotion. Without naming Woellner, Humboldt summarized an essential part of the edict on religion and even used the language of one of its prominent passages where the new rules were justified as a 'norm' ('Richtschnur') for the people.[15] In Humboldt's view, such an imposition of one form of religiosity or a canon of acceptable forms of religiosity entailed a degree of force that could only be harmful. As with all limitations of freedom, the consequences would be dependent, passive, and weakened individuals who would be unable to fulfil their full potentials.

Humboldt took on another part of the reasoning behind the edicts when he examined the question of whether it was legitimate or not for the state to impose certain forms of religiosity, even at the expense of losing freedom of thought if that led to a more orderly and moral conduct of the population.[16] Like many critics Humboldt questioned the validity of this nexus which was central to Woellner's political motivations and the arguments of his supporters. Because 'all true religious feelings' and 'every true systems of religion' proceeded from the 'inner structure of human sensibility', religious teachings that were imposed from the outside could never have the same effect on individual morality as those that emanated from within the person. Moreover, characters and sensibilities of individuals differed profoundly and the imposition of the same religious dogmas on different people would lead to different reactions and effects in each case.[17] Any attempts to further individual morality through imposition were therefore not only wrong but also futile. This argument was present in many variations in the Woellner debates, and it had also been essential to the defence of religious freedom for Apitzsch and the fellow members of his conventicle. For Humboldt, as for many writers in the Pietist tradition, the imperative of religious tolerance resulted from an understanding of religious experience as profoundly individualistic.

However, Humboldt also went beyond this intellectual tradition in one important respect. Religion, he argued, could play an important role for the development of moral individuals, but it was not the only way to achieve this end. Against the purely religious vision of the processes of introspection and rebirth that were part of the Pietist tradition, he posited a much broader view of human development in which morals developed independently of religion.[18] In this view all sensual and rational experiences contributed to the formation of individuals who were more rounded, autonomous, energetic, and social in the sense of being able and willing to engage with others in society while respecting their individuality. 'The greater the diversity and individuality of man's development,' Humboldt argued, 'the more sublime his feelings become' and with them man's qualities as a moral and social

---

[15] Frederick William II, 'Circulare an alle Inspectoren der Churmark, nebst Edict vom 9ten July, die Religions-Verfassung in den Preußischen Staaten betreffend.', *Novum Corpus Constitutionum Prussico-Brandenburgensium Praecipue Marchicarum (NCC)* (12 vols., Berlin, 1788), vol. 9, p. 2181.

[16] Humboldt, *Limits*, p. 64.

[17] Humboldt, *Limits*, pp. 62–3.

[18] Humboldt, *Limits*, p. 69. For the relationship of Humboldt's idea of individual development with the Pietist tradition see J. Burrow, 'Editor's introduction', in J. Burrow, ed., *Wilhelm von Humboldt: the limits of state action* (Cambridge, 1969), p. xix.

being. The state's role in this process was mainly to ensure the greatest possible freedom in order to allow for a maximum variety of experiences and forms of development. It was not specific ethical or religious teachings, but the freedom of individual development per se that was at the heart of the development of moral and social individuals: 'the greater man's freedom the more self-reliant and well-disposed towards others he becomes'.[19] Far from becoming a danger to society, the 'citizen who is wholly left to himself in matters of religion' would be more moral and law abiding than individuals subjected to state-led attempts at religious education.[20] In a conspicuous way Humboldt once again reverts to the language of the Woellner controversy in his considerations about religion when he refers to his ideal type of individual as a 'self-thinking head' ('selbstdenken Kopfe') or 'self-thinking and self-acting man' ('selbstdenkenden und selbsttätigen Menschen').[21] In contemporary debates, the language of 'self-thinking' was used by both Woellner and his critics, who saw the phenomenon respectively as the source of decay or as one of the proudest achievements of Prussian civil society. In the light of the historiographical debate about elitist tendencies in the contemporary Prussian public, it should be pointed out that Humboldt did not see moral edification through individual development as a path that was open only to the cultured and sophisticated members of society.[22] Perhaps in response to such views he explicitly pointed out that 'freedom of thought' and 'enlightenment' were not 'for a few only', but would unfold their beneficial effects in all parts of society. 'None are so hopelessly low on the scale of culture and refinement', he added, 'as to be incapable of rising higher.'[23]

Mill later shared Humboldt's suspicion of religiosity as the only or principal source of ethics and the preference for a more broadly defined approach to individual moral improvement. Going further than Humboldt, Mill even questioned whether Christianity offered comprehensive moral guidance, pointing out in particular that the New Testament represented more an elaboration and discussion of pre-existing moral codes than offering an original normative orientation. Quite apart from this problem, Mill argued in a similar way to Humboldt that the reliance and prioritization of one form of religiosity would inevitably lead to the formation

---

[19] Humboldt, *Limits*, p. 69.

[20] My translation differs from the English edition. 'Der in Religionssachen völlig sich selbst gelassene Bürger wird nach seinem individuellen Charakter religiöse Gefühle in sein Innres verweben oder nicht; aber in jedem Fall wird sein Ideensystem konsequenter, seine Empfindung tiefer, in seinem Wesen mehr Einheit sein, und so wird ihn Sittlichkeit und Gehorsam gegen die Gesetze mehr auszeichnen.' Oddly, the English version gives the last part of this passage as 'his system of ideas will be more consistent, and his sensations more profound, his nature will be more coherent and he will distinguish more clearly between morality and submission to the laws.' Wilhelm von Humboldt, *Ideen zu einem Versuch die Grenzen der Wirksamkeit des Staats zu bestimmen* (Stuttgart, 1967), p. 98. Humboldt, *Limits*, p. 69.

[21] I use my own translation here because the translation of the Burrow edition obscures the continuity of language that links Humboldt with the wider contemporary context. Humboldt, *Grenzen*, pp. 94, 178.

[22] Michael Sauter, *Visions of the Enlightenment: the Edict on Religion of 1788 and the politics of the public sphere in eighteenth-century Prussia* (Leiden, 2009), pp. 135–9.

[23] Humboldt, *Limits*, p. 68.

of a 'low, abject servile type of character, which submit itself as it may to what it deems the supreme Will is incapable of rising to or sympathising in the conception of Supreme Goodness'.[24] Mill thus agreed with Humboldt that a narrow reliance on religious ethics was pernicious, but on the whole the threat of imposed religiosity to liberty was a much less prominent issue in *On liberty* than in *Limits*. The context of Woellner's edicts certainly goes a long way to explain Humboldt's emphasis on this threat to individual liberty in the same way that Mill's focus on the tyranny of majority as a threat to liberty may be attributed to the rise of mass politics in the nineteenth century.

ON EDUCATION

The chapter preceding that on religion in *Limits* is equally related to the context of Woellner's edicts. It was published under the title 'On public education' in *Berlinische Monatsschrift* in 1792, the same year in which Woellner established the Immediatsexaminationskommission in order to implement more firmly his controversial policies to centrally control the teaching at schools and universities.[25] Humboldt rejected the underpinning notions of Woellner's educational policy as radically as he objected to his religious policies. 'I need only conclude from what has been argued here', he wrote at the end of the article, 'that public education systems lie wholly beyond the limits within which the State's activities should be properly confined.'[26] Parts of his argument resembled that on religion. Attempts to use education as a way to lift morality and produce loyal subjects were both pernicious and potentially futile. Perhaps the main problem that Humboldt discussed was that—as in the case of religion—state involvement in educational matters would inevitably give preference to certain forms of education and create a higher degree of uniformity. These were precisely the objectives that Woellner was trying to achieve at the time by means of imposing standard textbooks and disciplining teachers and professors. For Humboldt, such attempts by the state impaired individuality and meant that 'the man [is] sacrificed to the citizen'.[27] As with other forms of excessive state action, the result would be a society of weak and dependent individuals in which commerce, arts, and sciences were languishing. But in the case of education such a development also brought more far-reaching structural dangers. A society that was composed of citizens who had been moulded in the same way by public education became unable to counteract the power of the state. An excessive role of the state in education was thus bound to permanently alter the relationship between state and civil society.[28]

[24] Mill, *On liberty*, p. 52.
[25] Wilhelm von Humboldt, 'Ueber oeffentliche Staatserziehung', *Berlinische Monatsschrift*, (1792), pp. 597–606.
[26] Again I deviate slightly from the Burrow edition by translating 'öffentliche Erziehung' not as 'national' but as 'public education systems'. Humboldt, *Grenzen*, p. 74. Humboldt, *Limits*, p. 54.
[27] Humboldt, *Limits*, p. 51.
[28] Humboldt, *Limits*, p. 54.

Another problem pointed out by Humboldt was that while state interventions in education would engender many pernicious side effects they were unlikely to achieve their original objectives. For no matter how tightly the state controlled the teachings with which youths were imbued, the circumstances encountered by different individuals at different stages of their lives were varied and the way in which they interacted with the education they received was unforeseeable. Moreover, circumstances were bound to exercise a much stronger effect on the individual, thus rendering the efforts of teaching morality through education largely futile.[29]

Humboldt's views on education are of particular interest because of his political role during the reconstruction era and the lasting impact of his views on education on policies throughout the modern period. Moreover, education is perhaps the area where Humboldt's ideas in *Limits* differ most substantially from those of Mill and in some ways also from Humboldt's own later views and actions.[30] Humboldt had advocated that the state completely renounce any ambitions to provide or promote education with the only exception that tutors may be appointed where parents had completely failed to provide their children with an education. It remained unclear how the conditions for state intervention should be determined and how exactly the state should proceed in such cases. By contrast, Mill saw education as one of the areas where the states of his time were too reluctant to take action. In a way not dissimilar to Humboldt, he argued that the liberty of parents needed to be restricted in order to protect children. However, Mill proposed much more far-reaching and systematic interventions. While he rejected state-run education, he favoured state controls in order to ensure that children were being educated. Children were to be submitted to regular tests and parents were to be fined if progress was not satisfactory. In order to prevent these examinations from imposing uniformity of thought, children were only to be tested on their knowledge of 'facts and positive science'.[31] Matters of belief were open to interpretation and were to be kept out of the purview of assessment. The epistemological and practical difficulties associated with such arrangements were not a major concern for Mill. Humboldt's more categorical rejection of all forms of state action in education was, in part, certainly due to his greater emphasis on the sensual and emotional components of individual development which were not liable to such testing. However, even more than theoretical disagreement, concrete experience may have led Humboldt to remain suspicious of all forms of state involvement in education including types of oversight exercised by the state. In 1792 Woellner was gearing up to extending school inspections in which not only teachers but also pupils were quizzed and their level of knowledge judged according to standards set by state legislation.[32] This concrete experience with state oversight and the contemporary debate about Woellner's attempt to

---

[29] Humboldt, *Limits*, p. 53.
[30] Leroux, 'Humboldt et Mill', pp. 84–5.
[31] Mill, *On liberty*, p. 107.
[32] Paul Schwartz, *Der erste Kulturkampf in Preussen um Kirche und Schule 1788–1798* (Berlin, 1925), pp. 306–30.

legislate standards of truth in religion and education certainly contributed to Humboldt's greater emphasis on the problems associated with the theoretical premises and practicalities of such arrangements.

Differences in historical context may be cited to explain not only the different outlooks of Humboldt and Mill, but also an apparent change in Humboldt's views. When Humboldt was put in charge of reforming parts of Prussia's educational system in 1809, he oversaw what he had categorically rejected in 1792: a deep involvement of the state in shaping the content of curricula and, more generally, in the promotion of education and cultural progress that was at the root of the transformation of Prussia into a *Kulturstaat* (a state actively promoting cultural and educational development) in the course of the nineteenth century.[33] He seemed aware of this contradiction and continued to insist in official documents that all political actions in this area were to be undertaken under the premise that the state's involvement was per se potentially harmful. Fundamental doubts about the legitimacy of the office that he was asked to undertake may have contributed to his reluctance to accept the position in the first place. At the same time, he probably felt that the new political climate opened up the possibility to put many of his views about education and individual development into practice and he used this opportunity energetically and was able to establish structures that shaped education in Prussian and beyond in the long term. However, his resignation after only just over one year of tenure also points to his frustrations at the political obstacles to the implementation of his ideas. Despite the deviations from the more radical positions set out in *Limits* Humboldt's policies remained deeply rooted in enlightened and humanist traditions that were crucial to the efforts of reconstruction, but also encountered increasing resistance as a result of the reactionary backlash that began to form in this period.[34]

ON SCARCITY AND ABUNDANCE

Two further articles that were published in *Berlinische Monatsschrift* and in Friedrich Schiller's (1759–1805) *Neue Thalia* (*New Thalia*) in 1792 comprised most of the second, third, and eighth chapters of *Limits*.[35] The article published in *Neue Thalia* started out with general remarks about the relation between state and civil society, but then turned quickly to the specific question of the state's responsibility for the 'physical welfare' of its citizens. The other article argued the more specific question of whether the state should regulate certain forms of luxury consumption in order to protect the morality of the population. While Humboldt strove for originality in his answers, the questions were hardly new to the readers of the two

---

[33] Wolfgang Neugebauer and Bärbel Holtz, *Kulturstaat und Bürgergesellschaft: Preussen, Deutschland und Europa im 19. und frühen 20. Jahrhundert* (Berlin, 2010).

[34] Gall, *Humboldt*, pp. 138–225.

[35] Wilhelm von Humboldt, 'Wie weit darf sich die Sorgfalt des Staats um das Wohl seiner Bürger erstrecken?', *Neue Thalia* (1792), pp. 131–69. Humboldt, 'Staatserziehung'.

journals. Both questions had been central to the protracted debates associated with the demise of the Régie five years earlier.

Moreover, in a curious way the debates about the Régie were not only part of the intellectual context in which Humboldt wrote, but were also woven into his own biography. In 1791 Humboldt had married Caroline von Dachröden (1766–1829) and it was during the subsequent period, when the young couple lived on the estate of the bride's father Karl Friedrich von Dachröden (1732–1809), that most of the manuscript of *Limits* was written. At this time Humboldt's father-in-law lived as a man of independent but rapidly declining means and an author. However, Dachröden had previously served as *Kammerpräsident* in Minden until Frederick II dismissed him in 1771. The end of his career as an official was, in part, brought about by financial irregularities, but also by his critical views on the Régie. His outspoken criticism of the 'French migratory birds' and of the harm caused by the Régie to local businesses earned him repeated reprimands from Berlin. He was one of the addressees of the angry Cabinet Order cited in Chapter 4 in which Frederick instructed local officials not to side with merchants and to refrain from commenting on the Régie as these were matters beyond their competence.[36] It is impossible to know whether this curious family connection exercised any direct intellectual influence on Humboldt's ideas, but the connection still illustrates to what extent the events and debates associated with the Régie were part of the historical reality in which Humboldt wrote *Limits*.

In the *Neue Thalia* article Humboldt discussed the extent to which the state should be involved in efforts to 'augment the physical welfare of the nation', in particular 'the encouragement of agriculture, industry, and commerce' and 'of all regulation relative to finance and currency, imports and exports'.[37] In the second text, Humboldt questioned the legitimacy of sumptuary laws as a means to curb the negative effects of luxury consumption on the morality of the public. Taken together, the two articles thus explored the role of the state in protecting its citizens from the consequences of material scarcity and overabundance. The construction of the arguments differed in the two cases, but the conclusion was the same for both, namely that the state was to exercise the utmost restraint in its interventions.

Humboldt saw attempts to promote economic welfare by interfering with the freedom of individual citizens as one of the principal areas of state activity in his time. However, he warned that such provisions might be beneficial in the short term, but were likely to harm individuals and consequently the economic prospects of society and state in the longer term. States employed different means to guide individual behaviour in ways that were deemed useful to achieving prosperity. Among the tools used were direct force exercised through laws and orders, the creation of conditions that encouraged and discouraged certain forms of economic behaviour, and attempts to guide individuals by influencing their 'heart' and

[36] 'Französischen Zugvögel'. Dachröden cited in Ilse Foerst-Crato, 'Karl Friedrich von Dachröden', *Mitteilungen des Mindener Geschichtsvereins*, 49 (1977), pp. 131–6, at p. 134.
[37] Humboldt, *Limits*, p. 23.

'head'.[38] Although different in form these ways of interfering with individual freedom were all pernicious because of the uniformity and passivity that they imposed on the population. As a result individuals became used to tutelage and lost the power of imagination, energy, and strength that were associated with diversity. They were turned into subjects and, still worse, into 'machines' for the production of wealth.[39] In many ways this achieved what Humboldt described as the primary objectives of most states, 'prosperity and tranquillity' ('Wohlstand und Ruhe'), but it destroyed the creative powers of the nation.[40] Individuals were only able to pursue with full energy, intellectual capacity, and emotional attachment the activities that they had freely embraced. Ultimately, the strength of the state would suffer as a result of the damage done to the individual development of its citizens. Individuals paid for the greater abundance of goods in the short term, with a loss of their strength in the longer term.[41]

In the *Berlinische Monatsschrift* article Humboldt turned to considering the question of whether the state should intervene to limit excesses in consumption. Authors like Süßmilch had called for a return of sumptuary laws in order to curb the excesses of urban individualism and one of the main purposes of the Régie had been to use tariffs and monopolies in order to regulate individual consumption habits to suit the state's programme for economic development. Humboldt rejected all forms of interference with consumption, regardless of whether they were proposed in order to promote moral or economic welfare, because they were detrimental to the development of individual strength and morality. An important part of Humboldt's idea of individual development was the motivations and impressions provided by 'sensuousness' ('Sinnlichkeit'). Without it the 'greatest depth of thought and the treasures of wisdom are barren and lifeless'.[42] Individuals could only develop the strength and energy for great achievements, as well as the necessary taste and judgement, if they were exposed to a wide range of sensual experiences. Those who were left free to develop emotionally would eventually develop a strong sense of morality and benign social behaviour. In contrast, a population that was deprived of such experiences would be reduced to 'well-cared-for slaves'.[43] Humboldt rejected the widespread notion that the pursuit of pleasure was ultimately always a manifestation of selfishness that was likely to undermine social bonds. To the contrary, he argued that by contributing to the self-development ('Bildung') of the individual, sensual pleasures were beneficial for sociability and consequently for the stability of society.

Humboldt's radical rejection of state interference in economic matters was in some respects reminiscent of the critique that Mirabeau directed at the 'hothouses' that the government had erected over Prussia's cities. With its subsidies, tariffs, and

---

[38] Humboldt, *Limits*, p. 22.   [39] Humboldt, *Limits*, p. 24.
[40] Again I deviate from the translation in the Burrow edition. Humboldt, *Limits*, p. 24. Humboldt, *Grenzen*, p. 31.
[41] Humboldt, *Limits*, p. 23.   [42] Humboldt, *Limits*, p. 76.
[43] Humboldt, *Limits*, p. 79.

monopolies the Régie had embodied the attempts of the state to force, coax, and cajole individuals into behaving in a manner that the state saw as beneficial for economic development and individual health and morality. However, Mirabeau, like many others in the contemporary debates, looked at these matters from a perspective that was more narrowly economic than Humboldt's. Mirabeau insisted that economic freedom could not exist in isolation, but needed to be associated with other liberties, for example religious freedom. However, for him the economic problems that were caused by the excessive government control under Frederick II were related to the inability of individuals to take the right decisions in questions relating to consumption, production, and trade. Mirabeau's focus was on the immediate economic outcomes produced by restrictions on the economic choices of individuals. The effect of such limitations on individual development was much less of a concern to him, not least because he saw individual development as largely determined by climatic conditions and the laws of nature. In his view, the influence of governments on the development of individual and national characters was much more limited than Humboldt assumed. Mirabeau's position was perhaps closer to that of Frederick who had argued that government could alter national and individual characters, but only very slowly, and the main concern had to be to create government institutions that were adapted to the spirit of the nation as it was.[44]

The framing of Humboldt's critique was therefore closer to the approach that we find in Hamann's critique of the Régie. The 'Magus of the North' had repeatedly attacked Frederick for relying on the advice of 'political arithmeticians' whose coolly rational calculations about the maximization of state revenue eclipsed all other concerns of government. The establishment of the Régie was for him one of many signs announcing the dawn of a new era in which the 'Fredericks d'Or will shine brighter than the stars of the most brilliant winter night', and he deplored how the single-mindedness of government disregarded individual, religious, and moral development and crushed the 'will to live' of the citizens of Königsberg.[45] Like Humboldt he saw the oppression of individuality as the central problem which manifested itself in many forms including a lack of energy that led to the languishing of local trade and commerce.

Humboldt's holistic approach to the question of economic freedom also set him apart from subsequent writers like Mill. The question of economic freedom is not central in *On liberty* but it was discussed at some length in the *Principles of political*

---

[44] The position of the physiocrats has sometimes be described as 'antipolitical' (Pierre Rosanvallon, *Le capitalisme utopique* (Paris, 1979), p. 52). It is certainly true that their reliance on natural laws as an explanatory paradigm led them to disregard man-made historical and political developments. However, as Cheney has shown, even physiocratic authors such as Mirabeau did not always fully endorse this position (Paul Cheney, *Revolutionary commerce: globalization and the French monarchy* (Cambridge, MA, 2010), p. 151). Mirabeau's work on Prussia, for example, does not devote much attention to the historical developments, but political aspects of the Prussian reality are central to his analysis.

[45] Johann Georg Hamann, 'Lettre à un financier de Pe-Kim', in Josef Nadler, ed., *Sämtliche Werke/ Johann Georg Hamann* (6 vols., Vienna, 1951), vol. 3, p. 303. Hamann to Johann Friedrich Reichardt, 1777 (probably March), in Johann Georg Hamann, *Johann Georg Hamann Briefwechsel*, eds. Walther Ziesemer and Arthur Henkel (3 vols., Wiesbaden, 1955), vol. 3, p. 356.

economy (1848), published slightly earlier. Here, Mill supported a role for the state in a range of functions including the administration of justice, but he rejected other more far-reaching interventions such as monopolies, protective tariffs, and other efforts to increase prosperity associated with the 'mercantile system'. However, unlike Humboldt's, this rejection of state intervention was based mainly on considerations of economic efficiency. Mill's utilitarian approach meant that he was less inflexible in his rejection of state intervention and it led him to concede that protective tariffs and other measures from the toolkit of the 'mercantile system' could be justified if they were applied temporarily in a 'young and rising nation' in order to develop domestic industry.[46] He looked favourably on the tradition of infant industry protection so long as it represented a preparatory stage for full participation in free trade. It may be said that in this respect Mill was closer to the economic pragmatism of Frederick II and his French advisors, than to the inexorable views of Humboldt. One of Fredrick's primary concerns in his economic policies was to respond adequately to different local circumstances. Referring to the different development of Prussia's provinces with regard to trade, customs, and traditions he noted that 'it would be impossible to govern them according to the same principles in every detail'.[47] This view resulted in regional variations in economic policies in Prussia. Frederick pursued a much less interventionist approach in the more developed western provinces of Prussia, whereas he acted more heavy-handedly to promote manufacturing in the backward eastern part of his realm. Mill and the administrators of Frederickian Prussia thus shared an approach to economic policy that judged the necessity of state action in economic matters based on economic circumstance and outcomes. Humboldt's perspective was not only much broader, but it also led almost inevitably to a highly restricted economic role for the state. He argued that the freedom of individuality was likely to produce superior economic results, but these outcomes would only be visible in the long term and they were not amenable to control and evaluation because Humboldt remained vague in his description of the nature of these benefits. More importantly, superior results were not central to Humboldt's argument for economic liberty, which was mainly based on the notion that individual development, and with it the broader progress of society, was only possible if individuals enjoyed sufficient freedom. Because Humboldt—like Hamann—dismissed concerns with short-term results as reductionist, there was in practice no set of conditions or outcomes that could lead to a re-evaluation of his case for liberty. A lack of positive outcomes in the longer term might have convinced Humboldt to review his position, but he probably considered this possibility too outlandish to be given any serious consideration. Whereas Mill's utilitarian arguments and

---

[46] Andrew Walls, 'Self-development and the liberal state: the cases of John Stuart Mill and Wilhelm von Humboldt', *The Review of Politics*, 61 (1999), pp. 252–74, at p. 257. John Stuart Mill, *The principles of political economy* (Oxford, 2008), p. 302.

[47] 'Da sie unter verschiedenen Himmelsstrichen liegen und ihre Lage Handel, Sitten und Gebräuche bedingt, so wäre es unmöglich, sie bis ins einzelne nach gleichen Grundsätzen zu regieren.' Frederick II, 'Das politische Testament von 1752', in Gustav Volz, ed., *Die Werke Friedrichs des Großen* (10 vols., Berlin, 1912), vol. 7, pp. 115–94, at p. 127.

Frederickian pragmatism could lead to a range of policy options, only one outcome was ultimately possible in the context of Humboldt's argument. This disregard for short-term considerations of economic efficiency set his ideas apart from the tradition of liberalism as it developed among classical political economists from the late eighteenth century onwards and placed him closer to currents of liberalism that were associated with the writings of Herbert Spencer (1820–1903) in the nineteenth and Friedrich von Hayek (1899–1992) in the twentieth century. In his explorations of the genealogies of liberalism, Hayek emphasized the 'German roots' of this intellectual tradition and in particular the inspiration that Humboldt's and Goethe's ideas had provided for Mill. He also pointed to the distinctive character of the 'extreme position' that Humboldt held compared with other liberals.[48] Humboldt's 'evolutionary and individualist case against state interference' was in many ways closer to Hayek's own approach which explicitly distanced itself from the 'paleo-liberal' defence of economic freedom based on efficiency arguments and resorted to arguments about the long-term evolutionary benefits to social and individual development as a justification for economic liberty.[49] The neoliberal political reformers of the 1980s—some of whom were deeply suspicious of Germany and its Prussian heritage—would perhaps have been surprised to know about the Prussian roots of their rhetoric.

ON CHANGE

The evolutionary nature of Humboldt's approach was also apparent in his views on the development of government institutions in general and fiscal institutions in particular. Humboldt commented on fiscal matters in the parts of *Limits* that were not published at the time of writing and subsequently as a government official during the period of post-Napoleonic reconstruction. Despite the 'extreme position' that Humboldt took with regard to the extent of state action, he acknowledged that certain central tasks, mainly associated with the protection of individuals from being harmed by other citizens or foreign enemies, had to be carried out by the state and that the state needed to raise the necessary funds to fulfil these tasks. In his comments in *Limits* Humboldt made it clear that taxation was the preferable way to satisfy the financial needs of the state. Despite possible inconveniences, it was preferable to tax the revenues of private enterprise rather than having a state with direct ownership of productive resources. The political power of the state was already a substantial threat to individual liberty, and if

[48] Friedrich von Hayek, *The road to serfdom* (Chicago, 2007), p. 61. Friedrich von Hayek, *The constitution of liberty* (London, 1990), p. 297.

[49] Editorial note to Friedrich von Hayek, 'The legal and political philosophy of David Hume (1711–1776)', in W. W. Bartley and Stephen Kresge, eds., *The trend of economic thinking* (London, 1991), p. 104. For a nuanced picture of the transition from classical economic liberalism to neoliberalism see Ben Jackson, 'The origins of neo-liberalism: the free economy and the strong state, 1930–1947', *Historical Journal*, 53 (2010), pp. 129–51. For the use of the term 'paleo-liberal' see p. 141.

government was also equipped with economic power it was likely that the combination of the two would further shift the balance between state power and individual liberty in an intolerable way. This view was in itself rather radical considering the Prussian state still owned large stretches of land and derived a considerable income from these holdings. However, a perhaps even more surprising deviation from traditional views was the preference that Humboldt expressed with regard to direct taxation. A significant tradition in economic thought, dating back to the seventeenth century, had embraced indirect taxation as the less oppressive form. In the eighteenth century Montesquieu had formulated this view most influentially, when he argued in *Spirit of the laws* that indirect taxes were 'more natural to liberty'.[50] Humboldt's departure from this tradition is also noteworthy because most opponents of the Régie did not call for an abolition of the excise in itself, but only denounced the way in which it was collected. Humboldt's argument focused equally on the practical problems associated with the administration of indirect taxes, but arrived at a more radical conclusion. 'Experience teaches us', he wrote about indirect taxes, 'what multiplicity of institutions is required to arrange and levy them; and of all these, according to our previous reasoning [about the limits of state action] we must unquestionably disapprove.'[51] It may not be too far-fetched to see the twenty years of controversy about the vexatious controls implemented by Régie officials as the 'experience' evoked here. As a consequence Humboldt recommended direct taxes as the best form of fiscality. The experience of the political instability created by the lack of legitimacy of the Régie may also have influenced his views on fiscal reform plans after 1806. In 1817 Humboldt commented on the far-reaching fiscal reform plans that were part of the reconstruction in a series of government meetings and reports. As discussed previously, the new fiscal system was favourable to many groups of society who had been central to the resistance against the Régie. Nonetheless, Humboldt warned repeatedly not to put the plan into action without seeking approval from the estates for fear of alienating parts of the population and provoking new political rifts and conflicts.[52]

If the Prussian context had made him wary of radical political change, his observations of developments in France reinforced this view. In an article of 1792, Humboldt warned emphatically of the cool rationalism with which the revolutionary government introduced the most radical reform projects.[53] He later elaborated his views in *Limits* where he argued in favour of slow and gradual reform, rather than radical leaps, as the best way in which the institutions of the state should develop. Gradual institutional reform towards ever-greater freedom of the individual was to be implemented by the legislator but guided by civil society. The lawgiver's responsibility was to react with appropriate reforms to the extent

---

[50] Charles Louis Secondat Baron de Montesquieu, *The spirit of the laws* (London, 1914), bk 13, ch. 14.

[51] Humboldt, *Limits*, p. 129.

[52] See the edited documents in Wilhelm von Humboldt, *Wilhelm von Humboldt's gesammelte Schriften*, ed. Albert Leitzmann (20 vols., Berlin, 1916), pp. iii, 162–89.

[53] Wilhelm von Humboldt, 'Ideen über Staatsverfassung, durch die neue Französische Konstituzion veranlaßt', *Berlinische Monatsschrift*, (1792), pp. 84–98.

that society matured and demanded greater freedom. Only when restriction began to be perceived as 'shackles' should the legislator intervene by removing them and thus gradually creating an institutional framework that resembled Humboldt's ideal state. Inertia of the legislator as well as radical leaps that resulted in a degree of freedom for which individuals were not yet ready were both harmful.[54] Instead, it was crucial that an appropriate balance was kept between the level of maturity of the nation and the institutional framework of government. This language of 'balance' harked back to the debates about governance in the late eighteenth century in which both the defenders of royal prerogatives and the advocates of individual autonomy were concerned with gradual change and the preservation of harmony. Already in the early 1780s, Gedike had made explicit his suspicion against all 'rapid improvement coming from above'.[55] For many contemporaries, such views had been vindicated subsequently by the contrast between French and Prussian developments. While in France harmonious balance was first threatened by the unwillingness and inability to reform of the Bourbon state, it was subsequently threatened by the excessively radical change proposed by the revolutionary assembly. Prussia's parallel development in this period had steered a moderate course between these extremes which was much closer to Humboldt's ideal. Where civil society had demanded greater freedom, as in the fiscal and religious conflicts discussed here, the state had gradually given in to such demands, thus maintaining a healthy balance between institutions and development of civil society. From Humboldt's perspective the moderate Prussian model of development was far more satisfactory than the French radicalism, which he deeply mistrusted. Just as individuals were best left alone to develop in accordance with their own natures, so the development of the institutions of the state was best served by slow and gradual evolution. Humboldt's arguments about individual development were based on an evolutionary understanding of change and he also extended this view to all other areas of human activity, including the institutional development of the state. 'The best conducted human activities', Humboldt stated categorically in *Limits*, 'are those which most faithfully resemble the operations of the natural world.'[56]

ON THE LIMITS OF STATE ACTION

Looking at the individual parts of *Limits* separately makes it possible to place Humboldt's ideas in the context of contemporary debates and events, but this approach also obscures some of his achievements. Until now we have mainly ignored the chapter entitled 'On the solicitude of the state for security against foreign enemies', which was among those that Humboldt considered to be the most

[54] Humboldt, *Limits*, pp. 135–6.
[55] 'Ich bin gegen alle schnelle, von oben kommende Verbesserung'. Friedrich Gedike, 'Ueber Berlin, von einem Fremden (Briefe 1–3)', *Berlinische Monatsschrift*, 1 (1783), pp. 439–65.
[56] Humboldt, *Limits*, p. 10.

important of his work.[57] This short piece was published at the time as an article in *Berlinische Monatsschrift* and is not so much remarkable for his comments on the role of the state in warfare, but for the arguments about the effect of war on the individual. Unsurprisingly Humboldt endorsed national defence as an area appropriate for state action, but he also warned of the negative consequences of maintaining a standing army. The 'machine-like existence' that soldiers led, even in peacetime, was as harmful as any deprivation of freedom and created dulling homogeneity and equality among individuals. In the case of a standing army the consequences were particularly negative because war was one of the most important areas in which individuals could grow and excel by acts of bravery and skill.[58] The discipline and tactics of modern warfare eliminated this opportunity for individual development, and for this reason Humboldt advocated the reduction to a minimum of military preparations in peacetime and a greater reliance on the noble warrior spirit of free citizens in wartime. This argument bore a direct relation to the reality in which Humboldt had grown up. The superiority of the Prussian armies under Frederick II relied on their rigorous drill and organization. Also, as a result of the urban stationing and quartering the Prussian military had an unparalleled presence in civilian life. Nonetheless, public commentary or criticism of the military was rare and Humboldt's comments were not part of an extended contemporary debate. Occasional remarks about the excessive presence of soldiers can be found in commentary about urban life but only in very few cases is the question discussed in any detail.[59]

Our approach to place each of Humboldt's chapters in its contemporary intellectual context may also have obscured the fact that the whole text of *Limits* was in a way more than the sum of its parts. Humboldt reviewed and incorporated into his arguments concepts that had already been part of contemporary commentary and developed them further. However, his greatest achievement was in a way to bring these diverse considerations together under the single heading of the 'limits of state action'. We have pointed to some early attempts to connect discussions of the role of the state in religious matters with fiscal and other concerns in the Woellner debate. However, the range of Humboldt's consideration and the consistency with which he developed the central theme of individual development in these different contexts set his work apart from the debates on which he built. By joining considerations about state action in different spheres and by abstracting from specific detail—a process that we have tried to reverse in this chapter—he was able to write a text that spoke to readers beyond Prussia and beyond his time.

---

[57] Wilhelm von Humboldt, 'Ueber die Sorgalt des Staates für die Sicherheit gegen auswärtige Feinde', *Berlinische Monatsschrift* (1792), pp. 346–54.

[58] Humboldt, *Limits*, p. 47.

[59] An exception is the discussion of Prussia's military system in Mirabeau's writings, but unlike other parts of his works these comments were not part of a larger public debate in Prussia. Honoré Gabriel de Riqueti Comte de Mirabeau, *De la monarchie prussienne, sous Frédéric le Grand: avec un appendice contenant des recherches sur la situation actuelle des principales contrées de l'Allemagne* (4 vols., London [Paris], 1788), vol. 4. Honoré Gabriel de Riqueti Comte de Mirabeau, *Lettre remise à Fréderic Guillaume II, roi régnant de Prusse, le jour de son avènement au trône* (n.p., 1787).

Perhaps his main achievements lay in the way in which he summarized and reduced to their essence the outcomes of the protracted political conflicts and debates of late eighteenth-century Prussia and fed them into the larger context of the development of European liberalism. The editor of the modern English edition of *Limits* called Humboldt 'the lost leader of Prussia's liberal constitutionalist'.[60] However, to think of Humboldt as a leader—lost or not—might be partly misleading because it implies that he was ahead of his time potentially shaping events. But as we have suggested here, a different perspective may capture Humboldt's relation with the historical context more accurately: the political developments and debates of the second half of the eighteenth century shaped the ideas of the great Prussian thinker. Humboldt thus became the unlikely spokesman for a generation of angry Prussian brewers, merchants, smokers, coffee drinkers, and religious dissenters. He amalgamated their complaints, hopes, and achievements into a single vision and poured it into a prose that was moderate in tone, but radical in substance, and that found readers far beyond the geographical and chronological context that inspired it.

Nothing illustrates better the way in which Humboldt's text functioned as an interchange between different national debates than the polite exchange of epigraphs between three luminaries of the European history of political thought. In 1792 Humboldt opened *Limits* with a quotation from Mirabeau's *Work on public education* (1791).[61] The text was based on notes for a speech in the National Assembly but Mirabeau died before he was able to deliver it and his doctor published the text in the same year. In the passage that Humboldt chose for the epigraph the French revolutionary warned against the 'furore of governing' as 'the most calamitous affliction of modern governments'.[62] On one level, Humboldt used a text here that emerged from a specifically French context. Mirabeau had prepared it for the National Assembly and his views on government were part of the physiocratic debates that had dominated French intellectual life during much of the preceding decades. However, Humboldt could have found very similar comments in Mirabeau's works on Prussia. In the introduction to his *Of the Prussian monarchy*, Mirabeau warned that governments were constantly in danger of succumbing to the 'baneful affliction of wanting to govern too much' and pointed to the Prussian state as an example of excessive attempts to 'control', 'regulate', 'direct', and 'command everything'.[63] As the epigraph of his work, Humboldt thus chose a phrase from a French revolutionary who had developed his views in part against the backdrop of experiences in Prussia. Over half a century later, it was then Humboldt's turn to provide another political theorist with an epigraph. In 1859 Mill used a phrase from Humboldt's tract about the 'essential importance of human

---

[60] Burrow's comment cited on back cover of Humboldt, *Limits*.

[61] Gabriel de Riqueti Comte de Mirabeau, *Travail sur l'éducation publique trouvé dans les papiers de Mirabeau l'Aîné* (Paris, 1791). Humboldt was not the only German admirer of Mirabeau's work. See Otto Johnston, 'Mirabeau and Schiller on education to freedom', *Monatshefte*, 76 (1984), pp. 58–72.

[62] 'La fureur de gouverner, la plus funeste maladie des gouvernements modernes.' Humboldt, *Limits*, not paginated.

[63] 'Maladie meutrière de vouloir trop gouverner'; 'de tout surveiller, de tout réglementer, de tout prescrire, de tout ordonner'. Mirabeau, *De la monarchie prussienne*, vol. 1, not paginated.

development in its richest diversity' as an opening for *On liberty*. Mill's choice of epigraph was not less remarkable than Humboldt's. It was certainly not an obvious choice for one of the most prominent exponents of British liberalism, administrator of the East India Company, and later MP to use a phrase written over fifty years earlier by a Prussian noble under an absolutist regime on the European continent as the opening sentence of a tract on liberty. The extent to which Mirabeau, Humboldt, and Mill influenced each other is difficult to ascertain in detail but what emerges from this transnational exchange of epigraphs is that each of these authors had found a language in which they discussed the political problems of their time and place, that spoke powerfully to readers in other countries, even if circumstances there were seemingly radically different. Mill explicitly addressed the question of whether Humboldt's views could be understood in a British context and argued that ultimately the differences were smaller than they might appear.[64]

One may be tempted to attribute this fluent cross-border communication to the abstract and theoretical nature of the arguments and see this conversation as part of an elite discourse that was so far removed from political realities that different contexts could not get in the way of transnational communication. However, such a view would have to ignore the extent to which Mirabeau, Mill, and Humboldt and their writings were part of the political life of their countries. What is obvious in the cases of Mirabeau and Mill, and what has hopefully be shown convincingly here for Humboldt, is that their works were deeply rooted in the realities of day-to-day politics of their respective countries and that all three thinkers actively shaped these realities at different points in their lives. They were not only theoreticians, but also practitioners of politics. The appeal that their arguments had across borders can only be explained by the extent to which they saw historical developments in different European countries as unfolding along similar lines.

---

[64] Mill, *On liberty*, p. 58.

Conclusion: 'Le *Sonderweg* est mort, vive le *Sonderweg*?'

If contemporaries such as Mirabeau, Humboldt, and Mill had a common language in which to discuss the challenges and questions facing them, historians, too, need to use language that enables them to capture the structural similarities and connective nature of European history. Instead, there seems to be a tendency to respond to the demise of the notion of a German *Sonderweg* with a proliferation of European *Sonderwegs*. However, in this way historians risk depriving themselves of the capability to conceptualize the web of interactions, transfers, exchanges, and mutual observations between countries that—as we have tried to show in the case of Prussia—characterized the history of the eighteenth century. Such connections often also extended beyond Europe to North America and other parts of the world. And while the European context always remained most important for Prussia, more distant links became significant subsequently.[1]

In the context discussed here, but also in other periods, this type of connective development was often spurred on by wars. The Thirty Years War set in motion long-term structural change that led to similar challenges across Europe: the formation and continuous improvement of standing armies, the corresponding development of fiscal structures, and the redefinition of the relationship between state and religion were challenges that were faced across the European continent. Once states had begun to consolidate, the delimitation of their spheres of activity and relationship with civil society became crucial questions that could not be ignored anywhere in Europe. Such issues—for example about the relationship between state and religion or state and economy—have remained central throughout the modern period and are as important and controversial today as they were in the past.

Other wars of the early modern period such as the Seven Years War led to challenges that were perhaps more limited in scope but no less important for historical development. For all major European countries, this war resulted in a significant strain on public finances. Reactions and consequences differed, but it cannot be ignored that the fiscal implications of this war posed a simultaneous and structurally similar political and economic challenge across Europe. It would

---

[1] Among others Sebastian Conrad and Jürgen Osterhammel, *Das Kaiserreich transnational: Deutschland in der Welt 1871–1914* (Göttingen, 2004). Sebastian Conrad, *Globalisation and the nation in imperial Germany* (Cambridge, 2010).

certainly have baffled contemporaries not to think of such issues in European terms. If only for the reason that one country's fiscal crisis could quickly become another country's military opportunity, mutual observation and imitation were common practices and the associated movement of individuals, ideas, and practices was visible proof of the similarity of the challenges faced in different parts of Europe. The reason that both Smith and Hamann were eager to read Beaumont's study of fiscal systems in Europe was that contemporaries spoke about the same problems in the same languages no matter whether they were Scottish, Prussian, or French. And if the fiscal problems of Prussia could be solved by French administrators and if American and British tax payers revolted over some of the same issues that gave rise to heated exchanges in Prussia, reading their histories as separate and different stories is difficult to justify. The connective aspects of European history have received much attention and a substantial theoretical debate about transnationality, transfers, and exchanges has developed in this context.[2] As stimulating and necessary as this is, it must ultimately lead us to pose broader questions not only about connections but about the structural similarities of historical development across borders. The context that has been examined here certainly suggests that significant connections could develop because structural similarities existed. Claims about a common European heritage made by Europhiles or those warning of clashes of civilizations often turn out to be pompous misrepresentations after even cursory scrutiny. However, this should not lead historians to abandon the field, but, rather, to redouble their efforts to supply the public with a critically minded and empirically well-founded commentary on the common parts of Europe's past. None of this is to reduce the importance of national states. In particular, in the periods following the events that we have examined here, national states played an important role in virtually all areas of history. Nonetheless, as Ute Frevert has argued, even the German nation state of the modern period existed to a large extent in a historical context that was made up of transnational challenges and developments.[3] The two world wars, cyclical economic crises, and structural economic change that occurred in the modern period were challenges that transcended national borders in many ways.

However, if we return from these general considerations to the specific questions associated with the historical developments of the second half of the eighteenth century, are we not forced to acknowledge the existence of fundamental differences in the development of the relationship between state and civil society in Prussia and France, for example? We may argue that Habermas' view of the distinctive nature of this relationship in Prussia was in part based on assumptions about historical reality that have since been corrected, based on new research about the development of a critical public in Prussia. However, some of the most recent research once again

---

[2] See summaries and commentary in Holger Nehring and Florian Schui, 'Introduction: global debates about taxation: transfers of ideas, the challenge of political legitimacy and the paradoxes of state-building', in Holger Nehring and Florian Schui, eds., *Global debates about taxation* (London, 2007), pp. 1–18.

[3] Ute Frevert, 'Europeanizing German history', *GHI Bulletin*, 36 (2005), pp. 9–24.

suggests fundamental differences between the French and Prussian publics. The fact that the language of difference is now used to describe the French case is noteworthy and will no doubt attract the attention of historians of historiography in the future, but this does not change the diagnosis of a discrepancy along national lines. Critical questions must certainly be asked about the empirical basis of such arguments. In particular, some of the quantitative methods used are perhaps less convincing than they seem. Nevertheless, recent arguments about the authoritarian tendencies in the Prussian public are powerful and well supported and it is to be hoped that the present study has added some further facets to the analysis of concerns with social control present in the Prussian public. Yet does this not mean that we have to distinguish between an authoritarian Prussian public and a subversive one in France, ultimately leading us to acknowledge that national differences prevailed in the formation of European publics?

In large measure, the perception of the French and Prussian publics as opposites is predicated on a limited view of each. An examination of the authoritarian tendencies in the Prussian public is useful and important, but it sheds light only on a part of the historical reality. As this study has shown, significant developments associated with public debates and political events of this period point to a different direction. Prussian burghers challenged the authority of the state and sought to impose themselves politically in the defence of individual freedom. However, opposing voices made up a significant element of public debate at the time and we must conclude from this that different tendencies were present in the Prussian public. Authoritarian views that wished to instrumentalize the state for their exclusionary project existed alongside emancipatory arguments that aimed to contain or defeat the state for the purpose of carving out greater autonomy for individuals. A closer look at the French public reveals a similarly double-faced reality. The French public was clearly not exclusively populated by commentators who were committed enemies of the state. There is no space here to explore this more fully, but we have pointed to Voltaire's admiration of strong monarchs and ministers as promoters of progress and Turgot's readiness to work as part of the apparatus of state and in an authoritarian and oppressive way to achieve reform.

On one level, this heterogeneity simply confirms the observation that the public was politically 'multidirectional'. As we have argued, this did not reduce the threat that the public posed to the political stability of contemporary states. Rather, the co-existence of contradictory emanicpatory and authoritarian tendencies in the publics of Europe and sometimes in the writings of the same commentators points to a fundamental tension in the intellectual legacy of this period. As the controversy over the Woellner edicts but also the fiscal debates about the Régie show, contemporaries arrived at fundamentally different conclusions although they used the same Enlightened 'tool kit' to form and support their views. Adherence to common epistemological standards did not lead to common conclusions. In large part the emergence of a more harmonious vision was prevented by different views about individual and collective interests and their interrelation.

At the same time, the contradiction between liberating and authoritarian tendencies also reflects the deeper tensions that Max Horkheimer and Theodor

W. Adorno have discussed under the heading of the 'dialectic of the Enlightenment'. Rather than associating authoritarian and emancipatory tendencies of the Enlightenment with different national developments they—like Weber before them—pointed to the inherent contradictions within the intellectual foundations of the modern world.[4] As we have seen, these ambiguities were not lost on contemporaries themselves. The comments of Hamann, Humboldt, and others reflect a deep unease with the optimistic outlook that other contemporaries associated with the diffusion of Enlightened thought. These critical observers were well aware that a focus on concerns with procedural values such as rationality, empiricism, and efficiency was becoming the norm of European states and societies, but they were more doubtful than others that this new normality set humanity unequivocally on a path of progress. In other words, even before the history of the nineteenth and twentieth century had shown that modernity could be the worst enemy of humanity, contemporaries began to see that the normal path of development on which the western world had embarked was not necessarily and at all times a path that led to human progress.

---

[4] Detlev Peukert, *Max Webers Diagnose der Moderne* (Göttingen, 1989).

Bibliography

ARCHIVAL SOURCES

'Seiner königl.l Majestät in Preußen Allergnädigst neu approbirtes Reglement und Verfassung des ganzen Accise-Wesens, dero Vor- und Hinter-Pommerschen Städten wie auch Fürstenthum Cammin, imgleichen der Herrschaften Lauenburg und Bütow, wornach (!) die sämmtliche Accise-Bediente ihre Arbeit zu bestellen, die Accisanten abzufertigen, die dabey vorkommende Fälle zu entscheiden, und sich überhaupt allerunterthänigst zu achten haben. De dato Berlin, den 28. Febr. 1749.' Geheimes Staatsarchiv Preußischer Kulturbesitz (GStAPK), HA II, Abt. 12 Pommern Materien, General Accise Sachen, Nr. 20a.

'Circulair Verfügungen der Regie bereffend das Zoll und Transitowesen (in frz Sprache). Bd. I 1768–1772', GStAPK, HA II, Gen.Akzise/Zolldept., A Titel XLVII, Sect. 1, Nr. 2.

Franke, Heinrich, *Marc Antoine de la Haye de Launay im Kreis der Familie unter einem Portrait Friedrichs des Großen* (oil on canvas, Berlin, 1774). Deutsches Historisches Museum, Berlin, Gm 96/44.

PRINTED AND EDITED SOURCES

Adams, John Quincy, *Letters on Silesia, written during a tour through that country in the years 1800, 1801* (London, 1804).

Allied Control Council, 'Law no. 46. Abolition of the state of Prussia, 25 Feb. 1947', in Office of Military Government for Germany (US) Legal Division, ed., *Enactments and approved papers of the Control Council and Coordinating Committee* (1947), vol. 4.

Anonymous, *Oeconomia Major* (n.p., 1681).

Anonymous, *Beantwortung und Widerlegung der Schrift, Was ist für und was ist gegen die General-Tobaks-Administration zu sagen* (Berlin, 1787).

Anonymous, *Gedanken eines Patrioten über die Schrift: Was ist für und was ist wider die General-Tobacks-Administration zu sagen* (Berlin, 1787).

Anonymous, *Das Blendwerk der neumodischen Aufklärung in der Religion* (Frankfurt, 1788).

Anonymous, *Was ist Gewissensfreyheit? Und wie weit erstreckt sich die Macht des Monarchen in Religionssachen? Eine Antwort auf die Freymüthige Betrachtung über das Edict vom 9. Julius 1788 die Religionsverfassung in den preußischen Staaten betreffend. Von einem Auswärtigen Wahrheitsfreund* (Berlin, 1788).

Anonymous, *Apologie der unumschränkten Gewalt eines Monarchen in öffentlichen Glaubenssachen* (Rome [Weißenfels or Leipzig], 1795).

Anonymous, *Schreiben eines preußischen Patrioten, am sechs und vierzigsten Geburtstage seines Königs. Den 25sten September 1788* (Philadelphia [Berlin], n.d.).

Apitzsch, Samuel Lobegott, *Wir haben's nun alle gelesen eine Vertheidigungsschrift* (n.p. [Berlin], 1781).

Bahrdt, Carl Friedrich, *Mit dem Herrn Zimmermann Ritter des St. Wladimir-Ordens von der dritten Klasse deutsch gesprochen* (n.p., 1790).

Bahrdt, Carl Friedrich, *Zimmermanns Auferstehung von den Todten: Ein Lustspiel in einem Aufzuge vom Verfasser im strengsten Inkognito; ein Gegenstück zu dem Schauspiel Doctor Bahrdt mit der eisernen Stirn* (n.p., 1791).

Beaumont, Jean-Louis Moreau de, *Mémoires concernant les impositions et droits en Europe* (Paris, 1768).

Biester, Johann, 'Etwas über Benjamin Franklin', *Berlinische Monatsschrift*, 2 (1783), pp. 11–38.

Borcke, Adrian Heinrich von, *Was ist für, und was ist gegen die General-Tabaks-Administration zu sagen* (n.p., 1786).

Burke, Edmund, 'First speech on conciliation with America: American Taxation (19. April 1774, House of Commons, London)', in Paul Langford, ed., *The writings and speeches of Edmund Burke* (12 vols., London, 1981), vol. 2, pp. 406–63.

Büsch, Johann Georg von, *Abhandlung von dem Geldumlauf in anhaltender Rücksicht auf die Staatswirtschaft und Handlung* (2 vols., Hamburg, 1800).

Büsching, Anton Friedrich, *Anton Friderich Büschings Beschreibung seiner Reise von Berlin über Potsdam nach Rekahn unweit Brandenburg: Welche er vom dritten bis achten Junius 1775 gethan hat* (Leipzig, 1775).

Büsching, Anton Friedrich, *Topographie der Mark Brandenburg* (Berlin, 1775).

Büsching, Anton Friedrich, *Zuverläßige Beyträge zu der Regierungs-Geschichte Königs Friedrich II. von Preußen: Vornehmlich in Ansehung der Volksmenge, des Handels, der Finanzen und des Kriegsheers. Mit einem historischen Anhange* (Hamburg, 1790).

Chrysophiron, *Die Pflichten der G. und R. C. alten Sistems* (n.p., 1782).

Cranz, August, *Supplement zum ersten Stück der Chronika von Berlin, in einem Sendschreiben an den Weltmann in Berlin, wohmeritirten Tantenbelehrer und Verfasser der Briefe an einem [sic] Landgeistlichen das neue Gesangbuch betreffend von dem Verfasser der Bokiade* (Berlin, 1781).

de Launay, Marc Antoine de la Haye, *Friedrichs des Zweyten, Königs von Preussen, ökonomisch-politisches Finanzsystem gerechtfertigt: Eine Widerlegung der falschen Behauptungen des Grafen von Mirabeau, in seiner Schrift: Über die preuss. Monarchie (Nebst Anhang)* (Berlin, 1789).

de Launay, Marc Antoine de la Haye, *Justification du système d'économie politique et financière de Frédéric II., roi de Prusse: pour servir de réfutation à tout ce que M. le Comte de Mirabeau a hazardé à ce sujet dans son ouvrage de la monarchie prussienne* (n.p., 1789).

de Launay, Marc Antoine de la Haye and others, *Mémoire à consulter et consultation pour le Sr. De la Haye de Launay, Conseiller Intime des Finances de Sa Majesté le Roi de Prusse, & Régisseur Général de ses Droits; l'un des Associés dans l'Entreprise des Hôpitaux militaires des Armées Françoises en Allemagne, pendant les années 1758, 1759 & 1760. Contre les S.rs Ménage, Chardon, Fauveau & autres. Aussie Associes en la même Entreprise* (Paris, 1785).

Dohm, Christian, 'Ueber die Kaffeegesetzgebung', *Deutsches Museum*, 2 (1777), pp. 123–45.

Frederick II, 'Vorläufiges Declarations-Patent wegen einer für sämtliche königliche preußische Provizien, wo bishero die Accise eingeführt gewesen, vom 1ten Juni 1766 an, allergnädigst gut gefundenen neuen Einrichtung der Accise- und Zoll-Sachen. De dato Berlin, den 14ten April 1766', *Novum Corpus Constitutionum Prussico-Brandenburgensium Praecipue Marchicarum (NCC)* (12 vols., Berlin, 1766), vol. 8, pp. 293–308.

Frederick II, 'Des moeurs, des coutumes, de l'industrie, des progrès de l'esprit humain dans les arts et dans les sciences', in Johann D. E. Preuss, ed., *Oeuvres de Frédéric le Grand* (30 vols., Berlin, 1846), vol. 1, pp. 243–73.

Frederick II, 'Vers envoyés par Frédéric a un curé qui s'était avisé de célébrer le jour de sa naissance par une ode', in Johann D. E. Preuss, ed., *Oeuvres des Frédéric le Grand* (30 vols., Berlin, 1846–56), vol. 14, pp. 170–1.

Frederick II, 'De la superstition et de la religion', in Johann D. E. Preuss, ed., *Oeuvres de Frederic le Grand* (30 vols., Berlin, 1848), vol. 9, pp. 224–42.

Frederick II, 'Des mœurs, des coutumes, de l'industrie, des progrès de l'esprit humain dans les arts et dans les sciences', in Johann D. E. Preuss, ed., *Oeuvres de Frédéric le Grand* (30 vols., Berlin, 1848), vol. 9, pp. 243–73.

Frederick II, 'Dissertation sur les raisons d'établir ou d'abroger les lois', in Johann D. E. Preuss, ed., *Oeuvres de Frédéric le Grand* (30 vols., Berlin, 1848), vol. 9, pp. 9–37.

Frederick II, 'Essai sur l'amour-propre envisagé comme principe de morale', in Johann D. E. Preuss, ed., *Oeuvres de Frederic le Grand* (30 vols., Berlin, 1848), vol. 9, pp. 99–114.

Frederick II, 'Essai sur les formes de gouvernement et sur les devoirs des souverains', in Johann D. E. Preuss, ed., *Oeuvres de Frederic le Grand* (30 vols., Berlin, 1848), vol. 9, pp. 221–40.

Frederick II, 'L'antimachiavel, ou examen du prince de Machiavel', in Johann D. E. Preuss, ed., *Oeuvres de Frederic le Grand* (30 vols., Berlin, 1848), vol. 8, pp. 67–184.

Frederick II, 'Mémoires pour servir à l'histoire de la maison de Brandenbourg', in Johann D. E. Preuss, ed., *Oeuvres de Frédéric le Grand* (30 vols., vol. I, Berlin, 1848), pp. 1–202.

Frederick II, 'Mirroir des princes ou instruction du roi pour le jeune Duc Charles-Eugène de Würtemberg', in Johann D. E. Preuss, ed., *Oeuvres de Frédéric le Grand,* (30 vols., Berlin, 1848), vol. 9, pp. 1–8.

Frederick II, 'Les principes géneraux de la guerre', in Johann D. E. Preuss, ed., *Oeuvres de Frédéric le Grand* (30 vols., Berlin, 1856), vol. 28, pp. 1–108.

Frederick II, 'Das politische Testament von 1752', in Gustav Volz, ed., *Die Werke Friedrichs des Großen* (10 vols., Berlin, 1912), vol. 7, pp. 115–94.

Frederick William II, 'Declarations-Patent wegen Aufhebung der General-Tabacks-Administration und Caffeebrennerey-Anstalt auch Heruntersetzung der Cafee-Accise. De Dato Berlin den 6 Januarri 1787', *Novum Corpus Constitutionum Prussico-Brandenburgensium Praecipue Marchicarum (NCC)* (12 vols., Berlin, 1787), vol. 8, pp. 243–50.

Frederick William II, 'Rescript an das Cammer-Gericht, wegen Etablirung eines eigenen General-Fabriken- und Commerzial-, wie auch Accise- und Zoll-Departements des General-Directorii. De dato Berlin, den 2 Februar 1787', *Novum Corpus Constitutionum Prussico-Brandenburgensium Preacipue Marchicarum* (12 vols., Berlin, 1787), vol. 8, p. 294.

Frederick William II, 'Verordnung für sämmtliche Provinzen diesseits der Weser, wegen einer neuen Einrichtung des Accise- und Zoll-Wesens. De Dato Berlin, den 25sten Jan. 1787', *Novum Corpus Constitutionum Prussico-Brandenburgensium Praecipue Marchicarum* (12 vols., Berlin, 1787), vol. 8, pp. 255–68.

Frederick William II, 'Circulare an alle Inspectoren der Churmark, nebst Edict vom 9ten July, die Religions-Verfassung in den Preußischen Staaten betreffend.', *Novum Corpus Constitutionum Prussico-Brandenburgensium Praecipue Marchicarum (NCC)* (12 vols., Berlin, 1788), vol. 9, pp. 2175–84.

Frederick William II, 'Erneuertes Censur-Edict für die preußischen Staaten. Nebst Begleitungs-Rescript an das Cammer-Gericht vom 25. December. De Dato Berlin, den 19. December 1788', *Novum Corpus Constitutionum Prussico-Brandenburgensium Praecipue Marchicarum (NCC)* (12 vols., Berlin, 1788), vol. 9, pp. 2339–51.

Gedike, Friedrich, 'Klage eines jungen Ehemannes in Berlin an einen Freund', *Berlinische Monatsschrift*, 1 (1783), pp. 421–7.

Gedike, Friedrich, 'Ueber Berlin, von einem Fremden (Briefe 1–3)', *Berlinische Monatsschrift*, 1 (1783), pp. 439–65.

Gedike, Friedrich, 'Ueber Berlin, von einem Fremden (Briefe 4–6)', *Berlinische Monatsschrift*, 2 (1783), pp. 542–57.

Goudar, Ange, *Les intérêts de la France mal entendus dans les branches de l'agriculture, de la population, des finances, du commerce, de la marine, et de l'industrie* (Amsterdam, 1756).

Graumann, Johann Philip, *Gesammelte Briefe von dem Gelde; von dem Wechsel und dessen Cours, von der Proportion zwischen Gold und Silber; von dem Pari des Geldes und den Münzgesetzen verschiedener Völker; besonders aber von dem Englischen Münzwesen* (Berlin, 1762).

Hamann, Johann Georg, *Schriften*, ed. Friedrich Roth (8 vols., Berlin, 1821–43), vol. 1.

Hamann, Johann Georg, 'Au Salomon de Prusse', in Josef Nadler, ed., *Sämtliche Werke/ Johann Georg Hamann* (6 vols., Vienna, 1951), vol. 3, pp. 55–60, 423–4.

Hamann, Johann Georg, 'Lettre à un financier de Pe-Kim', in Josef Nadler, ed., *Sämtliche Werke/Johann Georg Hamann* (6 vols., Vienna, 1951), vol. 3, pp. 299–305.

Hamann, Johann Georg, 'Beylage zum 77., 78., 80., 87. Stück, 25., 28. Sept. 5., 30 Okt. 1775 (Hamann's translation of excerpts from *Discours sur le commerce des bleds*)', in Josef Nadler, ed., *Sämtliche Werke/Johann Georg Hamann* (6 vols., Vienna, 1952), vol. 4, pp. 389–404.

Hamann, Johann Georg, *Johann Georg Hamann Briefwechsel*, eds. Walther Ziesemer and Arthur Henkel (7 vols., Wiesbaden, 1955).

Hamilton, Alexander, 'Report on manufactures', in Henry Cabot Lodge, ed., *The works of Alexander Hamilton* (12 vols., New York, 1886), vol. 4, pp. 193–285.

Hayek, Friedrich von, *The constitution of liberty* (London, 1990).

Hayek, Friedrich von, 'The legal and political philosophy of David Hume (1711–1776)', in W. W. Bartley and Stephen Kresge, eds., *The trend of economic thinking* (London, 1991).

Hayek, Friedrich von, *The road to serfdom* (Chicago, 2007).

Hertzberg, Ewald Friedrich von, 'Réflexions sur la force des états et sur leur puissance relative et proportionnelle', in Académie Royale des Sciences et Belles Lettres, ed., *Nouveaux mémoires de l'Académie Royale des Sciences et Belles Lettres* (Berlin, 1782), pp. 475–86.

Hertzberg, Ewald Friedrich von, 'Sur la population des états en général et sur celle des états prussiens en particulier. Dissertation qui a été lue dans l'assemblée publique de l'Academie des Sciences & des Belles-Lettres à Berlin, le 27. de Janvier 1785 pour le jour anniversaire du Roi', in Académie Royale des Sciences et Belles Lettres, ed., *Nouveaux mémoires de l'Académie Royale des Sciences et Belles Lettres* (Berlin, 1785), pp. 417–42.

Hertzberg, Ewald Friedrich von, 'Sur la véritable richesse des états, la balance du commerce et celle du pouvoir. Dissertation qui a été lue dans l'assemblée publique de l'Academie des Sciences & des Belles-Lettres à Berlin, le 26. de Janvier 1786 pour le jour anniversaire du Roi', *Nouveaux mémoires de l'Académie Royale des Sciences et Belles-Lettres* (Berlin, 1786), pp. 407–38.

Hertzberg, Ewald Friedrich von, 'Discours qui a été lu dans l'assemblée publique de l'Académie des Sciences de Berlin le 26 Septembre 1788, Au jour de naissance du roi par le Comte de Hertzberg, Ministre d'État, Curateur & Membre de L'Academie', *Nouveux mémoires de l'Académie Royale des Sciences et Belles-Lettres* (Berlin, 1788), pp. 307–11.

Herz, Marcus, 'Die Wallfahrt zum Monddoktor in Berlin', *Berlinische Monatsschrift*, 2 (1783), pp. 368–85.

Humboldt, Wilhelm von, 'Ideen über Staatsverfassung, durch die neue Französische Konstituzion veranlaßt', *Berlinische Monatsschrift*, 1 (1792), pp. 84–98.

Humboldt, Wilhelm von, 'Über die Sittenverbesserung durch Anstalten des Staats', *Berlinische Monatsschrift*, 2 (1792), pp. 419–43.

Humboldt, Wilhelm von, 'Ueber die Sorgalt des Staates für die Sicherheit gegen auswärtige Feinde', *Berlinische Monatsschrift*, 2 (1792), pp. 346–54.

Humboldt, Wilhelm von, 'Ueber oeffentliche Staatserziehung', *Berlinische Monatsschrift*, 2 (1792), pp. 597–606.

Humboldt, Wilhelm von, 'Wie weit darf sich die Sorgfalt des Staats um das Wohl seiner Bürger erstrecken?', *Neue Thalia*, 2 (1792), pp. 131–69.

Humboldt, Wilhelm von, *Ideen zu einem Versuch die Gränzen der Wirksamkeit des Staats zu bestimmen* (Breslau, 1851).

Humboldt, Wilhelm von, *Wilhelm von Humboldt's gesammelte Schriften*, ed. Albert Leitzmann (20 vols., Berlin, 1916).

Humboldt, Wilhelm von, *Ideen zu einem Versuch die Grenzen der Wirksamkeit des Staats zu bestimmen* (Stuttgart, 1967).

Humboldt, Wilhelm von, *The limits of state action*, ed. J. Burrow (Cambridge, 1969).

Iselin, Isaak, 'Smith, A.: Untersuchung der Natur und Ursachen von Nationalreichthümern. Bd. 1.: Rezension', *Allgemeine deutsche Bibliothek*, 31 (1777), pp. 586–9.

Kant, Immanuel, 'Beantwortung der Frage: Was ist Aufklärung?', *Berlinische Monatsschrift*, 2 (1784), pp. 481–94.

Kant, Immanuel, 'What is Enlightenment?', in Lewis White Beck, ed., *Foundations of the metaphysics of morals* (Chicago, 1950), pp. 286–92.

Kästner, Abraham Gotthelf, 'Réflexions sur l'origine du plaisir, où l'on tâche de prouver l'idée de Descartes: qu'il naît toujours du sentiment de perfection de nous-mêmes', *Histoire de l'Academie Royale des Sciences et des Belles* Lettres (Berlin, 1751), pp. 478–88.

Klöden, Karl Friedrich von, *Jugenderinnerungen* (Leipzig, 1911).

Klose, Samuel Benjamin, 'Bemerkungen auf einer Reise durch die Lausitz und Sachsen', *Berlinische Monatsschrift*, 1 (1783), pp. 115–52.

List, Friedrich, *Das nationale System der politischen Oekonomie* (Stuttgart, 1841).

List, Friedrich, *The national system of political economy* (Philadelphia, 1856).

Malthus, Thomas, *An essay on the principle of population* (London, 1798).

Marenholz, Asche Christoph von, *Schmid, Johann Wilhelm* (Göttingen, 1744).

Mill, John Stuart, *Autobiography* (London, 1989).

Mill, John Stuart, *On liberty* (Cambridge, 2006).

Mill, John Stuart, *The principles of political economy* (Oxford, 2008).

Mirabeau, Honoré Gabriel de Riqueti Comte de, *Lettre remise à Fréderic Guillaume II, roi régnant de Prusse, le jour de son avènement au trône* (n.p., 1787).

Mirabeau, Honoré Gabriel de Riqueti Comte de, *Schreiben an Friedrich Wilhelm II. itzt regierenden König von Preussen, am Tage seiner Thronbesteigung* (Paris, 1787).

Mirabeau, Honoré Gabriel de Riqueti Comte de, *De la monarchie prussienne, sous Frédéric le Grand: avec un appendice contenant des recherches sur la situation actuelle des principales contrées de l'Allemagne* (4 vols., Paris, 1788).

Mirabeau, Honoré Gabriel de Riqueti Comte de, *Travail sur l'éducation publique trouvé dans les papiers de Mirabeau l'Aîné* (Paris, 1791).

Mirabeau, Honoré Gabriel de Riqueti Comte de, *Histoire secrète de la cour de Berlin. Avec des anecdotes plaisans et singulieres. Par le comte de Mirabeau.* (2 vols., London, 1792).

Montesquieu, Charles Louis Secondat Baron de, *The spirit of the laws* (London, 1914).

Nicolai, Friedrich, *Beschreibung der königlichen Residenzstädte Berlin und Potsdam und aller daselbst befindlicher Merkwürdigkeiten* (Berlin, 1779).

Nicolai, Friedrich, *Freymüthige Anmerkungen über des Ritters von Zimmermann Fragmente über Friedrich den Großen von einigen brandenburg. Patrioten* (Berlin, 1791).

Pott, Degenhard, *Commentar über das königlich preuß. Religionsedikt vom 9. Julius 1788* (Amsterdam [Halle or Leipzig], 1788).

Preuss, Johann D. E., ed., *Friedrich der Große: Eine Lebensgeschichte. Urkundenbuch zu der Lebensgeschichte Friedrichs des Grossen* (Berlin, 1833–4).

Quittenbaum, Johann Heinrich Friedrich, *Zimmermann der I, und Fridrich [sic] der II* (London, 1790).

Rachel, Hugo von, ed., *Die Handels-, Zoll- und Akzisepolitik Preußens* (Berlin, 1928).

Raymond, Daniel, *Thoughts on political economy* (Baltimore, 1820).

Raynal, Guillaume Thomas François, *Histoire philosophique et politique, des établissemens & du commerce des Européens dans les deux Indes* (6 vols., Amsterdam, 1772).

Richter, Johann Daniel, *Beyträge zur Finanz-Litteratur in den preussischen Staaten* (Frankfurt, 1781).

Richter, Johann Daniel, *Finanz-Materialien nach allgemeinen verbesserten und practischen Grundsätzen* (Berlin, 1789).

Römer, Karl Heinrich von, *Vertheidigung des neuesten preuß. Religions-Edikts gegen die Beschuldigungen und Besorgnisse des Verfassers der freimüthigen Betrachtungen über dasselbe* (Berlin, 1788).

Schmohl, J. C., 'Von dem Ursprunge der Knechtschaft in der bürgerlichen Gesellschaft', *Berlinische Monatsschrift*, 1 (1783), pp. 336–47.

Schopenhauer, Johanna, *Im Wechsel der Zeiten, im Gedränge der Welt* (München, 1986).

Schwager, Johann Moritz, 'Noch ein neuer Messias', *Berlinische Monatsschrift*, 1 (1783), pp. 266–76.

Semler, Johann Salomo, *D. Joh. salom. Semlers Vertheidigung des Königl. Edikts vom 9ten Jul. 1788 wider die freimüthigen Betrachtungen eines Ungenannten* (Halle, 1788).

Smith, Adam, *An inquiry into the nature and the causes of the wealth of nations* (2 vols., Oxford, 1976).

Spalding, Johann, *Predigt von dem, was erbaulich ist. Mit einer Anwendung auf das Gesangbuch zum gottesdienstlichen Gebrauch in den königl. preußl. Landen* (Berlin, 1781).

Struensee, Carl August von, 'Über den freien Getreidehandel in den preußischen Staaten', *Berlinische Monatsschrift*, 1 (1787), pp. 414–25.

Struensee, Carl August von, 'Über den neuesten Finanzzustand Frankreichs', *Berlinische Monatschrift*, 2 (1788), pp. 399–427.

Süßmilch, Johann Peter, *Der königl. Residentz Berlin schneller Wachsthum und Erbauung in zweyen Abhandlungen erwiesen* (Berlin, 1752).

Süßmilch, Johann Peter, *Die göttliche Ordnung in den Veränderungen des menschlichen Geschlechts, besonders im Tode durch einige neue Beweissthümer bestätigt u. gegen des Herrn von Justi Erinnerungen u. Muthmassungen in zweyen Sendschreiben an selbigen gerettet* (Berlin, 1756).

Süßmilch, Johann Peter, *Die göttliche Ordnung in den Veränderungen des menschlichen Geschlechts, aus der Geburt, dem Tode der Fortpflanzung desselben erwiesen* (2 vols., Berlin, 1761/5).

Teller, Wilhelm, *Drey Predigten bey Bekanntmachung und Einführung des neuen Gesangbuchs in der Peterskirche zu Berlin* (Berlin, 1781).

Tenzel, Friedrich Wilhelm, *Entdeckte Gold-Grube in der Accise* (Magdeburg, 1685).

Villaume, Peter, *Freimüthige Betrachtungen über das Edict vom 9. Julius 1788 die Religions-verfassung in den preußischen Staaten betreffend* (Frankfurt, 1788).

von der Lith, Wilhelm, *Politische Betrachtungen über die verschiedenen Arten der Steuern* (Breslau, 1751).

Zimmermann, Johann Georg von, *Vertheidigung Friedrichs des Grossen gegen den Grafen von Mirabeau: Nebst einigen Anmerkungen über andere Gegenstände* (Hannover, 1788).

Zimmermann, Johann Georg von, *Fragmente über Friedrich den Grossen zur Geschichte seines Lebens, seiner Regierung, und seines Charakters* (3 vols., Leipzig, 1790).

Historiography

Anderson, Gary, Shughart II, William, and Tollison, Robert, 'Adam Smith in the custom-house', *Journal of Political Economy*, 93 (1985), pp. 740–59.

Anderson, Perry, *Lineages of the absolutist state* (London, 1975).

Aner, Karl, *Die Theologie der Lessingzeit* (Halle/Saale, 1929).

Ashworth, William, *Customs and excise: trade, production and consumption in England, 1640–1845* (Oxford, 2003).

Bachmann, Johann Friedrich, *Zur Geschichte der berliner Gesangbücher ein hymnologischer Beitrag* (Hildesheim, 1970).

Barth, Karl von, *Die protestantische Theologie im 19. Jahrhundert ihre Vorgeschichte und ihre Geschichte* (Zollikon, 1947).

Baumgart, Peter, 'Friedrich Wilhelm I.—ein Soldatenkönig?', in Peter Baumgart, Bernhard Kroener, and Heinz Stübig, eds., *Die preussische Armee* (Paderborn, 2008), pp. 3–26.

Becker, Peter, 'Sprachvollzug: Kommunikation und Verwaltung', in Peter Becker, ed., *Sprachvollzug im Amt* (Bielefeld, 2011), pp. 9–44.

Beguelin, Heinrich von, *Historisch kritische Darstellung der Accise- und Zollverfassung in den preussischen Staaten* (Berlin, 1797).

Behrens, C. B. A., *Society, government and the enlightenment* (London, 1985).

Betz, John, *After Enlightenment: Hamann as post-secular visionary* (Hoboken, NJ, 2008).

Beutin, Ludwig, 'Die Wirkungen des Siebenjährigen Krieges auf die Volkswirtschaft in Preußen', *Vierteljahrschrift für Wirtschafts- und Sozialgeschichte*, 26 (1933), pp. 209–43.

Birtsch, Günter, 'Die Berliner Mittwochsgesellschaft', in Hans Bödeker and Ulrich Herrmann, eds., *Über den Prozess der Aufklärung in Deutschland im 18. Jahrhundert* (Göttingen, 1987), pp. 94–112.

Blackbourn, David and Eley, Geoff, 'Introduction', in David Blackbourn and Geoff Eley, eds., *The peculiarities of German history: bourgeois society and politics in nineteenth-century Germany* (Oxford, 1984), pp. 1–35.

Blaich, Fritz, *Die Epoche des Merkantilismus* (Wiesbaden, 1973).

Blanning, Tim, *The culture of power and the power of culture: old regime Europe, 1660–1789* (Oxford, 2006).

Bödeker, Hans, 'Lessings Briefwechsel', in Hans Bödeker and Ulrich Herrmann, eds., *Über den Prozess der Aufklärung in Deutschland im 18. Jahrhundert* (Göttingen, 1987), pp. 113–38.

Bödeker, Hans, 'Prozesse und Strukturen politischer Bewußtseinsbildung der deutschen Aufklärung', in Hans Bödeker and Ulrich Herrmann, eds., *Aufklärung als Politisierung* (Hamburg, 1987), pp. 10–31.

Bödeker, Hans, 'Journals and public opinion: the politicization of the German Enlightenment in the second half of the eighteenth century', in Eckhart Hellmuth, ed., *The transformation of political culture: England and Germany in the late eighteenth century* (Oxford, 1990), pp. 423–46.

Bödeker, Hans and Herrmann, Ulrich, 'Aufklärung als Politisierung—Politisierung als Aufklärung', in Hans Bödeker and Ulrich Herrmann, eds., *Aufklärung als Politisierung* (Hamburg, 1987), pp. 3–9.

Born, D., *Denkschrift über den Einfluß der Mahl- und Schlachtsteuer auf die gewerblichen Verhältnisse Berlins, besonders in Bezug auf die Arbeitslöhne und auf die Konkurrenzfähigkeit anderen Städten gegenüber* (Berlin, 1850).

Borsche, Tilman, *Wilhelm von Humboldt* (München, 1990).

Bradley, James and Van Dale, Kley, eds., *Religion and politics in enlightenment Europe* (Notre Dame, IN, 2001).

Breen, T. H., *The marketplace of revolution: how consumer politics shaped American independence* (Oxford, 2004).

Brewer, John, *The sinews of power: war and the English state, 1688–1783* (London, 1989).

Burrow, J., 'Editor's introduction', in J. Burrow, ed., *Wilhelm von Humboldt: the limits of state action* (Cambridge, 1969).

Cheney, Paul, *Revolutionary commerce: globalization and the French monarchy* (Cambridge, MA, 2010).

Chernow, Ron, *Alexander Hamilton* (New York, 2004).

Clark, Christopher, *Iron kingdom: the rise and downfall of Prussia, 1600–1947* (London, 2007).

Clark, Christopher, ' "Le roi historien" zu Füßen von Clio', in Bernd Sösemann and Gregor Vogt-Spira, eds., *Friedrich der Große in Europa* (Stuttgart, 2012), pp. 155–78.

Conrad, Sebastian, *Globalisation and the nation in imperial Germany* (Cambridge, 2010).

Conrad, Sebastian and Osterhammel, Jürgen, *Das Kaiserreich transnational: Deutschland in der Welt 1871–1914* (Göttingen, 2004).

Dann, Otto, 'Einleitung des Herausgebers: Die Lesegesellschaften und die Herausbildung einer modernen bürgerlichen Gesellschaft in Europa', in Otto Dann, ed., *Lesegesellschaften und bürgerliche Emanzipation* (Munich, 1981), pp. 9–28.

Delalande, Nicolas, *Les batailles de l'impôt: consentement et résistances de 1789 a nos jours* (Paris, 2011).

Delius, Walter, 'Zur Geschichte des berliner Gesangbuchs', *Theologia Viatorum. Jahrbuch der kirchlichen Hochschulen Berlin*, 9 (1964), pp. 5–31.

Deppermann, Klaus, 'Pietismus und die moderne Welt', in Kurt Aland, ed., *Pietismus und die moderne Welt* (Witten, 1974), pp. 75–98.

Droysen, Gustav, *Der Staat des Großen Kurfürsten* (3 vols., Leipzig, 1861–3).

Dyson, Anthony, 'Theological legacies of the Enlightenment: England and Germany', in Stephen Sykes, ed., *England and Germany: studies in theological diplomacy* (Frankfurt, 1982), pp. 45–63.

Eley, Geoff, 'Nations, publics, and political cultures: placing Habermas in the nineteenth century', in Craig Calhoun, ed., *Habermas and the public sphere* (Cambridge, MA, 1992), pp. 289–339.

Engel, Ernst, 'Die Ergebnisse der Classensteuer, der classificirten Einkommensteuer und der Mahl- und Schlachtsteuer im Preussischen Staate', *Zeitschrift des königlich preussischen statistischen Bureaus*, 8 (1868), pp. 25–84.

Engelen, Beate, 'Fremde in der Stadt. Die Garnisonsgesellschaft Prenzlaus im 18. Jahrhundert', in Klaus Neitmann and Jürgen Theil, eds., *Die Herkunft der Brandenburger* (Potsdam, 2001).

Engels, Friedrich, 'Letter to J. Bloch, 1 Oct. 1895', in T. Borodulina, ed., *On historical materialism* (Moscow, 1972), pp. 294–6.

Erlin, Matt, *Berlin's forgotten future: city, history, and enlightenment in eighteenth-century Germany* (Chapel Hill, NC, 2004).

Faden, Eberhard, 'Der Berliner Tumult von 1615', *Jahrbuch für brandenburgische Landesgeschichte*, 5 (1954), pp. 27–44.

Fidicin, Ernst, *Berlin, historisch und topographisch dargestellt* (Berlin, 1852).

Fidicin, Ernst, *Die Territorien der Mark Brandenburg oder Geschichte der einzelnen Kreise, Städte, Rittergüter, Stiftungen und Dörfer in derselben, als Fortsetzung des Landbuchs Kaiser Karls IV* (Berlin, 1858).

Fischer, Wolfram and Simsch, Adelheid, 'Industrialisierung in Preussen. Eine staatliche Veranstaltung?', in Werner Süß, ed., *Übergänge—Zeitgeschichte zwischen Utopie und Machbarkeit* (Berlin, 1989).

Foerst-Crato, Ilse, 'Karl Friedrich von Dachröden', *Mitteilungen des Mindener Geschichtsvereins*, 49 (1977), pp. 131–6.

Frevert, Ute, 'Europeanizing German history', *GHI Bulletin*, 36 (2005), pp. 9–24.

Fulbrook, Mary, *Piety and politics: religion and the rise of absolutism in England, Württemberg, and Prussia* (Cambridge, 1983).

Gall, Lothar, *Wilhelm von Humboldt ein Preuße von Welt* (Berlin, 2011).

Gawthrop, Richard, *Pietism and the making of eighteenth-century Prussia* (Cambridge, 1993).

Gay, Peter, *Voltaire's politics, the poet as realist* (New York, 1965).

Gellner, Ernest, *Nations and nationalism* (Oxford, 1983).

Gestrich, Andreas, 'The public sphere and the Habermas-Debate', *German History*, 24 (2006), pp. 413–31.

Gierl, Martin, *Pietismus und Aufklärung: Theologische Polemik und die Kommunikationsreform der Wissenschaft am Ende des 17. Jahrhunderts* (Göttingen, 1997).

Gleixner, Ulrike, *Pietismus und Bürgertum: Eine historische Anthropologie der Frömmigkeit, Württemberg 17–19. Jahrhundert* (Göttingen, 2005).

Gliemann, Benno, 'Die Einführung der Accise in Preussen', *Zeitschrift für die gesamte Staatswissenschaft*, 29 (1873), pp. 180–217.

Goldscheid, Rudolf, *Staatssozialismus oder Staatskapitalismus* (Vienna, 1917).

Graff, Paul, *Geschichte der Auflösung der alten gottesdienstlichen Formen in der Evangelischen Kirche Deutschlands* (Göttingen, 1937).

Groh, Dieter, 'Le "Sonderweg" de l'histoire Allemande: mythe ou réalité?', *Annales. Histoire, Sciences sociales*, 38 (1983), pp. 1166–87.

Habermas, Jürgen *The structural transformation of the public sphere: an inquiry into a category of bourgeois society* (Cambridge, 1989).

Habermas, Jürgen, *Strukturwandel der Öffentlichkeit. Untersuchungen zu einer Kategorie der bürgerlichen Gesellschaft; mit einem Vorwort zur Neuauflage 1990* (Frankfurt am Main, 2009).

Habermas, Jürgen, '"The political": the rational meaning of a questionable inheritance of political theology', in Judith Butler, Eduardo Mendieta, and Jonathan Van Antwerpen, eds., *The power of religion in the public sphere* (New York, 2011), pp. 15–33.

Hagen, William, 'Descent of the Sonderweg: Hans Rosenberg's history of Old-Regime Prussia', *Central European History*, 24 (1991), pp. 24–50.

Hagen, William, *Ordinary Prussians* (Cambridge, 2002).

Hahn, Peter Michael, *Struktur und Funktion des brandenburgischen Adels im 16. Jahrhundert* (Berlin, 1979).

Hamilton, Earl, 'American treasure and the rise of capitalism (1500–1700)', *Economica*, 9 (1929), pp. 338–57.

Harrison, Peter, 'Adam Smith and the history of the invisible hand', *Journal of the History of Ideas*, 72 (2011), pp. 29–49.

Hauc, Jean-Claude, *Ange Goudar: un aventurier des Lumières* (Paris, 2004).

Heinrich, Gerd, 'Der Adel in Brandenburg-Preußen', in Hellmuth Rössler, ed., *Deutscher Adel, 1555–1740* (Darmstadt, 1965).

Heinrich, Gerd, 'Staatsaufsicht und Stadtfreiheit in Brandenburg-Preussen unter dem Absolutismus (1660–1806)', in Wilhelm Rausch, ed., *Die Städte Mitteleuropas im 17. und 18. Jahrhundert* (Linz, 1981), pp. 155–72.

Heller, Gisela, 'Luise Henriette von Oranien, Kurfürstin von Brandenburg', in Jattie Enklaar and Hans Ester, eds., *Brandenburg-Preußen und die Niederlande* (Amsterdam, 1993), pp. 123–35.

Hellmuth, Eckhart, 'Aufklärung und Pressefreiheit: Zur Debatte der Berliner Mittwochsgesellschaft während der Jahre 1783 und 1784', *Zeitschrift für Historische Forschung*, 9 (1982), pp. 315–45.

Hellmuth, Eckhart, *Naturrechtsphilosophie und bürokratischer Werthorizont: Studien zur preußischen Geistes- und Sozialgeschichte des 18. Jahrhunderts* (Göttingen, 1985).

Hellmuth, Eckhart, 'Towards a comparative study of political culture', in Eckhart Hellmuth, ed., *The transformation of political culture: England and Germany in the late eighteenth century* (Oxford, 1990), pp. 1–38.

Henckel, M. von, 'Schlacht- und Mahlsteuer', in Johannes Conrad, ed., *Handwörterbuch der Staatswissenschaft* (Jena, 1893), pp. 571–6.

Henderson, William, *The state and the industrial revolution in Prussia, 1740–1870* (Liverpool, 1958).

Henkel, Arthur, 'Vorwort', in Walther Ziesemer and Arthur Henkel, eds., *Johann Georg Hamann Briefwechsel* (7 vols., Wiesbaden, 1955), vol. 1, pp. 1–14.

Hinrichs, Carl, *Preußentum und Pietismus* (Göttingen, 1971).

Hinrichs, Carl, *Friedrich Wilhelm I* (Darmstadt, 1974).

Hintze, Otto, 'Die Hohenzollern und der Adel', *Historische Zeitschrift*, 112 (1914), pp. 494–524.

Hintze, Otto, *Die Hohenzollern und ihr Werk: Fünfhundert Jahre vaterländischer Geschichte* (Berlin, 1915).

Hintze, Otto, 'Der Commissarius und seine Bedeutung in der allgemeinen Verwaltungsgeschichte', in Gerhard Oestreich, ed., *Staat und Verfassung* (Göttingen, 1970), pp. 242–74.

Hintze, Otto, 'Der österreichische und der preußische Beamtenstaat im 17. und 18. Jahrhundert', in Gerhard Oestreich, ed., *Staat und Verfassung* (Göttingen, 1970), pp. 321–58.

Hintze, Otto, 'Staatenbildung und Verfassungsentwicklung', in Gerhard Oestreich, ed., *Staat und Verfassung* (Göttingen, 1970), pp. 34–51.

Hinze, Kurt, 'Die Bevölkerung Preußens im 17. und 18. Jahrhundert nach Quantität und Qualität', in Otto Büsch and Wolfgang Neugebauer, eds., *Moderne Preußische Geschichte* (Berlin, 1981), pp. 282–315.

Hirschmann, Albert, *Exit, voice and loyalty: responses to decline in firms, organizations and states* (Cambridge, MA, 1970).

Hirschman, Albert, *The passions and the interests: political arguments for capitalism before its triumph* (Princeton, NJ, 1997).

Hont, István, 'The early Enlightenment debate on commerce and luxury', in Mark Goldie and Robert Wokler, eds., *The Cambridge history of eighteenth-century political thought* (Cambridge, 2006), pp. 379–418.

Hull, Isabel, *Sexuality, state and civil society in Germany, 1700–1815* (Ithaca, NY, 1996).

Hunter, Ian, 'Kant's religion and Prussian religious policy', *Modern Intellectual History*, 2 (2005), pp. 1–27.

Hunter, Ian, 'The history of philosophy and the persona of the philosopher', *Modern Intellectual History*, 4 (2007), pp. 571–600.

Im Hof, Ulrich, 'German associations and politics in the second half of the eighteenth century', in Eckhart Hellmuth, ed., *The transformation of political culture: England and Germany in the late eighteenth century* (Oxford, 1990), pp. 207–18.

Inama-Sternegg, Karl Theodor von, 'Der Accisestreit deutscher Finanztheoretiker im 17. und 18. Jahrhundert', *Zeitschrift für die gesamte Staatswissenschaft*, 21 (1865), pp. 515–34.

Jackson, Ben, 'The origins of neo-liberalism: the free economy and the strong state, 1930–1947', *Historical Journal*, 53 (2010), pp. 129–51.

Johnson, Hubert, *Frederick the Great and his officials* (New Haven, 1975).

Johnston, Otto, 'Mirabeau and Schiller on education to freedom', *Monatshefte*, 76 (1984), pp. 58–72.

Jones, Colin, *The great nation: France from Louis XV to Napoleon 1715–99* (London, 2002).

Jones, Colin and Spang, Rebecca, 'Sans-culottes, sans café, sans tabac: shifting realms of necessity in luxury in eighteenth-century France', in M. Berg and H. Clifford, eds., *Consumers and luxury: consumer culture in Europe, 1650–1850* (Manchester, 1999), pp. 37–62.

Kaiser, Michael and Kroll, Stefan, *Militär und Religiosität in der Frühen Neuzeit* (Münster, 2004).

Kantzenbach, Friedrich Wilhelm, 'Die Spätaufklärung: Entwicklung und Stand der Forschung', *Theologische Literaturzeitung*, 102 (1977), pp. 337–48.

Kemper, Dirk, *Mißbrauchte Aufklärung? Schriften zum Religionsedikt vom 9. Juli 1788. 118 Schriften auf 202 Mikrofiches. Begleitband* (Hildesheim, 1996).

Kemper, Dirk, 'Obskurantismus als Mittel der Politik. Johann Christoph Wöllners Politik der Gegenaufklärung am Vorabend der Französischen Revolution', in Christoph Weiß, ed., *Von 'Obscuranten' und 'Eudämonisten'. Gegenaufklärerische, konservative und antirevolutionäre Publizisten im späten 18. Jahrhundert* (St Ingbert, 1997), pp. 193–220.

Keynes, John Maynard, *A treatise on money* (2 vols., London, 1950).

Kiser, Edgar and Schneider, Joachim, 'Bureaucracy and efficiency: an analysis of taxation in early modern Prussia', *American Sociological Review*, 59 (1994), pp. 187–204.

Klaveren, Jacob van, 'Die historische Erscheinung der Korruption in ihrem Zusammenhang mit der Staats- und Gesellschaftsstruktur betrachtet', *Vierteljahrschrift für Sozial- und Wirtschaftsgeschichte*, 44 (1957), pp. 289–324.

Klaveren, Jacob van, 'Fiskalismus—Merkantilismus—Korruption. Drei Aspekte der Finanz- und Wirtschaftspolitik während des Ancien Régime', *Vierteljahrschrift für Sozial- und Wirtschaftsgeschichte*, 47 (1960), pp. 333–53.

Klippel, Diethelm, 'The true concept of liberty: political theory in Germany in the second half of the eighteenth century', in Eckhart Hellmuth, ed., *The transformation of political culture: England and Germany in the late eighteenth century* (Oxford, 1990), pp. 447–66.

Kocka, Jürgen, 'German history before Hitler: the debate about the German Sonderweg', *Journal of Contemporary History*, 23 (1988), pp. 3–16.

Kocka, Jürgen, 'Asymmetrical historical comparison: the case of the German Sonderweg', *History and Theory*, 38 (1999), pp. 40–50.

Koser, Reinhold, 'Die preußischen Finanzen von 1763–86', *Forschungen zur brandenburgischen und preussischen Geschichte*, 16 (1903), pp. 445–76.

Koser, Reinhold, 'Zur Bevölkerungsstatistik des preußischen Staates von 1756–1786', *Forschungen zur brandenburgischen und preussischen Geschichte*, 16 (1903), pp. 583–9.

Kries, Carl, 'Über die Mahl- und Schlacht-Steuer, die Einkommen- und Klassen-Steuer in Preußen', *Archiv der politischen Oekonomie und Polizeiwissenschaft*, 8 (1849), pp. 179–224, 227–324.

Kwass, Michael, *Privilege and the politics of taxation in eighteenth-century France: liberté, égalité, fiscalité* (Cambridge, 2000).

Kwass, Michael, 'Court capitalism, illicit markets, and political legitimacy in eighteenth-century France: the salt and tobacco monopolies', in D. Coffman et al., eds., *Questioning 'credible commitment': rethinking the origins of financial capitalism* (Cambridge, forthcoming).

Langford, Paul, *The excise crisis: society and politics in the age of Walpole* (Oxford, 1975).

Langford, Paul, *A polite and commercial people: England, 1727–1783* (Oxford, 1989).

Lawton, Richard and Lee, Robert, 'Introduction: the framework of comparative urban population studies in Western Europe, c. 1750–1920', in Richard Lawton and Robert Lee, eds., *Urban population development in Western Europe from the late eighteenth century to the early twentieth century* (Liverpool, 1989), pp. 1–18.

Lehmann, Max, *Preussen, und die katholische Kirche seit 1640* (Leipzig, 1885).

Lehmann, Max, 'Werbung, Wehrpflicht und Beurlaubung im Heere Friedrich Wilhelm's I', *Historische Zeitschrift*, 67 (1891), pp. 254–89.

Leroux, Robert, 'Guillaume de Humboldt et J.S. Mill', *Etudes Germaniques*, 6–7 (1951–2), pp. 262–74, 81–7.

Lüdtkeaus, Ludger, 'Karl Friedrich Bahrdt, Immanuel Kant und die Gegenaufklärung in Preußen', *Jahrbuch des Insrituts für deutsche Geschichte der Universität Tel Aviv*, 9 (1980).

Mann, Fritz Karl, *Steuerpolitische Ideale* (Jena, 1937).

Marschke, Benjamin, *Absolutely Pietist: patronage, fictionalism, and state-building in the early eighteenth-century Prussian army chaplaincy* (Tübingen, 2005).

Martin, Isaac, et al., eds., *The new fiscal sociology* (Cambridge, 2009).

Mathias, Peter and O'Brien, Patrick, 'Taxation in Britain and France, 1715–1810', *Journal of European Economic History*, 5 (1976), pp. 601–50.

Mathias, Peter and O'Brien, Patrick, 'The incidence of taxation and the burden of proof', *Journal of European Economic History*, 7 (1978), pp. 211–13.

McKay, Derek, *The great elector* (Harlow, 2001).

Melton, Edgar, 'The Prussian Junkers, 1600–1786', in Hamish Scott, ed., *The European nobilities in the seventeenth and eighteenth centuries* (London, 1995), pp. 71–109.

Melton, James van Horn, *Absolutism and the eighteenth-century origins of compulsory schooling in Prussia and Austria* (Cambridge, 1988).

Melton, James van Horn, 'Pietism, politics and the public sphere in Germany', in James E. Bradley and Dale K. Van Kley, eds., *Religion and politics in enlightenment Europe* (Notre Dame, IN, 2001), pp. 294–333.

Mintzker, Yair, 'What is defortification? Military functions, police roles, and symbolism in the demolition of German city walls in the eighteenth and nineteenth centuries', *GHI Bulletin*, 48 (2011), pp. 33–58.

Mittenzwei, Ingrid, *Preußen nach dem Siebenjährigen Krieg: Auseinandersetzungen zwischen Bürgertum und Staat um die Wirtschaftspolitik* (Berlin, 1979).

Möller, Horst, 'Wie aufgeklärt war Preußen?', *Geschichte und Gesellschaft*, Sonderheft 6 (1980), pp. 176–201.

Möller, Horst, *Vernunft und Kritik. Deutsche Aufklärung im 17. und 18. Jahrhundert* (Frankfurt, 1986).

Möller, Horst, 'Enlightened societies in the metropolis', in Eckhart Hellmuth, ed., *The transformation of political culture: England and Germany in the late eighteenth century* (Oxford, 1990), pp. 219–33.

Nachama, Andreas, *Ersatzbürger und Staatsbildung: Zur Zerstörung des Bürgertums in Brandenburg-Preussen* (Frankfurt, 1984).

Nash, Robert, 'The English and Scottish tobacco trades in the seventeenth and eighteenth centuries: legal and illegal trade', *Economic History Review*, 35 (1982), pp. 354–72.

Nehring, Holger and Schui, Florian, 'Introduction: global debates about taxation: transfers of ideas, the challenge of political legitimacy and the paradoxes of state-building', in Holger Nehring and Florian Schui, eds., *Global debates about taxation* (London, 2007), pp. 1–18.

Neugebauer, Wolfgang, 'Zur neueren Deutung der preußischen Verwaltung im 17. und 18. Jahrhundert in vergleichender Sicht', in Otto Büsch and Wolfgang Neugebauer, eds., *Moderne preußische Geschichte* (Berlin, 1981), pp. 541–97.

Neugebauer, Wolfgang, 'Bemerkungen zum preußischen Schuledikt von 1717', *Jahrbuch für die Geschichte Mittel- und Ostdeutschlands*, 31 (1982), pp. 155–76.

Neugebauer, Wolfgang, *Absolutistischer Staat und Schulwirklichkeit in Brandenburg-Preußen* (Berlin, 1985).

Neugebauer, Wolfgang, 'Brandenburg im absolutistischen Staat', in Ingo Materna and Wolfgang Ribbe, eds., *Brandenburgische Geschichte* (Berlin, 1995), pp. 291–394.

Neugebauer, Wolfgang, 'Staatsverfassung und Heeresverfassung in Preußen während des 18. Jahrhunderts', in Peter Baumgart, Bernhard Kroener, and Heinz Stübig, eds., *Die preussische Armee* (Paderborn, 2008), pp. 27–44.

Neugebauer, Wolfgang, 'Epochen der preußischen Geschichte', in Wolfgang Neugebauer, ed., *Handbuch der preußischen Geschichte. Das 17. und 18. Jahrhundert und große Themen der preußischen Geschichte* (Berlin, 2009), pp. 113–410.

Neugebauer, Wolfgang and Holtz, Bärbel, *Kulturstaat und Bürgergesellschaft: Preussen, Deutschland und Europa im 19. und frühen 20. Jahrhundert* (Berlin, 2010).

Niebuhr, Marcus von, *Geschichte der Königlichen Bank in Berlin von d. Gründung derselben (1765) bis zum Ende d. Jahres 1845; nach amtl. Quellen* (Berlin, 1854).

Nipperdey, Thomas, 'Verein als soziale Struktur in Deutschland im späten 18. und 19. Jahrhundert. Eine Fallstudie zur Modernisierung', in Thomas Nipperdey, ed., *Gesellschaft, Kultur, Theorie gesammelte Aufsätze zur neueren Geschichte* (Göttingen, 1976), pp. 176–205.

Nischan, Bodo, *Prince, people, and confession: the Second Reformation in Brandenburg* (Philadelphia, 1994).

North, Michael, *Material delight and the joy of living* (Aldershot, 2008).

Nugel, Otto, 'Der Schoppenmeister Hieronymus Roth', *Forschungen zur brandenburgischen und preußischen Geschichte*, 14 (1901), pp. 19–105.

O'Brien, Patrick, *Fiscal exceptionalism. Great Britain and its European rivals: from civil war to triumph at Trafalgar and Waterloo*. Working paper 65/1, Department of Economic History, London School of Economics (London, 2001).

Peitsch, Dietmar, *Zunftgesetzgebung und Zunftverwaltung Brandenburg-Preußens in der frühen Neuzeit* (Frankfurt, 1985).

Peukert, Detlev, *Max Webers Diagnose der Moderne* (Göttingen, 1989).

Posner, Ernst, ed., *Die Behördenorganisation und allgemeine Staatsverwaltung Preußens im 18. Jahrhundert* (16 vols., Berlin, 1932).

Press, Volker, 'Vom Ständestaat zum Absolutismus', in Peter Baumgart, ed., *Ständetum und Staatsbildung in Brandenburg-Preussen: Ergebnisse einer internationalen Fachtagung* (Berlin, 1983), pp. 280–336.

Rainer, Gömmel, *Die Entwicklung der Wirtschaft im Merkantilismus 1620–1800* (Stuttgart, 1998).

Rathgeber, Christina, 'The reception of Brandenburg-Prussia's new Lutheran hymnal of 1781', *Historical Journal*, 36 (1993), pp. 115–36.

Reinhard, Wolfgang, 'Zwang zur Konfessionalisierung? Prolegomena einer Theorie des konfessionellen Zeitalters', *Zeitschrift für Historische Forschung*, 10 (1983), pp. 257–77.

Reinicke, A., 'Resultate der Mahl- und Schlachtsteuer in der Periode von 1838 bis 1861', *Zeitschrift des königlich preussischen statistischen Bureaus*, 3, 4 (1863), pp. 217–35, 160–7.

Robling, Franz, 'Political rhetoric in the Enlightenment', in Eckhart Hellmuth, ed., *The transformation of political culture: England and Germany in the late eighteenth century* (Oxford, 1990), pp. 409–21.

Roche, Daniel, *France in the Enlightenment* (Cambridge, MA, 1998).

Rohrschneider, Michael, 'Leopold I. von Anhalt-Dessau, die oranische Heeresreform und die Reorganisation der preußischen Armee unter Friedrich Wilhelm I', in Peter Baumgart, Bernhard Kroener, and Heinz Stübig, eds., *Die preussische Armee* (Paderborn, 2008), pp. 45–71.

Rosanvallon, Pierre, *Le capitalisme utopique* (Paris, 1979).

Rosenberg, Hans, *Bureaucracy, aristocracy and autocracy: the Prussian experience, 1660–1815* (Cambridge, MA, 1958).

Rueschemeyer, Dietrich and Evans, Peter, 'The state and economic transformation: toward an analysis of the conditions underlying effective intervention', in Peter Evans, Dietrich Rueschemeyer, and Theda Skocpol, eds., *Bringing the state back in* (Cambridge, 1985), pp. 44–77.

Saine, Thomas, *Black bread—white bread: German intellectuals and the French Revolution* (Rochester, NY, 1988).

Sauter, Michael, 'The Prussian monarchy and the practices of enlightenment', in Hans Blom, John Laursen, and Luisa Simonutti, eds., *Monarchisms in the Age of Enlightenment: liberty, patriotism and the common good* (Toronto, 2007), pp. 217–39.

Sauter, Michael, 'The enlightenment on trial: state service and social discipline in eighteenth-century Germany's public sphere', *Modern Intellectual History*, 5 (2008), pp. 195–223.

Sauter, Michael, *Visions of the Enlightenment: the Edict on Religion of 1788 and the politics of the public sphere in eighteenth-century Prussia* (Leiden, 2009).

Schieder, Theodor, *Friedrich der Große* (Berlin, 1983).

Schilling, Heinz, *Höfe und Allianzen: Deutschland 1648–1763* (Berlin, 1989).

Schimmelpfennig, Friedrich, *Die preussischen indirekten Steuern oder die auf Produktion, Fabrikation und Konsumtion ruhenden Abgaben im Innern der preussischen Staaten. Eine systematisch geordnete Zusammenstellung der darauf Bezug habenden Gesetze und Verordnungen bis zum Schlusse des Jahres 1835* (Potsdam, 1840).

Schlobach, Jochen, 'Du siècle de Louis aus siècle de Frédéric?', in Christiane Mervaud, ed., *Le siècle de Voltaire—hommage à René Pomeau* (2 vols., Oxford, 1987), vol. 2, pp. 831–46.

Schmidt, Martin, 'Der Pietismus und das moderne Denken', in Kurt Aland, ed., *Der Pietismus und die moderne Welt* (Witten, 1974), pp. 9–74.

Schmoller, Gustav von, *Der preußische Beamtenstand unter Friedrich Wilhelm I.* (Berlin, 1870).

Schmoller, Gustav von, 'Die Epochen der preußischen Finanzpolitik', *Jahrbuch für Gesetzgebung, Verwaltung und Volkswirtschaft im Deutschen Reich*, 1 (1877), pp. 32–114.

Schmoller, Gustav von, *Das brandenburgisch-preußische Innungswesen von 1640–1806 hauptsächlich die Reform unter Friedrich Wilhelm I.* (Berlin, 1887).

Schmoller, Gustav von, 'Einführung der französischen Régie durch Friedrich den Grossen 1766', *Sitzungsberichte der Königlichen Preussischen Akademie der Wissenschaften zu Berlin*, 1 (1888), pp. 63–79.

Schmoller, Gustav von, *Die preußische Seidenindustrie im 18. Jahrhundert und ihre Begründung durch Friedrich den Großen* (München, 1892).

Schmoller, Gustav von, *Der deutsche Beamtenstaat vom 16–18. Jahrhundert. Rede gehalten auf dem deutschen Historikertag zu Leipzig am 29. März 1894* (Leipzig, 1894).

Schmoller, Gustav von, *Über Behördenorganisation, Amtswesen und Beamtenthum im Allgemeinen und speciell in Deutschland und Preußen bis zum Jahre 1713* (Berlin, 1894).

Schmoller, Gustav von, *Preußische Verfassungs-, Verwaltungs- und Finanzgeschichte* (Berlin, 1921).

Schmoller, Gustav von, *Das Merkantilsystem in seiner historischen Bedeutung städtische, territoriale und staatliche Wirtschaftspolitik* (Frankfurt, 1940).

Schmoller, Gustav von, *Deutsches Städtewesen in älterer Zeit* (Aalen, 1964).

Schrader, Wilhelm von, *Geschichte der Friedrichs-Universität zu Halle* (Berlin, 1894).

Schremmer, Eckart, 'Taxation and public finance: Britain, France, and Germany', in Peter Mathias and Sidney Pollard, eds., *The Cambridge economic history of Europe* (8 vols., Cambridge, 1966–89), vol. 8, pp. 315–494.

Schui, Florian, *Early debates about industry: Voltaire and his contemporaries* (Basingstoke, 2005).

Schui, Florian, 'Prussia's "Trans-oceanic moment": the creation of the Prussian Asiatic Trade Company in 1750', *Historical Journal*, 49 (2006), pp. 143–60.

Schui, Florian, 'Learning from French experience: the Prussian Régie tax administration, 1766–86', in Holger Nehring and Florian Schui, eds., *Global debates about taxation* (London, 2007), pp. 36–60.

Schui, Florian, 'French figures of authority and state building in Prussia', in Peter Becker and Rüdiger von Krosigk, eds., *Figures of authority: contributions towards a cultural history of governance from 17th to 19th century* (Oxford, 2008), pp. 153–76.

Schui, Florian, 'Observing the neighbours: fiscal reform and transnational debates in France after the Seven Years' War', in Gabriel Paquette, ed., *Enlightened reform in southern Europe and its Atlantic colonies, c. 1750–1830* (Farnham, 2009), pp. 271–86.

Schui, Florian, 'Tax payer opposition and fiscal reform in Prussia, c.1766–87', *Historical Journal*, 54 (2011), pp. 371–99.

Schultze, Walther, *Geschichte der preussischen Regieverwaltung von 1766 bis 1786, ein historisch-kritischer Versuch* (Leipzig, 1888).

Schumpeter, Joseph, *History of economic analysis* (New York, 1987).

Schumpeter, Joseph, 'The crisis of the tax state', in Richard Swedberg, ed., *Economics and sociology of capitalism* (Princeton, 1991), pp. 99–140.

Schwartz, Paul, *Der erste Kulturkampf in Preussen um Kirche und Schule 1788–1798* (Berlin, 1925).

Schwenke, Elsbeth, *Friedrich der Große und der Adel* (Burg, 1911).

Seligman, Edwin, *Essays on taxation* (New York, 1913).

Skocpol, Theda, 'Bringing the state back in: strategies of analysis in current research', in Peter Evans, Dietrich Rueschemeyer, and Theda Skocpol, eds., *Bringing the state back in* (Cambridge, 1985), pp. 3–43.

Spoerer, Mark, 'Wann begannen Fiskal- und Steuerwettbewerb? Eine Spurensuche in Preussen, anderen Deutschen Staaten und der Schweiz', *Jahrbuch für Wirtschaftsgeschichte*, 2 (2002), pp. 11–35.

Spoerer, Mark, 'The Laspeyres-Paradox: tax overshifting in nineteenth century Prussia', *Cliometrica*, 2 (2008), pp. 173–6.

Spoerer, Mark, 'The revenue structures of Brandenburg-Prussia, Saxony and Bavaria (fifteenth to nineteenth centuries): are they compatible with the Bonney-Ormrod Model?', in Simonetta Cavaciocchi, ed., *La fiscalitá nell'economia europea secc. XII–XVIII* (Florence, 2008), pp. 781–91.

Stange-Fayos, Christina, *Lumières et obscurantisme en Prusse* (Bern, 2003).

Straubel, Rolf, *Frankfurt (Oder) und Potsdam am Ende des Alten Reiches Studien zur städtischen Wirtschafts- und Sozialstruktur* (Potsdam, 1995).

Straubel, Rolf, *Kaufleute und Manufakturunternehmer: Eine empirische Untersuchung über die sozialen Träger von Handel und Großgewerbe in den mittleren preußischen Provinzen (1763 bis 1815)* (Stuttgart, 1995).

Straubel, Rolf, *Die Handelsstädte Königsberg und Memel in friderizianischer Zeit ein Beitrag zur Geschichte des ost- und gesamtpreußischen 'Commerciums' sowie seiner sozialen Träger (1763–1806/15)* (Berlin, 2003).

Straubel, Rolf, 'Heer und höhere Beamtenschaft in (spät-)friderizianischer Zeit', in Peter Baumgart, Bernhard Kroener, and Heinz Stübig, eds., *Die preussiche Armee* (Paderborn, 2008), pp. 96–106.

Stützel-Prüsener, Marlies, 'Die deutschen Lesegesellschaften im Zeitalter der Aufklärung', in Otto Dann, ed., *Lesegesellschaften und bürgerliche Emanzipation* (Munich, 1981), pp. 71–86.

Sweet, Paul, 'Young Wilhelm von Humboldt's writings (1789–93) reconsidered', *Journal of the History of Ideas*, 34 (1973), pp. 469–82.

Tilly, Charles, 'War making and state making as organized crime', in Peter Evans, Dietrich Rueschemeyer, and Theda Skocpol, eds., *Bringing the state back in* (Cambridge, 1985), pp. 169–91.

Tilly, Charles, *Coercion, capital, and European states, AD 990–1990* (Oxford, 1990).

de Tocqueville, Alexis, *L'ancien régime et la revolution* (2 vols., Paris, 1954).

Treue, Wilhelm, 'Adam Smith in Deutschland. Zum Problem des "Politischen Professors" zwischen 1776 und 1810', in Werner Conze, ed., *Deutschland und Europa* (Düsseldorf, 1951), pp. 101–35.

Ullmann, Hans-Peter, *Der deutsche Steuerstaat: Geschichte der öffentlichen Finanzen vom 18. Jahrhundert bis heute* (München, 2005).

Van Damme, Stéphane, '"Farewell Habermas"? Deux décennies d'études sur l'ancien régime de l'espace public', in Patrick Boucheron and Nicolas Offenstadt, eds., *L'espace public au moyen âge: débats autour de Jürgen Habermas* (Paris, 2011), pp. 42–55.

Van Dülmen, Richard, *Die Gesellschaft der Aufklärer* (Frankfurt, 1986).

Vierhaus, Rudolf, 'Die aufgeklärten Schriftsteller. Zur sozialen Charakteristik einer selbsternannten Elite', in Hans Erich Bödecker and Ulrich Herrmann, eds., *Über den Prozess der Aufklärung in Deutschland im 18. Jahrhundert* (Göttingen, 1987), pp. 53–65.

Vierhaus, Rudolf, 'The revolutionizing of consciousness: a German utopia', in Eckhart Hellmuth, ed., *The transformation of political culture: England and Germany in the late eighteenth century* (Oxford, 1990), pp. 561–78.

Vierhaus, Rudolf, 'The Prussian bureaucracy reconsidered', in Eckhart Hellmuth, ed., *Rethinking Leviathan* (Oxford, 1999), pp. 150–64.

Vilar, Pierre, 'Problems of the formation of capitalism', *Past and Present*, 10 (1956), pp. 15–38.

Vollmer, Ferdinand, *Friedrich Wilhelm I und die Volksschule* (Göttingen, 1909).

Wächtershäuser, Wilhelm, *Das Verbrechen des Kindesmordes im Zeitalter der Aufklärung* (Berlin, 1973).

Walls, Andrew, 'Self-development and the liberal state: the cases of John Stuart Mill and Wilhelm von Humboldt', *The Review of Politics*, 61 (1999), pp. 252–74.

Waquet, Jean-Claude, 'Les Fermes Générales dans l'Europe des lumières', *Mélanges de l'École Française de Rome*, 8 (1977), pp. 983–1027.

Weber, Max, *Economy and society* (2 vols., Berkeley, 1978).

Welke, Martin, 'Gemeinsame Lektüre und frühe Formen von Gruppenbildung im 17. und 18. Jahrhundert: Zeitunglesen in Deutschland', in Otto Dann, ed., *Lesegesellschaften und bürgerliche Emanzipation* (Munich, 1981), pp. 29–53.

Wiggermann, Uta, *Woellner und das Religionsedikt Kirchenpolitik und kirchliche Wirklichkeit im Preußen des späten 18. Jahrhunderts* (Tübingen, 2010).

Wilson, Peter, *War, state and society in Württemberg, 1677–1798* (Cambridge, 1995).

Wolff, Otto, 'Die Mahl- und Schlachtsteuer', *Vierteljahrschrift für Volkswirtschaft Politik und Kulturgeschichte*, 2 (1864), pp. 168–96.

Zaret, David, 'Religion, science, and printing in the public spheres in seventeenth-century England', in Craig Calhoun, ed., *Habermas and the public sphere* (Cambridge, MA, 1992), pp. 212–35.

Ziekursch, Johannes, *Das Ergebnis der friderizianischen Städteverwaltung und die Städteordnung Steins am Beispiel der schlesischen Städte dargestellt* (Jena, 1908).

Zschocke, Helmut, *Die Berliner Akzisemauer. Die vorletzte Mauer der Hauptstadt* (Berlin, 2007).

Index

Académie Royale des Sciences et Belles Lettres, *see* Royal Academy
Acta Borussica 15
Accise, *see* excise
Adams, John Quincy 99, 100
administration 11, 20–4, 28, 30, 38, 76–7, 79–80, 85, 90, 100, 102–13, 119–20, 122–6, 130–5, 169, 188, 190
Administration générale des accises et de péages 107; *see also* Régie
Age of Louis XIV 95
agriculture 57–8, 69, 185
Allgemeine Deutsche Bibliothek 57, 169
Allgemeines Landrecht für die Preußischen Staaten 43
Allied Control Council 1
Altena 148
American Revolution 141
Antimachiavel 78
Apitzsch, Samuel Lobegott 144, 149–52, 154, 164, 180
artisan 31–3, 53, 61, 80, 87, 123, 150–1
Asiatic Trade Company 92, 94

ban (on imports) 110
Beaumont, Jean-Louis Moreau de 121, 196
beer 26, 56, 109–10
Beguelin, Heinrich von 125, 131 *n.* 122
Behrens, Catherine 2
Berlin 15, 33, 36–7, 44, 50–6, 59–62, 72, 84, 86, 90, 93–5, 97, 99, 102, 108, 117, 125, 127–8, 131, 142, 145, 148–50, 152–4, 163, 166, 170, 179, 185
Berlinische Monatsschrift 49, 55, 61, 66, 71, 116, 127, 182, 184, 186, 192
Berlin Monthly, see *Berlinische Monatsschrift*
Bionval, Mangin de 142
Blackbourne, David 6
Borcke, Heinrich Adrian Graf von 128–30
Boston Tea Party 141; *see also* tea
Brandenburg 56
brandy 26, 56, 87, 110, 134
Breslau 51–2, 59–60, 93, 116, 151
brewer 34, 113, 177, 193
Britain 6, 109, 116, 118, 140–3, 177; *see also* England; Scotland
Bromberg 94
Brougham, Henry Peter (Lord) 96
Burke, Edmund 83, 102
Büsch, Georg 65
Büsching, Anton Friedrich 15, 53–9, 72–3, 128, 137, 163, 169

Calvinist, *see* Reformed
capitalism 12, 30, 89
Catholic 35–6, 40–1, 71, 162–3
Chaptal, Jean-Antoine 96
charlatan 66
Charlottenburg 147
Cheney, Paul 79
chocolate 59
Chodowiecki, Daniel 62, 66
civil society 69, 71, 76–7, 80, 86, 98, 103, 134, 154–6, 158, 160, 165, 171–5, 181–4, 190–1, 196
Clark, Christopher 14
class tax 138
clergy 3, 25, 27, 35–7, 68, 73, 115, 147–8, 155, 157, 159, 160, 161–4
Cleve, *see* Kleve
coffee 59, 109–10, 114–16, 128, 130, 134, 136–7, 167, 172, 176, 193
Colbert, Jean-Baptiste 24, 95–6, 175
commerce 3, 30–1, 49–50, 52, 55, 58, 60, 65, 70, 72, 78, 84, 93–5, 113 n. 42, 116–24, 129, 131, 133, 137, 182, 185, 187
Commisarius loci, see *Steuerrat*
Compte rendue 127
consumer 27, 29, 34, 48–9, 59, 60, 70, 73, 90–1, 99, 103, 109–10, 112 n. 36, 113, 116, 123, 129, 133–4, 136–7, 164, 167
consumerism 58–60, 64
contraband 102, 116–18, 123–4, 126, 133, 136–7, 172; *see also* smuggler; smuggling
Contribution 21, 26–7, 29, 85
conventicle 36, 40, 68, 71, 150–1, 159, 161, 163–4, 173, 180
corporation 30–1, 34, 41; *see also* guild
corruption 27, 103, 109, 119
cotton 56, 132, 134–5
Cranz, August Friedrich 152, 164
custom 78, 95, 120, 188
customs 26, 30, 90, 109, 115, 122, 129, 133, 139, 141
customs officers 118, 122

Dachröden, Caroline von 185
Dachröden, Karl Friedrich von 185
Danzig 114, 117
de Launay, Marc Antoine de la Haye 90–2, 94, 96–7, 107–8, 123–4, 130–3, 142
demographics 44, 50–1, 52, 53–4, 57, 69, 76–7, 78, 99, 143
devil 129, 146, 148

Discourse on the commerce of grain 121
Discourse on the reasons to introduce or abolish laws 78
Diterich, Johann Samuel 145–6, 148
Dohm, Christian 116
domain 19, 32, 58, 86, 101, 112, 140
Dorotheenstadt 154
Dressler (pastor) 147

East Prussia 17, 53–4
edict on censorship (of 25 December, 1788) 165; *see also* second edict
edict on religion (of 9 July, 1788) 157, 169, 171, 178, 180; *see also* first edict
Ediktenstaat 77, 171
education 5, 17, 25, 35, 37, 39, 40, 42, 44–6, 49, 68, 71, 73, 81, 103, 144, 146, 155, 177–8, 180–1, 183–4, 193
efficiency 4, 20, 76, 108 *n.* 23, 188–9, 198
Elbingen 59
Electoral Mark 21, 53–4, 58, 76
Eley, Geoff 5–6
Emden 92, 94
empire 17, 35, 42, 125, 140, 145
empiricism 5, 81, 198
Engels, Friedrich 12
England 1, 9 *n.* 21, 72, 96; *see also* Britain
Erlin, Matt 14
estate 123, 185
estates 18, 20–5, 27, 35–6, 93, 190
evil 64, 69, 73, 116, 146, 162
excise 25–30, 32–3, 80, 84–5, 90, 102–13, 116–19, 122–7, 129, 131, 133–42, 167, 173
excise officers 26, 104–5, 117, 122, 127, 150

Fabrikkommissar, see factory inspector
factory 49, 56–60, 65–6, 132
factory inspector 80
fashion 4, 50, 56, 58–62, 74, 76, 91, 114; *see also* tyranny of fashion
first edict (on religion, of 9 July, 1788) 155, 157, 160, 165; *see also* edict on religion
Fischer, Wolfram 79
flour 136, 138–9
Flour wars 175
France 1–2, 9, 13, 24–5, 53–4, 59, 71, 86, 95, 109, 114 *n.* 43, 116, 118, 124, 126–8, 135, 139–40, 142, 156, 163, 168–9, 174–5, 177–8, 190–1, 196–7
Francke, Hermann August 37, 173
Frankfurt (Oder) 93, 123
Franklin, Benjamin 127
Fredrick I 30–1
Fredrick II (the Great) 2–4, 16–17, 43, 49, 52, 55, 70, 75–86, 89–111, 115–20, 123–42, 144–8, 150, 152–5, 157, 164, 172–5, 185, 187–8, 192
Fredrick William I 18, 23–4, 30–1, 37–8, 43, 45–6, 80
Frederick William II 126, 130–4, 140, 145, 154, 164, 166, 169, 175

Frederick William III 171
Frederick William (the Great Elector) 18, 20, 25, 27, 29–30
freedom 4–6, 17, 25, 31, 35, 38, 40, 44, 47–9, 55, 65–6, 70–3, 82, 97–9, 101, 127, 129, 133, 141, 144, 150, 152–8, 160, 165, 167, 172, 179–81, 185–192, 197
French Revolution 142, 173, 177, 193
Frevert, Ute 196
Friedrichswerderstadt 154
Fulbrook, Mary 39

Galiani, Ferdinando 121
garrison 52–3, 55, 86, 88
Gay, Peter 174
Gedike, Friedrich 55–6, 69–71, 124–5, 191
Gellner, Ernest 135
Generaldirektorium 76
Generalkriegskommissariat 22
George William 17
Glatz 113
Glaucha 37
Gleixner, Ulrike 39
God 39, 98, 120, 145–6, 150–2, 162, 174
gold 65, 72, 89, 95, 120, 161
Goldscheid, Rudolf 8
Goudar, Ange 163
grain 26, 61, 109–10, 121, 134, 175
Graumann, Johann Philipp 92
Great Elector *see* Frederick William
guild 30–1, 41–2, 70, 135, 151; *see also* corporation

Habermas, Jürgen 5, 8–13, 196
Habsburg 101
Hagen, William 3
Halberstadt 59
Halle 37–8, 52, 170, 173
Hamann, Johann Georg 48, 58, 118–23, 126, 135, 187–8, 196, 198
Hamburg 65, 169
Hamilton, Alexander 96–7
Hartknoch, Friedrich 119
Haye de Launay, Marc Antoine de la, *see* de Launay, Marc Antoine de la Haye
Hayek, Friedrich von 189
Heinrich, Gerd 22–3
Herder, Johann Gottfried 119–20
Hermes, Herman Daniel 170
Hertzberg, Ewald Friedrich von 79, 86, 88–90, 92, 98, 128, 130, 132
Herz, Marcus 66, 68
Hillmer, Gottlob Friedrich 170
Hintze, Otto 7, 22–3, 157
History of the two Indies 120
Hohenzollern 2, 6, 13, 15, 17–21, 23, 27–35, 38, 44–5, 108, 140, 142, 145, 150, 156, 159, 165, 175
Honest considerations about the edict of 9 July 1788 165
Huguenot 55

Hull, Isabel 8, 62
Humboldt, Wilhelm von 6, 75, 82, 176–94, 198
hymnal 2, 144–55, 162–4, 172–3
Hymnal for the use in worship in the royal Prussian lands 145

immigration 38, 44, 55, 124, 125
impostor 49, 66, 68, 72, 163
individualism 4, 6, 24–5, 36, 40, 44, 48–9, 66, 70, 73–4, 76, 99, 102, 156, 159–60, 186
industry 48, 69, 70, 78, 80, 84, 90–1, 95–6, 123, 132, 185, 188
inequality 60
infanticide 43–4
Iselin, Isaak 57

Jesus 68, 146, 150, 152
John Sigismund 35
Jöllenbeck 68, 71
Journal des Luxus und der Moden 59
Journal of luxury and fashions, see Journal des Luxus und der Moden
Justification of the system of political economy of Frederick II 90

Kalvinistentumult 36
Kameralist 28
Kant, Immanuel 5–6, 66, 119, 122, 169–70
Kantonalsystem 33
Kästner, Abraham 64
Kemper, Dirk 157, 169
Keynes, John Maynard 89
Kleve 30, 111
Klöden, Karl Friedrich 103
Klose, Samuel Benjamin 116
Kolberg 93
Königsberg 6, 19, 24, 30, 51–2, 56–60, 69, 92–3, 113, 118–9, 121, 134, 137, 170, 187
Kontribution, see Contribution
Krefeld 111
Kreiskommissar, see Landrat
Kriegskommissar 22
Kurmark, see Electoral Mark

Laboulaye, Édouard 177
laissez-faire 133
Landrat 22–3
Langford, Paul 141
Lassalle, Ferdinand 138
Launay, Marc Antoine de la Haye de, *see* de Launay, Marc Antoine de la Haye
leather 56
Letter sent to Frederick William II reigning king of Prussia on the day of his ascent to the throne 130
Letters on Silesia 99
Levant Trading Company 135
liberalism 176–7, 189, 194
linen 56, 68, 88
List, Friedrich 96
literacy 3, 46, 157
Lith, Wilhelm von der 28

London 51, 72
loom 56, 60
Louis XIV 18, 95, 175
Lutheran 4, 35–8, 42, 145, 155, 157, 172–3
luxury 44, 49–50, 59, 62, 64, 69–70, 85, 91–2, 94, 99, 109, 115–16, 133–4, 136–8, 184–5
Lyon 57

Machiavelli, Niccolò 78
Magdeburg 24, 30, 55, 59, 60
magistrate 15, 21–2, 27–8, 33, 42, 80, 141
Mahlaccise, see milling tax
Malthus, Thomas 54
Mandrin, Louis 118
Marienwerder 59
Mark 111
Märkisch-Friedland 103
marriage 38, 41–2, 44, 49, 62, 64, 88
master 30–2, 41, 61
Mauvillon, Jakob 52, 58, 69–71
meat 26, 109–10, 112, 138–9, 167
Melton, James van Horn 39, 46
Memel 30, 92–3
Memoirs of the house of Brandenburg 95
mercantile system 69, 188
merchant 14, 28–9, 31, 33, 53, 84, 87–9, 92–4, 103, 105, 110–14, 119, 121, 123, 129–34, 136–7, 139, 149, 150, 164, 167, 176, 185, 193
Message to a worldling in Berlin 152
military 2, 3, 6, 13, 17–20, 22, 25, 32–5, 37, 52–3, 55, 77, 81, 84, 85–8, 90, 95, 97, 99, 101, 104, 107, 111, 140, 173, 177, 192, 196
military (the) 18–19, 21, 33–4, 38, 86, 88–90, 105, 112, 122, 125, 139, 175, 192
military-fiscal 4, 25, 34–5, 42, 45, 75, 81, 99, 102
Mill, John Stuart 6, 177–8, 181–9, 193–4, 196
milling tax 136, 138–9
Minden 93, 111, 185
minister 3, 79, 86, 88, 90, 95, 127–8, 145, 164, 168, 170, 175
Mintzker, Yair 14, 102
Mirabeau, Gabriel Riqueti Comte de 52–6, 58, 69–71, 75, 88, 90, 107, 115–16, 125, 130–2, 175, 186–7, 192 *n.* 59, 193–5
miracle 145
Mirror of princes 84
Mittenzwei, Ingrid 111, 134
Moers 111
Monddoktor, see moon doctor
money 19, 20, 34, 45, 52, 65, 70, 86, 92–3, 105, 118, 171
monopoly 13, 58, 86, 128–9, 134–5
moon doctor 66, 72
Moses 119
Mylius Hymnal, see Hymnal for the use in worship in the royal Prussian lands 145–6, 151

nation 45, 78–9, 97, 185–8, 191, 196
national 2, 7, 13, 49, 81, 97–8, 123, 125–6, 177, 187, 192–3, 196–8

nationalism 125, 135
necessities 59, 92
Necker, Jacques 86, 127
neoliberal 189
neologic 145, 150, 170
Netherlands 92
Neue Thalia, see *New Thalia*
Neugebauer, Wolfgang 18, 171
Neumark, *see* New Mark
New Mark 53–4, 61
New Thalia 184
Nicolai, Friedrich 57, 119, 131, 141, 169
Niemeyer, August Herrmann 170
Nimes 57
Nipperdey, Thomas 31, 40, 73–4
nobility 19, 20–3, 25, 85, 108
noble 21–3, 27, 33, 85, 93–4, 192, 194
North, Michael 59

Oberkriegskommissariat 22
Of the manners, customs, industry and progress of the human understanding in the arts and sciences 95
Of the Prussian monarchy under Frederick the Great 52, 76, 193
official 3–6, 11, 21, 26, 29, 30, 36, 61, 76, 79, 80–1, 83–5, 89–91, 94, 97–117, 119, 124–6, 131, 133, 141–2, 170, 172, 175, 185, 190
On liberty 176–7, 182, 187, 194
On the limits of state action 6, 176–9, 182–5, 189–93
opulence 52
original sin 146
Ostpreußen, *see* East Prussia
overshifting (of indirect taxes) 136–7

Packhof 112–13, 119, 137
paleo-liberal 189
Paris 51–2, 72, 163
parish 68, 144–5, 147–8, 153–4
pastor 35–7, 50, 68, 71, 145, 147–8, 163
petition 118, 148–54
Philippi, Johann Albrecht 135
physiocracy 175; *see also* physiocrat
physiocrat 52, 57
Pietism 10, 36–40, 45–6, 68, 150, 152; *see also* Pietist
Pietist 37–40, 46, 68, 71, 82, 145, 149, 150, 166, 172–3, 180; *see also* Pietism
Poland 35
Political testament (of 1752) 79, 84
Pommern, *see* Pomerania
Pomerania 53–4, 104
poor 29, 33, 49–50, 60–1, 64–5, 68, 84, 109, 133, 135–8
population 21, 23, 25, 28, 32–6, 44, 46, 48, 50–62, 65–6, 69, 71, 76, 79, 80, 86, 88, 90, 107–8, 110, 117, 135, 142–3, 158, 180, 184, 186, 190
porcelain 58

Potsdam 55
poverty 49, 60–1, 64
preacher 68, 148, 150, 152, 157, 160–1, 164, 169–70, 172, 179
price 26, 59, 61–2, 71, 88, 91, 110, 118, 134, 136–7
Principles of political economy 187
print 3, 6, 39, 50, 56, 59, 62, 72, 121, 126, 135, 141, 150, 156, 165, 168
privacy 28–9, 44, 106, 141, 151
privileges 12, 18, 21, 27, 42, 90, 137
protective tariff 30, 96, 110, 123, 132, 188; *see also* tariff
public 1–14, 27, 36, 38, 40, 43, 47, 55, 66, 73, 75–7, 80–1, 84–9, 97–8, 101, 106–11, 115–31, 134, 143–78, 181–2, 185, 192–3, 196–7

quartering 33–4, 97, 192

Rachel, Hugo 15
Rathäusliche Reglements 23
Rathgeber, Christina 147, 151
rationality 4–5, 75, 81, 97, 145, 147, 198
Raymond, Daniel 97–8
Raynal, Guillaume Thomas 72, 120–1
Reckahn 56
recruitment 32, 85, 104, 106, 108, 125, 143
Reformation 10, 35–6, 41–2, 46, 144, 172
Reformed 3, 35–6, 38 98, 155, 157, 170, 173
Régie 107–42, 144, 148, 150, 154, 167, 172–4, 176–7, 185–7, 190, 197; *see also* Administration générale des accises et de péages
Religion within the bounds of bare reason 169
religious freedom 4, 35, 38, 71, 82–3, 144, 150, 153–4, 157–8, 161, 179–80, 187
religious toleration 3, 5, 35, 38, 154, 159, 164, 175; *see also* tolerance
resistance 3, 5–6, 9, 11, 19, 23, 35–6, 102, 111, 115, 117–18, 125, 134–5, 141, 144, 147, 150, 154, 156, 158, 160, 163, 165, 167, 170–4, 184, 190
revolution 1–2, 6, 127, 139, 140–3, 169, 173–4, 177, 179, 190, 191, 193
rich 48–50, 60–1, 65, 68, 136–8
Ritterschaftliche Kreditwerke 93
Römer, Karl Heinrich von 167
Rosenberg, Hans 7, 135
Rosicrucians 161
Royal Academy 50, 64, 86

Säcken 43
Sauter, Michael 156, 158–9
Schlesien see Silesia
Schmoller, Gustav von 7, 14, 143
school 37, 45–6, 52, 74, 144–5, 169, 171, 182
Schopenhauer, Arthur 114
Schopenhauer, Johanna 113–14, 117
Schwager, Johan Moritz 68, 71
Schwartz, Paul 157

Scotland 68; *see also* Britain
second edict (on censorship, of 25 December, 1788) 155, 157–8, 168, 177, 179; *see also* edict on censorship
Secret history of the court of Berlin 52
serfdom 65
Seven Years War 5, 44, 48, 76, 81, 84, 92, 102, 107, 123, 125, 134, 139, 196
sex 40–4
Silesia 99, 101
Silesian War 101
silk 56, 58, 91, 132
silver 65, 89
Simsch, Adelheid 79
Skocpol, Theda 7, 23, 47
slaughter tax 97, 138–9, 117
Smith, Adam 57, 65, 68–9, 121–2, 196
smuggler 116–18, 123, 131, 134, 136–7; *see also* contraband; smuggling
smuggling 109, 112, 115–18, 124, 133, 135–6; *see also* contraband; smuggler
sociability 40, 73, 150, 152, 157, 186
soldier 18–19, 32, 33–4, 55, 86–8, 97, 102, 106, 192
Sonderweg, see special path
special path 1, 7, 13
Spencer, Herbert 189
Spener, Jacob 36–7
Spinner 56
Spirit of the Laws 141, 190
Stamp act 127
standing army 18–19, 32, 192
state building 3–4, 7–8, 10, 16–17, 19, 21, 23, 25, 30–1, 34–5, 40, 42, 48, 77
statistics 50, 53, 54, 56, 69, 76, 80, 86, 109 *n.* 25, 110, 123, 127–8, 132, 143, 168
Stein-Hardenberg reforms 138
Stendal 60
Stettin 55, 59, 60, 92, 93
Steuerrat 22–4, 26, 30, 80
stocking-maker 66
Stork (pastor) 148
Straubel, Rolf 14, 137
Struensee, Carl von 127
Süßmilch, Johann 50–62, 64, 69–71, 76–7, 162–3, 186
sugar 59, 94, 109, 115, 167
sumptuary laws 70, 185–6

tariff 26, 29, 97, 105, 109, 115, 134–7, 186, 187; *see also* protective tariff
taxpayer 8, 20–1, 26–8, 33, 84–5, 104–9, 111–13, 124, 126, 131, 138, 143
tea 59, 141; *see also* Boston Tea Party

textile 56–7, 64, 163
The divine order and the transformations of human kind 50
The duties of the Gold- and Rosicrucians of the old system 161
The interests of France misunderstood 163
The rapid growth and building of the royal capital Berlin 50
The state and its limits 177
Thirty Years War 3–4, 17–8, 22, 32, 34, 38, 44–5, 47, 53, 76, 81, 144, 156, 165, 173, 175
Three sermons on the announcement and introduction of the new hymnal 152
To a financier in Pe-Kim 120
tobacco 58–9, 110, 128–30, 134, 136–7
tolerance 38, 42, 66, 71, 82–3, 150, 152–6, 159, 161–2, 164, 180; *see also* religious toleration
To the Salomon of Prussia 48, 120
troops 17–8, 22, 33–4, 55
Turgot, Anne Robert Jacques 121, 135, 175, 197
tyranny 182; *see also* tyranny of fashion
tyranny of fashion 59, 60–2, 99; *see also* fashion; tyranny

Universal German Library, see Allgemeine Deutsche Bibliothek

veteran 106, 118
Villaume, Peter 165–8, 179
violence 3, 5, 11, 34, 147–8, 156, 164, 172
Voltaire 95, 174–5, 197

wage 53, 56, 61, 65, 88–9, 91, 110, 137
War of Austrian Succession 102
wealth 21, 27–30, 57–8, 60–1, 65, 69, 84, 93, 97, 109, 134–8, 186
Wealth of Nations 57, 117, 121
weaver 56, 66, 68, 163
Wesley, John 37
wine 26, 58, 109
wine merchant 113, 164
Woellner, Johann Christoph von 3, 73, 144, 155–83, 192, 197
Wolfenbüttel 92
wood 23, 26
wool 33, 56, 80, 88, 132
Work on public education 193
worker 34, 56–7, 60–1, 64–6, 68–9, 88, 92, 163

Ziekursch, Friedrich 14
Zimmermann, Johann 126, 130, 132